CAMBRIDGE LATIN AMERICAN STUDIES

41

DEMOGRAPHIC COLLAPSE

INDIAN PERU, 1520–1620

For a list of books in this series please turn to page 309.

DEMOGRAPHIC COLLAPSE

INDIAN PERU, 1520–1620

NOBLE DAVID COOK

Department of History
University of Bridgeport

CAMBRIDGE UNIVERSITY PRESS

Cambridge
London   New York   New Rochelle
Melbourne   Sydney

Published by the Press Syndicate of the University of Cambridge
The Pitt Building, Trumpington Street, Cambridge CB2 1RP
32 East 57th Street, New York, NY 10022, USA
296 Beaconsfield Parade; Middle Park, Melbourne 3206, Australia

First published 1981

Printed in the United States of America

Library of Congress Cataloging in Publication Data
Cook, Noble David.
Demographic collapse, Indian Peru, 1520–1620.
(Cambridge Latin American studies)
Bibliography: p.
Includes index.
1. Indians of South America – Peru –
Population.   2. Peru – Population – History –
16th century.   I. Title.   II. Series.
F3429.3.P68C66   304.6'2'0985   81–9950
ISBN 0 521 23995 8   AACR2

Contents

Tables, figures, and maps

Tables

Figures

Maps

Preface

Little did I realize when I first read Woodrow Borah's *New Spain's Century of Depression* in 1962 that I would begin a search for similar material for the Andean area of South America that would continue for almost two decades. Borah's description of the relationship between population and economy in Central Mexico stimulated my investigation for parallel patterns in Peru. While preparing my master's thesis, under the direction of Lyle N. McAlister at the University of Florida, I became aware of the limited knowledge of the dynamics of population change in colonial Peru. By 1969 I had completed much of the basic research on Peru's Indian population from 1570 to 1620 for my dissertation at the University of Texas with Thomas F. McGann and James Lockhart, but teaching duties, and revisions, led to a delay in completion until 1973. I have continued the search for supplementary materials since that date, conducting new research in Peru in 1973, 1974, and finally 1977. I have now reached the point where I feel continued investigation would provide only diminishing returns. Most of the population data for Indian Peru for the period prior to 1650 have already been collected. Census results, at least the totals, for almost 585 repartimientos – the primary local unit of Indian administration – for various dates provide the basis for the present study. Undoubtedly, other information will be found, but it is unlikely that the data base will be substantially modified.

Many people have assisted me during the course of research and writing. Woodrow Borah and William Denevan have read a draft of the present volume. I owe them special thanks for their comments and support. The work would have been substantially improved had I been able to incorporate all of their advice for the text. Robert Keith provided early citations for central coastal material. In Lima, Franklin Pease and Pablo Macera were a constant inspiration because of their unflagging interest in the colonial history of Peru, especially as it relates to the native population, but most of all they have been friends. John Fisher of Liverpool gave encouragement on numerous occasions. Nicolás Sánchez-Albornoz often guided me in the study of historical demography. To these, and to those whom I have not mentioned, I give my thanks.

Financial assistance came from several sources. A Fulbright–Hays grant funded original research in Spain in 1967. The Doherty Foundation supported investigations in Peru during most of 1968. I had partial help from the Ford Foundation briefly in 1973 and 1974. A Fulbright lectureship at the Catholic University in Lima allowed me to continue population research in 1974. My return to Peru in 1977 was sponsored by the Wenner–Gren Foundation for Anthropological Research. At that time I was working on social structure and population change in the Collaguas region of the south Peruvian Andes. The staffs of archives, libraries, and special collections were always courteous and quick in their assistance. In Spain I single out for mention the Archivo General de Indias in Seville, the special collections at the Biblioteca Central of the University of Seville, and in Madrid the Real Academia de la Historia, the Archivo Histórico Nacional, and the manuscript room of the Biblioteca Nacional. In Peru the following depositories were extensively consulted: the Archivo Nacional del Perú, the Archivo Arzobispal, the manuscript room of the Biblioteca Nacional, all in Lima, and provincial archives in Arequipa and Cuzco. In the United States I used manuscript collections and reference material at the University of Texas, Yale University, and the New York Public Library. The University of Bridgeport Computer Center staff was invaluable in facilitating data analysis. The maps were prepared by Valmor C. Philp of the Syracuse University Cartographic Laboratory, thanks to the generous assistance of David J. Robinson. I thank also the editors of the *Hispanic American Historical Review* for publishing the data base (volume 62, February 1982 issue).

Alexandra Parma Cook deserves more than thanks. She provided, first, the incentive; second, the time; and third, direct assistance. Her editorial work helped to clarify passages, and her critical questions and comments led to elaboration of areas that needed expanded analysis. The book owes much to her abilities. The sabbatical granted by the University of Bridgeport during the fall of 1979 permitted the extended time necessary to complete the manuscript. Typing assistance was provided by the funds of the Dr. and Mrs. Henry W. Littlefield Professorship in History. Finally, the appointment as Visiting Fellow in Latin American Studies at Yale University for the academic year 1979–80 gave me access to the facilities of that research center for final revisions.

I hope the book, for which I take full responsibility, is a modest contribution to our understanding of the impact of European expansion in the sixteenth century on the native population of the Americas.

Introduction: The problem in perspective

> We are now in a period of marked disagreement about the size of former Indian populations, both regionally and for the hemisphere, with a strongly realized need for resolution based on better techniques and evidence.
>
> William M. Denevan, *Native Population*, p. xix

The controversy over the size of the aboriginal population of the Americas on the eve of discovery has been heated in the last quarter-century and has become especially intense in the past decade. The battle is waged even though in most cases no mass of new documentary evidence has become available upon which to base unchallenged conclusions. Generally, historians agree on population totals for various regions fifty to one hundred years after contact. Figures for the 1550s to the 1650s are accepted, with provisions made for uncounted groups and the possibility of fraud.[1]

The numbers that are presented for the initial period vary widely. At both extremes – on the one hand, those who posit very high aboriginal populations and, on the other, those who accept only limited totals – the figures are held almost as a matter of faith rather than fact. The issue, in part, has become one over methods rather than evidence solely. Some recent historians have questioned whether the techniques of modern demographic analysis can be applied to preindustrial societies, where the sources were never intended for such study and are often fragmentary at best. Others ask how powerful statistical tools are for estimation of populations chronologically distant from acceptable censuses. Some historians argue that we can be sure only of the verifiable in the direct written record and that anything else approaches speculation. For such historians the construction of models is not a valid method of inquiry into the meaning of the past.[2]

The philosophical issue is also important in the debate over the contact Indian population. The Black Legend, about the nature of the Spaniards and the conquest of the New World, derives largely from the pen of Bartolomé de las Casas, defender of the Indians, who bemoaned the loss of so many millions of innocent lives. By implication, for Hispanophobes, the larger the population loss, the more evil were the Spanish in their destruction of the Indian. Conversely, if few natives died, the consequences of conquest were less vile and can be judged in the light of the fifteenth- and sixteenth-century European world. Furthermore, if the original residents of America are seen as generally not culturally advanced and if their population was not dense, then the Spaniard becomes the exemplary builder of a new Christian society, not the destroyer of great civilizations.[3]

No battle over the size of the aboriginal population is more vivid than that involving the island of Hispaniola. This island, almost the size of Portugal, was the first sector of the Caribbean to come under European occupation and control. Modern estimates of its 1492 population range from Verlinden's meager 60,000 to Borah and Cook's 8 million (their range is from about 4 to 14 million). Rosenblat and Amiama estimate 100,000; Lipschutz sets a range of between 100,000 and 500,000; Córdova estimates 500,000; and Moya Pons calculates 600,000. More recently, Zambardino projects 1 million, with a margin of about 30 percent. Although there is great disagreement on the initial number of Hispaniola Indians, there is little argument on the 1514 population (23,000 to 30,000). Nearly all scholars concur that by the end of the sixteenth century the Indians of the island had been decimated. Given the great variation in figures and the question of the reliability of the early sources for Hispaniola's demography, Henige has been led to conclude "that it is futile to offer any numerical estimates at all on the basis of the evidence now before us."[4]

The debate over the population of Central Mexico has also been heated. Since 1948, as a result of the combined scholarly efforts of Borah, Cook, and Simpson, our knowledge of Mexico's population history has gradually expanded. On the basis of thorough investigation of old sources and the discovery of new ones, the "Berkeley School" has provided a picture of a very dense aboriginal population of the area at the time of the arrival of Cortes. Cook and Simpson in 1948 projected a population of 11 million for Central Mexico in 1519. With new tribute records available, Borah and Cook reached a much higher estimate of 25.2 million in 1963. They pointed to a decline to 16.8 million in 1532, 6.3 million in 1548, then 2.65 million in 1568, 1.9 million in 1580, 1.375 million in 1595, and 1.075 million in 1605.[5] There is little controversy over the validity of their figures for 1568 through 1605, but there is great argument over the numbers for the first half-century after contact. The argument lies partly in the nature of early sources: It is necessary to convert figures for tribute goods into tributaries and then to convert these numbers into all categories of people. The process of conversion allows for the introduction of a series of human judgments that may lead to a substantial cumulative error. Rosenblat, using the same data for the later periods, estimates only 4.5 million for all of Mexico in 1519. Sanders, as a result of detailed study of the core of the Central Mexican area suggests that the Borah and Cook estimates are about double what he believes viable. Sanders's work is based on analysis of the written data and the carrying capacity of certain agricultural areas, plus archaeological evidence.[6] Whether or not the Borah and Cook projection of 25 million stands, it is clear that most scholars accept a much higher population for the area than was believed probable. An aboriginal Mexican population of about 4 million was deemed most likely by scholars of the 1940s. Currently, primarily as a consequence of Borah and Cook's detailed research during the past third of a century, most investigators believe that at least 10 million to 12 million people resided in Central Mexico in 1519.[7]

The controversy over the size of the aboriginal population extends to the other areas of the Americas. Central American populations have been reviewed by MacLeod, Sherman, Radell, and Daugherty.[8] The Amazon area has received the attention of Denevan, Sweet, and Hemming. Chile has been investigated by Mellafe, Carmagnani, and Larrain Barros.[9] Bolivia, especially during the seventeenth and eighteenth centuries, has been studied by Sánchez-Albornoz and Klein.[10] For Ecuador, Phelan suggested a conquest population of 500,000 to 750,000 for coast and highlands, with about 200,000 for the upper Amazon. Burgos-Guevara states that the late sixteenth-century population of the Audiencia was between 800,000 and 1 million. Hamerly continues preparation of a massive work on the same area.[11] Recently, several scholars have been at work on the early population of Colombia: Eidt, Parsons, Jaramillo Uribe, Ruíz Rivera, Villamarín, Colmenares, Padilla Altamirano, López Arellano, González Rodrígues, and Friede. The Chibcha population, and the Tunja, Quimbaya, and Pamplona areas have been extensively studied.[12] Yet most of the rest of South America has not received the scholarly attention it deserves. Venezuela, the whole of the La Plata region, and sectors of Brazil have seen only a reconnaissance. Denevan was correct in his assertion: "Certainly the Andes and South America in general have received less intensive study than has Middle America and hence offer a challenge to historical demographers."[13]

It is not my intention in this brief introduction to survey in detail the sources, methods, and conclusions of recent historical demographers in their study of the preconquest population of the New World. This has already been done to a lesser or a greater extent by Denevan, Borah, Rosenblat, Dobyns, and Sánchez-Albornoz.[14] I merely want to point out that the "polemic," as Rosenblat calls it, over the number of native Americans is reaching an important juncture. We owe much to the stimulating research of members of the Berkeley School, but we are entering a period in which there will be revision of estimates and publication of collections of new material for other areas of the New World. Indeed, I agree with Borah that "the materials for the demographic history of the viceroyalty of Peru in the sixteenth century may turn out to be more complete and better than those for Mexico."[15]

Historical research on preconquest populations of Peru occupies at present a prominent place in the field. Peru was the heartland of the Inca Empire, which extended almost five thousand kilometers from the southern part of present Colombia to the northern sectors of Argentina and central Chile. Cuzco, in the south Peruvian highlands, was the administrative capital of this vast Andean region. It was the permanent seat of the structure, where the Inca bureaucracy resided. Around its center lie the four quarters of the realm, each with its series of provincial units. A highway network that joined coast and highlands radiated outward and linked communities extending from Quito, Cajamarca, Pachacamac, Jauja, Lake Titicaca, and beyond. The Inca rulers were in the process of imposing a common administrative and religious structure on this extensive area when the Europeans arrived in the first third of the sixteenth century.

The Incas were recent rulers of the land. Their empire was elaborated during less than two centuries before Pizarro and his men first reached the northern fringes of the Andean world. The Incas were the inheritors of more than three thousand years of cultural evolution following the domestication of plants and animals in the area. The general outlines of the Inca precultures are well known, but new discoveries are filling in the panorama with greater detail. In both coastal and highland valleys various groups developed their own unique character, and at times valleys and regions were linked by the expanding influence of a strong center. About 900 B.C. the Chavín influence spread through most of coastal and north-central highland Peru. Around two thousand years ago major urban complexes rose, such as Tiahuanaco south of Lake Titicaca, Pucará to the north, and Huari, not far from modern Ayacucho. On the south coast were smaller cities in the Acarí, Nazca, Ica, and Pisco valleys. Irrigation agriculture, warfare, and the rise of cities and fortresses suggest the development of states during the era. Moche and Chicama expansion, Nazca conquests, a Topará state controlling the Pisco, Chincha, and Cañete rivers, and a Lima state uniting the Chancay, Rimac, and Chillón valleys are indicated by archaeological evidence. Beginning around A.D. 600 two empires rose and fell. The Huari included almost all of central coastal and highland Peru. The Tiahuanaco united highland Bolivia with southern Peru and northern Chile. Between A.D. 1000 and the Inca expansion a series of states based on valley combinations evolved. One of the most extensive was the Chimú of the Moche valley, which tied the border of southern Ecuador with the northern sector of the central Peruvian coast, the Supe valley.[16]

If a map of Peru's highlands and coast is superimposed on the central area of Mexico, we can see a band covering the area from Guadalajara and San Luís Potosí through Guatemala. If we lay a map of the Inca Empire over Central America, it will cover a strip from Panama to the California border. The area we are dealing with is vast.

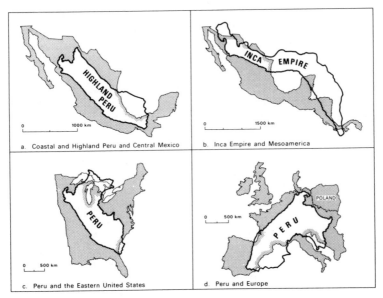

Map 1. Peru in perspective.

Contemporary Peru includes an area about the same size as the United States east of the Mississippi–Ohio rivers or Europe from the Pyrenees to central Poland. At the same time it must be admitted that not all of coastal and highland Peru is capable of sustaining agriculture. Large sections of the coast are arable only as a result of irrigation, and much of the sierra is too broken and too high in elevation to support crops. The central plateau of Mexico generally provides a wider area of favorable environment for dense population than does coastal and upland Peru. Peru is critical to our understanding of sixteenth-century population history, however. The demographic consequences of European expansion for this core area are important not only in their own right but also in their relevance for what happened in the rest of the Americas.

The purpose of the first part of the book is to establish, on the basis of the evidence and by an evaluation of various means of estimation, the size of the Indian population of Peru when contact with the Old World began. One of the limits to population growth is the carrying capacity of the ecological system of a particular society. We will examine the agricultural potential of Peru's economy in the first chapter. The present book is not a Peruvian paleodemography, but it is necessary to examine the archaeological evidence of Peru's Inca population to demonstrate the rise and fall of population densities in various sectors prior to the arrival of the Europeans (Chapter 2). Numerous scholars have attempted to estimate Peru's contact population by using the ratios of population change from political units where data are reasonably reliable. These I review and critique in Chapter 3. Other researchers have noted the relationship between the complexity of social and political organization and human numbers. In Chapter 4 we briefly discuss how these might relate to Peru. The mortality from epidemic disease can usually be predicted on the basis of the known experience of past populations. In Chapter 5 I attempt to apply such knowledge to the epidemiological and population history of the Andean region. Various census projections are made to estimate the contact population in Chapter 6. And in the following section I evaluate the methods and make my final projections of Peru's most likely preconquest population.

I examine what happened to that dense native mass in the century following contact in the next part of the book. The demographic experience of Peru's Indians varied with regard to environment and chronology. There were major differences between the coastal low-lands (Chapters 8 through 10) and the highlands (Chapters 11 to 13). The north coast was first to come into contact with the Europeans, and the consequences were rapid and catastrophic. Interestingly, however, the loss appears to have been arrested earliest. The central coast was dominated by the rise of Lima, the Spanish administrative center for all of South America, and the nearby coastal haciendas. The south coastal population was especially vulnerable to droughts and earthquakes. The northern highlands are comparatively low and broken. Depopulation there in the first century was especially quick. The lives of the central highland Indians were dominated by labor at the mercury mines of Huancavelica and the silver mines throughout the area. The south, containing Cuzco and about half of Peru's native population by the end of the sixteenth century, is still the land of the Indians. Mita service in the silver mines of Potosí, far to the south in what is now Bolivia, coca production along the eastern slopes of the Andes, and the high elevation pastoral economy were all characteristics of the Cuzco world, and each had a different impact on population decline. Part II is neither pure social history nor historical demography; rather, it is an attempt to delineate the collapse and stabilization of a once dense human population. I deal with the basic demographic variables, when data are available, and try to demonstrate migratory patterns, a changing population structure, the impact of epidemics on various segments of the population, and varying rates of population change, as well as differences in urbanizing areas and the impact of mining and forced settlement on total populations.

All historians are in one way or another constrained by the nature and availability of the sources. In the present work, not all subjects, areas, or chronological periods receive equal treatment in the analysis. Undoubtedly, some topics deserve a much more ample study than they receive, but in these cases the documentation is often meager or even nonexistent. Most of the material I have collected is fiscal: tributary counts to serve as the foundation for the repartimiento-encomienda system. In Peru these records are exceptionally abundant, especially during and after the administration of Viceroy Francisco de Toledo. In the viceroyalty, counts were taken not only of tributaries but also of females, men under tribute age, and elder, sick, or otherwise excused males. Thus, in Peru from the 1570s onward, all sectors of the native population were counted. This means, in general, that it is unnecessary to convert tributaries to total population by calculation of tributary indexes. The results for total population are therefore more realistic than in sectors of the Spanish Empire in America where this was not the case. For the present study I have not used to any great extent one other excellent source for demographic history: the parish registers. I have not done so for two primary

reasons. In the first place, local church records for Indian communities were unusual prior to the 1580s. In the second, there is still
no systematic survey of parish materials for Peru. I believe there are
extensive baptismal, marriage, and death records remaining from the
1680s to the present, but the earlier materials are few and far between.
Yanahuara, the Indian suburb of Arequipa, for example, was an important center from the beginning of the colonial era; unfortunately,
the first register has not been found, and the second register begins in
the early eighteenth century. The earliest registers for the Indian
community of Yanque, administrative center of the Collaguas Indians, date from the 1680s. There is a late sixteenth-century fragment
remaining from the nearby village of Coporaque. Parish records for
Indian residents of major Spanish cities are more accessible but are
more valuable for microdemographic studies than for a comprehensive
study of all of Indian Peru. [17]

In a macroanalysis it is impossible to cover all subjects. Among
topics and areas that have not received the attention they deserve are,
for example, the impact of the *obraje* on population decline; the role of
the *protector de los indios;* the variations among repartimientos held by
the Crown, by religious bodies, or by private colonists; unique developments in the Trujillo or Huamanga (Ayacucho) sectors; the
process of racial miscegenation. These and others all merit serious
inquiry. I hope, in spite of the limitations of the study, that the
salient features of the demographic collapse of the Andean area in the
century following the arrival of the Spaniards are clarified. The impact
of the Spanish conquest on the Andean world in the sixteenth century
was colossal. The European expansion not only caused a great decline
of the aboriginal population but also affected changes in Indian life
and culture that continue to the present.

PART I

Peru's preconquest population

The debate over the size of human populations in pre-Columbian America and the changes in them during the centuries of European domination has long been characterized by wide differences of opinion and much fervor. In recent decades the debate continues, if anything with greater participation and, one suspects, with no diminution of emotion . . . Involved also in the debate are differences over method, evidence, and basic philosophy that have much to do with the positions taken.

Woodrow Borah, "Historical
Demography: Attempt at Perspective,"
p. 13

The basic source for historical demography is the census. The Incas of Peru made periodic counts of their subjects and recorded the numbers on knotted-string mnemonic devices, which they called *quipus*. Pedro Cieza de León, writing in Cuzco in 1550, clearly explained why the native rulers wanted statistical information on the inhabitants and how the count was administered: "the principal men and their delegates in all towns and provinces of Peru had to keep track of the men and women who died and were born each year, for the purposes of tribute, and in order to know the number of warriors and defenders of the community." At the appropriate time the Inca sent an official called a *lunaquipo*, or *quipocamayo*, to each province. The leaders of each valley met the imperial representative at a central place. The quipu records of the previous census were brought, note was made of deaths and births, and a new division of the population was made into several age categories. During the inspection young girls and yanaconas were separated for special services and sent out of the area. In theory, if the population of an area became too large, a new administrative entity was established in order to maintain a rough numerical parity. In some cases groups (*mitimaes*) might be sent to entirely new sectors of the realm. Sequestering of Indians or falsifying the census returns in any other way was a serious crime.[1]

Not only were Inca censuses frequent, they were also detailed. The population was apparently divided by sex and by age. Early Spanish testimony on the age grades of the Inca counts is inconsistent. Some authors argue there were ten age classifications, in keeping with the Inca use of the decimal system. Others list twelve age categories. Confusion between the two groups exists primarily in the infant categories. For the age of 2 and up, most authors are in descriptive agreement. One of the early reports on the Inca classificatory system is that generated in 1558 during the inspection of the Chincha valley by Friar Cristóbal de Castro, vicar of the Dominican monastery, and corregidor Diego de Ortega Morejón. The eldest of the ten categories they outline is that for the *puñuloco*, old men, which they give as about age 60. The *chaupiloco*, ages 50 to 60, were exempt from military service and tribute but still tilled the fields. The *pouc*, or *puric*, were the able-bodied tributaries and warriors. In this case their age is listed as 25 to 40. The exempt young men, ages 16 to 20, are called *imanguayna*. The *cocapalla* (12 to 16) assist in the coca fields. The *pucllagamara* (8 to 10) play as children. The *tantanrezi* (4 to 6) are capable of reasoning, but the *machapori* (2 to 4) are not. Younger categories are the 4-to-8-month *sayoguamarac* and the 1-to-4-month "recently born" *moxocapari*. Another source gives the age of tributaries as 25 to 50; of the exempt youth, 20 to 25; of the cocapalla, 12 to 20. The key problem of using the Inca census classificatory system for demographic analysis is that the Inca described status, not exact chronological age. An even more obvious difficulty is that census quipus for the whole of the realm were lost or destroyed during the chaotic years of the conquest. The Inca probably knew the exact population of the area under their control, but we shall never know. Even if a cache of Inca quipu censuses is discovered, we can decipher only the numbers, not the categories counted.[2]

The quipus continued to be used in the Andes for statistical data well into the colonial period. In rare instances Inca quipus even survived into the mid-sixteenth century. One of the best-known cases is the retention of the census quipus for the province of Chucuito on Lake Titicaca. In a *visita* in 1567, undertaken by Spanish officials in order to set the tribute assessment, the local quipocamayos displayed their records of the last Inca census of the region. In this example the totals were entered into the written report. The numbers are not as revealing as one would hope, however. As we have seen, and as we shall examine in greater detail in Chapter 3, there is controversy over the "European" age of the enumerated adult male working sector of the population and the relation of the size of this group to the total population.[3]

The Mesoamericans possessed writing. Although the amount preserved is not overwhelming, what does exist provides rich insight into
religion, the calendar system, poetry and some history, and tributes.
Borah and Cook have attempted to use remaining tribute *matriculas* in
their reconstruction of the population history of the region. There is
no equivalent record for the Andean area of South America. The Incas
did not write. They did record numbers, but although the numbers
on quipus can be readily deciphered, there is no direct information on
the subjects counted – people, alpacas, or quantities of production of
maize, potatoes, cloth – or on where or when the count was made.[4]

The historical demographer would hope to have access to relatively
frequent censuses and a good series of birth, marriage, and death
records for his research, but it is a rare researcher who is fortunate
enough to have all. Moreover, the quality of the material that has
survived may not be as good as one would wish. As Hollingsworth has
written, "it is very natural that few societies in the past should have
good statistics on population, and, in particular, there are almost no
instances of entirely reliable data before 1700."[5] Parish records obviously tell us nothing of Peru's preconquest population. Had the conquistadores stopped their military operation in 1532 and taken count
of the inhabitants of the realm they were trying to subjugate, then we
might have a reasonably accurate idea of numbers. Even if this had
happened, however, the figures might not truly reflect the precontact
population. It is now evident that the contact between the Spaniards
and Incas long preceded the meeting of Francisco Pizarro and
Atahualpa at Cajamarca. European disease, spread from Indian to
Indian, passed down the Andean coast in the 1520s, as we shall see in
Chapter 5, with catastrophic results. The ruling Inca Huayna Capac
succumbed, as did the presumed legitimate heir, leaving a realm
contested by sons Huascar and Atahualpa.

The absence of an accurate population count of the Inca world in the
1520s and 1530s forces the historian onto unfamiliar ground. He
must use other disciplines to infer what was most likely to have been.
Studies of agricultural productivity, crop yields, the impact of irrigation and fertilizers, all give clues to the carrying capacity of an ecosystem. Archaeological research points out patterns of settlement, ur-
banization, and local population densities. From the relatively small
number of examples of the size of the population we have of the Inca
period, as in the case of Chucuito, we might be able to calculate a
depopulation ratio, then apply that mathematical formula to wider
regions. By studying the social and political complexity of the Inca
structure, we can estimate total populations. Epidemiological history

and the estimation of known mortality levels for certain diseases might be used to project population loss as a result of a series of epidemics recorded by Spanish contemporaries; or the historian might use demographic formulas to project earlier population totals on the basis of later rates of change, which can be calculated from reasonably accurate censuses.[6]

Some historians might argue that such methods cannot give solid answers and that the method is excessively speculative, that it might not be history at all. To these I reply that all history is speculative, especially when it deals with causation. We know *what* Bartolomé de las Casas wrote. We are less sure why he took the stands he did and why he modified positions over the years. We are familiar with the acts of the Spanish conquest of the New World, but when we deal with the motivations of the major actors in the drama, and the reasons for European success and Indian failure, we approach speculative areas. I propose to do in Part I what historians have always done: take fragmentary evidence from the past and from various disciplines, evaluate it critically, rejecting what appears to be least reliable, and try to present as accurately as possible the results of my investigation.

Recent estimates of the 1520 population of Peru have ranged from less than 3 million to approximately 32 million. The span is far too wide. The true figure likely lies somewhere between the two numbers. My purpose in Part I is to narrow the gap and present an estimate of the preconquest population that is most likely, based on new evidence and methods developed in recent decades. All scholarship is subject to revision, and I expect that my own conclusions will be carefully scrutinized, but I hope that the present volume will be taken as a point of departure and not as a piece to be quickly discarded.

I

The ecological approach

Surprisingly enough no authors (except for Kosok . . . in estimating coastal population) have used the carrying capacity of the present area encompassed as a check on maximum population.

> Richard Schaedel, "Formation of the Inca State," p. 123

Carrying capacity is, of course, an optimal concept – what *could* be if all constituent factors operated optimally.

> David Henige, "Contact Population of Hispaniola," p. 233

Human populations cannot expand forever. Densities are ultimately limited by the environment's ability to sustain them. One of the principal limits to population is the supply of essential foodstuffs. The population of Europe in the years prior to the Black Death in the mid-fourteenth century appears to have surpassed the limit and was suffering from a series of inadequate harvests and famine before the devastating epidemics of 1348. The population of Central Mexico under the Aztecs also seems to have exceeded the carrying capacity of its agricultural economy. Sherburne F. Cook has suggested that extensive practice of human sacrifice by the Aztecs was an implicit societal attempt to redress the balance between inhabitants and land. Study of the maximum carrying capacity of an ecological system can assist the researcher in establishing population bounds, but, as we shall see, there are many variables in the equation, and the estimated limits are far from precise.[1]

The human factor adds a major complication in assessing the ecological potential of a region. No two groups of people are exactly the same. Food intake of a population depends on its age structure, on the average physical size of residents, on sex, and on the climate and elevation. Further, caloric and protein intake is dependent on the amount of physical exertion required in subsistence activities. Recent efforts by United Nations agencies to establish minimal dietary requirements for various population units have not met with unqualified success.[2]

Wherever the ecological approach is attempted, the researcher must reconstruct the probable agricultural potentiality of various systems within the area studied. The amount of land that can be used for agriculture, the availability and seasonal distribution of water, the quality of the soil, the use of fertilizers, variation in temperature and the possibility of two crops per year, the need to leave fields fallow for certain periods, the differing yield of a variety of crops, are all factors that influence final agricultural productivity. Long- and short-term variations in climate and the impact of crop diseases and insects complicate the picture. The application of a carrying capacity model to estimate maximum levels of population works best on the local level, where the variables are easiest to control. For combinations of geographical units, the problem of calculating numbers is multiplied. It is clear that the margin of error in such a method is wide.[3]

The native Peruvian diet is a subject of great importance, which has not received the ethnohistorical and archaeological investigation it deserves. Recent research on the diet of inhabitants of Mesoamerica at the time of the arrival of the Europeans paints a favorable picture of diet in the New World in comparison with the late medieval European situation. The fact that the Americans did not have draft animals does not necessarily mean that they produced less than Old World residents. The use of the animal-pulled plow, or even modern mechanized agriculture, does not necessarily increase yields. Indeed, hand tillage is intensive agriculture, especially when coupled with terracing and irrigation. As Sanders has noted, "The densest rural populations today occur in portions of the Far East, where hand tillage is characteristic."[4] Further, the variety of native American crops was much greater than that available in fifteenth-century Europe. Maize was the staple of the Mesoamerican diet and was a prized crop in the Andes as well. Gibson, in a study of Central Mexico, states: "Among all the world's cereals maize ranks highest in its combination of nutritional quality, abundant yield, and adaptability to a variety of environments."[5] Maize yield per unit of land is roughly twice that of wheat; further, the American cereal matures quickly. Comparison of the caloric yields per hectare of the chief New and Old World crops (in millions of calories per hectare) gives the following results: for the New World, maize (7.3), potatoes (7.5), sweet potatoes (7.1), and manioc (9.9), versus, for the Old World, rice (7.3), wheat (4.2), barley (5.1), and oats (5.5). Beans, rich in protein, were also important. American varieties include the lima, French, frijol, string, snap, kidney, pole, butter, haricot, sieva, Burma, Madagascar, and Rangoon.[6]

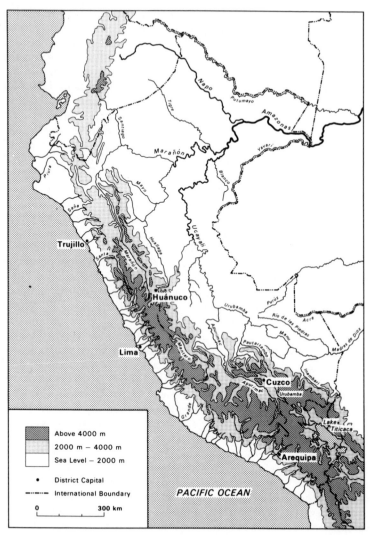

Map 2. Hydrographic map of Peru.

One of the best modern studies of the relationship between agricultural potential and population in the Americas was that of Sherburne F. Cook for the Teotlalpán valley north of Mexico City. Cook's analysis demonstrates both the strengths and the weakness of the carrying capacity argument. Cook suggested that 400 grams of total daily grain (corn, beans, and other similar products) intake was probably average at the conquest period in this region. Approximately 100 grams will provide 350 calories. From the "tribute record" he and Simpson estimated a 1519 population of 250,000. This number of inhabitants of the region would have required 100,000 kilograms of grain daily (0.4 × 250,000) when Cortes began conquest of the Aztecs. Total annual agricultural production of the region should, to sustain that population magnitude, have been 36.5 million kilograms. In 1930, however, there were 44,977 hectares of arable land in the area, with a low level of productivity; not quite 6 million kilograms of grain were harvested in 1930. Cook concluded that the difference between modern and ancient production of grain in the valley is a consequence of "the significant deterioration in agricultural capacity and soil fertility since the days of the conquest."[7]

In a more recent study, William T. Sanders examines the agricultural potential of the area he knows best: the Teotihuacán valley. More conservative in his assessment than Cook, he concludes, after comparison of pre-Hispanic and contemporary agriculture, that the indigenous system was at least as productive as the present.

> We will assume continuous land use over the 5,400 hectares that comprise the lower valley, delta, and adjacent northern portions of the Texcoco plain, with an average yield of around 1,400 kilograms. The average ration of maize per year, assuming an 80 percent dependence on maize in the diet, would be around 200 kilograms for each individual. This means that a hectare of land would feed seven persons.[8]

Sanders points out that other types of land produced less. Sloping lands without adequate irrigation probably did not exceed production of 600 kilograms for each hectare. For the total Teotihuacán valley Sanders doubts more than 150,000 to 175,000 people could have been supported by the agriculture system. He concludes 135,000 people as the likely number, a figure that allows for crop surplus. Borah and Cook had estimated 320,000 people for the same region, a figure that Sanders believes is too high.[9]

The ecological approach to population size that was applied to two Mexican valleys displays the nature of the difficulties we must face if we wish to use the carrying capacity model in the Andean region.

Present agricultural productivity is not indicative of fifteenth-century land capacity. Ecological changes have been substantial in some areas, and in many cases the impact has been a negative one. Badly eroded grazing lands cannot support the same population level as freshly cultivated fields. Furthermore, average caloric intakes are difficult to estimate and are subject to varying interpretations. In spite of its limitations, however, the carrying capacity approach has been attempted in Peru, predominantly for the coastal sector.

The list of crops cultivated in Peru in 1492 is long (see Table 1). I believe the ancient Andean residents had a definite advantage over their Mesoamerican relatives in available foodstuffs. In addition to cultivating all the North American staples, South Americans had the white potato, which could be grown at high elevations. Varieties of the potato were processed into the freeze-dried chuño, which then could be stored for long periods. The Peruvians also had the extremely nutritious high-altitude cereals, quinoa and *cañihua,* and the very productive root crops such as oca and ullucu. In addition, the Andean world had two important animal protein sources: guinea pigs (cavies) and the cameloids. Cavies are ubiquitous in the Andes, breed quickly, and act as excellent scavengers; they were kept by all households. Of the cameloids the llama was used as a beast of burden (the only one in the Americas) and occasionally for food.[10] The multitude of crops, the nature of production, storage and distribution in the Andes, and the diversity and proximity of ecological niches in the Andean area contributed to relative plenty. The native literature of Central Mexico mentions frequent periods of famine, starvation, and death. The preoccupation with famine is less apparent in the Andean world, except as a consequence of the catastrophic changes that occurred following the Spanish conquest. We will examine some of the changes in Part II.

Any ecological model applied to Peru must take into account the potentialities of several distinct productive patterns: coastal fishing and shellfishing, sunken-field agriculture, coastal irrigated valley systems, loma grazing, highland valley irrigation, highland terraced agriculture, and puna-level pastoral nomadism. Each type of subsistence pattern poses different challenges to Andean residents and elicits different responses. Peru's economic structure was and remains complex. Significant distribution of products took place, so that each ethnic group had access to agricultural commodities from various ecological systems.[11]

The possibility of estimating the coastal valley populations before the arrival of the Europeans by the amount of land in use has intrigued archaeologists for several years, and there is already an extensive litera-

Table 1. *Major Andean sources of food*

	Vegetable	Animal
Highest mountain valleys	potato	guanaco
	quinoa	vicuña
	cañihua	alpaca
	oca	llama
	ullucu	
	anu	fish
	mashua	
Lower highland valleys	maize	cavy
	tarwi	muscovy duck
	molle	vizcacha
	squash	deer
	chili pepper	
	amaranth	fish
	pacay	
	lucuma	
Coastal valleys	maize	fish and shellfish
	squash	
	bean	cavy
	peanut	
	gourd	
	manioc	
	sweet potato	
	achira	
	jíquima	
	pineapple	
	guanabana	
	cherimoya	
	guava	
	avocado	
	pacay	
	lucuma	
	pepino	
	cotton	
	chili pepper	
	cacao	
Montaña	maize	peccary
	manioc	tapir
	coca	turtle
	tobacco	monkey

Source: Lanning, *Peru before the Incas,* pp. 16–17; Bennett, "Andean Highlands," p. 5; and Rowe, "Inca Culture," pp. 210–21.

ture on the subject. The Virú valley has been especially well examined. The amount of land under cultivation along the coast is much easier to calculate than that in the sierra. The dividing line between desert and irrigated field is precise, and excellent aerial photographs and careful land surveys permit relatively accurate count of hectarage. Further, hydraulic research has provided information on river flow for each valley, a key factor in agricultural productivity. Annual variations in water flow are receiving increasing attention from agricultural historians. Most students of coastal agriculture conclude that the land under cultivation in .the early sixteenth century generally is similar to that of the mid-twentieth century.[12]

Robert G. Keith, using various early reports of household numbers in coastal valleys along with current cultivated hectarage, determined valley population densities (see Table 2). The total population figures for each valley are based on an estimated six-to-ten-person preconquest household for the coast, which Keith believes is a plausible assumption, given the Inca age category for the *hatunruna* of roughly 30 to 50 or 60.[13] Total coastal estimates can be derived by the extension of the density per hectare for the three valleys Keith studied to the total amount of land cultivated along the coast in the twenty-one major river agricultural systems. For establishing maximum and minimum densities I have used an appropriate span of densities of 2 to 12 for the three valley systems Keith analyzed in detail. The resulting figures for each valley and the maximum and minimum totals for the whole coastal region are listed in Table 3. The range is from slightly over 1 million to almost 6.5 million. It must be taken into consideration that the amount of land under irrigation is dependent on availability of water and also on surface area. In the Tumbez, Chira,

Table 2. *Central coastal population density, ca. 1530*

Valley	Households	Total population (thousands)	Irrigated land (hectares)	Density (per hectare)
Chincha	30,000	180–300	24,291	7.4–12.4
Lima–Pachacamac	25,000	150–250	72,874	2.1–3.4
Huarmey–Huaura	30,000	180–300	60,729	3.0–4.9

Source: Keith, *Conquest and Agrarian Change*, p. 23. The average figures are from Romero, *Geografía económica*, p. 175, and the multipliers for the total population are 6 and 10. Romero's irrigated land of the Rimac valley was doubled by Keith.

Table 3. *Land and water in the major coastal valleys, ca. 1960, and population estimates for 1520*

Valleys	Irrigated area (thousands of hectares)	Average flow of water (cubic meters per second)	Population density (thousands)	
			2	12
Tumbez	6	216	12	72
Chira	27	344	54	324
Piura	60	69	120	720
Lambayeque and La Leche	87	44	174	1,044
Saña	19	13	38	228
Jequetepeque	30	72	60	360
Chicama	40	42	80	480
Moche	20	14	40	240
Santa	9	192	18	108
Pativilca	21	55	42	252
Huaura	32	32	64	384
Chancay	22	12	44	264
Lima (Rimac and Chillón)	39	48	78	468
Cañete	24	60	48	288
Chincha	24	36	48	288
Pisco	25	34	50	300
Ica	21	15	42	252
Acarí	7	24	14	84
Camaná	8	72	16	96
Vítor	13	—	26	156
Moquegua	3	2	6	36
Total			1,074	6,444

Source: Romero, *Geografía económica*, pp. 62, 174–6; Keith, *Conquest and Agrarian Change*, p. 8.

and Santa valleys, for example, there are large amounts of water available but insufficient land to utilize it; hence, excess water is discharged into the sea.

Accurate study of the land under cultivation in the highland Andean valleys is much more difficult than a survey of coastal irrigated fields. Irrigation is not ubiquitous in the highlands. Seasonal rainfall in many areas provides adequate crop moisture, but annual differences in total rainfall result in variations in agricultural output. Nevertheless, good lands in the sierra may be exceptionally productive, and some areas can be double-cropped. On the coast, it is relatively easy to calculate crop hectarage; there are, after all, only twenty-one major systems that need to be analyzed. Crops may be grown throughout the highlands, however, wherever elevation is not too high, there is enough water during part of the year, and there is enough good level soil to support the efforts of the planters. Given Peru's geographic extent, exact calculation of the whole cropland cultivated in the highlands is a complex task.

The terraced hillsides and valley floors of the highland area provide a varied environment for the production of diverse crops. Corn will prosper in most places in Peru up to 3,300 meters in elevation. On protected lower slopes of Lake Titicaca it will grow at nearly 4,000 meters. In better areas corn will produce 1,200 to 1,600 kilograms per hectare. The yield of the potato is even greater: 7,000 to 9,000 kilograms per hectare. Long-term storage of Andean crops is possible. Root crops such as ullucu, oca, and mashua can be kept a year. The freeze-dried chuño can be stored for much longer periods.[14] Habas, rich in protein, will grow at elevations of 3,200 meters. The cereal quinoa will grow at higher altitudes. Fertilizer, either bird droppings from the coast (guano) or the dried dung of the cameloids, coupled with rich natural soil, allows agricultural use of the same land for centuries. Indeed, migratory currents in marginal areas appear to occur more as the result of rainfall and temperature variations than of soil depletion.[15]

Population is not limited to areas of lower elevation in the Andes. People have adapted physiologically to life at high altitude, and their economic systems have been modified to allow settlements in areas over 4,500 meters. High-elevation Andean life has been based on pastoral nomadism. This life style does permit reasonably large total populations scattered over vast expanses of otherwise nonutilizable lands.[16] The pastoralist's strategy for survival includes the attempt to maximize the number of animals as capital in time of crisis and to develop subsistence alternatives, such as exploitation of the animals for transportation, wool for trade, and some use of horticulture.[17] The question is: How many people could be supported by such an ecosystem? The key to the answer is the number of cameloids that could be sustained. Browman has studied the problem in the puna region of Jauja–Huancayo in the central highlands. There, one square kilometer will support 50 to 125 alpacas, with the llamas requiring slightly more space. After carefully weighing the evidence, Browman estimated the area could support 125,000 to 1.25 million animals.[18] This range illustrates simultaneously the ecological potential of puna-level herding and the difficulty of making precise human population estimates on this basis. If the family could retain a minimal livelihood with a herd of 125 animals, and if the family economy were supplemented by small-scale horticulture, then there could have been anywhere between 1,000 and 10,000 families in the Jauja–Huancayo puna when the Spaniards arrived. The range of 1:10 for the estimated population is too wide for projections of the total number of people who could have been supported by pastoral nomadism on the Peruvian puna.

One other type of highland agriculture should be mentioned. Highland ridged fields, used in flatlands for drainage of excess water, have been found in Peru, especially in the region of Lake Titicaca. In that area alone, some 82,056 hectares were once partly cultivated on ridges that were built up to two meters high and twenty-five meters wide. Much of the level or gently sloping land on Lake Titicaca's western shore was thus usable in spite of periodic flooding. Drained fields are associated with dense populations. In this case marginal land, by the heavy expenditure of labor, was reclaimed for agricultural purposes. Grazing replaced intensive cultivation in the Lake Titicaca basin during the demographic collapse of the sixteenth century. Only recently have there been some efforts to grow crops on the ridges, perhaps an indication of twentieth-century population pressure. Denevan, who has surveyed the region, believes it possible that the pre-Spanish population may have surpassed the carrying capacity of the better land. "Thus, preconquest populations of the Titicaca area may have been even greater than the present dense populations."[19] As we shall see in Chapter 2, sunken-field agriculture in some coastal valleys also indicates population pressure on resources.

At the simplest level, the transformation of figures of hectarage under cultivation to maximum populations that could be supported is a clear case of mathematical manipulation. A brief exercise illustrates the process. The Food and Agriculture Organization of the United Nations estimated that the total amount of land under cultivation in Peru (both coastal and highland) was 1.956 million hectares in 1961. It is possible to convert this figure to a total population, based on the number of people that could be supported by each hectare of cultivated soil. The major problem is to arrive at a reasonable figure for the carrying capacity of each land unit. It is, of course, also necessary to assume that the 1961 survey was accurate and, more important, that the land under cultivation in 1961 approximated the land under production in Inca Peru. Some scholars are willing tentatively to accept the second generalization.[20] If highland–coastal hectarage can be established, then what of the density per hectare? Steward and Faron reported that the terraced, irrigated, and well-fertilized land of the Inca inhabitants of Peru, whose farming was as intensive as anywhere in the New World, could support a family on one-half acre, about half that required for Mesoamerica.[21] If the average family size were four, then eight people could be supported on each acre of cultivated soil. There are 2.47 acres per hectare, so that the total population of Peru could theoretically have been 38,650,560 (2.47 × 1,956,000 × 8)![22] Numerous limitations are involved in such a simple method. Are the 1961 figures correct, for example? How close is 1961 hectarage to that of 1521? Has crop productivity increased or decreased in the post-Inca era? Is it possible to harvest the same land twice each year? What is the size of the family? The list of questions is long. The figure of twenty people (8 × 2.47) per hectare is much larger than the maximum of twelve we used in the calculations for coastal valley populations. Perhaps Steward and Faron's calculations of Andean productivity are overly optimistic or are applicable only in small, exceptionally fertile sectors of the country.

   More conservative figures can be derived using the carrying capacity model by applying the probable minimum and maximum coastal population densities to the 1.9 million hectares of currently cultivated land. The method yields totals of from 3.8 million to 22.8 million inhabitants for Peru. I consider the first figure to be minimal and the second unrealistically high. After a review of population density studies, I now believe that the figure of seven people per hectare that Sanders calculated for the better-irrigated alluvial flatland of the lower Teotihuacán valley of Mexico is most appropriate for maximum densities of High Civilization areas of the Americas.[23] The figure of seven is midway between the coastal Peruvian densities of two to twelve. By applying seven to the 1.9 million hectares, we reach a rough carrying capacity of 13.3 million inhabitants for Inca Peru. This figure is admittedly speculative and is obviously based on a number of assumptions that are difficult to verify. We shall reevaluate the 13.3 million carrying capacity figure in Chapter 7, in light of other models used to estimate the preconquest population.

   Did Peru's late Inca population reach the limits of the carrying capacity to sustain it? If the number of people exceeded the ability of the ecosystem to maintain them, then the "Malthusian checks" should have been set in motion to limit further population growth. There is no reason to believe, however, that the population of the Inca Empire had reached "critical density" before the arrival of the Europeans. The Spanish chroniclers report none of the devastating famines that frequently swept Central Mexico. Local famines occurred in Peru but were the result of temporary regional conditions.

When famines did beset sectors of pre-Spanish Peru, surpluses from unaffected areas could be redistributed. In theory, the Inca state collected from its subjects and stored (in tambos) tribute that could be used during emergencies. As Murra has pointed out, however, the goods were used predominantly by the royal family, the army, and workers on the great state projects (*mitayos*). Still, in grave emergencies the Inca did allocate foods to starving peoples. At the microlevel, an ethnic group was the key factor in the distribution of necessary commodities. The group had access to ecological zones of various altitudes, usually from the coastal fishing and tropical fruit and vegetable sectors to the high-level puna. Product failure at any single spot did not necessarily jeopardize the well-being of the whole. The Andean stress on reciprocity–redistribution, and the ecological safeguards, precluded truly permanent devastation emanating from catastrophic famine.[24]

The other demographic check – warfare – must also be considered. C. T. Smith has recently suggested that high casualties were associated with warfare during the rule of Huayna Capac and then during the strife between Huascar and Atahualpa. War-related deaths were high and in fact might have maintained a low or even negative growth rate.[25] Yet, was there enough population pressure on the environment to curb demographic growth? Richard Schaedel states: "The information on demographic trends in the last 1000 years of Andean prehistory is simply not adequate to warrant any inferences as to whether demographic pressures played a role in the early formation of the Inca state."[26] C. A. Rabell and C. S. Assadourian expand on the theme of militarism and its impact on population. There are few concrete examples of native mortality in pre-Spanish battles. Testimony in the 1567 Chucuito inspection reveals two estimates of Lupaca casualties: One respondent cites 6,000 deaths of 8,000 warriors; another 4,000 losses of 12,000. Assadourian and Rabell argue that the two cases might be illustrative of a wider pattern of mortality of about a quarter of the married male population. They argue that polygyny, restricted to the elite, would not provide the demographic substitute for widows and unmarried women necessary to maintain the population. "Demographically speaking, the increase in the number of 'definite widows' and in the mortality of future reproducers brings about a decrease in the birth rate on account of the interruption of many women's reproductive life, and also in the long run when the 'hollow generations' reach reproductive age."[27] Rabell and Assadourian fail, however, to take into consideration the levirate, which was common in the Andes and which allowed the commoner access to his brother's wife. Although formal polygyny was restricted, widows and unmarried women nevertheless had children. The 1562 census of the Chupachos of the Huánuco region demonstrates widespread concubinage. The practice existed in the early colonial period despite the efforts of Spanish missionaries to eradicate it. Concubinage must have also diminished the demographic consequences of a reduced number of males during the Inca period. Inca warfare was relatively "humane": The object was not to see how many enemies one could kill in a campaign but to subjugate a people with a minimum of force. Hence, the Incas usually relied on diplomacy before force. Likewise, the object of war was not to capture sacrificial victims. Human sacrifice of tens of thousands, an ultimate demographic check practiced by the Aztecs of densely populated Central Mexico, is not a characteristic of Inca culture. Conquered enemies in Peru were treated with reasonable restraint. Rather than being exterminated, groups of prior opponents might be settled in loyal provinces and allowed to retain certain parts of their cultural identity.[28]

The Andean mita also had an impact on population growth. Seasonal migration away from the native community for public work clearly restricted the time that married couples spent with one another. If wives did not follow the husbands, then the possible number of conceptions would be reduced. Furthermore, breastfeeding was the norm at least to the age of 2. Garcilaso de la Vega stated that the mother had no intercourse during this period. He wrote: "While women were breastfeeding they had no sexual intercourse because it was said to weaken the baby. Those sickly creatures were called *ayusca;* . . . which means, in its full meaning, the denied, and more properly the one who had been exchanged for another by his own parents."[29] Although such a practice would limit the number of births, it might also be expected to increase the likelihood of survival of the living infant.

Social factors conducive to population expansion include religious concepts of fertility: the moon, the sister of the sun and protectress of childbirth; and special huacas that assisted the woman to conceive. Prior to the birth itself, the mother confessed and petitioned the huacas for a successful delivery. Guamán Poma said the woman was withheld from heavy field labor during the child's initial twelve months. Youth was protected: Punishment for anyone killing a boy or girl was death by stoning or by being thrown over a cliff. The societal practice of celibacy might counteract these factors, but celibacy was not, as far as can be ascertained, significant. Women chosen as *mamaconas* to serve in religion were withdrawn from the fertile pool, but their number was probably not large:

> Early sources tell us they were numerous but this does not give us a basis for quantification. We might even suppose that the frequency with which the chroniclers mention the "Virgins of the Sun" is due to the interest occasioned by their resemblance to nuns, rather than to their numerical importance.[30]

Age at marriage has a clear impact on population growth. A woman who marries at the age of 18 can have a much larger completed family than one who marries at the age of 30. According to most chroniclers, the Inca expected all male workers to marry ultimately, but the age at which they married or the age of their wives is not clear in the testimony. Under the Inca, formal betrothal was a function of the state. During the annual inspection the official assembled males and females of marriageable age in opposite rows. At the appropriate time in the ceremony the boy chose his mate. If two young males contested the same woman the Inca representative decided the matter. When all couples were paired, the official gave the blessing of the Inca. The local marriage came later and followed area custom. The ethnic group, the ayllu, and the couple all participated in the process, so that what appeared to be a system tightly controlled by the state was in fact relatively free. At the same time that the betrothal took place, the state chose exceptional young women for religious service and as wives for the Inca and the curacas. The age of the specially selected young women was approximately 12. Three years of instruction followed before they married or entered temple service. The other women, the majority in fact, probably married before they reached 20. After a study of marriage age, Rabell and Assadourian conclude: "We can support the hypothesis that during the period of highest fertility, from 20 to 30 years, women were already married."[31]

Existing information on possible pre-Columbian checks on Andean population is contradictory and consequently provides little indication of whether Peru's population had exceeded carrying capacity. On the positive side, marriage age of women appears relatively low. Women and children were protected by social, juridical, and religious constraints. Polygyny was practiced, but it was limited to the elite. The state fostered marriage of all adult working inhabitants of the Empire. On the other hand, the mita and warfare temporarily or permanently resulted in the removal of males. There were large numbers of widows and unmarried women. Celibacy of females within the formal structure of organized religion was practiced. There were temporary social and religious taboos against sexual intercourse.

The main argument for very dense Andean populations is the archaeological evidence of widespread and impressive hydraulic systems: irrigation and terracing. Such massive irrigation projects obviously required a large labor force. At the same time, the agricultural works suggest that people made strenuous efforts to squeeze as much food from a limited area as possible. The reason for the need to extend agricultural land is clear: There is little arable land in the Andean region. The coast, viewed from the air, is a long expanse of grey and brown cut by infrequent thin ribbons of verdant green. The sea and its products permitted an economically significant but relatively small population. The agricultural valleys were the centers of dense populations. Much of the central highlands is too broken, high, and cold to permit agriculture. The land above 3,800 meters may be used for pasture. Important as the animals and their husbandmen were, however, populations based on the cameloid could not have been as dense as those relying on settled agriculture. In Peru one may find a group of people living in a valley that is completely irrigated and terraced, with perhaps a dense population of 30,000–50,000 or more, and then have to travel 100 to 135 kilometers over either deserts or puna before reaching another valley of similar settlement. The result is a pattern of populous valleys, separated by expanses of uninhabited or only slightly settled terrain. This is precisely the description of Peru that the sixteenth- and seventeenth-century Spanish chroniclers give. There is no large, open, flat country, as one finds in the central valley of Mexico, with a cover of almost continuous settlement.

The amount of irrigated cropland along the Peruvian coast, the productivity of highland agriculture, the populations supported by pastoral nomadism in the puna region, and coastal fishing and shellfishing all point to a high productivity for the Andean ecosystem. Population pressure on agriculture is suggested by extension to marginal lands, as in the ridged-field system of the Titicaca basin and coastal sunken-field farming. Yet total population estimates based on the ecological data diverge widely. The coastal estimates based on one model range from 1 million to 6.5 million; the number of families living off pastoral nomadism in the Jauja–Huancayo region could have been anywhere from 1,000 to 10,000; and the number of people living off highland agriculture has not yet been estimated satisfactorily. The ecological model has promising use for small geographical entities, but pan-Andean estimates are at present tentative approximations. In spite of the difficulties encountered in attempting to establish the carrying capacity of Inca Peru, we have derived a rough figure of 13.3 million for the coast and highlands. On the basis of what we have seen, it is unlikely that the population of preconquest Peru exceeded this figure.

2

Population and archaeology

Archaeology is a fascinating exercise, but reason has to set bounds to extravagant flights of fancy when seeking to interpret the evidence of inert matter.

Nicolás Sánchez-Albornoz, *Population of Latin America,* p. xiii

In 1965 I suggested that the pre-Spanish population of Peru could best be estimated by archaeologists after careful valley-by-valley investigation of sites and analysis of the productive capacity of ecological systems. As late as 1973 I continued to believe that archaeology held the key to an understanding of the native population. I overestimated, however, both the speed of archaeological fieldwork and the soundness of its methodology. Deriving population numbers from archaeological sources, whether skeletal remains, artifacts, remnants of foodstuffs, or mapping of settlement sites, is a very slow and painstaking process, fraught with major difficulties in the interpretation of the data. I have come to the conclusion that archaeological results covering large segments of the Andean region and providing noncontroversial population material will not be available in the immediate future.[1]

In this chapter we shall examine the general methods of paleodemographers and evaluate the potential of the information they can provide on prehistoric populations in the Americas as well as the limitations in their work. The chapter is organized thematically: We review the value of skeletal remains for population reconstruction, the relation of household dwelling area to the number of inhabitants, and human density and midden deposits; finally, we examine what monumental architecture and cities can tell us about population size. I shall attempt to limit the study chronologically to the two centuries preceding the arrival of Francisco Pizarro and his men on the South American west coast.

Modern archaeology can reveal many demographic characteristics of prehistoric peoples. Two general types of archaeological sources are relevant to population study: first, cultural records, including architecture, tools, and artifacts, agricultural systems, and refuse; second, skeletal remains. The first category enlightens us on social and political structure, household size, diet, and total population. The second kind of source may help the researcher to discern tendencies in longevity, the birth, death, and growth rates, and to ascertain the effects of some types of disease as well as to contribute to the estimation of the total population.[2]

Scientific study of skeletal remains is an exacting task. In large cemeteries, careful sampling techniques must be maintained. For sex determination, joint and skull size and pelvic details have been used. For age assessment, trained paleodemographers utilize such factors as the size and framework of the skull and bones and tooth eruptions.[3] The number of births experienced by a woman can be estimated from the normal changes that occur in the bony structure of the pelvis. Several types of disease and nutritional deficiencies can be diagnosed by their impact on bones and teeth. There is obviously much room for various interpretations of the data. Age assessment is especially difficult, except for the relatively accurate calculations made from normal patterns of tooth eruption to the age of 13. Henri V. Vallois, in an evaluation of age determination of skeletons, suggests that archaeologists can at best use bone and tooth structure to classify the population only in several broad categories: Infans I – children to the age of 6 years; Infans II – 6/7 to 12/13; Juvenis – 12/13 to 21; Adultus – 21 to 40; Maturus – 40 to 59; and Senilis – 60 and above.[4] Exactness is impossible. J. Lawrence Angel argues that "no two experts will agree precisely in judging a single skeleton, but their disagreements will usually average out to a closely similar assessment for a whole population."[5]

Skeletal research of desert coastal Peru offers unique possibilities for paleodemographers. Much may be learned of local disease, nutrition, fertility, mortality, and life expectancy because the climate has aided in the preservation of abundant data. Indeed, there is so much evidence concealed in the extensive cemeteries of the coast that the process of investigation appears overwhelming. In spite of, or rather because of, the large amount of information, there are limitations to what actually can be learned through skeletal study. In the first place, some coastal graveyards are so large that it would be impossible for a single archaeologist to analyze the entire universe. Scientific sampling is necessary, and the sampling technique chosen may influence the results. Second, burial sites were often used for several generations, and some were even utilized by different cultures. In such cases it is necessary to date each skeletal remain and artifact found in individual graves. Because of the complexity of the task facing paleodemographers, accumulation of new knowledge is very slow.

Household dwelling area provides another approach to population estimation. Naroll postulated a relatively constant relation between population size and the floor area of dwellings. In a study of eighteen cultures he reached a space requirement of approximately ten square meters per person.[6] Steven Le Blanc cited a study by Lyon of the small settlement of Wachipaeri in Paucartambo, Peru, who noted that the average roofed-over space per person in the community was 9.4 square meters. Not counting the community's chapel, the standard deviation was 4.7 square meters. Unfortunately, the population size is small (twenty-nine), but the approach should be further tested in Peru, on both contemporary and archaeological sites.[7]

Another way to estimate population using archaeology is by study of midden deposits. As early as 1909 N. C. Nelson pointed out the difficulty of making population projections on the basis of analysis of shell mounds because it is impossible to know how many were using the site at the same time.[8] Nevertheless, recent and more sophisticated analysis has opened up new solutions while at the same time presenting unforeseen problems.[9] Cook and Treganza studied four mounds, including one in the San Francisco Bay region, which had been examined previously by Nelson, and concluded a fairly constant relation between the area of a mound and the number of people who created it, "the logarithm of the population being about half that of the log of the mound's area in square meters"[10] A fully elaborated quantitative analysis was worked out by Robert Ascher based on research on a Zuma Creek, California, mound. During the Zuma fieldwork Ascher employed a screen to sort out materials taken by column sampling. He found that most of the weight in the site was from mussel shells. Ascher's method for reaching population size by shell deposits may be traced in general terms: Each mussel weighs about 2.5 grams; there are 1.065 grams of meat per mussel and 7.5 grams of protein in each 100 grams of meat. On the basis of deposits, 1,925,107 grams of protein were available to the inhabitants of the site during the time required to accumulate 0.3048 meters (1 foot) of deposits. Ascher assumed that about 5 grams of protein a day were consumed by each person. On the grounds of the depth of deposits and other investigations, he concluded the site was inhabited for twenty to fifty years. The population, therefore, could have been anywhere between twenty-one and fifty-three residents.[11] Ascher's results compare favorably with the figure derived by using Martin A. Baumhoff's formula based on the amount of shore frontage that is suitable for shellfish-gathering purposes: forty inhabitants. Application of the Cook–Treganza procedure to the same Zuma Creek site furnishes an estimate of thirty persons.[12] Ascher's models yield a range of population on the order of 1:2.5. This range is much narrower than, for example, the extent of calculations using architectural remains to serve as population estimates for both the Yucatán and Peru. Many of the Yucatán and Chan Chan population projections based on architectural and house counts range up to and even exceed 1:10. Ascher's work has been severely criticized by Glassow on two main counts: First, there were too many uncontrolled factors; and second, Ascher did not relate the population to the local ecosystem. There were nine variables in Ascher's model; some were subject to a wide margin of error. Glassow concluded: "If we submit to calculation the *extremes* of the ranges in the nine variables, the results in terms of population estimates vary from less than 1 to more than 200 individuals."[13]

Mark N. Cohen has outlined the difficulties in using middens to generalize about populations in Peru. From the coastal site of Lurín near Lima, Cohen made a single cut, 2 meters long by 1.5 meters wide by 1.5 meters deep. In that cut alone there were between 40,000 and 50,000 vegetable remains. In all there were about 100,000 items in the section. Richard S. MacNeish, in Central Mexico, had only 110,000 pieces of preserved matter for the entire Teotihuacán project. Cohen suggested, on the basis of the Lurín cut, that MacNeish may not have been even close to a significant sample in statistical terms. During work at the nearby Ancón Necropolis, however, Cohen took only 3,000 countable items from about 12 cubic meters of refuse. Cohen was forced to try to explain why there was a paucity of data at one coastal Peruvian location, yet at a site not far removed the remains were abundant. Obviously vegetable traces are highly sensitive to soil chemistry, but if there is a larger percentage of preserved animal matter, then the percentage figure for human consumption may be inaccurate. In view of the difficulties, Cohen's final statement is pessimistic:

> I was forced to conclude that, at least for the Peruvian coast, and probably for other regions as well, accurate quantitative measurement of organic remains is impossible; that only the most general of quantitative trends can be accurately envisioned; and that even those general trends can be reconstructed only tentatively until they have been reconfirmed by a large number of parallel lines of evidence.[14]

Midden analysis for Peru might be most valid for coastal shell-mound sites, which could have contained only a small percentage of the total population. As Cohen demonstrated, midden vestiges of vegetable foodstuffs, which would have been produced by Peru's agricultural society, would have decomposed to the point where quantitative analysis is difficult. The advantage of using shells to make population estimates is that they do not disintegrate readily. Analysis of mammal, bird, and fish bones in Peruvian middens might yield results of narrow ranges, save for the insurmountable difficulty of ascertaining the portion of animal to vegetable sources in the inhabitant's diet.

There is one almost indestructible artifact associated with the Peruvian population: ceramics. The remains of fired clay pots are available in all parts of highland and coastal Peru. Sherburne F. Cook outlined the promise and limitations of using these residues as an index of population in his comprehensive review of four southwestern United States sites. The first task using Cook's method is to count the number of shards in each volume unit or to take the weight of the residue. Sifting the mounds' remnants through a standard-size mesh speeds up the process. It is also necessary to calculate the volume of the mound from which the sample is taken. Results depend on what Cook terms the "mean annual production, or acquisition of pottery."[15] Past societies have used and discarded pots at varying rates. George M. Foster, working with modern peasants in the community of Tzintzuntzan, in Michoacán, Mexico, studied the utilization of ceramics in four households. He noted three main categories of use: daily, occasional, and storage and semiceremonial. The average lifespan of pots in daily use is estimated to be one year. For occasional cooking and eating purposes the pots lasted about eight years, and for storage about twenty. Cook believed Foster's data represent the maximum. He considered 5.75 kilograms to be the annual turnover for a family, 5 kilograms in "primitive" areas. Cook concluded that although there are difficulties in determining population size from pottery remains, reasonable ranges can be established. "Pottery residues, or indeed any residues can serve as an index to population provided the four cardinal parameters can be defined in numerical terms. These are . . . total amount of residue, turnover rate, duration of production and use, and association of unit quantity of residue with unit population."[16] Application of such a technique to Peruvian circumstances presents the same problems as midden analysis. Pot remnants are ubiquitous in Peru, yet are denser in some locales than in others. Careful sampling controls would have to be ensured, and even then the results would be subject to a relatively wide margin of error.

Archaeological evidence of human habitations and monumental

architecture provide another method of population estimation. The number of houses, house space, and the labor force required to construct great mounds, pyramids, and temples allow for tentative generalizations on population size. A very brief survey of the application of such analysis to one limited area of pre-Columbian America – the Yucatán – suggests the margin of error that may be involved. Oliver G. Ricketson and his associates reached a population density for the Yucatán of 104.5 persons per square kilometer. The estimate was based on archaeological counts of house mounds in a section of the urban complex of Uaxactúm. Ricketson calculated that five people were associated with each mound but that only one-fourth of the mounds were simultaneously settled; and he assumed that only one-half the surface of the Yucatán was habitable. With these qualifications, Ricketson concluded the peak Old Mayan population was about 13.3 million.[17] Morley set the range for the Yucatán at between 13.3 million and 53.3 million, believing that all house mounds were occupied at the same time.[18] Brainerd, in a revision of Morley, thought only one house in eight was inhabited concurrently, so the density could only be 52.5 per square kilometer (136 per square mile). Brainerd then argued that the figure should be further reduced to 24.7 to 17.4 per square kilometer for a total Yucatán population range from 2,216,666 to 3,325,000.[19] George L. Cowgill, basing his figures partly on an estimation of the minimum labor force required to erect the major monuments, set a minimum probable density for the area at 11.6 per square kilometer (30 per square mile).[20] Thompson pointed out that one of the problems encountered in making valid calculations for the Yucatán was that the Maya often buried a person in a house, then abandoned it. Population counts based on house mounds are consequently inaccurate.[21] Such a wide variation in demographic estimates for the Yucatán, which has been relatively well surveyed archaeologically, illustrates the difficulty in establishing the population of less well-studied and larger regions.

Recent reevaluation of archaeological data for the large complex of Chan Chan is illustrative of the intricacy of projecting population on the basis of Peruvian architectural remains. Chan Chan was the administrative capital of the Chimú state, which extended 1,000 kilometers along the coast north of the modern city of Lima. The state was highly organized, and its economy was based largely on irrigation agriculture. Chan Chan is situated in the Moche valley, not far from modern Trujillo. Although the dates are imprecise, it appears the Chimú state originated around A.D. 1000 and existed until conquest by the Incas in the 1470s.[22] Chan Chan appears from the air to be an impressive urban center, covering 24.5 square kilometers. It is well laid out in a gridiron pattern. High walls divide sections of the complex, and it contains numerous large mounds. There were a total of ten large rectangular enclosures, now called *ciudadelas,* oriented in a general north-to-south direction. These sections were entered by a single passageway from the north. The Rivera ciudadela, one of the larger units, had walls nine meters high and four meters thick at the base.[23] Otto Holstein in 1927 estimated the population of the complex to have been 200,000 at its height. Adolph Bandelier in 1948 calculated 40,000; but Donald Collier (1961) postulated 50,000.[24] Michael West, who studied the site in detail, concluded that approximately fifty-eight rooms were found in each 1,000 square meters of habitation. He believed a family of three occupied on the average three rooms and hence arrived at a total density of fifty-eight people per 1,000 square meters.[25] West argued the ciudadelas were used primarily not for habitation but rather for ceremony and storage. He concluded:

> I would postulate a very small population in and a low density for these massive structures, probably in the vicinity of 10,000 people or less for all of them. This would raise the minimum site population to 68,000. Taking this into account along with the possibility of other densely occupied areas not yet clearly defined, the site may have had a population in excess of 100,000 people.[26]

Michael E. Moseley, in a recent evaluation of Chan Chan as a preindustrial city, revised the population figures sharply downward. He argued that few Indians ever resided in the ciudadelas, except for a small number of retainers in the southern sectors of the compounds who supported the state's aristocracy. He stated: "In fact, at the close of the occupation only one royal enclosure was an active administrative center; the rest were mausoleums . . . It may be that at its height, Chan Chan housed less than 25,000 to 30,000 residents."[27] As can be seen, population estimates for this complex, perhaps one of the most thoroughly excavated of all the large coastal sites in Peru, range from 25,000 to 200,000. It is evident that further research and methodological refinements will be necessary before study of architectural remains will yield reasonably consistent and reliable population estimates.

Unfortunately, although archaeological investigations in Peru have continued at a relatively even pace over a period of several years, only a fraction of the sites have been surveyed. North coastal research has been limited usually to either very large or small settlements. Chan

Chan represents the first type. Because of the enormity of the complex, it will take several years of thorough investigation by various researchers before trustworthy results are obtained. Excavations of smaller sites bring more immediate fruits. The findings of Kautz and Keatinge for Medaños la Joyada, fourteen kilometers northwest of Chan Chan, are illustrative of the latter. La Joyada is made up of sunken gardens in a stabilized sand-dune region, which at one time was used to grow totora reeds for the making of mats and small rafts (caballitos) used by coastal fishermen. Many other crops were produced and consumed, and extensive marine resources were used by the Indians. The excavations allowed the research team to determine that the site was intensively occupied between 1476 and the early colonial period.[28] Further, Kautz and Keatinge found evidence that the site was left suddenly: "The preponderance of artifacts which were apparently abandoned in usable form along with the remains of foodstuffs does not seem to argue for an orderly or purposeful abandonment of the site." The authors suggested that Spanish enforcement of "encomienda policies" could have led to relinquishment. Kautz and Keatinge failed to point out that population loss suffered during a major epidemic could produce similar results.[29]

Farther to the south, Parsons and Psuty have examined in detail part of the Chilca valley. There, beginning around A.D. 800–1150 and continuing through the early colonial period, sunken-field agriculture was intensively practiced. Evidently, the demand for new croplands was great enough to stimulate development of the coastal plain. Significant manpower resources had to be invested to create the relatively large area of sunken fields. With no measurable rainfall and no major source of irrigation, crops were grown in depressions that were close enough to the water table to provide moisture for plant roots. When maize was planted in the Chilca sunken fields, a small fish was deposited with the kernel in order to provide fertilizer and perhaps moisture during germination. Of the Peruvian coast surveyed by Parsons and Psuty, the Chilca valley relied most heavily on the sunken-field method of agriculture. There, about 27 percent of the total irrigable land was devoted to this type of production. Other coastal valleys that used the technique were Pescadores, with 3.5 percent of the land being thus exploited; Asia, with 3 percent; Moche, with 1.8 percent; Lacramonte (Chimbote), with 1.6 percent; and Pisco, with 1.1 percent. Current evidence indicates that sunken-field agriculture developed relatively late and could perhaps have been due to population pressures in the nearby irrigated valleys.[30]

The archaeological examination of the ridged-field lands in the

Lake Titicaca basin and in some other parts of Peru, which we have surveyed in Chapter 1, suggest high population densities. William Denevan notes: "These were nuclear areas in terms of population growth and cultural evolution and were apparently characterized by the progressive utilization of new ecologic niches as population increased and new technology was developed; the most difficult habitats were brought into cultivation last, usually with elaborate reclamation."[31] The full extent of human occupation of the Titicaca area needs further archaeological investigation, however, before the total numbers that could have been sustained can be approximated.

Edward P. Lanning succinctly summed up the state of knowledge in Peruvian paleodemography by the late 1960s when he discussed the population of the Late Intermediate Period (1000–1476):

> As in other periods, there is no way of estimating population except by general impression. The ancient population had certainly reached its maximum at this time. Every archaeologist who has worked fairly widely in Peru has had the experience of finding Late Intermediate sites wherever he looks, whereas sites of other periods often take more effort to locate. There were a few valleys where the population seems to have declined, but they are rare exceptions to the general rule.[32]

Archaeological evidence does suggest that the population of the Virú valley of the north coast declined during the Late Intermediate Period, by perhaps as much as half. Important cities did flourish on the north coast, however: Pacatnamú, Chan Chan, Purgatorio, Apurlé, and Farfán, for example. New cities appeared in the Huancayo and Huánuco regions of the central highlands, and Pachacamac, Kuelape, and Kollor continued to be inhabited during the period.[33] John H. Rowe, in a study of Andean urban centers, refused to give precise numbers. He did suggest that cities and urban life rose and declined in Peruvian civilization before the arrival of the Europeans. Pachacamac on the central coast near modern Lima, for example, had been a large urban complex early in the Late Intermediate Period but had declined by the time of its conquest by the Incas. The huge urban complex of Cajamarquilla in the Rimac valley probably reached its maximum size during the Late Intermediate Period but was deserted by the time the valley was taken over by the Incas.[34] In an extensive part of southern Peru, Rowe saw "virtually no large cities in this area in the Late Intermediate Period and the Late Horizon." Large cities, however, had clearly existed in southern Peru earlier.[35]

Archaeological investigation of Cuzco might shed some light on its size under the rule of the last Incas. It is now clear that the city was neither large nor well laid out until the reign of Pachacuti (ca. 1438–71). Pachacuti's conquest made of Cuzco an imperial administrative center, and he undertook to rebuild it in keeping with its new greatness. Pachacuti is responsible for a number of developments. In order to increase the surface area, a large sector of swampy land near the core was drained, the magnificent Temple of the Sun was constructed, and the foundations of the great fortress of Sacsahuaman above the city were laid. Pachacuti probably followed a clay-model master plan in his efforts to construct the new city. Streets were relatively straight but did curve when necessary to fit the topography. They were paved with stone and had a water channel running down the middle. The center, between the Tullumayo and Huatanay streams, was used for palaces and temples of the major figures and was constructed using the best stone-working technology available. Other residents were scattered in communities in the valley surrounding the ceremonial core of Cuzco, with farm plots in the intervening open spaces. Dwellers of the capital were either indigenous or were transplanted from the provinces (mitimaes, or members of the provincial nobility). If they had come from the provinces, they were spatially distributed within the greater Cuzco complex in the approximate direction of their place of origin.[36] The Chachapoyas and Cañaris, for example, were in the northern sector in the direction of Carmenca. Cuzco was both the seat of an empire and a religious shrine. There were temples of the chief deities (Sun, Creator, Thunder) and lesser shrines. Even the shape of the urban complex had ceremonial significance: From the air the shape of a puma can be traced, with Sacsahuaman as its head. There were daily ceremonies relating to the sun and periodic ceremonies relating to the calendar and major events. Principal provincial cult objects were hostages in Cuzco. The compounds of the mummies and cults of the Inca ancestors composed a major part of the center. The convent of the Chosen Women was also situated in the core. The palace of the living Inca and the homes of the nobility and their servants complete the overview of the pre-Spanish urban site. But how many people inhabited the core between the Tullumayo and Huatanay rivers and the surrounding area below the Sacsahuaman fortress? Here archaeologists have not been able to provide good information. There are numerous problems in Cuzco archaeology. It is difficult to excavate and study a site that is currently occupied; digging in a densely populated area is prohibitive. Rowe stated: "Impressionistic estimates tend to be high, but there were evidently a lot of buildings. The archaeological evidence confirms this conclusion, but there has been so much destruction, and erosion on the hillsides, that we cannot use the archaeological sites to obtain more precise figures than the eyewitness estimates."[37] We shall examine the ethnohistorical evidence of Cuzco's aboriginal population in Chapter 13.

Many problems are involved in any attempt to use archaeology to generate population numbers. We have seen the difficulties in using skeletal remains to study demographic characteristics. In spite of the nature of Peru's coastal climate, which aids in the preservation of vegetable and animal remains, there are obstacles in the sampling technique and in interpretation of the articles. Another limiting factor is the vast area of the country. Perhaps more important is the extent of the chronological sequence we are dealing with, literally from the dawn of Andean prehistory, which is currently estimated to be in the neighborhood of 20,000 B.C., to the arrival of the Spaniards. The great time span means that only a small part of archaeological investigation will concentrate on the period in which we are most interested – the Late Horizon (A.D. 1476–1534). Indeed, most of present research is on sites that predate A.D. 1200. Further, only a sector of the archaeologist's interest concerns us in this chapter: paleodemography. Although archaeology has made major advances in Peru in the last generation, many important sites remain to be investigated. Even as the results of new studies become available, there is the obvious problem of interpretation. The range of population estimates for the complex of Chan Chan clearly demonstrates the question of inference of maximum occupation density. In concluding this chapter, I must concur with the assessment of a demographer, William Peterson, in his review of the population data generated by recent archaeologists:

> Increasingly during the past decade or two, archaeologists, prehistorians, anthropologists, and practitioners of related disciplines have grappled with the problems involved in deducing population statistics from various types of merely indicative data. The results have seldom been satisfying even to the authors themselves.[38]

3

Depopulation ratios

> Arguing by analogy with some known population (e.g. as in a model
> life-table) may help, assuming that the analogy is sociologically fair,
> but the society in question may be unique in history, and consequently
> not susceptible to such an analogy.
>
> T. H. Hollingsworth, Historical
Demography, p. 304

One of the simplest ways of estimating Peru's aboriginal population,
and one that has been frequently used by scholars, is the depopulation
ratio method. Use of depopulation ratios is straightforward. It does
not presume an extensive knowledge of statistics. The argument is
clearly understandable, and the manipulation of numbers gives an
impression of scientific accuracy. The procedure is logical: Known
population figures for precontact groups and later census figures for
the same population unit are used to derive a ratio. The ratio is then
applied to estimate the total regional population from a known census
total. In this chapter we shall examine the sources, techniques, and
conclusions of four recent investigators who have used depopulation
ratios to estimate the Andean native population: John H. Rowe,
Henry F. Dobyns, C. T. Smith, and Nathan Wachtel.[1]

John H. Rowe was one of the first modern scholars to utilize the
depopulation method to calculate the aboriginal population. His estimate is based on five samples: two (Rimac and Chincha) for the coast
and three (Yauyos, Huancas, and Soras) for the central highlands (see
Table 4). These five cases are employed by Rowe because there are data
for both the Inca period (ca. 1525) and the Toledo era (ca. 1571).
Rowe's results and sources are outlined in Table 4. Rowe's method
proved to be a major improvement over previous attempts to calculate
the Andean population; consequently, his work has been widely cited
and his total often accepted. Yet close scrutiny of Rowe's analysis
reveals some weaknesses. The key to any depopulation ratio method is
the validity of the figures that are used. Rowe's first example is
Rimac. The 1525 estimate of 150,000 is based on "the stated number
of *honokoraka*, or chiefs of 10,000 taxpayers, maintained in each

Table 4. *Rowe's figures for population change, 1525–1571*

| Province | Population | | Depopulation ratio |
	1525	1571	
Rimac (coast)	150,000	9,000	16:1
Chincha (coast)	50,000	2,070	25:1
Yauyos (sierra)	50,000	35,000	3:2
Huancas (sierra)	135,000	36,000	3:1
Soras (sierra)	20,000	15,159	4:3
Total	405,000	97,229	4:1

province by the Inca government."[2] The total number of inhabitants is reached by multiplying the amount of taxpayers by five, the approximate ratio of tributaries to the total population in two "samples" of 1571 data. It is hazardous to directly correlate the Inca "taxpayer" with the colonial tributary. Testimony from Chucuito in the 1560s illustrates the difficulty of establishing ages, in the European sense, of the Inca taxpayer. One witness reported the age of tributary in Inca times was from 30 to 50; others stated the range was 30–60.[3] The colonial system was precise: Tributaries were able males between 18 and 50 years of age. The application of a ratio of 1:5 is thus suspect. Furthermore, Rowe's 1:5 ratio is based on only two data sets: Soras and "Rucanas" for 1571. These are two of literally hundreds of Toledo figures. This is not an adequate statistical sample. In addition, the 1525 Rimac as well as the Chincha and Yauyos totals are based on the number of *honokoraka*. Three such officials for Rimac imply 30,000 taxpayers and convert to 150,000 inhabitants (1:5). Was Inca administration as exact as implied in such analysis? It is highly unlikely there were exactly 10,000 taxpayers under each official. Might not one official be in charge of 7,000 and another supervise 12,000? Further, Rowe's 1525 figure of 50,000 for Chincha is close to estimates of many sixteenth-century chroniclers of Chincha's preconquest taxpayer population, not the *total* population. Rowe's 1525 estimate for Huancas is based on a late sixteenth-century report that there were 27,000 "war Indians" there under the Incas (5 × 27,000 = 135,000 total). Rowe's 1525 estimate for Soras (20,000) is based also on a late sixteenth-century source, which related that there had been in the province "two-thirds more" Indians in Inca times than found during Viceroy Toledo's census.[4] Rowe miscalculated, however, and added one-third to Toledo's figure of 15,159 instead of two-thirds. A corrected depopulation ratio for Soras would be near 5:3 instead of Rowe's 4:3. In addition, most of Rowe's 1571 figures are not the correct Toledo numbers. The exact figures have long been available to scholars, yet Rowe apparently did not consult them. When the repartimientos of the Rimac valley are totaled their population reaches 5,367 (Rowe's figure is 9,000), Yauyos totals 16,677 (versus 35,000), and Huancas totals 37,661 (not 36,000).[5] On the basis of the five samples and the overall depopulation ratio of 4:1, Rowe estimated the total population of the Inca Empire at 6 million. He justified his sources and his use of them:

> This table includes all the reliable estimates of Inca population that have been preserved for our area, and, as the tribes listed were selected by the historical accident of this preservation, the group can be fairly called a random sample. It is also a representative group, for it includes two of the provinces known to have suffered worst between 1525 and 1571 (Chincha and Rimac) and two that escaped relatively unharmed (Yauyos and Soras).[6]

Aside, however, from objections already raised as to the handling of the data, it must also be pointed out that the "random sample" of two central coastal and three central highland regions, of *hundreds* possible, does not provide a solid footing for historical generalizations. As shall be seen, both Dobyns and C. T. Smith reevaluate Rowe's data and method.

Henry F. Dobyns also used the depopulation ratio method and reached a total estimate of between 30 million and 37 million for the same area. After a study of Indian depopulation throughout the Americas following the introduction of European disease, Dobyns concluded that "the depopulation ratio of 20 to 1 appears to be a sound, if perhaps conservative, total to employ as a hemispheric minimum."[7] The higher estimate (37.5 million) is based on a possible depopulation ratio of 25:1. Dobyns was very much influenced in his investigations by the findings of Woodrow Borah and Sherburne F. Cook for the Mexican region and by his own research of the recorded rapid depopulation of some American Indian tribes. The direct evidence that Dobyns mustered for Peru is meager. He took the Rowe depopulation ratios for Chincha (25:1) and Rimac (16:1), which he believed to be more representative than Rowe's highland ratios, and the data on the quota of mitayos to serve in the Potosí mines. Toledo's mita assessment for Potosí in the 1570s was 95,000; in 1663 the Potosí mitayo assessment was reduced to 40,115, and by 1689 to only 10,633. Dobyns believes that the decline in the number of mitayos was paralleled by a general Indian population decline.[8] The resulting depopulation ratio is about 9:1. Unfortunately, although the Potosí draft was set at one-seventh of the tributary population, the number of mitayos bore little resemblance to the number of tributaries. It is clear (see Chapter 13) that when Indians migrated from their native *corregimientos* their status changed to forastero, and thereby they became exempt from the draft. Such an inducement was often great enough to create a flood of migration in corregimientos subject to Potosí mita. By 1689 over half the inhabitants of some corregimientos subject to the mita were forasteros.[9] Thus, although the quota dropped, it did not reflect the true population change of the region. Further, the Potosí mines were declining in productivity in the late seventeenth century, and the labor need was being increasingly met by paid wage earners.

Dobyns used one other source for Peru: a 1685 report, which stated that on the road between Paita and Lima there were once 2 million Indians but that only 20,000 remained. This is evidence enough for Dobyns to suggest a depopulation ratio of 100:1. The report was made by Gabriel Fernández de Villalobos, who became Marqués de Varinas.[10] Unfortunately, the Varinas "evidence" is difficult to verify. Two million coastal inhabitants between Lima and Paita before the Spanish arrived are possible, but Varinas wrote 150 years after the fact. Was his figure an estimate? If so, it should be noted that the author was a polemicist and was arguing the cause of the Indian, charging the European with excessive exploitation. Varinas's figure for 1685 must also be scrutinized. Is it based on Viceroy Palata's returns of the 1680s for the coastal region (see Chapter 6)? Does the 20,000 include Indians living within Trujillo and Lima? The biography of the Marqués de Varinas is the story of a man of action, a soldier of fortune. He was a soldier, farmer, slave trader, merchant, smuggler, shipwreck survivor, and on occasion a prisoner in both Brazil and Spain. His career does not suggest a man who was careful in his figures.[11] The point is that Dobyns based his Andean estimates primarily on the experience of an inadequate sample of population change in a small number of geographical regions. His hard evidence for high depopulation ratios for Peru is fragmentary. Further, Dobyns did not ferret out all the evidence.

C. T. Smith arrived at an estimate using a depopulation ratio model that is more convincing than either Rowe's or Dobyns's. The model is based on the Garcí Diez de San Miguel visita of the province of Chucuito in 1566.[12] At the time of the inspection the Spanish requested information on the number of tributaries in Chucuito during the administration of the last Incas. Don Martín Cari, curaca of the Hanansaya moiety of the village of Chucuito, produced quipus that recorded the last Inca census. The results obtained from the quipus were listed in the visita by moiety and village and included most of the administrative units of the province (see Table 5). The totals for the 1525 population of Chucuito comprise 4,129 Urus and 15,778 Aymaras, for a total tributary population of 20,280. The visita results of 1566 report a total of 15,404 tributaries (see Table 6). In 1571 there were 17,779, and, according to Smith, there were 13,364 about "1628."[13] Smith assumed that the low point in the population curve was reached around 1628. To find the depopulation ratio between 1520–5 and 1571 it was necessary for Smith to estimate the total populations at those dates. Instead of using the Toledo 1570s figures for Chucuito, Smith used the results of the 1566 census: The total recorded population was 63,012. He then calculated a multiplier (4:1) on the basis of the data. Smith then had to estimate the total Inca population from the quipu tributary data of 20,280.

The difficulty was in ascertaining the age categories for the Inca census. We have seen that, when asked what age tributaries were in Inca times, Martín Cari replied that they were 30 to 60. Other witnesses concurred. One Chucuito informant reported, however, that the age was 30 to 50, and another elaborated that before the Spaniards arrived the tributary was an adult married male with his own house and fields.[14] This conflicting testimony suggests that in Inca times the criteria for tributary status implied more than strict chronological age in the European sense. Other testimony implies that status depended more on "function" than on age. The Europeans, as they viewed Inca census categories, did what they believed was correct: They tried to assign a true age to the native term. This in fact explains the many inconsistencies in European descriptions of the native census. If this be the case, the Inca tributary was a healthy, working, married, adult male with house and fields. When the European asked, "How old?" the Indian generally chose what appeared to be a European age equivalent. This is probably the type of much testimony from the 1540s to 1570s. The curacas of Chucuito in 1566 must also have been aware of the fact the Europeans were weighing the evidence to permanently set the colonial tribute age categories. They must also have been aware of the 18–50 age category that had been elaborated elsewhere in the Spanish Indies. For self-interest, the Indians might state a high beginning age for tribute under the Inca system in order to avoid payment as long as possible. Here John Murra's critique is apropos: "What the Europeans translated as *tributario* ap-

Table 5. *Inca census of tributary population, Chucuito, ca. 1520–1525*

District	Uru	Aymara	Others	Totals
Chucuito				
Parcialidad de Anansaya	500	1,233	0	1,733
Parcialidad de Lurinsaya	347	1,384	0	1,731
Total	847	2,617	0	3,464
Acora				
Parcialidad de Anansaya	440	1,221	0	1,661
Parcialidad de Lurinsaya	378	1,207	0	1,585
Total	818	2,428	0	3,246
Ilave				
Both parcialidades	1,070	1,470	0	2,540
Juli				
Parcialidad de Anansaya, + 153 Indians of Chinchasuyo, mitimaes of the parcialidad de	158	1,438	153	1,749
Lurinsaya	256	1,804		2,060
Total	414	3,242	153	3,809
Pomata				
Parcialidad de Anansaya, + 20 Canas, mitimaes of the	110	1,663	20	1,793
parcialidad de Lurinsaya	183	1,341		1,524
Total	293	3,004	20	3,317
Yunguyo				
Both parcialidades	381	1,039	0	1,420
Zepita				
Parcialidad de Anansaya	186	1,112	0	1,298
Parcialidad de Lurinsaya	120	866	0	986
Total	306	1,978	0	2,284
Sama				
Yungas native Indians, both parcialidades	0	0	220	200
Recorded total	4,119	16,151		20,270
Actual total[a]	4,129	15,778	373	20,280

[a] The discrepancy between recorded and actual totals is a result of incorrect addition.
Source: Espinosa Soriano, *Visita de Chucuito,* from Smith, "Depopulation of the Central Andes."

Table 6. *Age–sex structure of the population of Chucuito, 1566*

| | Aymara | | Uru | | |
	Men	Women	Men	Women	Total
Married couples, ages 17–50	8,707[a]	8,707[a]	3,199	3,199	23,812
Widowers and bachelors with their own houses, ages 17–50	2,110		394		2,504
Marriageable men in the houses of their relatives, ages 17–50	841		189[b]		1,030
Married couples over 50	626	626	196	196	1,644
Widowers and bachelors over 50	257		58		315
Widows and spinsters with their own houses, ages 17–45		4,401		1,241	5,642
Spinsters in the houses of their relatives, ages 17–45		1,027		190	1,217
Widows and spinsters over 45		2,768		738	3,506
Boys and girls, 11–16 years	2,930		725		3,655
Boys and girls, 10 and less	14,869		4,708		19,577
Blind and others unable to work but of tributary age, 17 and over		96		14	110
Total	47,965		15,047		63,012
Total of tributary males[c]					15,404

[a] Given in the text as 8,607 in roman numerals but as 8,707 in arabic.

[b] Given as 89 in arabic but as 189 in roman numerals.

[c] 11,658 Aymara and 3,782 Uru, less 36 caciques (all Aymara and not subject to tribute).

[d] Thus, the ratio between total and tributary population is 4.1:1.

Source: Data from Espinosa Soriano, *Visita de Chucuito,* from Smith, "Depopulation of the Central Andes."

proaches only marginally the social and economic condition of the *hatun runa,* the able bodied, married, male household head . . . for the same reason I would hesitate to use any arithmetic expression of the household leader's age."[15]

Smith, aware of the difficulties of Inca age classification, opted for 30–50 or possibly 30–60. It was then necessary for Smith to estimate the total Inca population. To do this, he used two methods to convert the adult male population to the total population. First, he used the proportion of the male population in the 30–60 and 30–50 age groups in the 1940 Chucuito census; second, he used the rough proportion of tributary males in the 1566 census. In 1940, 9.25 percent of Chucuito's population were males 30–50, and 12.2 percent were males 30–60. "Applying these proportions to the tributary popula-tion of late Inca times, then, estimates may be reached of 219,240 people (assuming the tributary age range was 30–50) or 166,230 people (assuming the tributary age range was 30–60)."[16] Smith be-lieves the 1940 census is a good population model to use because it was taken before the impact of modern medicine on the region, the count was of a modestly growing population, and it was previous to the contemporary exodus to the coast and urban centers. A case can be made, however, against use of the 1940 census as a model. There was a severe underenumeration of infants in the 1940 Peruvian census, the population at that period was growing more rapidly than Smith be-lieved, and migration was a relatively important factor.[17] In the 1566 data the age–sex structure was not complete, so for the second model Smith was forced to interpolate the 30–50 age group on the basis of the 17–50 totals. (In the 1560s the male began tribute payment at the age of 17. Toledo modified the age to 18, where it remained to the end of the colonial period.) For interpolation Smith turned again to the 1940 census. In 1940 males ages 30–49 composed 51.1 percent of all males between 17 and 50. On the basis of that figure, Smith calcu-lated that 12.6 percent of the population were males between 30 and 49 years of age in 1566. If this percentage is applied to the 1520–5 figures, the Inca total population of Chucuito would have been 160,800. Smith's mean figure for the two methods outlined above is 190,000; consequently, the depopulation ratio for the province be-tween 1520–5 and 1566 is 3:1.

On the basis of this depopulation ratio Smith proceeded to revise Rowe's estimates. The chief line of attack is on Rowe's multiplier of 5 for the whole Andean region in 1520–5 and 1571. According to Smith the ratio of tributaries to the total population of Chucuito in 1566 was 1:4. In order to strengthen his argument, Smith took data to calculate multipliers from several other provinces. There are four-teen multipliers in his universe (seven are for Otavalo in Ecuador in 1582), the range is from 3.4 to 6.2, and the mean is 4.75. Smith employed the mean figure to revise Rowe's estimates for the early 1570s. Then, for the 1520–5 figures, Smith "corrected" Rowe by use of a multiplier of 9, his result for the case of Chucuito (see Table 7). The sample populations in the highlands examined by Smith are Yauyos, Huancas–Hatun Xauxa, Soras, Huamanga, and Chucuito; for the coast he used Rimac and Chincha. The calculated highland depopulation ratio is 3.4:1, and the coastal ratio is 58:1. Then, to estimate the total Peruvian population in 1520–5, Smith multiplied 284,040 highland tributaries in 1571 by 4.75 to reach a total 1571 population of 1,349,190, then multiplied that by 3.4 to arrive at 4,641,200 in 1520–5. In the calculations for the coast, tributaries of 1571 were converted to the total number (27,217 × 4.75 = 129,281), then multiplied by the depopulation ratio (129,281 × 58) to reach 7,498,298. When coast and sierra were added, the estimated population in 1520–5 was 12,139,498.[18] Although Rowe and Do-byns made estimates for the whole Andean civilization area, Smith's estimate appears to be for only the "central Andes" (Peru?). Unfortu-nately, Smith failed to cite his source for the 1571 highland and coastal populations. It should be noted that his sample coastal popula-tion (1571) was only 1,309 of a total 27,217, and the highland sample was 31,816 of 284,040. The samples are rather inadequate. Certainly Smith's use of depopulation ratios is interesting; his model is more rigorous than that of Dobyns, and he is in most ways more convincing than Rowe. Glaring problems remain, however. Smith's use of 9 as tributary multiplier for 1520–5 can be taken to task. The figure 9 should be considered "maximal"; it is likely a true figure lies between Smith's 9 and Rowe's 5. Smith's sample is too small. Fur-ther, his use of the 1940 Chucuito census can be attacked; and the sources for his 1571 figures for highlands and coast are not cited, nor do we know to what area they apply, except broadly the "central Andes."

Nathan Wachtel also used depopulation ratios to estimate the preconquest population of the Inca Empire. The key dates in Wachtel's analysis are 1530, 1560, and 1590. Wachtel approaches the problem by first establishing the 1560 and 1590 populations and rates of depopulation. The 1560 figures are based on comparative study of the 1561 data in the Muñoz collection (396,000 tributaries, incomplete), Matienzo (535,000 tributaries), and López de Velasco (680,000 faulty, revised to 495,000). Wachtel picked approximately

Table 7. *Revised estimate of population, Central Andes, ca. 1520–1525*

	1571			1520–5			Depopulation ratio
	Tributary Indians	Multiplier	Total	Inca tribute payers	Multiplier	Total	
Sierra (sample populations)							
Yauyos	7,000	4.75	33,250	10,000	9	90,000	2.7:1
Huancas–Hatun Xauxa	6,953	4.75	33,027	27,000	9	243,000	7.3:1
Soras	2,459	6.2	15,159			25,265	5:3
Huamanga			35,500			71,000	2:1
Chucuito (1566)	15,404	4.1	63,012	20,280	9	190,000	3:1
Total			179,948			619,265	3.4:1
Coast (sample populations)							
Rimac	897	4.75	4,261	30,000	9	270,000	63:1
Chincha	412	4.75	1,957	10,000	9	90,000	43:1
Total			6,218			360,000	58:1
Total populations							
Sierra	284,040	4.75	1,349,190			4,641,200	3.4:1
Coast	27,217	4.75	129,281			7,498,298	58:1
Total	311,257		1,478,471			12,139,498	

Source: Smith, "Depopulation of the Central Andes."

500,000 tributaries for 1560, and a total population of 2.5 million, based on five persons per tributary. Wachtel chose the 1561 census rather than the more reliable Toledo results because he mistakenly concluded that only fragments of the Toledo inspection were available. His generalization that "it is not until about 1590 that we find country-wide estimates" is likewise erroneous.[19] The 1590 figure is based on the 1586 "census" of Canelas de Albarrán and the data of Luís de Morales Figueroa (1591). Wachtel recognized that Morales included Toledo census results for some repartimientos but failed to make the appropriate adjustments in the Morales figures when he concluded that the 1590 population was between 1.3 million and 1.5 million. The population thus declined about 40 percent between 1560 and 1590. Wachtel noted major regional differences in the process: The north (Quito region) declined 60 percent; the center (most of Peru), 30 percent; and the south (southern Peru and Charcas), only 13 percent. Elsewhere Wachtel incorrectly dated and used Vázquez de Espinosa data for "1630."[20]

Wachtel, with the 1560 estimate in hand, proceeded to calculate the 1530 population. "Without contemporary estimates, we have to make do with doubtful extrapolations, by calculating on the basis of precise but isolated examples, the probable rate of population decline between 1530 and 1560." Wachtel cited Rowe's use of a 75 percent decline for the period but cautioned that "the examples on which he bases his hypotheses are still disputed."[21] Wachtel then presented his own case. The 1530 estimate is based on the "recorded" experience of four groups: the tributary population of Chupachos was 4,000 in 1530 and 800 in 1562; Hananhuanca was 9,000 in 1530, 1,700 in 1548, and 500 in 1571; Yucay was 3,000 in 1530 and 780 in 1558; and Chucuito was 20,000 in 1530 and 15,000 in 1567. Wachtel calculated an average decline of over 75 percent from 1530 to 1560 for the first three cases (the correct calculation is near 85 percent). In the last case the decline is 25 percent, but the Chucuito Indians experienced "privileged conditions"; therefore, the first three "appear to be more representative of the overall trend," but he admitted "they represent groups too small to serve as a reliable basis for generalization."[22] Nonetheless, Wachtel built his final argument on these three cases:

> If, hypothetically, we accept an intermediary rate of overall decline of 60 to 65 percent from 1530 to 1560, we obtain totals of 7 to 8 million for 1530. Given the inadequacies of the sources (essentially census figures of tributaries some of whom fled to avoid registration) we might reasonably propose an estimate of about 10 million inhabitants.[23]

Several criticisms may be directed at Wachtel's method. First, no attempt is made to determine what population the 1530 figures referred to in the four cases. C. T. Smith attempted at great lengths to correlate Inca and Spanish "tributary" data. Wachtel only glossed over the problem of the statistical meaning (especially the age category) of the 1530 data. Second, there are no coastal examples in Wachtel's group, although it is widely believed that the coastal rates of change varied significantly from highland figures. Third, the statistical sample is inadequate. The total "tributary" population of the three cases cited by Wachtel reaches only 16,000, yet he used that figure to derive a total population estimate of 10 million. Fourth, his projection is for 1530, yet the first contact (through European disease) took place several years before.

There is another way of applying the depopulation ratio model to estimate the preconquest population of Peru – by direct analogy with the depopulation of Mexico, an area carefully examined by the "Berkeley School" of Latin American historical demographers. Borah and Cook, after several years of detailed study, have estimated that the rate of population decline for the coastal area averaged −6.87 percent yearly between 1534 and 1573. During that same period the highland population of Central Mexico declined at an annual rate of −3.74 percent. Borah and Cook concluded that in less than a century after contact with Europeans only 4 percent of the preconquest population remained. Viewed another way, the population in 1519 was roughly ten times what it was in 1568 – 25.3 million versus 2.6 million (see Table 8).[24] If we take a similar overall ratio of decline for Peru, with

Table 8. *Borah and Cook estimates of the Mexican population*

Year	Number in millions
1519	25.3
1523	16.8
1548	6.3
1568	2.6
1580	1.9
1595	1.3
1605	1.0

Source: Borah and Cook, *Aboriginal Population of Central Mexico.*

our "solid" estimate of 1,290,680 for 1570 (see Table 18), the pre-conquest population might be approximately 12 million; or, if we use the rates for the Mexican coast and highlands, with the Peruvian coastal and highland population figures of 1570, the Peruvian totals may be calculated (see Table 9). The total population projected by this method is 14,400,640.

There are three major weaknesses in this depopulation model. First, the Borah and Cook figures for Central Mexico have not been accepted by all critics. Angel Rosenblat has posited a maximum Mexican conquest period figure of about 4 million and has consistently refused to accept higher estimates. The majority of researchers, however, recognize that the Borah and Cook work is the most accurate and hence the most reliable of what we now have. Nicholás Sánchez-Albornoz implied there is no effective challenge to their conclusions. Henry F. Dobyns based part of his 1966 estimates of the aboriginal population of the hemisphere on Borah and Cook's studies.[25] Second, the Mexican rates are for the 1534–68 period. The time span is chronologically similar to Peru (1530–70); however, the historical experience in Peru concerned the *initial* contact and subsequent events. In Mexico the equivalent historical period would have been about 1520–60. The coastal–highland rates of decline could have been very different in the 1519–34 period in Mexico. The third methodological weakness is the problem of the applicability of the Mexican experience to the Peruvian case. Although essential similarities cannot be denied, Peru is certainly not Mexico. It is true that both areas were relatively densely populated at the time of contact, that neither native group possessed immunity to European disease, and that both peoples were conquered in a short time and then exploited within the Spanish colonial system. The contrasts cannot be overlooked, however. European diseases probably spread more rapidly in Mexico than in Peru. In Mexico the highland population was

Table 9. *Peru's 1520 population, based on the Mexican rates of decline*

	1570 population	Rate (Mexican experience)	1520 estimate
Coast	245,530	−6.87	7,619,140
Highlands	1,045,189	−3.74	6,781,500
Total			14,400,640

concentrated in the central plateau in villages with relatively easy access to each other. A network of markets and roads resulted in easy communication and transport of products. The coastal population of Mexico was also tied into the system. In Peru, by contrast, the coastal populations were concentrated generally in east–west river valleys, often widely separated by stretches of deserts. The highland populations were also scattered, with difficult access, in mountain basins. The sierra settlements were located in north–south direction, in contrast with the east–west coastal valleys. Further, the average elevation of Peru is significantly higher than that of Mexico. Elevation affects people and also influences disease. Relatively more isolated and living at higher elevations, the native Peruvians may have suffered slightly less from the consequences of epidemics than did their Mexican counterparts.[26]

Review of the findings of Rowe, Dobyns, Smith, and Wachtel leads to the inescapable conclusion that there must be a better way to estimate Peru's 1520 population than to use depopulation ratios. All four had difficulties in obtaining accurate data and misjudged part of the numbers they did use. They encountered problems in converting tributary to total populations, especially during the Inca regime. Here Smith was most successful. All suffered from what I consider to be a totally inadequate sample on which to base reliable population projections. The final figures for the four are: Rowe's Inca Empire, 6 million; Dobyns's 30 million to 37 million for the same area; Smith's 12 million for the "central Andes"; and Wachtel's 10 million for the area presumably controlled by the Incas. The probable Empire estimate for the four ranges from 6 million to 37 million. For the sake of comparison, I have projected figures for Peru alone, using depopulation ratios for Central Mexico and applying these to the Andean scene. These estimates extend from 12 million to 14 million. In spite of the simplicity of the depopulation ratio method and the manipulation of numbers that appear at first glance to be trustworthy, the technique is useful only at a certain level. The method unfortunately gives us the results we expect. Researchers who anticipate large totals get them, and those who envision a more moderate population project intermediate figures.

4

Estimates from social organization

Social scientists have long been aware that a relationship exists between the size of a society in terms of population and its degree of sociocultural complexity.

Robert L. Carneiro, "On the
Relationship between Size of
Population and Complexity of Social
Organization," p. 234

Population estimation on the basis of social organization is one of the least accurate of the methods we shall examine. At best, we can only infer in general terms how high populations were at various levels of societal complexity. It is obvious that a people supported by a hunting, fishing, and gathering technology would be smaller than a group living by intensive irrigation agriculture. The basic differences in the population characteristics of primitive, agricultural, and industrial economic systems have long been a subject of investigation of historical demographers. In the present chapter we shall review some recent developments in the study of social structure and population size, then examine applications of the method to Incaic Peru.[1]

Robert L. Carneiro has documented a relationship between the number of organizational traits of a society and the size of the group. As societies become larger they become structurally more complex. The relationship is direct, but structural complexity does not increase as rapidly as population. Indeed, for Carneiro, growth provides the very impetus for societal development. "The pressure brought about by the quantitative increase of like units leads inevitably to a critical point at which the system must either fission or advance to new levels of organization by undergoing a qualitative transformation."[2]

D. E. Dumond goes so far as to suggest that population is the independent variable and that any change in social organization is dependent on population size. Michael J. Harner attempted to test by analysis the relationship between population pressure and social evolution. Harner studied 1,170 societies, became thoroughly convinced that there indeed is a relationship between the two, and con-

curred with Dumond that societal evolution takes place as a consequence of population pressure. Yet Dumond admitted that the exact
level of social complexity reached is not predictable: "It appears, that
although an increase in the density of population will bring on altera-
tions in social organization, this increase in density cannot certainly
be expected to result in the degree of centralization associated with the
term civilization."[3]

The relationship between population and social structure is implicit in Julian H. Steward's classificatory system of culture areas,
with population densities in high civilization empires sharply larger
than among the hunters, fishers, and gatherers. It may also be seen in
his developmental sequence for areas of early civilization. Steward
suggests that as culture areas go through the stages of hunting and
gathering, incipient agriculture, formative, regional florescence, and
cyclical conquests the population increases.[4]

The question that must be answered in any attempt to apply the
method to Peru under the Incas is not whether there was a complex
social and political structure that might signify a high population but
how·large that population was. The complexity of Andean social
structure gives few clues to exact numbers, but there are simple ways
in which numbers can be assigned to political or social units. Philip
Ainsworth Means found one such way in his famous study of the Inca
Empire. He took idealized population numbers for variously sized
Inca administrative units and added them to reach a total estimate for
the realm. His line of argument and conclusions are worth repeating
in their entirety:

> The *Puric* household has been variously estimated to contain
> from five to ten individuals. From this it follows that the *Chunca*
> contained from 50 to 100 people, the *pachaca* or Incaized ayllu
> from 500 to 1,000, the *huaranca* from 5,000 to 10,000, the
> *hunu* from 50,000 to 100,000, and the *guamán* or province ruled
> by a *tucuiricuc* consisting of four *hunu-cuna* from 200,000 to
> 400,000. In an attempt to arrive at some notion of the total
> population of the realm at the time of its greatest extension we
> are hampered by a lack of knowledge as to how many *guamán-
> cuna* were contained in each of the four *suyu-cuna* or quarters
> ruled by the four viceroys or *apu-cuna*. A careful study . . . con-
> vinces me that each *suyu* must have contained at least twenty
> *guamán-cuna*. This figure gives to each *suyu* a population of
> between 4,000,000 and 8,000,000 and to the Empire of
> Ttahua-ntin-suyu a population of between 16,000,000 and
> 32,000,000. Assuming, for caution's sake, that it was much

closer to the lower of these figures than to the higher, we find that the population of the empire was approximately twice as great as that of the same territory today.[5]

Means, like many other western scholars, was impressed by the obvious administrative ability of the Incas. Their empire seems to have been as well put together as their stone temples, palaces, and fortresses. The Inca technique of transferring the inhabitants of a peaceful area to a bellicose region, and vice versa, is well known. Frequent censuses and elaborate age classifications were admired by sixteenth-century Spanish colonial bureaucrats, who described them in detail. A conscious effort of the Incas to "balance" the population, to ensure subservience to the state, and also to provide full utilization of natural resources was part of their successful policy. Yet, did the system function in reality in the fashion described by Means? J. Alden Mason, in his study of the prehistory of the Andean area, noted that it was unlikely that the system outlined by Means really existed. The normal sequence of births and deaths would have required almost constant shifting of population to maintain the theoretically described balance.[6] Dobyns reports that the criticisms of the system outlined by Means "are undoubtedly valid insofar as one might attempt an exact reconstruction of peak Inca Empire population, yet they do not seriously impute the utility of Means' method for obtaining an approximation of the actual population."[7] Another recent scholar, in a reevaluation of Means, does not accept a rigorous decimal organization of the Inca state. Yet Richard Schaedel states:

> There does seem to be growing archaeological and ethnohistorical confirmation for the existence of a principle of ordering the populations of provinces within decimal magnitudes which would account for disaggregation (as in the case of the Chimú state with 3/4 million inhabitants) and the aggregation of the small chiefdoms into the Huánuco province.[8]

Other population estimates can be derived from social–political structures. One such method would be to use the tribal units of which the Inca state was composed. In each of the approximately fifty-seven tribal areas, or provinces, that made up the territory of what is now modern Peru, there lived 200,000 people in Inca times. The assignation of this number is based on Wendell C. Bennett and Junius B. Bird: "The ideal province had 40,000 workers representing about 200,000 inhabitants."[9] Multiplication of this figure by 57 would give a total population estimate of 11.4 million for preconquest Peru. Such a figure has no basis in fact, however. It is only an idealized picture of what the population might have been, not what it was in reality. The efforts of Means and others who wish to use the political–social structure model to estimate the preconquest population must end in frustration.

Henry F. Dobyns, in reviewing the possibility of population projections on the basis of aboriginal social structure reconstruction, states:

> The really serious limitation on the use of the method of estimating population upon the base of an ideal socio-political structure is simply the extreme scarcity of hierarchically organized states whose administrative structure is based upon a theory of uniformly populated governmental entities. An ancillary limitation on the use of this method is the rarity of state boundaries which coincide with those of cultural or geographic areas whose population an investigator wishes to discover.[10]

I am not as optimistic as Dobyns. It is not the scarcity that concerns me but the applicability of what I consider to be a methodologically unsound approach. It would be impossible to maintain anything resembling numerical parity of provinces or tribes in the very complex Andean region. Certainly the Incas were the most competent administrators of ancient America, but the requirements of a system of continuous redistribution of people could not likely be met by the Inca administrative structure. Furthermore, the Inca did not force people to conform to a pure statistical population model. People were distributed as a result of the immediate and long-term requirements of the state, not on a need to maintain an ideal number of 100 *hatunruna* in a given territory.

5

Disease mortality models

When the isolation of the New World was broken, when Columbus brought the two halves of this planet together, the American Indian met for the first time his most hideous enemy: not the white man nor his black servant, but the invisible killers which those men brought into their blood and breath.

Alfred W. Crosby, *Columbian Exchange,*
p. 31

Modern medical researchers are able to project the time, place of appearance, rate of infection, and mortality for disease epidemics. The projections are not completely accurate; nonetheless, predictions of impending outbreaks of potentially dangerous epidemics are taken seriously by public health officials. Indeed, modern disease control is based on the premise of predictability. In this chapter we shall attempt to project a preconquest population figure on the basis of estimated mortality for known epidemics that swept Peru in the sixteenth and early seventeenth centuries.

Numerous complicating factors confront the researcher of early colonial epidemics in America. First, descriptions of epidemics are conflicting. It is often difficult to ascertain the correct disease agent that is called various names by colonial eyewitnesses. Second, the American Indians apparently lacked immunity to common European diseases. Measles, for example, which had a low mortality rate for Old World residents, had very high rates for the virgin American Indian population. Third, general health and diet affected the mortality rate for those who became ill. Warfare, famine, and overwork contributed to the death rate for those who contracted the disease. Fourth, it appears that elevation affected the course and outcome of several types of epidemics. This factor is especially important in the Andes. Fifth, either diseases or humans or both evolved during the century after the first contact. Indians may have become gradually more resistant, or diseases less virulent.

Thanks to the research of José Toribio Polo, Juan B. Lastres, and Henry F. Dobyns, we now have a relatively good idea of the chronol-

Table 10. *Peruvian epidemics, 1524–1635*

Dates	Disease	Mortality, comments	Source (pp.)
1524–6	Hemorrhagic smallpox (*sarampion viruelas*)	"Great part"; "may well have been halved"	Dobyns (497) Polo (51–4)
1530–1	Smallpox (*bubas*)	Not general for Spanish, but through all Peru	Polo (54)
1531–2(?)	Measles	From Panama?	Dobyns (499)
1539	"Peste" (typhus), famine	Popayán	Polo (55)
1544–8	Sarna	Two-thirds of livestock died	Polo (55)
1546	Typhus (?) or plague (peste)	Uncounted died	Dobyns (499) Zinnser (256) Polo (56)
1558–9	Influenza, hemorrhagic smallpox (smallpox & measles)	"Many died"	Dobyns (500)
1560	Epidemic (*mortifera*)	Potosí	Polo (58)
1560–1	Peste	Potosí	Polo (58)
1585–91	Smallpox, measles, mumps, typhus, influenza	High mortality during the period	Martínez y Vela (23–5)
1588–9	Smallpox	Quito: women suffered more than men; 4,500 died but not one Spaniard; thousands, esp. children	Dobyns (500–8) Polo (62–4)

Date	Disease	Location / Notes	Source
1606	Measles, smallpox (*contagio*)	Cavana y Huandoval, Castrovirreyna	Polo (68); Lastres (2:179)
1614	Diphtheria, scarlet fever	Cuzco-centered (May–Sept.); affected every household Sp. & Indian; all ages	Dobyns (508–9); Lastres (2:179); Polo (68)
1615	Diphtheria (probable)	Potosí	Polo (68)
1618–19	Measles		Dobyns (509); Lastres (2:179)
1618–19	Measles	Lima, Copacavana; generalized	Polo (69); Lastres (2:180)
1619	Bubonic plague?	Trujillo; rats were thick	Lastres (2:180)
1625	"Tabardillo"	Lima	Lastres (2:180); Polo (70)
1628	Measles, generalized		Lastres (2:180)
1631	Smallpox	Chavín	Polo (70)
1632	Smallpox	Huánuco	Lastres (2:180)
1633	Smallpox	Chavín	Polo (70)
1634–5	Measles		

Sources: Dobyns, "Andean Epidemic History"; Polo, "Apuntes sobre las epidemias"; Zinnser, *Rats, Lice, and History*; Lastres, *Medicina peruana*; Martínez y Vela, *Anales de Potosí*.

ogy of early colonial epidemics in the Andean area.[1] Certainly, it is difficult to be totally accurate in the diagnosis of the historic epidemics. Frederick F. Cartwright warned that the large group of childhood infections, principally measles, smallpox, chicken pox, scarlet fever, and German measles, "are characterized by a rash, and our forefathers had great difficulty in distinguishing one from another."[2] Yet there is at least general agreement on diagnosis among those who have studied the early Peruvian epidemics. A list (Table 10) based on the research of Dobyns, Lastres, and Polo and on additional findings presents a relatively complete chronology of the worst epidemics for the period. In the years between 1524 and 1526 hemorrhagic smallpox, introduced from Panama and preceding the Spanish conquerors, swept through the Inca Empire. Huayna Capac, his son the legitimate heir to the imperial office, and tens of thousands of Indians perished. In 1530-2 a series of epidemics, probably smallpox and measles, passed through all of Peru. In 1546 plague, or typhus, beset the inhabitants of the region. From 1558 to 1560 an influenza epidemic perhaps coincided with a recurrence of hemorrhagic smallpox. The 1585-91 period was characterized by a series of epidemics: smallpox, measles, mumps, typhus, and influenza. Mortality, especially for children, was high. In 1606 there was a recurrence of smallpox and measles, but it appears to have been confined to areas that had been spared during the 1585-91 period. A diphtheria epidemic raged in Cuzco and Potosí in 1614-15. In 1618-19 measles returned, especially in Lima. Smallpox and measles epidemics were also recorded that year for the area of Lake Titicaca.

Infectious diseases vary in the way they are spread. The acute community diseases, such as chicken pox, smallpox, measles, mumps, rubella, and cholera, pass from person to person and are specific to man. Such diseases "require minimum host populations for permanent maintenance; if the sizes fall below the threshold levels, the infections die out."[3] In other diseases the agent may remain for long periods in the host and be infective for varying periods. Amoebic dysentery, typhoid, leprosy, pinta, and trachoma are of this type. Other diseases, such as malaria and filariasis, can be infective in the host for a long period and are passed by intermediate vectors, such as insects. In the high Andes and on the coastal desert, malaria did not become a major hazard.[4]

The conditions necessary for a widespread epidemic are now recognized. Immunologists agree that major epidemics take place only where there is a concentration of susceptible individuals. Dr. Jacques M. May stated:

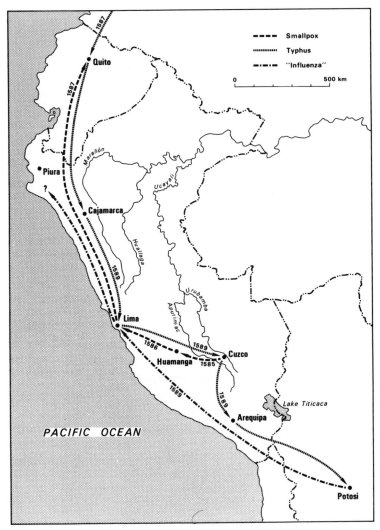

Map 3. The 1586–9 epidemics in Peru. (*Source:* Wachtel, *Vision of the Vanquished.*)

In order for an epidemic to occur, a critical percentage of the population must be susceptible. This percentage is supplied chiefly by new generations coming into contact with the virus, and is determined by cultural conditions. After a human population group has had measles, it takes some time for the number of susceptibles to reach the critical point again.[5]

Another researcher, Frank MacFarlane Burnet, elaborated: "Measles under modern conditions can persist only in large communities and could neither have developed nor survived among small isolated groups."[6] It is evident that the question of the "threshold size" has not been adequately answered by medical researchers. T. Aidan Cockburn suggested that, for measles, the cycle can be continuous in a city with a population of about 1 million.[7]

In order to apply the disease mortality model to estimate Peru's contact population, it is necessary to ascertain the rates of mortality for the major disease epidemics that struck the Andean populations during the period. Little direct evidence is available for mortality during the sixteenth and seventeenth centuries. One way around the problem is to apply the analogy of known mortality rates for more recent epidemics. In Iceland, for example, during a smallpox epidemic that lasted from 1707 to 1709 approximately 18,000 of a total of 50,000 inhabitants died. Crosby stated: "Analysis of figures for some twenty outbreaks of smallpox shows that the case mortality among an unvaccinated population is about 30 percent."[8] It is evident that when a smallpox epidemic occurs in an isolated population, which had never contracted the disease, almost everyone is infected, as the Iceland case of 1707–9 illustrates. Friar Toribio de Benevente (Motolinía) in the 1541 *History of the Indians of New Spain* vividly described mortality in that area during the initial biological contact between the Aztec and Old World resident:

> The first plague was an epidemic of smallpox. It broke out in this manner. Hernando Cortés was Captain and Governor at the time when Captain Panfilo de Narváez landed here. On one of his ships came a Negro striken with smallpox, a disease that was unknown in this land. New Spain was thickly populated at this time. When the smallpox began to infect the Indians, there was so much sickness and pestilence among them in all the land that in most provinces more than half the people died, whereas in others the number was somewhat smaller.[9]

Mortality from smallpox could be high, even for the Europeans. In England, for example, eighteenth-century mortality for smallpox was about one in five cases.[10] Smallpox mortality in fact varies from about

1 percent for *variola minor* to about 30 percent for classical smallpox (*variola major*).[11] Cowpox (*variola vaccinae*) is another form. An attack of any of the three provided the European at least temporary immunity against the other two. It appears that in the Americas Indian mortality during the first epidemic of classical smallpox must have ranged from a minimum of 30 percent to much higher, perhaps 50 percent, as Motolinía reported for some sectors of New Spain. The medical historians Zinnser and Cartwright also accept a mortality of 50 percent for New Spain.[12]

Measles was also a serious disease for the native American, even though it was a common childhood illness in the Old World. Even for European children, measles was potentially dangerous, because of the risk of contracting pneumonia.[13] There is also a strong possibility that pregnant women who contract measles may give birth to deformed or stillborn infants. There is also a good chance that the offspring will be partially or totally deaf. In the sixteenth century in Peru, it appears that several measles and smallpox epidemics coincided. It is therefore difficult to differentiate deaths caused by one or the other of the two diseases during an epidemic period. In more recent epidemics among susceptible populations, high measles mortality has been documented. The introduction of measles to the South Pacific Fiji Islands in 1875, for example, resulted in the death of about 40,000 of the 150,000 inhabitants. The registered mortality rate in the Fiji case is about 27 percent.[14] Zinnser suspects that the 1531 New Spain epidemic (probably of measles) had a lower mortality than the 1519–20 smallpox epidemic.[15] Elsewhere, measles caused large population losses. In the third quarter of the nineteenth century the Yahgan population of the Tierra del Fuego region at the tip of South America numbered between 2,500 and 3,000. In 1881 a precipitous decline was initiated, and by 1884 the population stood at about 1,000. By 1886 there were only 400 Yahgans; by 1899 there were 200; by 1902, only 130; in 1913, less than 100; and by 1933, some 40. The causes for such incredible mortality are relatively well documented. Initial respiratory infections in the early 1880s were followed by a severe measles outbreak in 1884. Whooping cough, typhoid, and smallpox followed shortly thereafter. Further, the introduction of European clothing, shelter, food and alcoholic beverages, and labor regimen contributed to the destruction of the Yahgans' culture.[16] A similar decline took place in the population of the Ona living near the Yahgans. In the last quarter of the nineteenth century there were 2,000 Ona, but by 1940 fewer than 50 remained. In this case the decline was speeded by the invasion of Ona territory by sheep ranchers and gold seekers in the early 1880s. The invasion ultimately contributed to a bitter campaign on the part of the invaders to exterminate the Ona.[17]

In the Faroe Islands no measles had been experienced between 1781 and 1846. The total population of the island was 7,864. About 6,100 inhabitants came down with the disease when an epidemic was introduced in 1846. The rate of mortality was about 1.6 percent for those infected. Measles returned to the Faroes in 1875, but only those under the age of 30 contracted the disease.[18] Measles was also introduced into the Hudson Bay region of Canada in 1846. During a six-week epidemic in one Indian group, 145 were infected and over 40 died, for a mortality rate of about 25 percent.[19]

When measles and smallpox occurred concurrently, as often was the case, mortality could be especially high. This fatal combination probably struck several repartimientos in the Cuzco region in 1606. Two sets of tributary data that remain, counts made in 1602 and 1609, allow calculation of mortality for the period. The results are recorded in Table 11.[20] Such high rates of mortality, almost 60 percent, can suggest the disastrous effect on populations when the two diseases coincided. High mortality in this area of Peru may be the result of the region's escaping the 1589–91 epidemics, leaving these populations highly susceptible to the 1606 outbreak. To the northwest, the populous repartimiento of Andaguaylas la Grande did experience the earlier epidemics and declined at a rate of −10.57 percent annually between 1591 and 1594, for a mortality total of about 31.71 percent. Yet Andaguaylas increased its population from 1603

Table 11. *Mortality during the 1606 epidemics (smallpox, measles)*

Repartimiento	Annual rate of change, 1602–9	Maximum epidemic mortality
Guaytara	−13.30	93.1
Quichuas Aymaraes	−20.43	61.3
Tanquigua	−5.26	36.8
Soras	−6.75	47.3
Andamarcas	−9.79	68.5
Lucanas	−8.81	61.7
Quinua	−5.83	40.8
		Mean: 58.5
		Median: 61.3

to 1608 at a rate of 4.55 percent yearly. There were apparently enough people immune to the diseases in 1606 so that no major local outbreak recurred.

An influenza epidemic passed through Peru in 1558–60. According to available evidence, it appears that a smallpox epidemic swept the area concurrently. Influenza is caused by a virus and is a highly communicable disease, spreading from person to person by "infective droplets." Mortality varies, according to the type of virus. Unfortunately, the strain of virus producing almost all historic epidemics is unknown, for the influenza virus was not isolated by scientists until 1933. In the last great pandemic in 1918–19, mortality was high: 500,000 died in the United States, and in Europe more succumbed from the disease than died in actual combat in the four years of World War I. The influenza outbreak hit young adults especially hard, not only in the United States but elsewhere as well.[21] D. I. Pool, in a study of influenza mortality among the Maori of New Zealand, found sharply higher rates for natives than for nonnatives of the island (crude death rates of 22.6 per 1,000 as opposed to 4.5 per 1,000). Further, among the Maori the male death rate was much higher than the female (27.7 versus 16.3). The 30–34 age cohort experienced heaviest mortality (106.5 per 1,000 for males and 56.6 for females). The result was that a high percentage of marriages were dissolved by the death of at least one partner. The child–woman ratio declined for the next several years. In the attempt to explain higher native than nonnative mortality, Pool hypothesized: "Because exposure of Maoris to influenza mortality prior to 1918 had been for only two relatively brief periods, there may have been little chance for 'genetic drift' such as would develop in a population with immunity acquired by those means."[22] Katz, in an attempt to analyze mortality differences for age and ethnic groups in the United States, found that the highest death rate was among the young adults of recent immigrants. "Living in isolated, rural communities where contact with outsiders was rare, they would not have been exposed to the man-to-man droplet contact, the crowding, and the constant influx of new infective vectors vital to the spread of influenza. Consequently, they would not have had the chance to develop immunity."[23]

These conclusions are relevant to the experience of the Indian in Peru. With the introduction of the influenza virus around 1558, the infection spread relatively rapidly among still densely settled groups. The disease probably reappeared during the 1585–91 epidemic period, perhaps coming from the direction of Potosí in 1589 and spreading in a northerly direction to Lima and on toward Piura. Levels of mortality from influenza alone for the Peruvian population cannot be ascertained. A rate similar to the highest experienced by the Maori males (about eleven per hundred) would be possible during the 1558–60 outbreak in Peru, as there was not likely to be immunity as a result of previous infections. Influenza, coupled with smallpox and measles, could easily have led to a high mortality level for that epidemic period.

In 1546 a new epidemic reached the Andean area. There is disagreement on the type of disease. Fever and bleeding nostrils were two symptoms noted by observers. Some reported the malady was the *peste,* a word meaning specifically "plague" or generally "epidemic."[24] Zinsser suggested it could have been typhus (*tabardillo*). There was probably a typhus epidemic in New Spain in 1545, with recurrences in 1576, 1588, and 1595. Zinsser found it "highly probable" that typhus existed in Central Mexico before the Europeans arrived.[25] Contemporary medical evidence suggests that Peruvian Indians are resistant to typhus. In the community of Pusi, on the edge of Lake Titicaca, about half the adults carry typhus antibodies. Body and head lice infestations there are ubiquitous.[26] If typhus has been endemic in the Andean area for several centuries, then it is unlikely to have had as high a rate of mortality as some of the diseases that were introduced into the New World.

Malaria in Peru also seems generally less likely to cause death than other diseases. Mosquitoes, the key vector in the medical history of malaria, are most prevalent in Peru in the Amazon basin and montaña. Health investigators, in a recent study of the distribution of mosquitoes in four areas of Peru, found probable malaria carriers were rare. The *Anopheles darlingi* is the main vector in the Peruvian Amazon, but in the sierra malaria is infrequent. Medical researchers in Peru have concluded: "The percentage of persons who have positive malaria histories in interviews decreases as the altitude of the village increases."[27] Malaria in the desert coastal Peru is and was less frequent than in the humid Amazon basin. The community of Yacango, in the coastal section near Arequipa, has a rate of malaria history of about 12.6 percent for males; the village of San Antonio, on the Marañón River, has a rate of 25.3 percent; and highland Pusi on Lake Titicaca has a rate of only 0.7 percent for the mid-1960s. Although current research in medical history suggests the New World "appears" to have been free of malaria before European expansion, the fact has not been definitively established.[28]

There is little information on diphtheria during the colonial period in Peru. There is evidence that there was an epidemic in 1614–15; and it has been reported that there were six diphtheria epidemics in Spain from 1581 to 1638.[29] But no specific studies have been made on diphtheria mortality in colonial South America. Because evidence is lacking, it is necessary to make an estimate of diphtheria mortality based on the few available data. Were there a census of a repartimiento immediately preceding and another following the passage of an epidemic, calculation of the rate of mortality during the period would be a simple matter. Unfortunately, censuses were not taken annually. To further complicate the matter, there were epidemics of smallpox and measles in Cavana and Huandoval and the surrounding area in 1606, and there was a general measles epidemic in 1618. To estimate mortality for diphtheria in the 1614 period, we need a population unit with a census following 1606 and preceding 1618. Of the 585 Peruvian repartimientos, only two such cases exist. Lunahuana's tributary population of 320 in 1608 fell to 265 in 1617. Huachos Chocorvos had 572 tributaries in 1608 but only 440 in 1616. If the loss in populations in both is ascribed solely to diphtheria mortality during 1614, then the rate for the first repartimiento is 17 percent and for the second is 23 percent. The average of both is 21 percent. Diphtheria mortality varies and is dependent on the type contracted. In an epidemic period that spanned 1735 to 1740 in the Anglo-American colonies of New England and the Middle Atlantic, diphtheria "may well have caused the death of more than 20 percent of the entire population under 15 years of age in those regions where it occurred."[30] In a major European outbreak in 1927 some 600,000 became infected, and, of these, 150,000 died. The disease is communicated by contact with nose and mouth droplets or via infected utensils, so that isolation and quarantine can slow down or stop its spread.[31] It is unlikely that diphtheria swept all of the Peruvian viceroyalty in 1614–15; therefore, a conservative estimate of a 10 percent mortality level seems more plausible than 20 percent.

A preconquest population estimate using disease mortality is founded on three basic premises: First, in the vast majority of cases, the cause of Indian death in the century following contact was disease; second, mortality levels for the various diseases can be established with relative accuracy; and third, there was little population growth between epidemic periods. Unfortunately, epidemic mortalities have to be estimated because absolute levels cannot be calculated on the basis of extant evidence. The disease mortality model here employed (Table 12) provides two alternatives: one of "high" mortality and another of "low" mortality. The rates are only estimates. A smallpox mortality rate between 30 to 50 percent among people who have not

Table 12. *Possible population loss due to epidemics, 1524–1619, with "maximum" and "minimum" mortalities (base population of 1,000)*

Epidemic	Dates	"Maximum model"			"Minimum model"		
		Rate	Deaths	New population	Rate	Deaths	New population
Smallpox	1524–6	50	500	500	33	333	667
Smallpox, measles	1530–2	30	150	350	25	167	500
Plague or typhus	1546	20	70	280	20	100	400
Influenza, smallpox	1558–60	20	56	234	18	72	328
Smallpox, measles, et al.	1585–91	60	140	94	30	98	230
Diphtheria	1614–15	10	9	83	10	23	207
				83:1000			207:1000

contracted the disease before appears to be reasonable in comparison with known experiences elsewhere. A measles mortality of between 25 to 30 percent likewise appears tenable on the basis of known evidence. The combination of the two diseases, which occurred in 1585–91, warrants a 30 to 60 percent mortality figure. A similar combination in 1530–2 took place too soon after the 1524–6 epidemic to justify such a high rate of death. Further factors suggesting exceptionally high mortality in the 1585–91 series are reports of probable epidemics of mumps, typhus, and influenza alongside the smallpox and measles. The 1546 rate of 20 percent for typhus is an estimate based on the similarity of European and Indian mortality for this malady. The 10 percent mortality for diphtheria is an estimate, founded on the two examples and on analogy of diphtheria mortality elsewhere. Using the minimal rate of epidemic mortality model, an Indian community with a population of about one hundred would have been reduced to twenty in the century following 1520. In the maximal model, only eight would remain of the original hundred. It is clear that in the application of the epidemic mortality model the range of total population estimates is narrowed considerably, in comparison with the possibilities when archaeological or ecological models are used. If we take a calculated base in 1620 of 671,505, the "maximal" 1520 population on the basis of the model is 8,090,421, and the minimal population estimate is 3,243,985.

Epidemics affect some sectors of the population much more than others. Population change would be minimal twenty to thirty years after an epidemic that carried away only adults over 50 years of age. On the other hand, an epidemic that killed most children under 5 but no adults would have an impact on the population as that cohort decimated by disease passed through its childbearing cycle several years later. In Peru, epidemic mortality for children was high, but almost all couples whose infants died during an epidemic were new parents the following year. The normal pattern of spacing children was broken during epidemics. The recuperation in the population could in such a case be rapid, especially if the following five-year cohort constituted a larger than normal population, as often appears to be the case. Conversely, if mortality is constantly high among the adult childbearing population, the group can become virtually extinct. The overall rate of mortality is a less critical factor than age-specific mortality in determining future population trends.

Ultimately, some type of immunity must have passed to remaining Indians. The mechanism by which immunity to a disease is acquired is a matter of investigation for medical researchers. Resistance to disease may be of three basic categories: "active immunity, in which the body reacts specifically against the invader; passive immunity, in which antibodies are passed from the mother to the offspring via the placenta, milk or egg; and genetically inherited nonspecific resistance."[32] The third type may be illustrated by the African's resistance to malaria, which is often lethal in Europeans. Unfortunately, the African's abnormal hemoglobin causes sickle-cell anemia; thus, the ability to ward off the very dangerous malaria was gained at the cost of a greater risk of sickle-cell anemia. It was the third type of resistance that permitted low rates of death during frequent epidemics of measles and smallpox among the Europeans; lacking such resistance, the Indians suffered very high mortality.[33]

If the Indian suffered consistently high mortality from measles and smallpox he would have soon become biologically extinct, but extinction, except in the cases of small tribes, did not occur. In part, the survival of the Peruvian Indian was due to active and passive immunity. The number of survivors of epidemics who either contracted the disease or acquired a partial resistance during its passage increased rapidly during the sixteenth century. The frequent recurrences of epidemics and the new infection of susceptible inhabitants helped to establish some immunity and prevented total decimation of the population. Partial immunity was also passed by the recently resistant mother to her offspring. Both smallpox and measles became endemic in the Andean world, causing a decline in mortality from these diseases.

Part of the answer to the survival of some groups may lie in genetic mixture. A mestizo should inherit part of the immunity of the European parent. A mestizo living as an Indian might not be distinguished as a separate census category. If the ability of the Indian to survive was due to racial mixture, then the process needs explanation. Using test mice, Sabin in 1952 discovered that resistance to yellow fever was inherited in Mendelian fashion.[34] Human populations reproduce relatively slowly. Any type of biological immunity must take place over a long period.

Another explanation of mortality decline may lie in the natural selection of less virulent measles and smallpox viruses. The introduction of the myxomatosis virus into the wild rabbit population of Australia for control purposes is illustrative of what might have happened to the measles and smallpox viruses in America. In the first epizootic in Australia, rabbit mortality was between 97 and 99 percent; in the second, 85 to 95 percent; and in the third, 40 to 60 percent. Natural selection could favor rabbits with resistance to the disease, but there must also have been a "selection for comparatively nonviolent strains of the myxomatosis virus."[35] The selective premium is on the virus that does not destroy the host; otherwise, the disease would ultimately destroy itself. The implication is obvious: A virus that has spread from an initial center, through tens of thousands of hosts and across thousands of kilometers of territory, should be less virulent than it was at the center of the original infection. It would be interesting to test this theory were adequate census and vital statistics available. Certainly, if the hypothesis were true it would help explain a relatively low population loss in the Andes of southern Peru.

Further, humans have adapted physiologically to the requirements of high-altitude life in the Andes. If a lower oxygen level, intense cold, and higher radiation influenced the biological evolution of people, there is no reason to expect that disease vectors would be unaffected by the same factors. T. D. Stewart argued that temperature has played an important role in the response of the native American to Old World diseases:

> The cold of the Far North has been characterized as a screen serving in past times to prevent the flow of many pathological germs along with the movements of their human hosts. There is much evidence to support this generalization even in this day of rapid transportation. Apparently the cold screen explains why at the time of the first European contact the Indians lacked many disease entities common to the Old World, and hence were so vulnerable to the diseases introduced by the Europeans and their African slaves.[36]

The high elevation of the Andean puna has adversely affected outsiders. Soroche, or altitude sickness, commonly afflicts residents of sea-level environments who venture into the highlands. Heavy exertion severely taxes the respiratory–circulatory system of the unassimilated. Monge found that Spaniards had difficulty reproducing at elevations over 4,000 meters and that blacks suffered environmental stresses. R. B. Mazess noted that postnatal death rates increase directly with elevation. The native resident of the Andes survives because of a larger lung capacity, a high count of red blood cells, and a large myoglobin content in the muscle. Physiological adaptation has allowed the Andean people to persist in the twentieth century in an environment that is often hostile to the outsider. As Paul T. Baker states:

> The Andean population is also biologically unique in the history of the Western Hemisphere. Of all the major Indian populations living in areas amenable to the agricultural practices of Euro-

peans, only the highland Quechua and Aymara have not been either displaced or mixed to a major extent with intrusive peoples. The strong continuity of the culture and biology of this human group suggests that they had attained an adaptation to their environment which incoming populations have so far not been able to match.[37]

The present attempt to study the numerical effects of disease on populations is not unique. One of the first applications of mathematical models to disease was in the last half of the eighteenth century in France. In 1760 David Bernoulli statistically tried to evaluate smallpox mortality and the effectiveness and risk of inoculation. Biomathematicians currently study "epidemics, recurrent epidemics, endemics, spatial factors, carrier models, host–vector and parasitic disease models, multistate models, interference phenomena, immunization programs, and public health control." Norman T. Bailey recently reviewed the growing literature on mathematical concepts in epidemiology in his standard work on the subject. Due to deficiencies in knowledge of sixteenth-century Peruvian epidemics and levels of mortality in virgin American populations, I presented in this chapter a rather simple model. Further researchers might wish to incorporate the powerful mathematical tools described by Bailey in cases where the evidence is found to be reliable.[38] Nonetheless, the minimal and maximal estimates generated via the disease model method deserve consideration: Three-and-a-quarter million to 8 million residents for coastal and highland Peru in 1520 fall within the general outlines of aboriginal population estimates.

6

Census projections

Of course, statistical analysis is possible only if there is a great number of variables. The more causes that combine to generate an effect, the more dependable that effect will be. In particular, extrapolation assumes that the trend observed over a period can be depended upon not to change too much shortly before and after that period; the more the causes responsible for the trend, the more reliable this assumption will be.

> R. A. Zambardino, "Critique of David Henige's 'On the Contact Population of Hispaniola,'" p. 706

Demographers have for a long period of time estimated populations for dates on which no census was taken. Even if national censuses were available for 1920, 1930, and 1940, for the purpose of analysis it might be important to know the total population at intervening dates. If accurate and complete vital registration were available, estimating the total population at a point in time would be a simple process of addition and subtraction; but an adequate system of vital registration is rare, even in the twentieth century, especially in underdeveloped portions of the globe. Therefore, for the purpose of estimating population in the past or future the standard formula for population change becomes a necessary analytical tool.

The formula $P_2 = P_1 e^{rt}$ represents change as a continuous process, which is indeed true of population movement. The curve of population growth, positive or negative, is an exponential curve, not a straight line. The process reflected by the formula is the same as that for the continuous compounding of interest. If we know, for example, the 1930 population (P_1) and the 1940 total (P_2), we obviously know the number of years between the censuses (t) and can solve the equation for the rate of change (r). With a value for the rate, we can estimate the total population for any date between 1930 and 1940. The results should be relatively reliable, because it is unlikely that major demographic changes were taking place during the short time span. The formula has been widely used to project future populations on the basis of current growth rates. Over a long term, however, growth rates will change. Several factors contribute to variation: changing patterns of mortality and fertility and migratory currents. A modern projection of Peru's population for the year A.D. 2,000 based on the 1961–72 growth rate may miss the true population by several million, if major changes in the variables take place. Yet the formula remains a relatively good tool for estimating population.[1] In the first section of this chapter we shall examine the quality of the early colonial census; then we shall use various methods of census projections to estimate the aboriginal population.

The validity of the census projection method is in large measure dependent on the completeness and reliability of the data on which the estimates are based. Scholars unfamiliar with the sixteenth-century Spanish bureaucracy and the interest in good statistical data on the new discoveries and colonial territories integrated into the Empire have argued that valid demographic and economic information is not available until the eighteenth century. As we shall see, this conclusion is wrong. Data are available, but they must be collected, properly dated, and carefully analyzed. Uncritical use of published population materials is the principal reason for past difficulties of many researchers.

The earliest Peruvian population counts emanated from the need of the Spanish administrators to know the number of tribute-paying subjects being granted to colonists. The encomienda, or *repartimiento de indios,* was an award made by the government for services rendered by individual conquistadores or other persons or institutions important in the colonizing effort of the Spanish Crown. The gift entitled the holder to a monetary payment and, at first, labor services of the charges. In theory, the recipient of the grant was obligated to Christianize, civilize, and protect the inhabitants under his jurisdiction. In practice, exploitation replaced the implied reciprocity of the repartimiento–encomienda system.

The population counts in the first thirty years of the colonial regime in Peru were infrequent and incomplete. The chaos of the period prior to the late 1560s explains the poor statistical information on the pre-Toledo era. Francisco Pizarro had attempted to launch a general count around 1538, and a few copies of local tributary lists or tribute assessments remain from the early 1540s. The assassination of Francisco Pizarro in 1541, and the rebellion of Gonzalo Pizarro from 1544 to 1548, created the instability that made normal administrative activities difficult, if not impossible. With peace restored, however, Pedro de la Gasca prepared an official list of encomiendas in 1549 and called for a complete reassessment of Peruvian encomiendas. For some grants, the approximate number of tributaries was recorded. Viceroy Antonio de Mendoza continued the process in 1551–2 with similar partial results. In 1561 the secretary of the Audiencia of Lima, Pedro de Avendaño, prepared a master list of grants in the viceroyalty, which in some cases included an estimated number of tributaries. All this early data, though useful, cannot be compared with the post-1570 population counts and must be rejected as a foundation on which to build a reliable set of census projections.[2]

The most important single data source for a study of the historical demography of late sixteenth-century Peru is Viceroy Toledo's general census and tribute assessment. Because that record is of fundamental importance in the present analysis, a critical evaluation of the *visita general* is appropriate. Philip II, in his orders to the newly appointed viceroy (28 December 1568), asked the official to draw up a tax register (*libro de tasa*) for repartimientos. The register was to include a list of encomenderos, the amount and type of tribute they received, and the number of tributaries. Supplementary information on the past history of the local assessment was also requested. Shortly after he arrived in Peru, however, Toledo decided a more comprehensive inspection of the viceroyalty was necessary. He named sixty-three secular and ecclesiastical inspectors for the realm, one or more for each chief administrative district, and ordered them to ascertain how many curacas (chieftains) and *parcialidades* (divisions, often ayllus and sometimes moieties) were in each repartimiento. The register had to include married tributaries and their legitimate and illegitimate children, all other children in the village, the blind, ill, crippled, or otherwise incapacitated males of tribute ages, and old and unmarried women. Nonpresent males had to be included on the register, and their length of absence and new residence were to be listed. Next, Toledo's instructions dealt with tribute. The quantity, type, frequency, and place of payment were to be recorded. The *visitadores* were then ordered to inspect local parish registers of baptisms, marriages, and deaths to check whether curacas were attempting to defraud the Spanish government.[3]

Few complete census schedules for individual repartimientos during Toledo's inspection have been located. If all returns for the census were available for the approximately 585 repartimientos that made up the territory of the modern republic of Peru, they could fill a small archive. There exist, fortunately, several summary copies based on the aggregate population and tribute records. The section dealing with the repartimiento of Los Collaguas in Toledo's visita general is illustrative: 4,026 tributaries (ages 18 to 50) were counted, 2,499 of Hanansaya and 1,527 of Hurinsaya. There were 641 older males (including the ill or those unable to pay tribute); 3,966 young men, 17 and under; and 8,915 women. The total population of the repartimiento was 17,548.[4]

Similar censuses were conducted in the late sixteenth and early seventeenth centuries. Most counts were made as a result of rapid population loss and the inability of Indian communities to continue to remit tribute at the Toledo assessment level. European epidemic diseases spread rapidly in the Spanish-style villages in which Toledo had forced the Indians to congregate. Severe droughts and floods brought havoc to some coastal valley systems. Due to a series of particularly serious epidemics from 1589 to 1591, most repartimientos had to be reassessed. These *revisitas,* comparable in format and content to the Toledo inspection, provide the second-best set of population data for the sixteenth century.

The results of the revisitas of the 1589–91 period were compiled for Viceroy García Hurtado de Mendoza, second Marqués de Cañete, by the Audiencia secretary, Luís de Morales Figueroa. This official kept on file all documents relating to each new tribute assessment. It was consequently relatively easy for Morales Figueroa to prepare a summary report of the number of tributaries in each repartimiento and the amount of tribute. He states that the compilation is based on the "Libro de las tasas de la visita general" of Francisco de Toledo and on subsequent reassessments of repartimientos made prior to 1591. Many new quotas were assigned during the administration of Cañete because of the disastrous epidemics. Administrative and financial documents of the period reveal that in the regions where disease mortality was the highest the remaining Indians were incapable of paying tribute at the previous rate. In some regions the corregidores jailed the curacas for noncollection of tribute and confiscated their land and property. In the areas most severely affected, Viceroy Cañete exempted tributaries from payment for one year.[5]

A significant percentage of the Morales Figueroa totals date from the 1570–5 period. The consequence of accepting his figures for the 1591 population is a severe overestimation of the true population of that date. Any population curve constructed for the 1570s to the 1590s would as a result be much flatter than it should be. Kubler generalized that what he calculated as the lower rate of decline during the period was due to "the administration reforms of the viceregal government of Francisco de Toledo."[6] Instead of decreasing the rate of decline, however, the Toledo reforms, especially the forced *reducciones* of Indians into a small number of large settlements, actually raised the rate of depopulation, because European disease mortality was heightened by concentrated populations. The village structure, with a much higher population density than indigenous patterns, allowed a more rapid spread of the European diseases and thus a higher mortality. Others who have inappropriately used the Morales Figueroa material include Angel Rosenblat, Alberto Tauro, Günter Vollmer, and Daniel Shea.[7]

Census manuscripts of the sixteenth and seventeenth centuries may still be found. In 1974, for example, actual returns for the repartimientos of Los Collaguas province were located in parish archives and in depositories in Lima and Arequipa. Although some folios of the visitas are missing, a wealth of information is available. Each inhabitant is named and classified by moiety, ayllu, and family. The sex and age are given, and the land, crops, and herds are catalogued. Major censuses were taken of most of the repartimientos of the valley in 1591, 1594, 1603, 1615, 1626, and 1654. At the conclusion of each manuscript schedule is a summary of the number of inhabitants. These summaries are compatible with those of the last major compilation of repartimiento population figures for the early seventeenth century: the compendium of Vázquez de Espinosa.[8]

Antonio Vázquez de Espinosa, a Spanish Carmelite friar, was born in Jerez de la Frontera sometime in the last half of the sixteenth century and resided in Peru from 1615 to 1619. In 1622 he returned to Spain from the Americas and there probably wrote the *Compendio y descripción de las Indias occidentales.*[9] He died in Seville in 1630. In the *Compendio* Vázquez de Espinosa lists each repartimiento in the viceroyalty, with the number of tributaries, boys under 18, old and disabled men, and women. The value of the tribute is also given. Vázquez de Espinosa probably collected many of the figures during his residence in Peru. He generally used the most recent census totals available for each repartimiento. His *Compendio* contains a wealth of population information but has no chronological meaning. The inhabitants of one repartimiento could have been counted in 1610, and in another repartimiento a census might have been taken in 1591. In many cases Vázquez de Espinosa did not have access to population data other than Viceroy Toledo's of the 1570s. Unfortunately, the Carmelite did not record the census dates along with his figures. The consequence is a hodgepodge of information that at the outset appears accurate, yet on close examination is highly misleading.

Yet it is commonly believed that a general census of all Peru was made sometime between 1610 and 1628 and that the results were recorded by Vázquez de Espinosa. Several examples illustrate the point: Alberto Tauro put forward a census date of 1625 for the Vázquez de Espinosa figures. This is clearly incorrect. Tauro recorded the same population totals for the repartimiento of Atavillos for 1581 and 1625, which should have led him to a more critical review of the figures.[10] Angel Rosenblat examined the Vázquez de Espinosa material and reported that it was a valuable source for Peruvian historical demography. He did recognize that some of the data were based on the visita general, but he avoided the question of the correct dating of the friar's repartimiento figures for his calculations of the population.[11] Günter Vollmer in his study included the totals by corregimiento and used 1615 as the probable date of a Vázquez de Espinosa census. His final population estimates must therefore be considered approximate.[12] George Kubler in "The Quechua in the Colonial World" assumed that an entirely new census was made in 1628 and listed the totals by corregimiento.[13] Nathan Wachtel used the Vázquez de Espinosa figures to ascertain the "1630" population, although he allows that some figures may "go back to as far as 1610–20."[14]

The present work is based predominantly on Viceroy Toledo's visita general and on subsequent revisitas. I was able to locate in Spanish and Peruvian archives numerous repartimiento censuses. By careful analysis it was possible to establish either exact or approximate (within the administration of a particular viceroy) census dates for each population unit. The repartimiento figures included in the Morales Figueroa and Vázquez de Espinosa compilations were used only when a census date could be assigned. Generally, the greater the number of censuses, the more accurate and informative the returns will be. In many cases several censuses of the population were made between 1570 and 1630. Illustrative of one of the best sets of data is the case of the repartimiento of Jequetepeque on the north coast, inspected in 1575, 1580, 1581, 1582, 1591, 1599, 1609, and 1610. Lunaguana on the central coast provides another good series; its population was counted in 1575, 1591, 1608, 1617, and 1625. Such data form a solid foundation for population estimates for the 1570–1620 period.[15]

Although the frequency of censuses in many locales was good, it is possible that some people escaped enumeration. The number who might not have been counted is difficult to ascertain. Archbishop Mogrovejo's 1591 pastoral inspection sheds light on the problem. In the pueblo of Magalena de Cao the archbishop reported 169 tributaries, 25 *reservados* ("exempt from tribute"), 530 *de confesión* ("confessed"), and 715 *ánimas* ("souls"). Within the jurisdiction of the pueblo were several other settlements: an estancia of Alonso Díaz Vejete with nine mitayos and ten married yanaconas, a second Díaz Vejete estancia with six mitayos, a married yanacona with three children, and one Spaniard; an estancia of Bartholomé de Miranda with six mitayos and two married yanaconas with their children; and finally, Pedro Carrera's estancia with four mitayos and twenty married yanaconas. The reservados and curacas were recorded on the fiscal lists for tribute purposes. Mitayos were part of the tribute-paying group and were noted on the tribute lists of their home repartimiento. Yanaconas, however, were exempt from paying tribute and were often not recorded. Therefore, in some regions a large segment of the total Indian population could have escaped enumeration. Mogrovejo, for example, lists thirty-three male yanaconas living within the jurisdiction of the pueblo of Magalena de Cao. There were 169 tributaries in the village at the same time. Thus, about 20 percent of the working male population of Magalena de Cao in 1591 might not have been recorded in the fiscal data for the repartimiento.[16] But how large was the yanacona group elsewhere?

The number of yanaconas in Peru in the sixteenth and seventeenth centuries has been hotly debated. In the preconquest era yanaconas were a special group of personal servants or dependents of the Inca. In the chaotic period during the conquest and in the early colonial period, a substantial number of yanaconas became retainers of the Spanish. Other Indians, who found the status and privilege of the yanaconas appealing, assumed the position. The new yanaconas left their lands, traveled and fought beside the conquerors, and ultimately settled with the Europeans in colonial cities or on estates in the countryside. Yanaconas enjoyed a special status: They were apparently free of tribute payment and mita service and could exercise their trade in cities. The number of yanaconas had been carefully regulated and restricted by the Inca, but under the Spanish thousands entered their ranks. George Kubler has even suggested that after the 1537–8 Indian uprising there could have been as many yanaconas as tributaries.[17] It is doubtful, however, that there were that many; and certainly by the end of the century the number of yanaconas was curtailed. Viceroy Toledo was instrumental in this process. In 1571 repartimiento Indians were no longer allowed to become yanaconas. A series of measures prohibited the employment of yanaconas by non-Spaniards (black, mulatto, or vagrant mestizos) without special authorization. All yanaconas not having an overseer were assigned one, and those yanaconas who worked the mines had to stay there. The yanacona was forced to remain in his existing employment unless he received official authorization to change his position. Spaniards who allowed their charges to go about drunk or idle could be fined and their yanaconas could be expropriated. The family of the yanacona was protected by a provision prohibiting separation of husband and wife. Karen Spalding, in studying the yanaconas of the province of Huarochirí, noted that most were settled into communities, given lands, and generally incorporated into local rural society by the Toledo reforms. Some in Huarochirí did manage to escape the process, however, and a number·continued to move onto nearby Spanish haciendas and become yanaconas through the eighteenth century.[18]

Before the administration of Viceroy Toledo there were a significant number of yanaconas in Peru, especially on coastal estates and in Spanish cities and mining centers; but under Toledo members of the group lost much of their special status, and their number began to decline. The experience in the city of Arequipa illustrates the process: During the visita general of Toledo in 1572, there were 514 yanaconas living in the city, in 1586 there were 286, and in 1593 there remained only 190. The transformation is similar in Cuzco. Part of the reason for the decline in Arequipa's yanaconas was the same as for the decline of the Indian population throughout the viceroyalty: epidemic mortality. Urban mortality was exceptionally high. The other reason for the decline in the number of yanaconas appears to be their less attractive status after the Toledo reforms. It is also true that the yanaconas could have rapidly merged with the lower segments of the Spanish population and thus escaped enumeration.[19] There is little doubt, however, that following the 1570s the yanacona population of the viceroyalty was small in relation to the total Indian population.

There were at least two other groups of Indians exempt from tribute: The Cañaris and the Inca. The Cañaris tribe was famous for its brave warriors. These Indians originally lived in territory now part of southeastern Ecuador and were conquered by the Inca before the arrival of the Spaniards. Part of Inca military policy dictated the systematic resettlement of "safe" subjects in unstable or newly conquered areas and the corollary, the establishment of unruly elements in tractable locations. As part of that policy, approximately fifteen thousand Cañaris warriors, with wives and children, were moved by the Inca to Cuzco and some ultimately became so loyal that they acted as special guards of the royal family. The Cañaris were apparently on the side of the Cuzco faction during the civil war after the death of Huayna Capac and were persecuted by Atahualpa following his victory over Huascar. Fortunately for the Europeans, the Cañaris

joined them during the Indian siege of Cuzco in 1536. As a reward for
their help, the Cañaris were granted permanent exemption from tribute and the mita. There is consequently little information about the
Cañaris in the fiscal record, but some information does appear elsewhere. López de Velasco, probably referring to the late 1560s, reported that on Holy Thursday some three hundred of the Cañaris
customarily paraded through the streets of Cuzco, carrying their
lances as they marched in the religious procession. The Cañaris also
supplied eight men nightly to serve as the corregidor's bodyguard,
and they were often used as messengers. It is known that as late as
1613 there were at least two Cañaris living in Lima who had never
paid tribute to the Spaniards. There also exist several court cases
dealing with the Cañaris: Whenever colonial officials attempted to
collect tribute or force the Cañaris to labor in the mita draft, representatives of the group would appear in court and exhibit documents
granting exemption. The size of the Cañaris population in Peru after
the 1570s could not have been substantial, however. It is unlikely
they numbered more than a few hundred.[20]

Descendants of the Inca, a special group, were also freed from
tribute. It is difficult to ascertain just how far this exemption went.
During the early colonial regime Inca "puppet" rulers and their close
relatives were automatically exempt. Inca "princesses" were acceptable marriage partners for the conquistadores. The mother of Garcilaso
de la Vega and Doña Beatriz Coya are good examples. Many marriages
or common-law unions between natives and Europeans took place,
and their children were exempt as mestizos. Many of the lesser Inca
nobility in local communities became curacas, or *principales,* and were
free of both tribute and mita service. The total number exempted
presents a difficult problem.[21] In the village of Coporaque, which had
been the Inca administrative capital of the Collaguas province, two
adult males claimed exemption in the 1594 census, "por ser Incas."
Yet they were included in the population count of the repartimientos,
being added under the category of reservados. Parish registers in the
nearby pueblo of Yanque include some death entries for persons who
did not pay the usual burial fees "por ser descendiente de los Incas,"[22]
but I believe it unlikely that the number of "Incas" with special
privileges could have been large.

The forastero category poses another dilemma. Forasteros were
simply those Indians who emigrated from their local communities
and settled in other villages or even provinces. When they permanently abandoned their native territory they lost their right to lands.
Because the land in their new home was already largely distributed to

members of the local community, the immigrant had very limited access to it. The forastero therefore was exempted from tribute and the mita. In provinces subject to dangerous mining mita requirements, the inducement to migrate to another area was great.[23] On the other hand, in order to meet the labor demand as a consequence of fewer and fewer mitayos, mine and smelting operators offered excellent benefits to attract wage earners. Reasonable labor conditions and high salaries were ample enough to entice some laborers to settle permanently in or around the mining centers. Owners of the mines and the smelting firms recognized the value of these workers and tried to ensure their supply. Shortly after Toledo's general inspection of Peru, Philip II, in the decrees of Badajoz (1580) and Lisbon (1582), exempted from tribute forasteros and *advenedizos* laboring in the mines. It was suggested that "One of these Indians provides more useful service than twenty tributaries." There were some "indios aventureros," evidently forasteros, in the silver-mining city of Potosí in 1603. By the mid-seventeenth century, however, there were enough Indians who had become forasteros to influence negatively the number of mitayos and tribute payments. To increase the working force the Miner's Guild in Potosí in 1646 requested the viceroy to order yanaconas and forasteros to be called up to provide labor.[24] By the late seventeenth century a large percentage of the population in some regions was composed of forasteros. Viceroy Palata recognized the problem and ordered a new general census, beginning October 1683, to determine exactly how many Indians fell in this category. Ultimately, the viceroy issued two orders: All Indians were required to pay tribute where they resided, thus ending the special status of the forasteros; and all Indians had to return to their original homelands. To ease the return, lands that had been taken away from the forasteros during their absence and rented or sold were to be restored to the original owners. A special order providing for a six-month period to move and take up the lands was promulgated.[25] It must be remembered, however, that the effort failed and that even in the mid- and late eighteenth century a large percentage of the population remained forastero (see Table 13). Indeed, archival evidence suggests that in 1692 Viceroy de la Monclova revoked Palata's orders, and the forastero remained in a category separate from the *originario* tributary. Officials apparently believed there were enough Indian workers available. At any rate it is unlikely that there were as many forasteros in the provinces exempted from labor in the larger mines such as Potosí, Castrovirreyna, Carabaya, and Huancavelica as there were in the districts required to contribute mitayos. The parish registers of the village of Yanque, colonial capital of Los Collaguas province, reveal

Table 13. *Originarios and forasteros in Peru, 1680s–1690s*

Repartimiento	Date	Originarios	Forasteros	% Forasteros
Tanquiques[a]	1694	28	13	46
Quichuas[a]	1694	186	7	4
Hurin Vilcas[a]	1694	90	4	4
Papris[a]	1694	270	28	10
Hanan Vilcas[a]	1694	72	13	18
Lari[b]	1688	979	0	0
Cabana[b]	1688	256	0	0
Yanque[b]	1688	885	72	8
Total		2,766	137	5

[a] BNL, B1477.
[b] BNL, C1156.

that in 1688, of thirty-nine baptisms recorded, only three of the parents came from outside the repartimiento. These three parents were from neighboring villages. In the 1683 Palata census it was found that, of the sixteen provinces subject to the Potosí mita, including those within Cuzco and Arequipa, slightly less than one-half of the adult males were classified forasteros (31,348 of 64,581). Viceroy Palata recorded 2,116 originarios and 72 forasteros in Los Collaguas in 1688. That province was not subject to the Potosí or Huancavelica mitas.[26]

Nicolás Sánchez-Albornoz, in a study of the tributary in Upper Peru, concludes that "it is evident that the fiscal information – with the forasteros omitted – is a poor reflection of the true dimension of the population."[27] In Upper Peru, by the time Viceroy Palata finished his count in the 1680s, forasteros exceeded fifty percent of the population. The forastero population did not reach such proportions overnight. Forastero status, especially in corregimientos subject to the Potosí mining mita, was desirable, in spite of the fact that the individual's claim to land was forfeited. Data are still inadequate for Peru proper to calculate the forastero population – only sections of the 1680s census are available – but the results of the comprehensive census of around 1754 illuminate the forastero issue. (The totals are presented in Table 14.)[28] The results for Peru may be visually presented (see Figure 1) to illustrate the likely evolution of the forastero–originario dichotomy.

As the previous discussion of the visita general has shown, it is

Table 14. *Forasteros and originarios, ca. 1754*

Ecclesiastical unit	Originarios	Forasteros	Total	% Forasteros
Cuzco	20,711	12,053	32,764	37
Arequipa	3,083	667	3,750	18
Huamanga	8,587	1,933	10,520	18
Lima	17,720	5,371	23,091	23
Trujillo	12,788	5,387	18,175	30
Total	62,889	25,411	88,300	29
Chuquisaca	11,589	15,359	26,948	57
Mizque	3,182	506	3,688	14
La Paz	10,550	13,644	24,194	56

Source: Sánchez-Albornoz, *Indios y tributos*, p. 52, based on Fuentes's *Memorias de los virreyes,* 4:7–15.

reasonable to believe that at the time of Viceroy Toledo the number of forasteros was insignificant and that almost all natives had been placed under the fiscal regime. Certainly the Indians excluded from the census are limited. The real reason for the expansion of the forastero group after the 1570s was the administrative order of Toledo, which formalized the operation of the mining mitas. By Toledo's decrees, forasteros were exempted from the tribute and mita service. The viceroy would not have excluded a large part of the native population from fiscal obligations; rather, the exemption was a recognition that there were *some* forasteros but that their number was small. Toledo never expected that the position of the forastero, without lands and local ties, would be appealing in a society where community and land

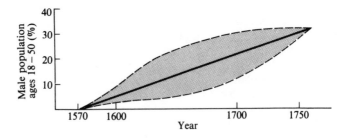

Figure 1. Possible evolution of the tribute-exempt class.

were above all else basic. Yet tribute and mita service, especially for Potosí, became so onerous that men did break with their roots.[29] The question remains: When did the new class comprise a notable percentage of the adult working male population? The percentage for Upper Peru was quite large by the 1750s. Even then, however, Arequipa, Huamanga, and Lima were different, with less than one-quarter in the forastero category. The documents are inadequate to give a definitive answer, yet several factors may be noted. In the first place, as Sánchez-Albornoz demonstrates, in the era of Viceroy Palata in the 1680s corregimientos subject to the Potosí mita in Upper Peru had large proportions of forasteros. The percentages parallel those of the 1750s. Unfortunately, as yet the Palata census summaries are available only for Upper Peru. For Peru proper one is forced to work with a small statistical sample. Table 13 presents data for the late 1680s and early 1690s from repartimientos in the central and southern highlands. In these units the percentages of forasteros are quite low, in contrast to Upper Peru. They are, in fact, even lower than the overall percentages from the 1750s data. At present, it can only be concluded that the number of forasteros in the repartimientos subject to the Potosí mita was quite large, even before the 1680s. It is doubtful that the transformation of originario to forastero took place in arithmetic fashion. The growth must have been very rapid at first and then probably leveled off by the 1680s. The growth phase took place sometime between Toledo and Palata.

Within less than a decade after Viceroy Toledo, officials recognized that Quito became a focus of migration for residents of the entire west coast of South America: Nueva Granada, Popayán, and Peru. According to the Dominican friar Miguel de Monsalve, by 1610 Charcas had attracted twelve thousand advenedizos from Nueva Granada, Loja, Quito, Chile, Paraguay, and Tucuman. In his final administrative report Viceroy Luis de Velasco (ca. 1604) commented that Toledo's settlement policy in Upper Peru was threatened because of the death of many Indians and the flight of others who hoped to escape the mita and personal service. He lamented that the runaways had established themselves in rugged terrain and were difficult to remove.[30] The forastero never becomes ubiquitous and obviously does not appear with the same speed in all locations. Close scrutiny of the census of the nearly two thousand Indians living within the city walls of Lima in 1613 does not reveal use of the term "forastero," although certain individuals could be categorized as such.

No final solution of the dilemma is possible. It does seem, however, that a rapid increase in the forastero group immediately following Viceroy Toledo did occur and was most evident in repartimientos subject to Potosí or other especially loathsome mitas. By the 1620s, however, it is highly unlikely the percentage of the population of this category exceeded the percentage found in the returns of the 1750s. The information on yanaconas found in the religious census of Archbishop Mogrovejo in the 1580s points in the same direction. Indians were ultimately excluded from tribute lists. They appeared in a new status: as dependents on a Spanish estate, free wage laborers in the mines, forasteros renting lands in an adopted Indian community, urban artisans. Nonetheless, within Peru itself only a fraction of the Indians had managed by 1620 to make the transformation.

Another problem facing the researcher investigating the historical demography of the period is fraud. Several scholars have questioned the value of pre-twentieth-century statistical returns for Latin America. George Kubler, for example, in 1946 singled out fiscal data as especially unreliable. Kubler argued:

> The good intentions of Colonial governors were perverted by a conspiracy among the curacas, the encomenderos, and the religious doctrineros to secure reductions on assessments, all the while levying tribute at an older, higher rate: failing to remunerate the Indians for personal services and failing in general to comply with the ethical provisions of colonial legislation.[31]

More recently, Nicolás Sánchez-Albornoz points out groups that could have benefited from fraudulent tributary counts. Based on material from the 1680s, his conclusion is that there was widespread deception. Curacas often hid Indians in order to provide an adequate labor force for themselves. Corregidores obfuscated the true number of tributaries because the Crown held them responsible for the collection of the full assessment. Corregidores also wanted workers at their disposal. Spanish hacendados often obscured the true number living on their estates, for any amount of tribute paid to the Crown ultimately cut into their own potential revenues.[32]

The present work is based primarily on the fiscal data, in spite of the arguments mentioned above. My own research has led me to conclude that, at least for the 1570–1620 period, fraud was kept to a minimum during the tribute assessments. Priests, curacas, encomenderos, tributaries, corregidores, *protectores de los indios* (Indian protectors), and other officials were interest groups with often conflicting aims. They checked and balanced each other during the time of inspection. Close reading of the census returns indicates the care that was taken to ensure a correct count. The published 1562 visita of Los Chupachos provides evidence similar to that found in other, as yet unpublished sources. The visitador was persistent in his efforts to account for all inhabitants of the repartimiento, even those who had migrated to other provinces for seasonal labor. Priests, curacas, principales, and others were called before the inspector to testify. The new census return was carefully compared with the previous one and checked against the parish records of baptisms, marriages, and deaths. Often, at the end of a document it can be seen that the inspector came back to the community a few days later and added people missed during the initial inspection. The appended lists include not only tributaries but also newly born infants, the ill, and the elderly – hence, all segments of the population.[33] Such care suggests that residents who avoided the census must have made up only a small percentage of the repartimiento population. Indeed, many returns demonstrate a diligence often exceeding that of twentieth-century census takers.

It is true that the frequency of repartimiento population counts was less than satisfactory; however, modern documentation is not necessarily better. There was no general census in Peru between 1876 and 1940.[34] In the period from 1570 to 1620, 429 of 585 repartimientos were enumerated at least twice (see Table 15). In some repartimientos six or more counts were made, as we have already seen.

Between 1570 and 1620 Indian population counts during repartimiento reassessments were relatively accurate. There is no doubt that there was some fraud, but competing interest groups helped keep the level of deceit to a minimum. It is also true that some Indians, such as the Cañaris, the Inca, the yanaconas, and increasingly the forasteros, avoided fiscal enumeration due to their special status. It is

Table 15. *Repartimiento population counts, 1570–1620*

	Number of repartimientos	Number without at least 2 censuses
North coast	61	5
Central coast	44	2
South coast	40	23
North sierra	130	18
Central sierra	50	3
South sierra	260	105
Total	585	156

unfortunately impossible to calculate the exact number of people who escaped count. As we have seen, however, the Crown's fiscal agents applied constant vigilance to limit the growth of the exempt class. Indeed, let us shift from the negative to the positive. Given more than four centuries for documents to be lost or destroyed and the general lack of interest in the "statistical" in sixteenth-century Europe, the amount and quality of the information that remains are surprisingly high. There were frequent censuses; they included almost all native segments of the population; and, with the exception of jungle territory outside European control, all areas within the modern boundaries of Peru were enumerated.

Model 1. The census projection models are based on the statistical data we have just reviewed. In the first model the data are for the 1570s and 1600s. Model 1 is based on several assumptions. First, population change can be relatively accurately represented by the standard demographic formula $P_2 = P_1 e^{rt}$. Demographic historians have used other formulas. Even a normal arithmetic rate can suffice for short time periods; however, the standard formula most correctly represents true population change. Projection of the population requires a rate of change and population figures for two censuses. Fortunately, these data are available for our estimates of the tributary population of two-thirds of Peruvian repartimientos and for slightly over two-fifths of the estimates for the total population (Method A). The population of the repartimiento of Copiz on the north Peruvian coast, for example, was counted by officials in 1575 and 1602. The census results are 123 and 95, respectively.[35] The number of years (t) between the counts is 27. The annual rate of calculated change is -0.957. With this information, it is possible to estimate the population of the repartimiento at any date between the two censuses. The 1580 estimated population is 117, for example; for 1590 it is 106; and it is 96 in 1600. The population can also be projected into the future or the past. An estimate for 1630 is 71; for 1530 it is 193.

In approximately one-third of the repartimientos, however, the tributary population figures are available for only one of the two decade intervals. In such a situation, the method of calculation is to use the figures for the median rate of change for the region in which the repartimiento was located (see Table 16), and the first tributary count after 1570, to estimate the tributary population for the desired dates. The total tributary population of Peru at decade intervals can then be found by summing the repartimiento population within each region (Method B). In order to estimate the total number of inhabitants of repartimientos that lacked a total population figure for any

Table 16. *Median rates of change for the Indian population, 1570s–1600s*

Region	#Rep	#r Trib.	% Sample	mr Trib.	#r Tot.	% Sample	mr Tot.
North coast	56	51	91.1	−2.6	18	32.2	−2.2
Central coast	44	35	79.5	−2.4	30	68.2	−3.1
South coast	39	15	38.5	−3.5	14	35.9	−3.8
North sierra	130	77	59.2	−1.9	39	30.0	−1.2
Central sierra	50	47	94.0	−1.3	36	72.0	−1.4
South sierra	253	144	56.9	−1.1	102	40.3	−1.2
Total	572	369	64.5	−1.6	239	41.8	−1.5

Note: #Rep = repartimientos; #r Trib. = number of repartimientos with available tributary rates of change; mr Trib. = median rate of change for tributaries; #r Tot. = number of repartimientos with total rates of change available; mr Tot. = median rate of change for total population.

date (only thirty-five of Peru's repartimientos fall into this category), a further calculation must be made. It is essential to determine the tributary index for each region (the total population, divided by the tributaries, equals this figure). The regional tributary index may then be used to estimate the total population of repartimientos with deficient data. The final step is the addition of repartimiento estimates by date and region. Table 17 presents the frequency with which each

Table 17. *Methods of estimating the total population, 1520–1630*

Region	Number repartimientos	Method[a]		
		A	B	C
North coast	56	18	22	16
Central coast	44	30	13	1
South coast	39	14	24	1
North sierra	130	39	83	8
Central sierra	50	36	14	0
South sierra	253	102	142	9
Total	572	239	298	35

[a] A = rates of change for the total population calculated from available data; B = median rates of change used on a regional basis; C = total population estimated from median number of tributaries by region.

method was used in determining the total population at decade intervals. Method A is statistically most reliable; Method C is least reliable
but had to be used in a handful of cases.

The median rather than the mean rate-of-change figures for each
region are used in the calculations because the data are highly skewed.
Of the forty-seven repartimientos classified in the central highland
region, for example, the range of tributary rates of change is from
−3.7 to +0.5. With highly skewed data the median is as effective a
measure of central tendency as the mean, and it is easier to calculate.
The mean or "average" rate of change for the north coast is −1.4
percent, compared with a median figure of −1.3 percent, which
demonstrates that the two figures are, in any case, relatively close.
Estimated populations for the central highlands, using the mean
instead of the median for calculations, are only slightly different.

The large number of Peruvian censuses taken between 1570 and
1610 provide several thousand sets of population figures. All the
mathematical procedures performed during the course of analysis
(over 14,000) could not easily be handled by individual hand calculations. The following illustration is indicative of how many operations
are required: For several repartimientos, six sets of tributary figures
are available for the period and, for most, two sets of tributary/
muchacho/viejo/female figures are recorded. For the 585 repartimientos that have sets of data several mathematical functions are necessary
to calculate the rates of change of the tributary population, the age
and sex composition, the ratio of tributaries to the total population,
and the estimated tributary and total population projected forward
and backward in time. The mathematical requirements of this investigation were sufficiently complex to justify computer assistance.
After the elaborate computer program was designed and tested, it was
possible to calculate in minutes what would have taken months.[36]

Data are uniformly stored on standard computer data cards. An
effort was made to find each population unit on modern maps. It was
possible tentatively to identify and locate most northern and central
coastal repartimientos, with the exception of four in the corregimiento of Piura and one in Lima. On the south coast there are two
densely packed clusters, which made it impossible to distinguish
individual locations (see maps in Part II). The modern position of
repartimientos in the northern highlands could not be found in
enough cases to make individual locations within corregimiento
boundaries meaningful. Many of the repartimientos in the district,
especially those in the corregimientos of Chachapoyas, Luya, and
Moyobamba, are on or near the headwaters of the Amazon. These

repartimientos were among the last to be granted in Peru. Many are small, including a dozen or so tributaries, and quickly disappeared during the initial population decline. Other repartimientos, because of the impermanent nature of slash-and-burn agriculture, periodically moved from one site to another, thus making identification difficult. There was little difficulty in finding the approximate location of central highland repartimientos. Most repartimientos in the southern sierra could be located, but they were closely packed. In the corregimiento of Chilques more than twenty repartimientos were situated within a twenty-five-kilometer radius of the center.[37] The lines dividing the regions are generally based on natural geographical and administrative boundaries. Four repartimientos are often located within a dozen miles of each other, near the line intersecting four regions, yet each unit is classified as totally separate for the purposes of the present analysis. Individual designations may be contested. Some repartimiento boundaries reflect the pre-Spanish attempt to provide a single ethnic group with a series of microclimatic lands so that the group could be agriculturally self-sufficient, producing tropical, temperate, and highland crops. The Callejón de Huailas is included in the northern highlands, even though the Santa River flows into the nearby Pacific and not the Amazon. Huarochirí and part of Arequipa could, on the basis of ecology, also be considered highland repartimientos but are classified "coastal" because in administration, communications, and economic interchange they were more closely tied to the coast than to the sierra.

Most documents included the date of the census. Unfortunately, some sources state only that the count was made during the administration of a certain viceroy. In this case, a date midway through the known viceroy's official tenure was assigned; or, if a datable census was taken of other repartimientos in the same corregimiento, then the known census date is assigned. This procedure is generally sound, because most counts were made on a corregimiento-wide basis.

The estimated total population of Peru of 3.3 million derived in Model 1 is found in Table 18. For the decades of 1560, 1550, 1540, 1530, and 1520 the projections are based on the same rate of change as for the 1570–1600 period. I consider that the figures are relatively accurate for dates near the actual censuses. In the case of most repartimientos the calculations are "reliable" for dates between 1560 and 1620. With each decade prior to 1560, the estimate becomes more and more questionable. Factors that influenced demographic change in the 1520–30 period were in most cases quite different from those acting in the 1580–90 period. The 1530s and 1540s were charac-

Table 18. *Estimated total Indian population of Peru, 1520–1630*

Region	1520	1530	1540	1550	1560	1570
North coast	320,638	257,318	186,270	137,857	104,117	80,123
Central coast	667,947	489,904	323,149	227,545	168,134	128,820
South coast	245,854	168,130	109,268	73,719	51,259	36,587
North sierra	421,608	373,933	317,702	273,631	238,187	209,057
Central sierra	512,707	445,726	379,370	324,412	278,724	240,604
South sierra	1,131,820	1,003,832	872,999	764,383	673,054	595,528
Total	3,300,574	2,738,673	2,188,626	1,801,425	1,513,396	1,290,680

	1580	1590	1600	1610	1620	1630
North coast	62,706	49,975	40,449	33,263	27,787	23,578
Central coast	101,399	82,044	67,710	56,942	48,715	42,323
South coast	26,406	19,883	15,394	12,164	9,844	8,168
North sierra	180,753	163,366	146,274	131,034	117,737	106,125
Central sierra	207,094	180,992	159,071	140,052	123,776	109,801
South sierra	528,315	471,946	423,104	380,578	343,655	311,557
Total	1,106,662	968,197	851,994	754,024	671,505	601,645

Note: Because of the way the estimated totals were generated by the computer, the sum of the regional figures varies slightly from the total for each date.

terized by civil wars, conquest, and rebellion. They were also years of disease, famine, and dislocation. The years around 1520, 1546, and 1558 were all marked by high epidemic mortality. The total population estimate of 3,300,574 derived from Model 1 should therefore be considered near the absolute minimum that the Peruvian population was likely to have been in 1520.[38]

In 1976 Daniel E. Shea attempted a census projection model based on the same formula for population change. Shea used a sample of data from ten "towns" (should be repartimientos) for Guamanga, fourteen for Cuzco, twenty-four for Lima, eight for Huánuco, and ten for La Paz for 1581 and used 1613 "censuses" to calculate the annual rate of change for the viceroyalty. His 1581 "census" is that of Morales Figueroa, and the 1613 one is the Vázquez de Espinosa compilation. We have already seen the possible error introduced by Rowe, Smith, Dobyns, and Wachtel through reliance on those data sets. The Morales Figueroa repartimiento results may cover the period from about 1571 to 1591, and those of Vázquez de Espinosa from about 1571 to the date he compiled the manuscript (ca. 1620). By using these data and assigning census dates of 1581 and 1613, Shea's calculated rate of change was low and the population curve flat. Shea's estimated rate is −0.612 percent yearly. My own calculated rates of Model 1 are over twice that large for approximately the same period. Shea next uses the rate and my 1973 data for Peru in 1580 to project the 1535 and 1520 population. The resulting estimate for Peru alone in 1520 is 1,343,143. Using the mean rate plus one deviation, he estimated the maximum 1520 Peruvian population to be 1,944,753. For the central Andean region (Lima, Quito, and Charcas), the estimate using the mean is 2,026,108, and the mean plus one deviation is 2,933,670.[39] Shea's results must be rejected on two main counts: First, he did not use all data at his disposal. The correct Toledo figures with census dates are available in Cook.[40] Shea's creation of 1581 and 1613 censuses is misleading and inaccurate and contributes to an artificially low rate of depopulation between the two dates. Second, as we shall see, Shea's supposition that the rate of decline prior to 1581 paralleled the rate following that date is unfounded.

Model 2. The second census projection model is based on the assumption that the 1520–70 period had an exceptionally high rate of mortality, compared with later decades, but that relative decline was proportionately similar between the various geographical sections of Peru in the two periods. With Model 2, the critical question is: How rapid was the rate of depopulation in the early period? No final answer is possible. The evidence for that time is inadequate, as has been made

Table 19. *Estimated Peruvian population in 1520, based on rapid initial decline*

Region	Rate of change, 1570s–1600s	Estimated 1520–1570 rate (2x)	Population, 1570	Estimated, 1520
North coast	2.2	4.4	80,123	723,111
Central coast	3.1	6.2	128,820	2,859,540
South coast	3.8	7.6	36,587	1,635,480
North sierra	1.2	2.4	209,057	694,094
Central sierra	1.4	2.8	240,604	975,697
South sierra	1.2	2.4	595,528	1,977,220
Total				8,865,142

clear. The historical record does suggest, however, that the rate of decline in the 1520–70 period was higher than the rate from 1570 to 1620. Mortality in civil wars, the first major epidemics, rebellions, and crop failures was severe. How rapid the early rate of mortality was is still controversial. The initial mortality could have been easily double that which followed. Were the rate much higher than twice that of the later period, then it appears the impact on the society would have been much more devastating than the historical evidence pictures. I have consequently chosen an initial rate of decline for each region of Peru twice the rate of the 1570s–1600s. After that key assumption is made, it is possible to calculate the total population of each of the six major geographical sectors in 1520 by using the standard formula. The resulting figure (Table 19) of almost 9 million is not minimal. Neither can the projection be considered a maximum one. We will reevaluate the result of Model 2 at the conclusion of this chapter.

Model 3. The third model is based on the "recorded" historical data on Indian population units in two decades: the 1540s and 1570s. Unfortunately, the sample is small and is of only the tributary sector of the whole population. It is very likely, however, that the rate of change of the entire population was relatively similar to the rate of change of the tributary population. Material in Table 18 suggests that for at least the period from the 1570s to the 1600s this supposition is relatively valid. In most regions the 1540s sample is very small. The north coast figures are based on twenty-one sets of data; central coast on twelve; south coast on nine; north sierra on eighteen; central sierra

Table 20. *Estimated Peruvian population in 1520, based on recorded rates of 1540s–1570s*

Region	Tributary rates of change		Estimated total population	
	1570s–1600s	1540s–1570s	1570	1520
North coast	−2.6	−5.3	80,123	1,134,060
Central coast	−2.4	−1.1	128,820	223,278
South coast	−3.5	−0.6	36,587	49,387
North sierra	−1.9	−0.8	209,057	311,876
Central sierra	−1.3	−0.5	240,604	308,942
South sierra	−1.1	−1.2	595,528	1,085,120
Total				3,112,663

on fourteen; and the south sierra on five. The rates of change (see Table 20) are very low with the exception of the north coast. It is clear that the reason for the low rate of population change estimated for the period is due to the nature of the early data. The source of most of the figures for the 1540s is the tributary report of the La Gasca division of repartimientos. The 1549 date corresponds to the year when the *relaciones* were gathered by local officials and presented to Pedro de la Gasca for a new distribution of repartimientos after Gonzalo Pizarro's defeat. The original reports were not dated; some could have referred to estimated populations at the time of the first Indian grants, as early as those made under Francisco Pizarro. The La Gasca population data are approximate, being rounded off to the nearest tens, hundreds, and even thousands. It appears that the majority of the tributary figures extant for this period are based on estimates by colonial officials after at best a rapid tour of the territory involved, or even on figures provided by local curacas, and are not the result of true censuses. Model 3 gives us a projected total of 3,112,663 inhabitants for Peru in 1520. I consider that projection to be lower than the population was likely to have been.

Model 4. In order to arrive at the minimum and maximum estimates of Model 4, we need to use the rates of change recorded for the decades of the 1530s and 1540s for the six geographical divisions of Peru. With these rates of decline at hand (they are generally high), the population can be projected with the aid of the 1550 base population estimates of Model 1. As has already been discussed, the 1570s–1600s rate of decline was similar to the rate from 1550 to 1570, but a much higher rate of population loss occurred in the first two decades following European contact. Unlike Model 2, which is based on a similar set of assumptions, the rate of decline for the first period was significantly more than double that of the later period (see Table 21). The "maximum" estimate for each region is calculated by taking the highest rate of change for a repartimiento in that region for the 1530s–1540s period and applying that rate to all the repartimientos of the region for the 1530–50 dates. The "minimum" estimates are calculated in the same fashion. The maximum and minimum rates for the north coast are the same (− 17.918) because only one rate (Paita y la Silla between 1532 and 1542) is available for the whole region. There were no figures for the 1530s–1540s for the central sierra, so those maximums and minimums are based on repartimiento data for the 1534–75 period. Model 4 yields a 1530 maximum population of slightly less than 32 million and a minimum of about 13.5 million. Projected to 1520, the rates result in a statistical maximum of slightly more than 200 million and a minimum of almost 68 million. Such high estimates for 1520 are far beyond the range of probability. Mortality levels of 17 to 20 percent a year for a three-year epidemic period are likely, but such a high level of mortality could not have been sustained for more than a brief span of years. Further, the ecological and historical evidence in no way supports figures such as 30 million for the north coast, 48 million for the central coast, or 131 million for the northern sierra.

Another difficulty with Model 4 arises from the inadequate statistical sample. If 10 percent of the rates for a region could be calculated for the 1530s–1540s period, then the method would be helpful. Only one example, however, is available for the north coast; two for the central coast; three for the south coast; four for the northern highlands; and only two for the southern highlands. Little confidence can be placed in the estimates of Model 4, although other researchers using different methods have approached the "maximum" 1530 estimate of 32 million. We have seen that P. A. Means, using the theoretical or "ideal" size of Inca administrative units, calculated the full Empire's population as between 16 million and 32 million. F. A. Loayza posited, on the basis of what he believed to be the recorded depopulation between the conquest and Toledo's epoch, an Inca population of 45 million. H. F. Dobyns reached an estimate of between 30 million and 37.5 million for the entire Andean region.[41] Current high estimates of the contact Andean population, however, are not convincing.

Model 5. Stable population theory and the model tables recently

Table 21. *Estimated Peruvian population of 1520 and 1530, based on maximum–minimum rates of change for the 1530s–1540s*

Region	Rates, 1530s–1540s		Population, 1550	1530 population		1520 population	
	Maximum	Minimum		Maximum	Minimum	Maximum	Minimum
North coast	−17.918	−17.918	137,857	4,963,250	4,963,250	29,780,700	29,780,700
Central coast	−17.806	−16.838	227,545	8,010,820	6,600,810	47,531,500	35,551,868
South coast	−5.676	−0.855	73,719	229,398	87,466	404,665	95,274
North sierra	−20.569	−1.112	273,631	16,740,400	341,785	130,938,000	381,985
Central sierra[a]	−4.185	−3.095	324,412	749,206	602,456	1,138,550	820,993
South sierra	−1.744	−0.688	764,383	1,083,410	877,142	1,289,830	939,614
Total				31,776,484	13,472,909	211,083,245	67,570,434

[a] Maximum and minimum rates for central sierra based on 1534–75 period.

elaborated and refined by the demographers Ansley J. Coale and Paul Demeny have been utilized by a handful of historians in their analysis of population characteristics. At the base of stable population theory is the fact that the age distribution does not change in a "closed" population (no migration), which has a constant growth rate as the consequence of constant birth and death rates. The theory has major applications in the study of modern developing nations, with census data that make possible analysis of age distribution and the intercensal growth rate but with no good data on fertility and mortality levels, a consequence of an inadequate system of vital registration.[42]

In Model 5, two relatively accurate censuses, that of Huánuco in 1562 and of the Yanaconas of Yucay in 1571, will be used in conjunction with stable population models in order to arrive ultimately at population totals for the two areas in 1531–2. Close examination of the ten-year cohort population pyramids of Huánuco and Yucay (Figure 2) reveals that in both cases the female population above the age of 50 appears inflated. In both, the number of women is substantially greater than the number of men. In Yucay, a woman born in 1521 would be 50 at the time of the 1571 census. The 50-year-old woman in Huánuco in 1562 would have been born in 1512. In both cases the cohorts above these ages would have already passed the period of high childhood mortality by the time the Europeans arrived. The women would have been young adults in 1532 and would have been the least likely to succumb to the ravages of disease or starvation. Further, the young women would have been the least likely sector of the population to die in warfare. They probably would have engaged in active combat neither in the civil war between the Cuzco and Atahualpa factions nor in the armed resistance against the European invaders. We might, therefore, conclude that the female population above the age of 50 in 1562–71 would be the group "least" affected by the unusually high mortality associated with epidemics, war, and famine in the contact period. Consequently, this cohort best represents the "true" size of the population.

Taking these factors into consideration, a standard population model that best represents the characteristics of our group must be selected. The "choice" is extensive: Coale and Demeny and their associates have provided us with several models, based on different mortality levels and therefore different life expectancies. The model I have chosen for our use is the "west" stable population model at Level 3, where the life expectancy of the woman at birth is twenty-five years (see Table 22). This model is of a population with a moderately high rate of mortality but certainly not the highest possible. A high level

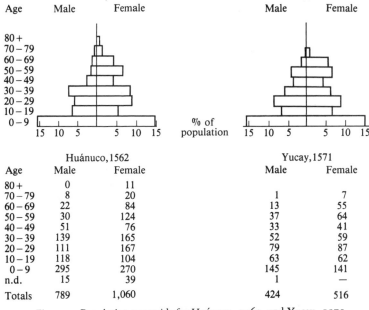

Figure 2. Population pyramids for Huánuco, 1562, and Yucay, 1571.

| | Huánuco, 1562 | | Yucay, 1571 | |
Age	Male	Female	Male	Female
80+	0	11		
70 – 79	8	20	1	7
60 – 69	22	84	13	55
50 – 59	30	124	37	64
40 – 49	51	76	33	41
30 – 39	139	165	52	59
20 – 29	111	167	79	87
10 – 19	118	104	63	62
0 – 9	295	270	145	141
n.d.	15	39	1	—
Totals	789	1,060	424	516

of infant mortality is to be expected. If we used, for example, the model for the maximum level of mortality, the life expectancy at birth for the woman is twenty years. A calculation of the average age of women in Yucay was made on the basis of the 1571 census: The result was approximately 27 years. Rénique and Trelles calculate the average age of women in Yanque–Collaguas at 27.65 in 1591.[43] On the Level 3 model stable population the average age of females is 27.3 for the zero rate of growth column we are using for the calculations. It is also necessary to reach a decision about the magnitude of the growth rate in the precontact era. We lack evidence on the rate of population change for the period before the conquest, but it is clear that migration either into or out of the Inca Empire was statistically insignificant. We must assume that migration had little impact on the growth of the region preceding the 1530s, and any population change had to be principally the result of births and deaths. Although there were internal population shifts during the Inca period, a relative overall demographic stability appears likely. For this reason I have selected a population model that represents a nil rate of growth. Table 23 is a

Table 22. "West" model stable populations arranged by level of mortality (annual rate of increase)

Level 3: females ($e_0 = 25.00$ years)

Age interval	-0.010	-0.005	0.000	0.005	0.010	0.015	0.020	0.025	0.030	0.035	0.040	0.045	0.050
						Proportion in age interval							
Under 1	0.0241	0.0279	0.0321	0.0365	0.0412	0.0461	0.0511	0.0564	0.0617	0.0672	0.0727	0.0783	0.0840
1-4	0.0733	0.0840	0.0954	0.1072	0.1194	0.1320	0.1447	0.1575	0.1703	0.1831	0.1957	0.2082	0.2204
5-9	0.0850	0.0953	0.1057	0.1162	0.1266	0.1367	0.1466	0.1560	0.1650	0.1734	0.1812	0.1885	0.1951
10-14	0.0846	0.0924	0.1000	0.1072	0.1139	0.1200	0.1254	0.1302	0.1343	0.1377	0.1403	0.1423	0.1437
15-19	0.0841	0.0896	0.0946	0.0989	0.1024	0.1053	0.1074	0.1087	0.1093	0.1093	0.1087	0.1075	0.1059
20-24	0.0823	0.0856	0.0881	0.0898	0.0908	0.0910	0.0905	0.0893	0.0876	0.0854	0.0829	0.0799	0.0768
25-29	0.0795	0.0806	0.0809	0.0805	0.0793	0.0776	0.0752	0.0725	0.0693	0.0659	0.0624	0.0587	0.0550
30-34	0.0760	0.0752	0.0736	0.0714	0.0686	0.0654	0.0619	0.0581	0.0543	0.0503	0.0464	0.0426	0.0389
35-39	0.0719	0.0693	0.0662	0.0626	0.0587	0.0546	0.0504	0.0461	0.0420	0.0380	0.0342	0.0306	0.0273
40-44	0.0674	0.0634	0.0590	0.0544	0.0498	0.0452	0.0406	0.0363	0.0322	0.0284	0.0249	0.0218	0.0189
45-49	0.0626	0.0575	0.0522	0.0470	0.0419	0.0370	0.0325	0.0283	0.0245	0.0211	0.0181	0.0154	0.0130
50-54	0.0570	0.0510	0.0451	0.0396	0.0345	0.0297	0.0254	0.0216	0.0183	0.0153	0.0128	0.0106	0.0088
55-59	0.0497	0.0434	0.0375	0.0321	0.0272	0.0229	0.0191	0.0158	0.0130	0.0107	0.0087	0.0070	0.0057
60-64	0.0404	0.0344	0.0290	0.0242	0.0200	0.0164	0.0134	0.0108	0.0087	0.0069	0.0055	0.0043	0.0034
65-69	0.0296	0.0245	0.0202	0.0164	0.0133	0.0106	0.0084	0.0066	0.0052	0.0041	0.0031	0.0024	0.0019
70-74	0.0188	0.0152	0.0122	0.0097	0.0076	0.0059	0.0046	0.0035	0.0027	0.0021	0.0015	0.0012	0.0009
75-79	0.0095	0.0075	0.0059	0.0045	0.0035	0.0027	0.0020	0.0015	0.0011	0.0008	0.0006	0.0004	0.0003
80+	0.0043	0.0033	0.0025	0.0019	0.0014	0.0011	0.0008	0.0006	0.0004	0.0003	0.0002	0.0001	0.0001

Age						Proportion under given age							
1	0.0241	0.0279	0.0321	0.0365	0.0412	0.0461	0.0511	0.0564	0.0617	0.0672	0.0727	0.0783	0.0840
5	0.0974	0.1120	0.1274	0.1437	0.1606	0.1780	0.1958	0.2139	0.2320	0.2503	0.2685	0.2865	0.3044
10	0.1824	0.2072	0.2331	0.2599	0.2872	0.3147	0.3424	0.3699	0.3970	0.4237	0.4497	0.4750	0.4995
15	0.2670	0.2996	0.3331	0.3670	0.4010	0.4347	0.4678	0.5001	0.5313	0.5613	0.5900	0.6173	0.6432
20	0.3511	0.3893	0.4277	0.4659	0.5035	0.5400	0.5752	0.6088	0.6406	0.6706	0.6987	0.7248	0.7491
25	0.4334	0.4748	0.5158	0.5557	0.5942	0.6310	0.6656	0.6981	0.7283	0.7561	0.7815	0.8048	0.8259
30	0.5129	0.5555	0.5967	0.6362	0.6736	0.7085	0.7409	0.7706	0.7976	0.8220	0.8439	0.8635	0.8808
35	0.5890	0.6306	0.6703	0.7076	0.7422	0.7739	0.8028	0.8287	0.8518	0.8723	0.8903	0.9061	0.9197
40	0.6608	0.7000	0.7365	0.7702	0.8009	0.8285	0.8531	0.8748	0.8938	0.9103	0.9245	0.9367	0.9470
45	0.7282	0.7633	0.7955	0.8247	0.8507	0.8737	0.8938	0.9112	0.9261	0.9387	0.9494	0.9584	0.9659
50	0.7908	0.8208	0.8477	0.8716	0.8926	0.9107	0.9263	0.9395	0.9506	0.9598	0.9675	0.9738	0.9790
55	0.8478	0.8717	0.8929	0.9112	0.9270	0.9405	0.9517	0.9611	0.9688	0.9752	0.9803	0.9844	0.9878
60	0.8975	0.9151	0.9303	0.9433	0.9542	0.9633	0.9708	0.9770	0.9819	0.9858	0.9890	0.9915	0.9934
65	0.9379	0.9495	0.9593	0.9675	0.9742	0.9798	0.9842	0.9878	0.9906	0.9928	0.9945	0.9958	0.9968
						Parameter of stable populations							
Birth rate	0.0299	0.0347	0.0400	0.0456	0.0516	0.0579	0.0644	0.0712	0.0782	0.0853	0.0926	0.0999	0.1074
Death rate	0.0399	0.0397	0.0400	0.0406	0.0416	0.0429	0.0444	0.0462	0.0482	0.0503	0.0526	0.0549	0.0574
GRR (27)[a]	1.88	2.15	2.46	2.80	3.19	3.62	4.12	4.68	5.31	6.01	6.81	7.70	8.71
GRR (29)	1.92	2.21	2.54	2.93	3.36	3.86	4.43	5.07	5.81	6.64	7.58	8.65	9.86
GRR (31)	1.95	2.27	2.64	3.07	3.56	4.13	4.78	5.53	6.39	7.34	8.50	9.79	11.26
GRR (33)	1.99	2.34	2.75	3.22	3.78	4.43	5.18	6.06	7.08	8.26	9.63	11.22	13.06
Average age	31.3	29.2	27.3	25.5	23.8	22.2	20.7	19.3	18.0	16.9	15.8	14.9	14.0
Births/population 15–44	0.065	0.075	0.087	0.100	0.115	0.132	0.151	0.173	0.198	0.226	0.258	0.293	0.333

[a] GRR = gross reproduction rate.
Source: Manual IV, p. 96.

Table 23. *Proportion of women in cohorts of ten years, west model level 3 for females*

Age	Proportion of females	Huánuco, 1562	Yucay, 1571
80+	0.0025	11	0
70–9	0.0181	20	7
60–9	0.0492	84	55
50–9	0.0826	124	64
40–9	0.1112		
30–9	0.1398		
20–9	0.1690		
10–19	0.1946		
0–9	0.2332		

simplified version of the west stable population model at Level 3 mortality, which provides the information on the proportion of females within each ten-year cohort, then the data for Huánuco in 1562 and Yucay in 1571. Using the proportions, we can estimate what the 1562 and 1571 population of Huánuco and Yucay *should have been,* based on the survivors of the precontact period: The expected 1562 and 1571 populations are 2,979 and 1,571; but the recorded populations were 1,849 and 940, respectively. The difference between the census figures and the "expected" populations is the result of the exceptional mortality of the postconquest period (see Table 24 for calculations).

We have now estimated what the population of Huánuco and Yucay should have been in 1562 and 1571, based on elderly female survivors. By applying what we have learned to all of Peru, then the 1570 base period population figures should be adjusted upward by approximately the same percentage as the figures for Huánuco and Yucay (61 percent and 67 percent). The adjustment would involve an approximate 64 percent increment for the 1570 base figure of 1,290,680. The "corrected" 1570 population estimate is 2,116,715. That is, the Peruvian Indian population in 1570 should have been 2.1 million, if the mortality experience for all the population was the same as that of the cohorts of women who were in their youth or slightly older at the time Pizarro entered Cajamarca. These women, however, must also have suffered a higher rate of mortality than was normal for the Andean region prior to the arrival of the Europeans.

Clearly, using this method, the aboriginal population of Peru had

Table 24. *Calculations to adjust for "real" populations of Huánuco (1562) and Yucay (1571)*

Age	Proportion	Huánuco, 1562		Yucay, 1571	
		Number	Total female estimate	Number	Total female estimate
80+	0.0025	(11)	4,400	(—)	
70–9	0.0181	(20)	1,105	(7)	387
60–9	0.0492	(84)	1,707	(55)	1,118
50–9	0.0826	(124)	1,501	(64)	775
$\Sigma 50+$	0.1524		1,568	(126)	827
Total male population (based on estimated sex ratio of 90)			1,411		744
Total population			2,979		1,571

to have been at least 2.1 million, even if the annual rate of decline were zero between 1520 and 1570. The native population must have been much higher, however. There is no solution to the question of the overall mortality rate for the fifty years following 1530. One alternative is to use the same regional rates of decline that we used in Model 1 and the adjusted 1570 population; the resulting estimate is almost 5 million (see Table 25). Or, we might apply the maximum coastal rate (−3.8 percent) to the 1570 revised coastal figure of 402,670; the adjusted 1520 coastal estimate is 2,692,210. Application of the highland rate of −1.4 percent to the 1570 figure (1,714,110) yields a highland 3,451,790 and a combined total of 6,144,000. Or, simply applying the lowest regional rate to the 1570 adjusted total (−1.2 percent) gives a minimal contact population of 3,856,910. Using a rate of change of −3.8 percent, the highest regional rate in the 1570s–1600s period, provides what I believe to be a maximal estimate of 14,152,100.

Model 5 is highly speculative. The female population above the age of 50 is not the ideal group to use for stable population analysis, but we must necessarily focus our attention on this small sector. The choice of stable population model for Level 3 mortality is hypothetical and is partly the consequence of measurements of the average age of the female population of Huánuco and Yucay. The selection of a zero

Table 25. *Estimated Peruvian population in 1520, from the adjusted 1570 figures*

Region	1570 recorded	1570 adjusted	Rate of change	1520 adjusted estimate
North coast	80,123	131,402	−2.2	394,753
Central coast	128,820	211,265	−3.1	995,369
South coast	36,587	60,003	−3.8	401,174
North sierra	209,057	342,853	−1.2	624,719
Central sierra	240,604	394,591	−1.4	794,609
South sierra	595,528	976,666	−1.2	1,779,600
Total				4,990,224

growth rate is arbitrary and is based on the assumption of stable populations in two units in the late Inca period. In spite of the obvious shortcomings, I nevertheless consider the method a step in the right direction. The figures of 4 million to 14 million that we derived for Peru set a reasonable minimum and maximum boundary, which we shall reexamine in Chapter 7. We shall also review the projections of 5 million and 6 million.

Evaluation. In Model 1 we projected a 1520 population of 3.3 million for Peru, utilizing the reliable data of the 1570 and 1600 decades. The result is dependent on the assumption that the 1520 to 1570 rate of decline was similar to the 1570 to 1600 period. I believe this estimate is at the low of a possible range. Model 2, based on the possibility that the rate of decline for the first half-century was double that of the later period, provides an estimate of 8.9 million. The result is tenable. Model 3, because of the faulty data for the 1540s, results in a low figure of 3.1 million. Model 4, using an inadequate number of cases and unreliable figures for the decades of the 1530s and 1540s, provides unrealistically high totals, which must be discarded. In Model 5, I adjust the 1570 figures according to stable population theory, then project the 1520 population using the assumptions of Models 1 and 2. In this manner we arrive at a figure of approximately 4 million to 14 million residents for Andean Peru in 1520. The last model yields what I consider to be a reliable range for the true preconquest population.

The census projection models we have examined in this chapter do not provide a single answer to the question of the size of Peru's aboriginal population. Totals have varied depending on the method. Yet census projection models seem more appropriate than some of the techniques outlined in previous chapters. In the next chapter we shall reexamine the results of the various models before arriving at a final conclusion.

7

Conclusion

In the previous chapters we examined a variety of approaches to making population estimates of the native population of Peru before first direct contact with the Old World invaders or the diseases that preceded the Europeans. Some of the avenues are less useful than others, and we had to discard them outright.

The ecological model, or a study of the carrying capacity of pre-Columbian Peru, may best suggest the limits of population growth. There is certainly a maximum population that may be sustained by an ecosystem. Due to the nature of Peru's coastal agriculture, it is easier to establish theoretical maximums for coastal valleys than for the highlands. The maximum 6.5 million that we reached (Table 3) for the coastal population is, in my view, a valid high point, but the total productivity of the highlands is not well enough known to establish a limit for that area. At best, we might apply seven people per square hectare as the carrying capacity of Peru's total cultivated land in 1961 to arrive at a figure of 13.3 million. This highly tentative number is about as good as any other figure one is able currently to derive from the method, given the large number of variables and the insufficient evidence. The question of whether the Empire reached the limits of the agricultural base is not yet fully answered. Evidence that it did comes from the extension of cultivated lands into marginal areas: ridged fields in floodplains, sunken fields along the coast, extensive terracing of the hillsides. Warfare did not seem to be a significant check on growth, however, nor did famines. Indeed the redistributive aspects of the state precluded permanent local disasters. State and societal marriage practices, if anything, stimulated expansion of the aboriginal population.

Archaeological evidence still holds future promise for providing good results, although many methodological problems must be faced. At local levels archaeology improves our understanding of preconquest patterns of longevity, birth and death rates, disease, and nutrition, and careful study of sites should narrow the now wide range of population estimates for many regions of Peru. Yet, currently, population estimates for Chan Chan, one of the most thoroughly explored

Peruvian sites, range from 25,000 to 200,000 residents. Pan-Andean population estimates on the basis of archaeological data will not be possible in the foreseeable future. The area is too extensive and the difficulties too formidable to be quickly surmounted.

Depopulation ratio models have been widely used in the past to estimate Peru's population, but their use has produced a large range of estimates. Dobyns's maximum of up to 37.5 million for the Andean region may be contrasted with Rowe's estimate of about 6 million. Wachtel's 10 million and C. T. Smith's 12 million are intermediate results. The problem with all past investigators who have attempted to use depopulation ratio models is that they have generalized from an inadequate statistical sample.

Political and social structure models such as that of Means are based on the European's idealized concept of the structure of the Inca world. Means reaches a range of 16 million to 32 million. Application of the ideal number of inhabitants in each Empire province yields about 11.5 million, but the concept has little basis in fact.

The disease mortality model is a new approach to the problem and provides evidence that must be considered. Using a "maximal" mortality model and a base population of 1,000, eighty-three people would remain a century after contact. With "minimal" mortality, about 207 might remain of the original thousand. The estimated range on the basis of this model is 3,243,985 to 8,090,421. It must be cautioned, however, that the rates of mortality for the various epidemics are only estimates. The vital statistics do not exist. Further, the model does not take into account possible population growth between epidemic periods. The population pyramids for Huánuco in 1562, Yucay in 1571, and Yanque Collaguas in 1591 do suggest that, although severe epidemics took place frequently, mortality was highest for children under 5, and the population tended to recuperate fairly rapidly after the epidemics. Peruvian Indian society was devastated but not destroyed by disease.

Census projection models provide one of the most promising avenues of approach to answering the problem of the size of the aboriginal population. For Peru, the major difficulty with the census projection models lies in the fact that the relatively complete and accurate census returns generally begin in 1570. The most reliable way of projecting earlier populations is to use post-1570 rates for the preceding half-century. With this method, however, the 1520 population is projected to be 3,300,574. This estimate should be considered minimal. Given the probable high mortality during the fifty years between 1520 and 1570, the initial population is likely to have been higher,

but how much higher is not at all clear. Major epidemics swept Peru
in the 1520s, 1530–2, 1546, and 1558–60. In some areas in the
1520s, adult males among the proponents of Atahualpa and Huascar
suffered high combat mortality. With the entrance of the conquistadores, there was substantial mortality between 1531 and 1534, then
heavy mortality in locales most involved in the great uprising of
1536–7, and exceptional mortality during the Gonzalo Pizarro revolt. Further, before the institutional safeguards to protect the Indians became effective, roughly in the 1560s, many repartimiento
Indians were mercilessly exploited. Thus, it is safe to assume that post-
1520 mortality was higher than mortality following 1570. A model
using a double rate for the first fifty years projects a 1520 population
of 8,865,142. Although the case for a higher rate of mortality for the
early period may be defended, the choice of a specific rate, such as
double, cannot. One might as well claim the rate was three, four, or
five times as high. Another method of census projection is to take the
rate of change between the 1540s and 1570s. With these rates the
1520 population projection is 3,112,663. The population figures
recorded in the 1540s are low, however, lower than they should have
been, because of the nature of the Gasca census and tribute assessment; and the statistical sample for the 1540s is unsatisfactory. There
are data to calculate rates of change of selected repartimientos in the
1530s–1540s. During this period a sharp decline in the population
was recorded; in many cases these reports provide data for a fourth
model of census projection. With this method a minimal estimate of
68 million and a maximum of 211 million for 1520 are reached. Once
again, though, the statistical sample is inadequate, and the results
must be eliminated from our consideration of alternatives. The fifth
model, based on stable population theory, applied to Peru's total
population and using recorded regional minimum and maximum
rates of change in the 1570s–1600s period, presents a minimum
population of 3,856,910 and a maximum of 14,152,100. I believe
these limits to be valid.

What then has this exercise contributed to our historical understanding of the size of the aboriginal population of Peru? In the first
place, a base minimum population appears to be clearly demonstrated. There is a remarkable convergence of four estimates, which
may be considered conservative, between 3 million and 4 million.
The epidemic disease model, using minimal mortality rates for
known epidemics, based on the 1620 population, yields a result of
3,243,985. The projection of 1570–1600 depopulation rates to 1520
using a known base population in 1570 gives an initial figure of

3,300,574. The low rates of the 1540–70 period projected to 1520 provide a population of 3,112,663. Use of an "adjusted" 1570 population on the basis of analysis of the population pyramids of Huánuco (1562) and Yucay (1571) and projection of that figure to 1520, using the minimal rate of regional decline for the 1570–1600 period, result in a total of 3,856,910. On the basis of this evidence, any estimate lower than approximately 3.2 million for the precontact population of Peru's highlands and coast is suspect.

At the upper end of the scale, two projections converge at the 8–9 million level and two at the 12–14 million figure. The "maximum" disease mortality model results in an estimate of 8,090,421; and regional rates of double the 1570–1600 loss provide a total of 8,865,142. The model using an "adjusted" 1570 population on the basis of stable population analysis and a maximal regional rate of change from the 1570–1600 period gives a 1520 population of 14,152,100. The analogy with the rates of decline for Mexico gives an estimate of 14.4 million. Further, preliminary study of the carrying capacity of the coastal ecosystem suggests a limit there of approximately 6.5 million. A coastal–highland "balance" would result in a maximum of about 13 million. The density of seven people per hectare of tilled land yields 13.3 million. One social structure model, based on ideal provincial size, gives 11.5 million. The maximums are speculative and, in the current state of research, should not be considered definitive.

Before a final estimate of the aboriginal population of Peru can be reached, it is necessary to adjust for the number of inhabitants of the region east of the Andes: the montaña and edges of the Amazon basin. Even the twentieth-century population of the region, which makes up almost half the territory of the nation, is a matter of conjecture. For the 1961 census part of the data was provided by aerial "counts" and missionary and government "reports." The National Office of Statistics admitted the possibility of major error. For the aboriginal population estimate for this region I rely on the recent investigations of William M. Denevan.[1] After an examination of his method (ecological) and review of sources, I am convinced Denevan's estimates are the most reliable available. Denevan calculates a contact population of 477,940 for that region (see Table 26).

Addition of the figures for eastern Peru to those for the highland and coast makes it unlikely that the total Indian population of the area in 1520 was less than 4 million or more than 15 million. This should be a valid "range" for the work of future investigators. Such a range may be too wide, however, to satisfy those looking for a single figure.

Table 26. *Denevan's aboriginal population, estimated by habitat areas, for eastern Peru*

Habitat	Area (km^2)	Density (km)	Population
Floodplain	11,700	14.6	170,820
Upland forest	157,000	1.2	188,400
Lowland forest	573,100	0.2	114,620
Superhumid upland	41,000	0.1	4,100
Total	782,800	0.61	477,940

Source: Denevan, *Native Population,* p. 228.

As I pointed out in the beginning, the "exact" population of Peru in the sixteenth century will never be known. It was even impossible to establish the "exact" population of the United States in 1970, using a census staff of thousands, sophisticated techniques, and advanced computers. The underenumeration in the 1970 U.S. census was estimated to be 2.5 percent. On the basis of the research, I will hazard an estimate for the 1520 Indian population of Peru that is admittedly subject to a much wider margin of error.[2]

I have pointed out repeatedly that I consider the lower figure to be "minimal." The figure of 4 million is based on a constantly low mortality rate for nearly the whole of the first century after European–Indian contact. I am not at all convinced that the rate of mortality between 1520 and 1570 was only equal to the rate for the following half-century. The Toledo and post-Toledo epochs were characterized by formalized yet overtly stable relations between the races. With the exception of the localized resistance and ultimate execution of Tupac Amaru I and his companions, there were no major uprisings or bloody wars of extermination between the newcomer and the native. Combat fatalities had taken a toll during the previous fifty years. Thousands were involved in the fighting between Atahualpa and Huascar in the 1520s. Combat mortality continued as the Spanish first defeated one side, then played one group against the other. Some areas, especially Lima, Jauja, and Cuzco, suffered heavily as a result of the Indian uprising of 1537. Then Indians were enrolled as either combatants or auxiliaries and transport and supply personnel during the conflict between the Pizarrists and Almagrists, and later between the encomenderos under Gonzalo Pizarro and the royalists under

Pedro de la Gasca. Conflicts continued into the 1550s. One of the main reasons for the small number of elderly males in Huánuco and Yucay in the 1560s and 1570s must be combat mortality during this chaotic period.

Further, by the Toledo era the relation between tributary and encomendero had been well established by law and custom. The encomenderos were generally under close control of authorities, especially the corregidores, the protectores de los indios, and the parish priests. In the first decades after Cajamarca there were usually no checks to the exactions of the encomenderos. Marched from place to place, often between high elevation and low, acting as human beasts of burden, working in mines, Indians unquestionably died by the thousands. Although the use of the Indian as a carrier of goods largely came to an end by the time of Toledo, mine labor did not. The mita for Huancavelica, Potosí, Castrovirreyna, and lesser mining centers was closely regulated, however, and prescribed percentages of the population were required to work for specified periods and under supervised conditions. Certainly, the mining mortality was not eliminated by the Toledo administration, but it was limited.

As time went on, population density decreased. Epidemiologists agree that population density is a key factor in the spread of disease. Toledo temporarily reversed the process by settling the Indians in large villages. The consequences were new major epidemics in the late 1580s and a gradual decline in population density. Moreover, with the passage of generations, either the Indians were more resistant to diseases or less virulent strains of the disease persisted.

For these reasons I believe the estimate of 4 million is minimal and is probably significantly less than the actual 1520 population. It seems to me likewise unlikely that the true population reached what I consider "limits" of 12 million to 15 million. The question remains: What was the population likely to have been? I now consider that the "maximum" disease epidemic model (8,090,421) and the census projection model using a double rate of change for the 1520–70 period (8,865,142) provide reasonable results. The two projections based on the stable population model, one using the adjusted 1570 population and the 1570s–1600s regional rates and the other using the maximum coast and highland rates, also warrant consideration (4,990,224 and 6,144,000). By adjusting the four figures upward by 477,000 for the eastern region of Peru we reach estimates of from about 5.5 million to 9.4 million. We must also consider the possibility that some Indians escaped enumeration and hence have been left out of our calculations. The true aboriginal population could have been more or less than the range of 5.5 million to 9.4 million, but on the basis of what we have seen I believe the burden of proof for numbers outside these bounds to be on the scholars who posit them. My final estimate of 9 million, which is at the upper edge of the range, is based on the maximal epidemic disease model and on the assumption that the rates of decline in the period from 1520 to 1570 must have exceeded rates during following decades. Although choice of 9 million may appear to be arbitrary, it is made after careful weighing of the evidence, rather than being purely an act of faith.

The figure of 9 million for Peru's pre-Spanish population underscores the demographic collapse of the native Andean world. We shall see in the next section that in the next half-century the population fell to slightly over 1 million and by 1620 stood at about 600,000. The overall decline was approximately 93 percent for the century following contact between the European and Andean inhabitant. The collapse along Peru's coast was total. The native resident was almost completely wiped out and was replaced by the Spanish colonist and African slaves. Only migration of highland Indians toward coastal haciendas and urban centers prevented extinction of Indian influence on the coastal strip. On the coast remaining Indians were transformed, as they became part of the lower level of colonial Hispanic society. By contrast, the sierra Indian was not decimated by the expansion of Europe in the sixteenth century. In spite of disease and outright exploitation by the Spaniards, the highland Indian persisted. Peru is today very much influenced by the biological and cultural legacy of that survival.

PART II

Demographic collapse

The point to be stressed here is the obvious one that this relationship between the size of a population and the organization of that population is such that a drastic reduction of the population size undermines the existing social organization in virtually all its aspects. Thus a case of so-called cultural devolution may be attributable to nothing more complex than extensive depopulation caused by elements beyond the immediate control of the society involved.

D. E. Dumond, "Population Growth
and Cultural Change," pp. 319–20

In the preceding pages we attempted to gauge the magnitude of Peru's preconquest population. By any standards the Inca population was large. Perhaps 9 million people resided within the limits delineated by Peru's contemporary boundaries. The number of inhabitants remaining a century after contact was roughly a tenth of those that were there when the Europeans invaded the Andean world. In the following chapters we shall examine the transformations that were taking place as a result of the demographic collapse of native America.

The impact of population change varied from one place to another within Peru. Some Indian communities were wiped out. In a few cases numbers actually increased, in spite of the general downward tendency. We shall examine these developments in as great detail as possible. Analysis is within the framework of major geographical regions. We have already seen the differences between coastal and highland change. More subtle variations are discernible as one moves southward, down the Peruvian coast. Although on occasion such a structure becomes too rigid, the results are useful for comparative analysis. Each population unit is studied in the context of the chronological evolution of that locale, and at the conclusion to each section I attempt to provide an overview of the major regional developments.

We have discussed the type and reliability of the data on which our analysis is based in Chapter 6. Population projections at ten-year intervals are found in Table 18. The tributary estimates for the same

Map 4. Peruvian corregimientos.

areas for the period extending from 1570 to 1620 are shown in Table 27. We shall return to these figures during the course of our examination of Peru's population decline. Map 4 outlines the six sectors we shall be reviewing. The corregimiento units (Piura, Saña, Jaén, and so on) are also depicted. More detailed regional maps are included within each chapter.

Demographic collapse

Table 27. *Estimated tributary population of Peru, 1570–1620*

Region	1570	1580	1590	1600	1610	1620
North coast	20,398	15,359	11,769	9,170	7,262	5,844
Central coast	25,189	20,567	17,082	14,331	12,140	10,374
South coast	8,711	6,403	4,936	3,925	3,193	2,668
North sierra	42,677	34,544	30,224	26,002	22,372	19,356
Central sierra	41,994	36,966	33,070	29,802	26,965	24,539
South sierra	121,584	108,738	97,944	88,611	80,500	73,462
Total	260,544	222,570	195,017	171,834	152,424	136,235

Note: The total for each date varies slightly from the sum of the regions. The difference is the result of rounding off to the nearest digit of population estimates for each repartimiento.

My purpose is to impart to the reader not only a concept of the demographic experience of a people at a critical juncture in its history but also an understanding of the dynamics of change. We shall view the extent of population loss; the impact of epidemic disease; the role of exploitation in mines, haciendas, and public works projects; possible changes in family structure and size; the importance of elevation as a factor in population change; the short- and long-term consequences of disasters such as floods, droughts, and earthquakes; and the importance of migration. The north coast of Peru was the region that experienced the first contact between the conquistadores and the Inca Empire. It is here that our study begins.

8

First contact: north coast

The infinite abundance of humanity, during the passage of many years, which this New World propagated, was such that there scarcely remained a corner, however remote or hidden it might be, that the native inhabitants did not search for, discover, and settle, . . . there came an abundant multiplication of people, which gave such a filling of this section of the world, that men were not lacking for land, but land for people.

Miguel Cabello de Balboa,
Miscelánea antártica, pp. 220–1

There are three distinct ecological systems in Peru: the coast, the highlands, and the montaña with the Amazon basin. Each of the regions has its own set of unique characteristics and is subject to its peculiar internal divisions.[1] Common to all the Peruvian coast, and the factor that contributes to its special climate, is the Humboldt current. That broad river, flowing in a counterclockwise fashion in the eastern South Pacific, sweeps cold Antarctic water along the South American coast. The prevailing westerly winds push the air, cooled by the water, against the unbroken Andean chain, which in places surpasses 6,000 meters in elevation. The result is an area of high barometric pressure. Almost no rain falls along the mid-Chilean to north Peruvian coasts. The consequence is a narrow desert strip some 3,000 kilometers in length. As the air rises along the western Andean slopes, moisture condenses. In some areas, at roughly 600–1,500 meters in elevation, the moisture forms a fog or *garua*. At higher altitudes there is seasonal rainfall and at the highest points snow, which provide the water for coastal rivers and irrigation systems. In almost all cases, the river flow varies sharply from dry to wet seasons, and often rivers that are raging torrents at the height of the rainy period disappear during the dry season.

The only major break in this coastal climatic pattern occurs when for reasons not yet fully understood the Pacific current shifts and a countercurrent, called the Niño, flows southward from equatorial regions. This warm, moisture-laden current causes rapid temperature rises along the coast. The climate shifts from temperate to tropical, as the latitude would suggest; and heavy rainfall strikes the coast, destroying irrigation systems and sun-dried brick structures. It is during these periods that major ecological crises take place.

The north Peruvian coastal ecology parallels that of the central and southern regions: a narrow coastal desert strip; foothill areas (lomas) at higher elevations, where there is enough air moisture part of the year to produce vegetation for grazing of animals; and high Andean slopes, usually 3,200 meters or more, which provide enough rainfall for seasonal farming. Yet there are important differences along the north coast. The Piura region, for example, is at just about the point where the Humboldt current sweeps westward; thus, the water temperature is warmer and the air is more moist. There is enough water in Tumbez near the Ecuadorian border to allow growth of cacti and mesquite. The Chira River, second largest of the coast, cuts too deep a chasm to permit extensive irrigation. The Piura valley, the first to be settled on a permanent basis by the Spaniards, represents the first in a series of coastal valleys with dense populations. Beyond lie the great Sechura desert and, even farther, the Lambayeque valley. At Lambayeque began the first great population concentration, perhaps the largest of the north coast: It included the Lambayeque along with the Leche and Motupe river complexes. Farther southward are the Saña, Jequetepeque, Chicama, Moche, Virú, Santa, Nepeña, Casma, and Huarmey river valleys. Each valley had its own irrigation system. At times, when valleys became politically and culturally linked, irrigation canals tied one or more units together. A good example was the Chimú unification of the Chicama and Moche inhabitants, and the interconnection of the Lambayeque, Saña, and Jequetepeque valleys in a vast network that extended more than 150 kilometers north to south. Each valley, however, retained its distinct economic characteristics.[2]

The aggregate population figures for the north Peruvian coast for the period from 1570 to 1620 illustrate a general pattern of rapid depopulation. The number of tributaries in the half-century fell from slightly more than 20,000 to less than 6,000 and the total population declined from approximately 77,000 to 23,000. In spite of the relatively rapid loss of people during the period, however, some north coastal populations actually managed to maintain a relative stability. Individual differences deserve close attention.[3]

The first region of Peru to be touched by the Europeans was the north coast. Just south of the Gulf of Guayaquil, in modern Ecuador, lay the northernmost outposts of the Inca Empire encountered by the

Spanish. Preliminary reconnaissance in that area extended from Tumbez, just south of the Ecuadorian border, for about 250 kilometers to what became the first foreign settlement in 1532: San Miguel de Tangarara (later moved to Piura). Early contact was intermittent, beginning in 1528 at Tumbez. The first Europeans to land in the area were probably Pedro de Candía and Alonso de Molina. The earliest report of Tumbez referred to the Indian settlement as "a well-ordered town."[4] Zárate, the famous chronicler who arrived in Peru in the early 1540s, suggested that Tumbez was the site of a major palace of the "lord" of Peru and that the whole was "One of the finest sights in the country until the Indians of Puna island destroyed it." In fact, in the previous decades warfare between the Indians of Puna and Tumbez was frequent. During the 1528 expedition one or more Spaniards were left in Tumbez while the main European force returned northward.[5]

The importance the Spanish ascribed to Tumbez is illustrated the following year. In 1529, Francisco Pizarro, while in Spain, negotiated the contract with the Crown to discover "Peru." The resulting agreement named Almagro "Commander of Tumbez" and Hernando de Luque "Bishop of Tumbez."[6] Yet, when the Europeans finally reached the site again late in 1530 or early 1531, the city was desolate. Local informants reported the change was a consequence of a civil war within the Inca Empire, but there had also been a renewal of fighting between the natives of Puna and Tumbez before the Spaniards returned. Puna probably was victorious in the conflict, for when Pizarro took Puna there were "more than six hundred men and women of Tumbez, including one chieftain, . . . held prisoner on the island of Puna." The figure of 600 illustrates the problem of early reports of population recorded by the chroniclers. Was the number generated by an actual count made by the conquistadores or by a guess based on a superficial glance? Or could the Spaniards have relied on reports of local Indian leaders who may have taken an accurate enumeration? In this case we have an approximate number; but how many Tumbez residents avoided capture? What percentage of the total original population of the city was killed by the attackers from Puna or fled? How many had died from European disease that preceded the actual arrival of the conquerers? The figure, like so many early numbers, can be at best only a reflection of the true population. The Spanish freed the prisoners from Tumbez and allowed them to return to their homes. But Tumbez was clearly deserted when the Europeans arrived, and the entire region was in arms. The inhabitants of Tumbez, to thank Pizarro for freeing them from Puna and helping them go back to their homeland, sacrificed three Spaniards. Shortly thereafter the Europeans inflicted heavy punishment on the Indians responsible for the excessive act of "gratitude." Ultimately, the curaca of Tumbez sued for peace and presented the Spanish with gifts of silver and gold.[7]

Pizarro and the Spanish forces spent several weeks at Tumbez, during which time some Indians returned to their partially burned-out houses. Other early reports also described the community as a relatively important city when the Europeans first arrived. Miguel de Estete reported it was a major settlement but one that the natives quickly abandoned to the Spanish. Estete wrote that the Temple of the Sun was especially impressive: "a great structure, and all inside and out painted with great paintings of a rich variety of color."[8] An early anonymous account of the conquest published in France in 1534 reports that the cacique of Tumbez, Chilemaza, led an uprising against the Europeans and that Pizarro and the Spanish forces therefore destroyed much territory and "killed many inhabitants."[9]

It is clear that the process of population collapse in the Tumbez region began before the arrival of the foreigners. Warfare was a major cause of decline, initially between natives of Tumbez and the island of Puna, then probably against the forces of the Inca Empire. There followed direct confrontation with the Spanish and further combat mortality. There is no report of the number of Indians at Tumbez in 1528, but it is unlikely that the six hundred prisoners from Tumbez held by the natives of the island of Puna composed the total population of the former settlement at that date. Spanish descriptions suggest that there remained a large number of original inhabitants of Tumbez who had fled to the interior to avoid capture by the Puna Indians. The contract for exploration and discovery with the Spanish government entitled Almagro to the first European control over the native residents of Tumbez. That power was broken in the conflict between the Almagro and Pizarro factions. By the 1540s Gonzalo Pizarro granted to Francisco de Villalobos some four hundred "Indians" there, which is likely to mean that there were about four hundred married working males in Tumbez at that time.[10] Their true age is unclear, but it is probable they were between 25 and 50 years old. At the time of Viceroy Toledo's general inspection in the 1570s there were 217 tributaries (18 to 50 years of age) and a total population of 553 in the village of Tumbez. They made up the repartimiento of Gonzalo Farfán. There were in addition 20 tributaries and a total of 95 people of Mancora, which comprised the repartimiento of Gonzalo Prieto Dávila, concurrently living in Tumbez. By the end of the century there appear to have been only a dozen or so tributaries left in the city.[11]

The full extent of the depopulation of Tumbez in the century between 1528 and 1628 is not clear. The early evidence is too fragmentary to assign a definite contact figure. Archaeological investigations may help find the answer. It is evident, however, that Tumbez was a major population cluster before the Europeans arrived. Early descriptions of the city and the fact that Almagro was made "commander" and Luque bishop point to a reasonably dense population as well. The captives from Tumbez at La Puna in 1530 at least suggest what must have been a sizable original population. The number of 400 in the 1540s is not to be trusted. It appears that figure is relative only and that the Spaniards were attempting to obscure the true size of their holdings from the watchful eye of royal authorities. Although no report of the precontact population of Tumbez has been found, I estimate that the 1520 number of inhabitants was in the neighborhood of 1,000 tributaries, with a total population of 5,000. The Tumbez population fell to about 250 tributaries and 650 inhabitants in the 1570s and to 12 tributaries in the 1600s. Such a rapid population loss for Tumbez resulted in the effective disintegration of the structure of native society. Many other coastal pre-Columbian centers went through the same disintegrative process. That crisis will be studied in the context of other communities along the coast.

After his temporary residence at Tumbez, Pizarro marched southward and ultimately attacked the inhabitants of the Chira valley. It was in this area that he established San Miguel de Tangarara, which was the forerunner of Piura. Estete's description of what became Piura is especially revealing: "The Tallana River was very populated with pueblos and a very good fruit growing sector of a better kind than Tumbez; there is an abundance of foodstuffs and native livestock. All the area to the sea was explored because it appeared to have a good port."[12] It was here, near the pueblo of Puechos that San Miguel was founded. The 1534 French account suggests: "There are many pueblos and settlements of Indians, and near the river is a large tall and attractive structure made of stone in the manner of a fortress, and near the structure is a large and beautiful city from which the inhabitants approached the Christians with a great abundance of commodities."[13]

Francisco Pizarro granted a relatively large number of small repartimientos to his followers at Piura in 1532. This was the first of a set of Indian grants made by the conqueror, primarily to Spaniards who were too old or too sick to continue on the southward march toward the temporary Inca highland headquarters of Atahualpa at Cajamarca.

A list of the repartimientos of Piura compiled for Pedro de la Gasca's general distribution after the successful defeat of the rebels

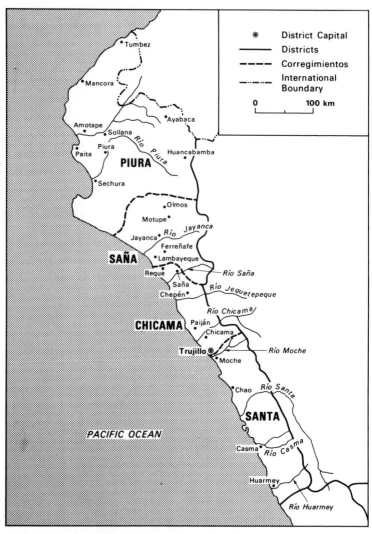

Map 5. North coast of Peru.

under Gonzalo Pizarro is illustrative of the approximate size of the Indian population of that region in the 1540s (see Table 28).[14]

By the 1560s, the site of San Miguel had been moved from Tangar-ara in the Chira valley to Piura. Part of the reason for the transfer of the settlement was excessive heat and the unhealthy nature of the original site. Fevers and eye infections were especially prevalent among Euro-pean children. The new location, by the 1560s, consisted of about one hundred Spanish houses, with twenty-three resident encomenderos. Within the jurisdiction of San Miguel were six thousand tributaries, not yet living in pueblos. Europeans related that the area was excellent for growing not only fruit, including oranges, figs, apples, *membril-los,* grapes, and melons, but also grain, as, for example, wheat, corn, and oats. There was enough grazing land for cattle, goats, sheep, and pigs. There was at least one sugar mill in the valley, and in Piura an Indian hospital and a Mercedarian monastery were located. For the royal cosmographer, López de Velasco, the six thousand Indian trib-utaries were situated in numerous "repartimientos and pueblos" (see Table 29).[15]

Francisco de Toledo's reduction of Indians into a small number of population clusters in the district of San Miguel de Piura in the 1570s simplified the human geography of the region and contributed to further population decline. By the time of Viceroy Toledo, there were twenty-seven repartimientos in the jurisdiction of Piura, held by a total of sixteen encomenderos, including Catacaos, which was in the hands of the Crown. Generally, the encomendero put together enough repartimientos to provide a reasonable tribute, if at all possi-ble. With two grants, for example, Rodrigo Méndez controlled 83 tributaries; Francisco Cornejo did better with 113; Gonzalo Prieto Dávila managed to oversee 98 tributaries in three grants; Gaspar Troche had 117 in three; Rui López Calderon had access to 171; and Gonzalo Farfán had 285 (see Table 30). It must be noted, however, that the total number of tributaries at the time of the visita general, according to a document in the Marqués del Risco collection in Seville, was only 2,400. In Vázquez de Espinosa's *Compendium,* roughly three decades later, there were only 1,500 tributaries! At the turn of the century the population of Piura was concentrated in the interior at higher elevations.[16] The coastal sector of Piura was practi-cally destitute of its aboriginal inhabitants a century after European contact. Although the census dates for Piura are imprecise, the number of tributaries fell from roughly 14,250 in 1545 to 6,000 in 1560, to 2,400 in 1575, and finally to 1,500 in 1600. It should also be noted that the tributaries of 1545 and 1560 constituted a smaller

Table 28. *Pedro de la Gasca's distribution of repartimientos in Piura*

Name	Holder	Location	Size (tributary males)
Puianca (c.)[a]	Francisco Lobo, Diego Palomino[b]	Llanos	2,000
Motape (c.)	Francisco Palomino	Llanos	400
Controilico (c.)	Diego de Serra	Llanos	500 }
Penachi (c.)	Diego de Serra	Sierra	
Copez (c.)	Francisco Bernaldo de Quiroz	Llanos	200
Tabaconas	Francisco Bernaldo de Quiroz	Sierra	500+
Serrán (c.)	Gonzalo de Gujera	Llanos	300
? (c.)	Gonzalo de Gujera	Sierra	500
Chumala (c.)	Baltasar de Carbajal	Llanos	100
Moscala (c.)	Diego de Fonseca	Llanos	300 }
Suntotora (c.)	Diego de Fonseca	Llanos	
Pabor (c.)	Minor son of Juan de Trujillo and Maria de Paz	Llanos	400 }
Guama Tabacona (c.)	Minor son of Juan de Trujillo and Maria de Paz	Sierra	
Xibraque (c.)	?	Llanos	
Picol (c.)	?	Sierra	900 }
Malatacos (c.)	?	Sierra	
La Apullana de Catacedos	Miguel de Salcedo, by death of Fernando Carrasco (married widow)	Llanos	600
Apullana de Catacedos, half of Valle of Catacedos	Miguel de Salcedo, by death of Fernando Carrasco (married widow)	Llanos	300
Valle de Dipatera	Melchior de Montoia[b]	Llanos	500
Comboco	Melchior de Montoia	Sierra	400
V. Dipatera, Cosegra (c.)	Fernando de Ceballos[b]	Sierra	100
Sexillo (c.)	Monastery la Merced	Llanos	30
Menonque (c.)	Miguel Ruiz	Llanos (fishermen)	400

Place	Region	Encomendero	Number
Conchira (c.)	Llanos	Francisco de Lucera	⎱
Tanguacila (c.)	Llanos	Francisco de Lucera	400
Castillo de Puerto Paita	Coast	Francisco de Lucera	⎰
Paita y Lisilla (c.)	Coast	Vacated	60
Colin (Puerto de Paita)	Coast	Vacated	60
Xinaba (c.)	Coast	Francisco Martín Albarrán	⎱
Bitonera (c.)	Coast	Francisco Martín Albarrán	800
Motape (c.)	Llanos	Francisco Martín Albarrán	
Colana (c.)	Sierra	Francisco Martín Albarrán	⎰
Chirma (c.)	Llanos	Juan Farfán	600
Mitimaes de Maicabelita	Llanos	Vacated	100
Cocolan (c.)	Llanos	Pedro Gutiérrez de los Rios	⎱ 400
Half of Chuparra	Sierra	Pedro Gutiérrez de los Rios	⎰
La Apullana de Poechos	Llanos	Diego de Santiago	100
Tumbez (c.)	Coast	Francisco de Villalobos	400
Pariña (c.)	Coast	Francisco de Villalobos	⎱ 200
Mancoia (c.)	Coast	Francisco de Villalobos	⎰
Ibaco (c.)	Sierra	In daughter & wife of Aguilar, now married to Capt. Fernando de Cardenas	600
Caxas (c.)	Sierra	Isabel de Caravantes (wife of Christóbal de Coto[b])	800
Guanacabamba (c.)	Sierra	Diego Palomino	⎱ 1,300
Guamian (c.)	Sierra	Diego Palomino	⎰
Total			14,250

Note: Spelling of names that appear in the tables follows the spelling in the original source. There are numerous variations; for example, Copez, Copiz.

[a] c. = curaca.

[b] Deceased.

Sources: Real Academia de la Historia, Mata Linares Collection, vol. 82; Loredo, *Repartos*, pp. 265–75.

Table 29. *Distribution of Piura inhabitants in the 1560s (6,000 tributaries)*

Guancabama	Motripemoscala	Paita	Mancora
Caxas	Xayanca	Sechura	Catacaos
Caxas	Piura	Chira	Isonto
Serran	Malingas	Motapesolana	La mitad de Catacaos
Ayabaca	Cocolan	Bitonera	Chumalaque
Olimos	Catacaos	Guarna	Paiuor
Penachepo	Marycabelica	Paita	Sechura
Ochos	Colán	Zilla	Colán
Copiz	Tangarara	Tumbez	Catacaos
Xayanca		Parina	

Note: López de Velasco often lists the same community more than once, usually signifying that Indians were granted to different Spaniards.

percentage of the total population than in the time of Viceroy Toledo and onward because of the shift in the Crown guidelines concerning the ages for which males were subject to tribute payment. The Piura decline was about 90 percent in approximately fifty-five years. Such a catastrophic decrease did take place in other coastal regions, as we shall see, but the decline is selective. Depopulation in the Lambayeque complex, in the next major valley to the south, was apparently not so pronounced.

In pre-Columbian times the "Lambayeque complex" consisted of an interconnected irrigation system bringing together the Lambayeque, Leche, and Motupe valleys. There were also irrigation links with the Saña and Jequetepeque valleys farther to the south. The connections were broken with the Spanish conquest, and there is now less irrigated land area than there was four centuries ago. There had been heavy internal conflict before the Europeans reached the area. The chronicler of the north coast, Cabello de Balboa, reported that the people of Jayanca had just terminated a war with the inhabitants of Tucuma when Pizarro arrived. Ethnohistorical research led Paul Kosok to conclude that the area was only weakly held by the Incas.

A complicating factor in dealing with the Lambayeque complex is that the Spanish divided it administratively. Most of the sector north of the pueblo of Lambayeque was administered as part of the corregimiento of Saña, located in the next major river valley to the south. Yet, in the south of the irrigated Lambayeque complex were the repartimientos of Cinto y Chiclayo, Chuspocallanca, Reque, and

Repartimiento	Pueblo	Encomendero	Tributaries	
			Toledo	Vázquez de Espinosa
Tumbez	San Nicolás de Tumbez	María Muñoz	47	12
Mancora		Gonzalo Prieto Dávila	20	4
Amotape		Gonzalo Farfán	34	9
Paita la Silla		Gonzalo Farfán	41	27
Colán		Rodrigo Méndez	51	30
Guaura		Francisco Cornejo	52	45
La Chira		Francisco Cornejo	61	17
Sechura y la Punta		Rui López Calderon	79	40
Sechura y Muneli		Gaspar Troche	78	72
Malingas		Diego Carvajal	26	3
Tangarara		Gaspar Troche	25	9
Ayabaca	N. S. de Pilar	Diego Vaca de Sotomayor	237	234
Guancabamba	San Pedro	Gaspar de Valladolid	377	420
Frías Chalaco		Pedro de Saavedra	209	93
Chinchachara	Sondor Serrán	Capt. Hernando Lamero to Gabriel de Miranda	203	45
Solana		Gonzalo Farfán	217	60
Nauguala Socolan y Polchos, Catacaos	San Juan de Catacaos	Crown	212	145
Pariña y Cosio		Gonzalo Prieto Dávila	63	48
Mechatomecomo (Sochiman)		Alonso Gutiérrez	56	24
Malaca		Gonzalo Prieto Dávila	15	18
Menon		Rui López Calderon	74	40
Camacho		Rui López Calderon	18	14
Mecache		Alonso de Vega	48	31
Moscalaqui	San Sebastián del Valle	Diego de Sandoval	82	10
Marcavélica		Rodrigo Méndez	32	16
Castillo	(Puerto de Paita)	Gaspar Troche	14	16
Vitonera		Gonzalo Farfán	27	18
Total			2,398	1,500

probably Collique. These were part of the larger corregimiento of Chicama, which included Chimú, Guanchaco, Mansiche, Licapa, Jequetepeque, Chepén, Moro, and Cherrepe. The four repartimientos in Lambayeque were all north of Saña and by logic should have been administered by nearby Lambayeque instead of by Chicama. Kosok suggests that one of the reasons Saña was chosen was because the best port in the area was at Caleta Cherrepa and the flow of goods to the sierra was via the Saña valley. Possibly the ancient road to Cajamarca was up that valley and not alongside one of the rivers of the Lambayeque system. In 1604 Lizárraga reported that Saña was "the richest valley between Jayanca and Trujillo and that the town of Saña was an important trading center."[17] Vázquez de Espinosa described the "Villa of Saña" in the beginning of the seventeenth century as having a cathedral, monasteries of the Dominican, Franciscan, and Augustinian orders, as well as other churches and a hospital. The city was bustling with business activity: Sugar and leather products and conserves were sent to other parts of Peru; wine, wheat, corn, and other agricultural products were also exported.

Vázquez de Espinosa wrote that the pueblo of Lambayeque was "the greatest in all the llanos of Peru" with a church with four priests to administer the sacraments. There were abundant fruits and also fresh fish, which were caught along the nearby coast. Wine, olive products, melons, and other food crops were grown. Cotton was a major commodity, and textiles were exported to all parts of Peru. Reed mats and hats and soap were also among the important items produced and sold. In addition there were large numbers of goats, which fed on the leaves and fruit of the algarrobas (carob trees).[18]

When compared with other coastal valleys, it appears that a relatively large number of natives remained in the region at the end of the sixteenth century. Within the valley, as elsewhere in Peru, some repartimientos declined more rapidly than others (see Table 31). Lambayeque, a Crown repartimiento, declined least of all, by sixty people of a total population of about six thousand between 1575 and 1602. Lambayeque had the largest tributary population of the north coast in the 1570s (1,584). Not far up the valley was the large (6,668) grant of Jayanca of the encomendero Francisco de Barbarán. Jayanca's population fell at a rate of −4.9 percent yearly during the same period. By 1602 Jayanca was third in size in the region instead of first as it had been in the 1570s. There clearly must have been out-migration from Jayanca during those years. Could it have been in order to escape the control of the encomendero? Between Lambayeque and Jayanca was Lorenzo de Zamudio's large grant of Tucuma (1,554

Table 31. *The Lambayeque complex*

	1575	1602	Rate of change
Motupe	2,320	988	−3.2
Penache (Salas) (1573)	793	730	−0.3
Jayanca	6,668	1,753	−4.9
Pacora	945	364	−3.5
Illimo	3,335	1,479	−3.0
Tucuma	5,779	3,176	−2.2
Ferreñafe	1,985	746	−3.6
Lambayeque	5,854	5,794	−0.0
Cinto y Chiclayo	2,373	no data	—
Chuspocallanca	2,972	1,339 (1600)	−3.2
Reque	2,572	1,934 (1599)	−1.2
Collique	2,325	1,869 (1595)	−1.1
Total	37,921	22,545[a]	

[a] Includes estimate of 2,373 for Cinto y Chiclayo.

tributaries and 5,779 inhabitants). Tucuma ranked approximately second with Lambayeque in 1575 and was a solid second in 1602, declining least rapidly of the private encomiendas at a rate of −2.2 percent annually. There was a substantial internal movement of population in the irrigated complex. The relative stability in the size of the repartimiento of Lambayeque must be partly the consequence of immigration and perhaps also of better conditions for the Indians living within the Crown holding. The declines of the Crown repartimientos of Chucuito and Yanque Collaguas, far to the south, are also low.

Sex ratio figures demonstrate heavy immigration of working males in some parts of the region. The three repartimientos of Cinto y Chiclayo, Chuspocallana, and Reque had substantially more males than females, with sex ratios of 110 in 1579, 115 in 1600, and 126 in 1594. These repartimientos were situated within seventeen kilometers of each other, almost directly on the coast. For those dates their sex ratios indicate immigration of males who may have worked in the vineyards, olive orchards, and cotton plantations located between Lambayeque and Collique. During the early colonial era the Lambayeque area became one of the most highly productive sectors of the northern region. Keith concludes: "The prosperity of Lambayeque thus rested not on the expansion of Spanish agriculture but on the survival of a relatively large Indian population (compared to the rest of the coast) which was able to adapt its traditional economic patterns to colonial circumstances."[19] Unfortunately, although the size and complexity of the Lambayeque system demonstrate its importance on the coast, it has received neither the archaeological nor the ethnohistorical investigation it deserves. That 17 × 80 kilometer complex had a total population of 38,000 in 1575 and managed to have about 22,545 residents of a total north coastal population of 40,000 in 1600. Lambayeque represented the densest Indian population on the entire Peruvian coast in the sixteenth century, and the area requires substantial future investigation.

The repartimientos of Olmos and Copiz in the northern sector of Saña provide an exceptional case of population change. Indians of both repartimientos were situated in the village of Santo Domingo Olmos. The largest of the two at the time of Toledo's inspection was Olmos, with a tributary population of 382 and a total of 1,598 inhabitants. Olmos was a Crown repartimiento, which dwarfed the grant of Copiz of Nicolás de Villacorta with 41 tributaries and 123 inhabitants. Olmos was located north of Lambayeque in the extensive Sechura desert, yet deep pools or wells provided water for a reasonably modest population. Further, Olmos was situated on the north–south coastal highway and provided an oasis stop for travelers. After the conquest Olmos was converted into a center for mule production. Many of the region's residents became expert muleteers for the booming overland Paita–Lima route. Such a favorable economic environment is paralleled by a slow rate of population change between the 1570s and 1600s: −0.2 percent yearly! A Spaniard named Olmos had been the first encomendero, his son was confirmed successor by Vaca de Castro, but by the time of Toledo the repartimiento had reverted to the Crown. Between censuses of 1575 and 1602 the tributary population fell only from 382 to 305, and the total declined from 1,598 to 1,521. Yet Villacorta's private encomienda of Copiz dropped from 41 tributaries to 13, with a concurrent drop in the total population of 123 to 95. It appears that tributaries of Villacorta were fleeing the control of their encomendero in substantial numbers. The case of Olmos demonstrates, as does Lambayeque, that an area that is able to develop and maintain a strong economic base is less severely affected by depopulation.[20]

The Spanish city of Saña was established in 1563. Contemporary documents relating to that formulation refer to the supposed Indian population of the valley three decades earlier, when the Spanish first arrived. One report suggests that around 1533 there had been 3,000 Indians, and by internal evidence it appears the number in the report referred to married, adult working males. By 1563 there remained only 400; most of this group were fishermen. The local population provided an inadequate base for the construction of the European community. Consequently, Indians from surrounding repartimientos in 1564 were required to provide mita service. The number of mitayos reflects the size and importance of nearby population centers. Saña was required to produce 30; Reque, 25; Collique, 30; Suspo, 25; Cinto, 20; Lambayeque, 40; Tucuma, 50; Illimo, 15; Jayanca, 40; Ferreñafe, 20; and Pacora, 20. The total of 315 mitayos were to be paid a daily stipend and receive food. Colonial authorities suggested service in Saña was preferable to the Trujillo mita draft because of the proximity of the new Spanish center. Curacas of the repartimientos were allowed house lots in Saña, theoretically to have a place of residence among the approximately forty Spanish settlers. No political jurisdiction over land beyond the head of the valleys was allowed Saña in 1564. Colonial officials already recognized that highland Indians should be separated from coastal inhabitants "because they were of a contrary climate, and it is not good for them to descend to the llanos were they become ill." By 1575 there were only 320 tributaries in the repartimiento of Saña, but there were also 317 down-river in the repartimiento of Motupe; consequently, the full valley depopulation may be less than first appears. Saña, a narrow valley but with a high river discharge, deserves closer future study.[21]

The recent study of Manuel Burga of the socioeconomic development of the Jequetepeque valley is illustrative of changes in nearby north coastal valleys. Jequetepeque is situated about 650 kilometers north of Lima and 200 kilometers north of Trujillo. The city was outside close range of the chief Spanish centers in the early colonial period. For the first half-century the valley did not appear to offer the rewards that might be expected elsewhere in Peru. Yet in 1534 Pizarro distributed two grants of Indians in the valley: Jequetepeque and Cherrepe. Jequetepeque, probably the richest of the two, went to Pedro González de Ayala, and in 1585 it was taken over by the Crown. Cherrepe was granted to Francisco Pérez de Lescano, then passed to his wife María de Mendoza; as late as 1611 it was held by his daughter Graciana de Lescano. In 1568 two other repartimientos were partly created through the fragmentation of Cherrepe. Located slightly away from the coast toward the sierra in an area of lower population density, they represented more complete Spanish control of the native inhabitants. Not only did rapid depopulation occur in the area in the early colonial period, but there were also major internal population movements. According to testimony of 1540, there was significant migration of Indians from the Moro region to the neighboring sierra, but in 1565 the flow reversed, with Indians returning to the coast. A similar movement took place in Chepén, with a current to the highlands in 1567 and a later reversal. The founding of an Augustinian monastery in 1561 provided the first true Spanish nucleus in the valley. Eleven years later the visitador Juan de Hoces conducted a census, and following the orders of Viceroy Toledo he settled the inhabitants in a relatively small number of villages. The repartimiento of Cherrepe (293 tributaries), for example, had originally been made up of three Indian villages, Noquique, Cherrepe, and Guadalupe, and smaller settlements, which were converted by the visitador into two Indian towns: Cherrepe and Guadalupe. After 1572 Guadalupe rapidly lost its Spanish flavor. At the same time, in Guadalupe, the Indian small landholdings were dissipated in the process of the expansion of the Augustinian monastery. Between 1572 and 1582 there was a rapid drop of the population in the four repartimientos in the valley. The decline was selective, however, affecting some repartimientos more than others.

One of the principal reasons for the population loss in this decade was the impact of the heavy rains and floods of 1578. That year the irrigation canals were destroyed, and the local economy was severely disrupted. The impact on Moro was especially great; instead of rebuilding, the inhabitants emigrated. Chepén underwent a similar process. Yet the repartimiento of Cherrepe did not collapse as did Moro, probably because of internal migration and the availability of land, especially for carob trees. The part of the valley nearest the coast, with the densest native populations and an economy based on small and medium-size properties, fell least rapidly. The area was also part of a royal repartimiento, which might have influenced the less rapid depopulation.

Two years after the floods of 1578 the encomenderos of Moro and Cherrepe called for a substitution of money instead of agricultural products for tribute. The question that faced local inhabitants was this: How could a smaller number of remaining Indians find the required money? In testimony the estanciero Juan Rodríguez suggested it would be easy for Indians to earn money working on Spanish lands. Another estanciero reported Indians could earn a wage and food and save up to twelve pesos a year. The new tribute assessment of 1582 placed the quota required in cash at about 50 percent. Between the 1580s and 1609 the tribute income from the repartimientos declined rapidly. In slightly less than thirty years about 45 percent of the revenues of the repartimientos were lost. Yet population decline was more substantial than the loss in tribute. One way the Spanish maintained incomes was via fixed payments for agricultural products. The value of wheat, for example, had been established during the Toledo assessment at four tomines (one-half peso) per fanega. That rate was retained. Yet the sale value in the Spanish center of Trujillo was as follows: 1551, 13.5 tomines; 1567, 13.5; 1598, 17; and 1603, 16. The difference between the rural and the urban price of the wheat was pocketed by the encomendero. The same possibility for significant extra profit for the European was provided by sale of a variety of other tribute products.[22]

The population pyramid for the inhabitants of the repartimiento of Cherrepe in 1572 (Figure 3; Table 32) illustrates the likely demographic experience of other Indian residents of the valley. Of special note is the small size of the population in the cohorts 10–19 and 20–29. These cohorts are nearly decimated, especially those encompassing ages 10 to 19. Members of the cohorts were born between 1542 and 1562. Those years were critical for Andean residents, who experienced the rebellion of Gonzalo Pizarro, Gasca's pacification, and two sets of severe epidemics. Typhus or plague began in 1546, with heavy mortality; and an epidemic series that included influenza,

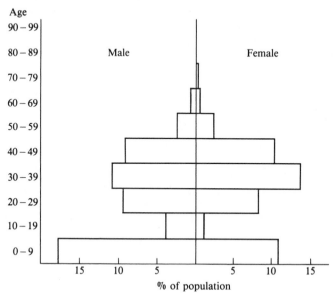

Figure 3. Population pyramid for Cherrepe, 1572.

Table 32. *Age and sex distribution*
of Cherrepe in 1572

Age	Males	%	Females	%
70–79	0	—	2	0.2
60–69	5	0.5	4	0.4
50–59	22	2.4	22	2.4
40–49	84	9.2	85	9.3
30–39	100	10.9	124	13.5
20–29	86	9.4	78	8.5
10–19	33	3.6	10	1.1
0–9	164	17.9	99	10.8

Note: Estimated on the basis of Burga's five-year cohort
population (*De la encomienda a la hacienda capitalista*).

measles, smallpox, and the "peste" lasted from 1558 to 1561. One
other characteristic of the pyramid should be noted: the dearth of
people over 59 years of age. There were many fewer survivors of the
generation born before 1513 than one would expect in a population
the size of Cherrepe. Further, the population structure of Cherrepe in
1572 is such that internal population decline could be expected to
continue for some time. There are far fewer children than necessary to
maintain the population level constant. The child–woman ratio, for
example, is 41, or $(P_{0-4}/f_{15-44}) \times 100$. The sex ratio is 116.5, which
may reflect immigration of working males. The small number of
females under 19 could produce the same effect, however. Indeed, the
pyramid probably reflects substantial underenumeration of girls.

The area around the Spanish colonial administrative center of
Trujillo is especially interesting. Trujillo is located just north of the
Moche River and was established less than seven kilometers from the
coast. The Moche River marked the southern boundary of the corregimiento of Chicama. Just across the river lay the repartimiento of
Moche, jurisdictionally part of Santa. The ancient center of Chan
Chan is located about four kilometers northwest of Trujillo. About
forty kilometers north of the Moche River is the Chicama. In the
preconquest era canals connected the two systems and provided water
for a much more extensive irrigated area than today. Chan Chan is
located roughly where the flows of the Moche and Chicama canals
met. The irrigated area of the Chicama valley is approximately three
times that of the Moche, and one might expect that the Chimú capital

would have been in that valley and not the Moche. Kosok suggests the Moche was intermediate in size, small enough to be able to politically unify early, yet large enough when unified to subjugate more extensive but politically weak valleys.[23] Chan Chan was probably significantly smaller when the Spaniards arrived than when conquered by the Incas, around A.D. 1465–75. There are few mentions in the chronicles of this process. Perhaps the best is Cabello de Balboa:

> But it is known with great certainty that the army of the Yngas attacked suddenly those of the wide and spacious valley of the Chimo, and held its inhabitants in fear, and shut in for many days behind their high walls, from here without having achieved results for the time being they proceeded to the lands irrigated by the river called Pacaz mayo, and they upset all these valleys and by the upper part of the Nepos they returned to Cajamarca.[24]

The Inca campaign was ultimately successful. It is possible that under Yupanqui, during a siege of the capital, the city's source of water was discovered and destroyed, thus forcing the inhabitants to surrender. It is also likely that many of the defenders were either executed or forced to resettle in other parts of the realm. This development helps explain the low native population of the valley in the mid-sixteenth century.[25]

The Spanish chose the Moche valley for their administrative capital of northern Peru in late 1534 or early 1535 and picked a site very close to ancient Chan Chan and the largest Moche pyramid, the Huaca del Sol. Vázquez de Espinosa stressed the importance of that site as a native pilgrimage center. The huaca was "one of the greatest sanctuaries that existed in the realm, where from many parts Indians came in pilgrimage and to comply with their vowes and promises."[26] It appears the reason for the choice of Trujillo as a center was similar to that for the choice of Lima: proximity to a major pre-Spanish shrine and population center, which would make it easier to maintain control over the conquered population. Trujillo was founded by Diego de Almagro and Diego de Mora under orders of Pizarro. The large number of burial sites in the area that could be ransacked provides another reason for the choice of the Moche valley. Miguel de Estete may have laid out the actual site, and there were approximately eighty founders of the Spanish city. A nearby port and gold mines in the vicinity clinched the decision of the conquerors for the placement of the settlement. Encomiendas dominated the first years of settlement. In 1535 some twenty-two large grants were made to Spaniards. Around 1555, when Zárate wrote, Trujillo was "built on an ordered and regular plan and housed three hundred Spanish families."[27] Captain Diego de Mora, probably the most important encomendero in the Trujillo area, received the repartimiento of Chicama. In the 1540s Captain Miguel de la Serna was recorded to have controlled a curaca of Chimo, and Marshal Alonso de Alvarado had others in Chimo. A second part of Chicama was held by a Spaniard named Fuentes in 1548. Paiján was received by Francisco de Fuentes in 1534. By the 1570s Diego de Mora ruled both Chicama and Paiján and dominated Chimo, Mansiche, Guanchaco, Cao, and Chocope. This important encomendero thus controlled 1,605 tributaries and a total of 6,637 inhabitants. By roughly 1600 the population of those units had fallen to 4,210. When Vázquez de Espinosa described Trujillo at the beginning of the seventeenth century he reported 400 Spanish *vecinos* in a city of a major cathedral and Dominican, Franciscan, Augustinian, and Mercedarian monasteries and a convent for the nuns of Santa Clara. Corn, wheat, various types of beans, peanuts, and other products were grown in the Moche valley, along with grapes and sugarcane. Fruits such as bananas, avocados, pineapples, apples, pears, peaches, figs, and apricots were also available. There were many sugar mills in the valley. The Chicama valley's products were similar, with inhabitants specializing in sugar.[28]

Indian tribute provided economic stimulus for Trujillo as long as the native population remained large, but declining numbers resulted in lower revenues for the encomenderos. About 80,000 pesos were collected in 1563; by 1591 the yearly amount was approximately 50,000 pesos. Another development paralleled the decline in population. The water system, which had been carefully maintained in the pre-Spanish era, fell into disrepair. By 1571 the traditional canal-clearing rituals were abandoned by local Indians. Then, in 1578, a major disaster hit the Trujillo sector in the form of heavy rains. The Niño, which concurrently afflicted the Jequetepeque valley, had come. Homes and croplands were destroyed. Indians fled to high ground and waited for the waters to subside. Crops that had been planted and food in storage were lost. The floods deposited heavy clay on the fields, and the irrigation system was wiped out. The following year, between one thousand and two thousand Indians were engaged in repairs. Unfortunately, the crops that were planted that year were hard hit by locust infestation. The young plants – including cotton, which encomenderos required in tribute – were consumed by hoards of insects. The price of a fanega of wheat and corn rose from the normal one-half peso to three or four and, in spite of the high price, was in very short supply. Alonso de Lucio, defender of the Indians, presented a petition on behalf of his charges to suspend tribute collection for 1578 and 1579 and recommended that two additional years of exemption be allowed so the economy could stabilize. According to testimony, however, the "majority of Indians fled to other valleys."[29] Other years of floods in Trujillo include 1624, 1701, 1720, and 1728.[30] Katherine Coleman, who studied the urban development of the provincial capital, notes that "by 1600 the main canal was so badly blocked, and the controls on irrigation outside the city so lax that there was a severe water shortage in the city."[31] In the 1560–80 period there was Spanish migration away from Trujillo, partly as a result of competition from the newly founded villa of Saña. Trujillo was devastated by earthquake in 1619. Diego de Cordoba Salinas reported that "no building nor any house was left standing, or without its foundation destroyed; its churches . . . all fell to the ground, without leaving a single stone on top of another."[32] About 390 residents died. A plague of insects and rats added misery to survivors of this major disaster. The seventeenth century witnessed frequent depredations of foreign corsairs who raided Peruvian coastal settlements. There was pressure for Spaniards in the Trujillo area to move inland. Guamachuco and Cajamarca were favored destinations. Another major earthquake demolished the complex in 1687, and this was followed by a series of poor grain harvests, a consequence of the introduction of wheat smut.

Trujillo's early demographic development is poorly understood. According to Coleman, two population counts are available: 1575 and 1604. The two "censuses" were compared and contrasted by Coleman to outline Trujillo's demographic transformation during the era.[33] Unfortunately, comparative analysis is not possible. Careful checking of the published reports reveals that there was only one count, at least for most sectors of Trujillo's population. On 22 February 1604 the corregidor, Felipe de Lazcano, prepared a list for several categories of the city's inhabitants. It is not clear whether the corregidor took an actual census or merely derived totals from an earlier count, perhaps the Toledo one. Consequently, it is premature to assign a date for the material, other than broadly – the last sixteenth to the early seventeenth century. Nonetheless, the remaining record is a useful one.[34] (See Table 33.)

What can we glimpse of the demographic structure of colonial Trujillo from the Lazcano tabulation? First, roughly a third of the residents are Indians. The sex ratio is 108. There is a larger number of unmarried men and boys than in the same female categories. This is probably the result of the immigration of a sizable number of young

Table 33. *The urban population of Trujillo from the 1604 list of Lazcano*

Category	Number	Comments
Spanish and mestizos		
Married men	108	4 wives absent
Married women	133	28 husbands absent
Solteros	185	
Mestizo soltero servants	20	
Solteras	208	78 doncellas, 40 widows, 31 solteras, 59 mestiza servants
Boys	143	45 orphans
Girls	128	44 orphans
Total	925	
Others in area	96	
Negroes and mulattoes		
Slave males	387	
Slave females	381	
Slave boys	91	
Slave girls	93	
Total slaves	952	
Free males	32	
Free females	49	7 mulattas married to absent Spaniards and mestizos are included
Free boys	20	
Free girls	20	
Total free	121	
Total	1,073	
Indians		
Married men and women	622	
Unmarried men and boys	309	
Unmarried women and girls	263	
Total	1,194	456 in houses of vecinos, 738 in own houses, solares, and huertas

Note: The list of Felipe de Lazcano may have been prepared from a 1575 count. See *Revista histórica* 8 (1925):91–3.

working males to the urban center. We shall see a similar process exemplified in the Lima census of 1614. Further, we find almost twice as many Indians dwelling in their own houses rather than living in the residential unit of a Spanish vecino. Unfortunately for our purposes, whites and mestizos are lumped together in a single category by

Lazcano. This in itself may illustrate the relative ease of passage of the mestizo into the Spanish class in early provincial society. The sex ratio for this group is 97. Several interesting features of Trujillo's population stand out: One-third of the Spanish–mestizo children were orphans! There is no equivalent figure for blacks or Indians. Of course we lack data on legitimacy, but it might be expected that a sizable portion of orphans were bastards. We have only two indications of the size of the mestizo element. In the soltero group there were twenty mestizo servants and fifty-nine mestiza servants in the same female category. Thus, a minimum 20 percent of the solteros in the white–mestizo sector are mestizo. The true figure could be higher. Approximately one-third of Trujillo's population was black. Of these, about 12 percent were free blacks and mulattoes. The sex ratio for black and mulatto slaves was 101, but the ratio for the free colored population was 75, which is illustrative of the greater ease of manumission of female slaves. Seven of forty-nine mulattas were married to absent Spaniards and mestizos. Children constitute 33 percent of the free black population but only 19 percent of the slave sector. It appears from these figures that free blacks had a substantially larger number of children than the slave population. Children constituted 29 percent of the Spanish–mestizo category, so, if the age bracket for children in the enumerator's list is the same for all racial sectors, free blacks and mulattoes had the largest number of births. Unfortunately, the same type of information for the Indians is unavailable.

The river valleys near Trujillo illustrate the close relationship of man, land, and water along the Peruvian coast. Almost no rain falls directly on the Pacific coastal strip. Agriculture depends on the use of irrigation from rivers bringing water from the upper slopes of the western Andes. The waterflow is dependent on the amount of rainfall in the mountains. Precipitation varies from year to year and from one watershed to another, and there appear to be long-term cycles of heavy rain followed by periods of scant moisture. Studies of the annual water discharge of the Chicama River from 1913 to 1948 demonstrate the pattern in the twentieth century (see Figure 4). Much lower than average flows occurred in 1924, with a prolonged drought from the late twenties to 1931, then 1935, 1937, 1942, and 1947.[35] During these years crop failure might be expected. The Indian population of the Moche valley was not large in 1575. Chimo and Guanchaco had a combined population of 1,660, and the figure of 364 for Moche at that time placed the valley population at just over 2,000. At the same time, the two repartimientos of the connected Chicama system, Chicama with 2,937 and Paiján with 1,040, totaled just under 4,000

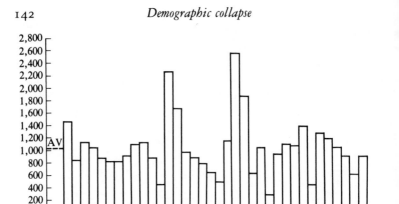

Figure 4. Annual water discharge of Chicama River, in millions of cubic meters, according to agricultural year (October rise in river to following September). (From Kosok, *Life, Land, and Water*, p. 29.)

Indian inhabitants. If the preconquest population of Chan Chan were in the neighborhood of 100,000 as some observers have reported, then an exceptionally catastrophic demographic decline affected the region. Yet the rates of decline for the 1575–1600 period are not especially high: Chicama (−0.7); Chimo and Guanchaco (−0.9); and Moche (−2.4). Indeed, the rates suggest immigration from other areas. In 1600 the sex ratios of Chicama and Chimo y Guanchaco were 101 and 102, respectively. Such ratios are usually indicative of immigration of males.

The aggregate figures for the north coastal region of Peru also provide insight into the nature of population change. There is information, for example, on the composition of the north coastal population, which is relatively good for the decades of the 1590s and 1600s. The low percentage of males under 18 in the 1590s (20.1 percent) was probably a result of the high mortality of the youthful population during the 1589–91 epidemic period. In the 1600s there was a larger number of young males, 22.7 percent of the population. This increase placed the northern coast in the position of having the largest percentage of young males of any of the six major regions in the 1600s. The rapid recovery in the number of small children after the 1589–91 epidemic suggests a high birth rate, just as the large percentage of old and infirm males (8.4 percent in the 1590s) reflects the debilitating effects of the epidemic. By the 1600s the percentage of old and disabled males had fallen to 6.7 percent. The north coastal records for the 1600s, which demonstrate a relatively low percentage of the old and infirm and the largest percentage of young males for any part, indicate that the north coastal region, with the earliest and most severe population changes as a result of European contact, might have been the first area to undergo population stabilization.[36]

There are several reasons for the rapid population loss of the north coast. Population density is a major determinant in the spread of epidemic disease. The immunity of a population is another factor. There was virtually no natural immunity to European disease among the native inhabitants of the Americas in 1492. Coastal areas, where the population was concentrated in relatively narrow irrigated river valleys, provided ideal conditions for maximum mortality during epidemics. An entire valley could be infected by a disease carrier, foreign or native, traveling along the coast. In cities as densely settled as Chan Chan once was, epidemics occurred rapidly and wreaked extreme devastation. Highland valleys, in contrast, are more isolated by geographical barriers than the coastal valleys. The passage of disease was slowed. Further, some diseases, particularly those carried by insect vectors, are more quickly spread in warm climates than in cool ones. Temperature appears to be a factor influencing the speed with which disease agents reproduce themselves. Warmer climates at low elevations provide a better environment for most disease carriers than the cool sierra.

It is also evident, on the north coast, that population decline preceded the arrival of the Europeans. Warfare between indigenous groups took its toll. The inhabitants of Puna and Tumbez were hurt by conflict in the immediate preconquest era, as is likely to have occurred in the case of the Jayanca–Tucuma strife. Chan Chan and much of the area around what became the Spanish center of Trujillo were decimated by the Inca expansion. Archaeologists generally concur that the north coastal population reached its apogee before Pizarro arrived. Yet there is no agreement on the date or size of the north coastal population at its maximum extent.[37]

On the basis of the study of repartimientos of the region, generally the larger units were demographically most stable. The population of the Lambayeque complex, which had the highest concentration of native residents in the area, fell minimally in the 1570–1620 period. Some repartimientos with strong economic foundation remained relatively stable or in some cases actually increased in population. The village of Lambayeque, for example, was a center of production for foodstuffs, cotton, textile products, and reed mats and hats. It lost only a handful of residents between 1575 and 1602. Tucuma, with a population of just under 6,000, fell at only −2.2 percent yearly during the same period. Olmos, center for northern transportation, was also relatively stable in population. It was located on the major coastal highway and provided mules and muleteers for the Paita–Lima overland trade.

The Crown repartimientos also seem to have been losing population less rapidly than those held by individuals. Jayanca of Francisco de Barbarán was declining at a higher rate than other large repartimientos of Lambayeque: −4.9 percent annually. There seems to be a parallel development in other private repartimientos in comparison with nearby Crown holdings. The low rate of change of Olmos, a royal repartimiento, compared with the rapid loss of Copiz is a similar case. Perhaps conditions were less severe on the royal grants.

Spanish colonial urban centers also influenced local population characteristics. San Miguel de Piura had limited appeal for Indian migrants in the late sixteenth century, but Saña and especially Trujillo, with substantial numbers of Spanish vecinos, became focal points of migration. As administrative headquarters and as centers for the production of important agricultural commodities, both cities attracted various types of immigrants. By the early seventeenth century many sugar mills were operating in the Trujillo area; and corn, wheat, grapes, and other fruits were grown in commercial quantity.

The population pyramid of Cherrepe, approximately in the middle of the north coast and near Saña, may reflect the demographic experience of other population units of the region. First, epidemics clearly took their toll. The consequences of the typhus or plague epidemic of 1546 and the 1558–61 series, which included measles, smallpox, and influenza, are quite evident in the small number of survivors. The heavy rate of mortality is also apparent for Indians born before 1513. The preconquest generation suffered heavy losses. Further, the small child–woman ratio holds little hope for rapid recuperation during the sixteenth century. Nonetheless, the north coast may have been the area that first reached a relatively stable population in the first half of the seventeenth century.

9

Center of Spanish control: middle coast

The hacienda system developed on the Peruvian coast in response to social and economic changes which took place during the century after the conquest. Of these changes, three were of primary importance: (1) the growth of the Spanish population, which was stimulated initially by the news of Cajamarca and later by the attractions of the coastal climate and new economic opportunities; (2) the rapid decline of the Indian population in the disastrous epidemics of the sixteenth century, and later as a result of the pressures generated by economic development; (3) the rise of agrarian markets to supply the needs of a sizeable Spanish urban population.

Robert G. Keith,
Conquest and Agrarian Change, p. 130

The central Peruvian desert coast extends southward through several valley systems. The major rivers that descend to the Pacific and break the desert are the Pativilca, Huaura, Chancay, Rimac and Chillón, Malay, Cañete, Chincha, Pisco, Ica, and Nazca. At the time of the conquest, most residents of the central coast subsisted on the basis of irrigation agriculture, with food supplemented by marine resources. Most of the area was brought into the Inca Empire through conquests between 1460 and 1480. Pachacamac was the most important center in that sector of the Peruvian coastal region. It contained a relatively dense urban population and, as the chief ceremonial shrine along the entire coast, attracted a large number of temporary residents. Pachacamac seemed important enough for the Spaniards to send Hernando Pizarro as a special emissary in 1533, but the colonial administrative capital, as in the case of Trujillo, was to be situated near the aboriginal site rather than within it. In this chapter we shall focus on developments in the Huaura valley as an example of coastal changes and on the rise of Lima, the "City of Kings," which was to become the core of the Spanish Empire in South America. We shall also review the evolution of the population of several important valleys south of Lima.[1]

The tributary population of the central coast was declining sharply.

145

It fell from 25,189 in 1570 to 10,374 in 1620. Although the decline was rapid, it was not as fast as the rate of change for the north and south coasts. The central coastal population was dense before the conquest, in spite of the fact that there, as in the north, a process of contraction could have been taking place in the century or two preceding the arrival of the Europeans. By the end of the sixteenth century, the population of the central coast was declining less rapidly than the Trujillo or Arequipa coastal sectors. The tributary population of the central coast was falling between the 1570s and 1600s at a much slower rate than the total population (-2.4 percent annually versus -3.1 percent), which indicates heavy immigration of adult working males.

The repartimiento of Végueta provides a good example of coastal migration. Végueta was situated on the Pacific coast about 12 kilometers north of the Huaura River mouth, in an excellent sugar- and wheat-growing region. Corn, wine, and olives were also produced on haciendas in the valley and shipped to the Lima market, some 120 kilometers to the southeast. It is likely that a single family held the repartimiento during the course of the sixteenth century. Francisco Pizarro had granted Indians to Nicolás de Rivera el Mozo.[2] By the time of Toledo in the 1570s the repartimiento was held by Sancho de Rivera. In 1607 Nicolás de Rivera possessed the grant. By 1622 Végueta was jointly administered by Sancha de Rivera Verdugo and Fernando de Castro. The total population was 505 at the time of the visita general; in 1607 it was only 258, and in a census of 1623 there were 179 inhabitants. Between 1607 and 1623, however, the tributary population actually increased in spite of an overall population decline. The reason for the increase was migration of laboring males. In 1608, seven of the fifty-six tributaries of the repartimiento were forced to appear in Lima for the summer mita. Six others were required to participate in the mita de plaza of Chancay, and one had to serve as a minor church official. By 1623 about 40 percent of Végueta's population was male between 18 and 50 years of age. The 1623 census provides no information on the origin of migrants to the valley, but it might be inferred that a significant percentage came from higher up the Huaura toward Canta. The repartimiento of Canta, situated on the western Andean slopes about 100 kilometers inland from Végueta and approximately 80 kilometers northeast of Lima, was also held by the Rivera family. The repartimiento of Canta was large, about ten times the size of Végueta, and the Rivera family had theoretical access to a substantial labor pool for lowland haciendas.[3]

The 1623 population pyramid for Végueta (Figure 5; Table 34) is

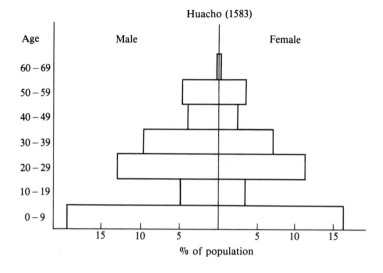

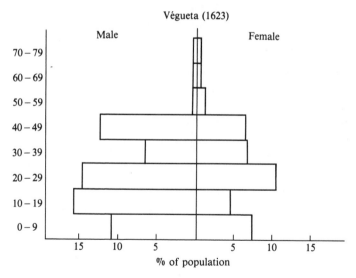

Figure 5. Population pyramids for Huacho, 1583, and Végueta, 1623.

Table 34. *Age and sex distribution of Huacho in 1583 and Végueta in 1623*

Age	Huacho (population)		Huacho (% distribution)		Sex ratio	Végueta (population)		Végueta (% distribution)		Sex ratio
	Male	Female	Male	Female		Male	Female	Male	Female	
70+						1	1	0.56	0.56	100
60–69	2	1	0.20	0.10	200	1	1	0.56	0.56	100
50–59	46	34	4.63	3.42	135	1	2	0.56	1.12	50
40–49	38	24	3.83	2.42	158	22	11	12.29	6.15	200
30–39	96	70	9.67	7.05	137	12	12	6.70	6.70	100
20–29	129	113	12.99	11.38	114	26	19	14.53	10.61	137
10–19	49	35	4.93	3.52	140	28	8	15.64	4.47	350
0–9	195	161	19.64	16.21	121	21	13	11.73	7.26	162
Total	555	438			127	112	67			167

interesting for several reasons. Although the total population of Végueta at that date was slightly less than two hundred, several features
stand out. In the first place, there is almost a total lack of people over
49 years of age. It was as though the older generation, those born
before the reductions of Viceroy Toledo, did not exist. Furthermore,
the 30–39 cohort was not large either. Members of this group would
have been born between 1583 and 1592, and their small number is a
result of 1589–91 epidemic mortality. The relatively small size of the
0–9 cohort suggests high mortality following 1613, perhaps during
the general diphtheria epidemic. At almost all levels, there are more
males than females, and the overall sex ratio is 167, which is indicative of heavy immigration of working-age men.[4]

The repartimiento of Huaura, located near the river, and only 7 or 8
kilometers from Végueta, also merits special attention. The area had
first been part of a vast encomienda of Diego de Almagro. After
Almagro died the grant was taken by Francisco Pizarro, then later
subdivided into five smaller repartimientos: Huaura, Végueta, Supe,
Barranca, and Huarmey. Huaura was held for a time by Ventura
Beltran, oldest son of a member of the Council of the Indies. Thanks
to an inspection of Huaura, located by Nathan Wachtel among the
manuscripts in the National Library in Lima, we have a fairly good
picture of local conditions there in 1583. The encomendero Juan
Bayon de Campomanes "imposed on the inhabitants of the valley a
totally arbitrary despotism." Exactions included labor in the encomendero's field, even on religious days, work in the inn at Arnedo,
and mita service in Lima and Chancay. Indians were compelled to
work under threat of violence. One Indian related that he was forced
into the plaza of the town, a rope around his neck, and flogged. The
encomendero's control over his charges was facilitated by the complic-
ity of the curaca Don Pedro Payco. Furthermore, the Indians saw their
lands taken from them piecemeal. The encomendero encroached on
either communal or private fields without providing the owners com-
pensation. Although the area of the Indians' personal land continually
diminished, they had no time to work it, because of the numerous
mita services. The traditional planting, cultivating, and harvesting
cycles were broken. Huaura Indians were short of land, short of time,
and – worst of all in this arid country – short of water, for the
encomendero seized control of it and prevented the Indians from
irrigating their soil. They used the canals secretly, by night, and
complained that they could work their own plots only by going
without sleep![5]

The 1583 population pyramid for Huacho, the major Indian community of the valley (Figure 5; Table 34) illustrates several demographic characteristics of the area. First, it should be noted that the total population is relatively large, approximately 1,000 inhabitants, so the universe is ample to allow for reasonably valid generalizations. Noteworthy is the abundance of males in all cohorts. The sex ratio is 127, and other evidence suggests immigration of men. Given the local economy, it is apparent that males were entering the region to work on Spanish estates. Two cohorts are distinctly smaller than they should be: The 10–19 and 40–49 groups appear to have suffered especially high mortality. The elder of the two cohorts would have been born between 1534 and 1543, and clearly the initial disruptive consequences of the conquest and the first major smallpox epidemic left their scars. The younger of the cohorts was born between 1564 and 1573. No major epidemic was recorded for this period; hence, we must search for other possible causes for the small size of the group. One simple possible explanation is that the small number is the result of the births of the "shrunken" 1534–43 generation. Women born during the 1534–43 period would be passing through their childbearing cycle at precisely this time. A small generation has a small number of children. The effects of a demographic catastrophe are experienced long after the initial impact. Yet the child–woman ratio for Huacho is approximately 83.6. That ratio is large for two reasons: first, the relatively large number of women at the height of their reproductive years and, second, an era apparently free of major epidemics affecting children in the late 1570s and early 1580s.

The Rimac valley of the central coast obviously acquired special importance because the Spanish established their administrative capital there early in 1535. A reasonably good port, protected from the wind and current flow, with access to the highlands was a key factor in the ultimate choice. Nearness to the great pilgrimage site of Pachacamac in the next valley to the south also was important. The Rimac was probably less populated when the Europeans arrived than some other coastal valleys. Yet, at one time, as the extensive ruins of Cajamarquilla attest, the valley was densely inhabited.

Almost from the day Lima was established, on 1 January 1535, it attracted migrants. The Ciudad de los Reyes, or City of the Kings as it was first named, was the administrative center for the Spanish Empire in all South America until the eighteenth century, when two new viceroyalties were created out of its territory: New Granada and the Rio de la Plata. The city was also a thriving commercial and transportation center that attracted European traders and fortune seekers by the thousands, and as the city grew, Indians and Negro slaves moved in to serve their Spanish masters.[6]

The broad outlines of the demographic growth of Lima have been traced, thanks to a series of censuses and a number of eyewitness accounts. By the second decade of the seventeenth century the population of the capital was truly cosmopolitan, with settlers and traders from various European nations, African slaves and free black artisans and workers, American Indians from as far away as Mexico and Chile, and migrants from the Orient: the Philippines, Macao, and Singapore. Viceroy Montesclaros ordered a census of the residents of the city. The count, initiated late in 1613 and completed early in 1614, presents a vivid picture of the nature of Lima in its ninth decade of growth.[7] The census clearly demonstrates the preponderance of black and white (see Table 35). The complexion of this part of the coast had been altered by the new European-dominated order. The Africans ranked first, with 42 percent of the city's population. The whites followed, with 39 percent. There were substantially more European males than females, but the ratio was reversed for the blacks. Mulattoes constituted a growing segment, with 3 percent of the inhabitants. The sex ratios of white and black, and the slave owner's control over his "property," played a part in the process. The substantially larger number of female mulattoes as opposed to male offspring may reflect a greater ease of social upward mobility for the mulatto woman. The male child might be more readily classified as black and therefore slave by the master. Indians living within the city walls of Lima made up only 8 percent of the city's residents and counted slightly less than 2,000 of 14,000 inhabitants. There were fewer Indian women than men. Further, there were fewer than 200 mestizos in the whole urban complex, if the census returns are valid.

Only part of the 1614 Lima census has been located; fortuitously for our purposes, it is the Indian schedule that remains. The enumerator was Miguel de Contreras. In the count Contreras was assisted by local Indian officials and members of the religious brotherhoods. The in-

Table 35. *Population of Lima in 1614*

Category	Men	Women	Percentage
Spanish	5,271	4,359	38.9
Negros	4,529	5,857	41.9
Indians	1,116	862	7.9
Mestizos	97	95	0.8
Mulattoes	326	418	3.0
Religious	894	826	6.9

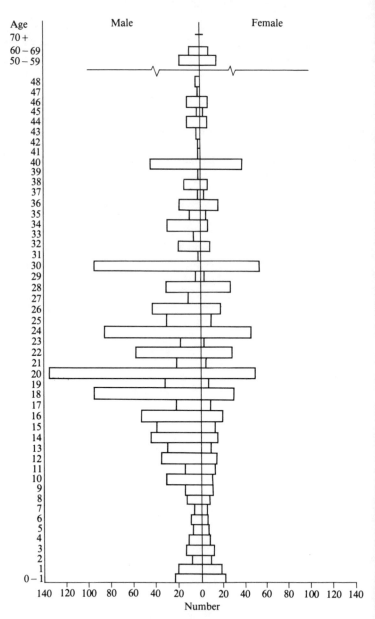

Figure 6. Population pyramid for Lima, 1614.

formation in the census includes the name, age, sex, occupation, place of origin, and years of residence of each city dweller. Because of the fiscal requirements of the tribute system, the names of encomenderos and curacas were also noted. Contreras made strenuous efforts to make sure all Indians were accounted for, even those who had temporarily left the city.[8]

The population pyramid (Figure 6) reveals several characteristics of the Indian residents of Lima. In the first place, there is a marked abundance of males of working age. The tendency toward a large male population is first apparent at the ages of 10 and 12. Rough parity between the number of males and females is not reached until the age of 38. Most of the young men living in Lima were migrants, and most were artisans. One shoemaker, for example, was born in Nazca in 1577. He migrated to Trujillo and in 1610 moved to the capital. Another shoemaker was born in Guayaquil, then worked in Cuzco before finally settling in Lima. Women were usually domestic workers and resided in the house of their employers. The large number of domestics and the imbalanced sex ratio meant that relatively few families were established. And the size of existing families was relatively small, at least as far as the single census suggests (see Table 36). There were slightly less than 250 couples of a total Indian population of about 2,000. Nearly two-thirds of the couples had no offspring at all! Only one of the couples had as many as five children. The average number of children per family was calculated to be 0.61. Further, the child–woman ratio was calculated at 37.4. The Indians living within Lima were not having enough children to maintain population stability. In fact, there would have been a very rapid internal collapse of Lima's Indian population, had it not been for migration.

Lima acted as such a strong magnet for Indian immigrants that the demographic catastrophe of the 1589–91 epidemic period is obliterated from the record. In no other extant population pyramid for Peru for the period do we find this to be the case. Only in the 2-year-old cohort do we see any possible impact of exceptionally heavy mortality, in this case probably from a diphtheria epidemic. The impact on this group is visible because immigration of infants was inconsequential.

Table 36. *Family size in the Lima Indian population, 1614*

Number of children in family	0	1	2	3	4	5
Number of families	150	66	20	8	4	1

Demographic collapse

The origin of Lima's Indian immigrants can also be outlined, on the basis of the 1614 census (see Table 37). The northern highlands contributed the largest number of migrants (463), approximately one-quarter of all Indian migrants to the city. The reason for the large influx from the Peruvian north is not clear. The geographical structure of Peru, which promoted a smooth flow in the southwesterly direction, might be part of the answer. Further, there was no local strong focus for migration in the northeast. No Spanish city in that area equaled the respective attractions of Trujillo, Lima, Guamanga, Arequipa, or Cuzco for their hinterlands. The cities of Cajamarca, Chachapoyas, Jaén, and even Huánuco had limited appeal for Indians,

Table 37. *Origins of the population of Lima in 1613*

Region	Number	Percentage of total Indian population in Lima
North coast	80	4.1
Central coast	268	13.8
South coast	34	1.7
North sierra	463	24.0
Central sierra	262	13.6
South sierra	103	5.3
Charcas	22	1.1
Tucuman	2	—
Chile	81	4.1
Quito	45	2.3
Guayaquil	22	1.1
Loja	19	1.0
Puerto Viejo	12	0.6
Bogotá	12	0.6
Cuenca	4	—
Tunja	2	—
Popayán	1	—
Riobamba	1	—
Zamora	1	—
Mexico	1	—
Migrants of undetermined origin	42	2.2
Those probably born in Lima	453	
Total	1,930	100.0

Note: Dashes indicate an insignificant percentage.

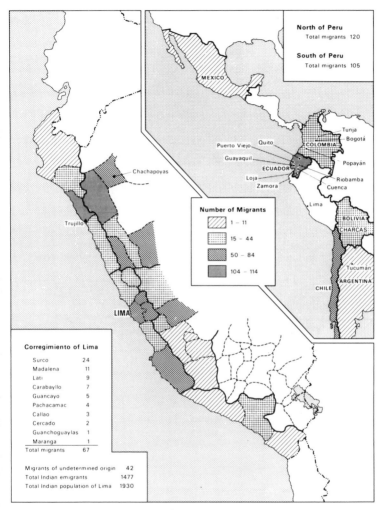

Map 6. Indian migrants to Lima, 1613.

in comparison with the other major cities of Peru. As might be expected, large numbers of Indians migrated to Lima from the central region, either the coast or highlands. Nearby in the mountains, Jauja provided the greatest number. The close connection between Jauja and Lima in trade and communications is a clear reason for the large number of immigrants from the corregimiento. On the central coast the largest number of migrants quite obviously came from the corregimiento of El Cercado. The communities of Surco and Madalena provided substantial numbers. The number of migrants to Lima from the north and south coasts is small. Their own populations were small, and their respective capitals created their own focuses. Few immigrated from the southern highlands. Distance and the attraction of Cuzco and the mining centers have to provide the major explanation for the low number of southern immigrants.[9]

A number of "foreign" Indians resided in Lima in 1614. Most were from the Andean culture area: Quito, with 45 representatives; Guayaquil and Charcas, with 22 each; Loja, with 19; Bogotá and Puerto Viejo, with 12 each; and 81 from the captaincy-general of Chile. Most of the Chileans were youngsters and were engaged in Spanish households, rather than as artisans. Perhaps they had been captured during European–Indian conflict on the southern frontiers.

Indian migration to Lima was not without its risks. With luck, perseverance, and skill the Indian might become a success in his craft as carpenter, shoemaker, tailor, or silversmith. He could become a useful member of the lower ranks of urban Hispanic society. The Indian faced a much higher rate of mortality than the European, however. During the first weeks of residence on the Peruvian coast the risk was extremely high, especially if the migrant were from mountain areas of Peru. One colonial observer wrote in 1574 that yearly over one-half the highland mitayos sent to Lima, Trujillo, and other coastal towns died. Lima drew its mitayos from as far away as Jauja to serve on the mita de plaza of the city. Following a journey of up to ten days, the Indians were subjected to hard labor in the sea-level climate of Lima. Their bodies, genetically adjusted to life at an elevation of 3,500 meters or more, suffered severely. Contemporary migration from the highlands to the coast and vice versa is followed by lowered resistance to disease and often respiratory and vascular infections. Although one would suspect that the sixteenth-century observer exaggerated the number of migrants from the highlands who died each year, it is nevertheless true that mortality among the Indians increased, at least for a short period, after they moved from one ecological level to another and very different one.[10]

Indian migration to Lima was heavy but not great enough to fill the manpower needs of the growing urban center. High Indian mortality along the Peruvian coast made it necessary for the European rulers to resort to massive importation of Negro slaves in order to fill a growing labor shortage. The much larger black population in Lima was similar to that of other coastal regions. As we have seen, in the city of Trujillo approximately one-third of the population was Spanish and mestizo (1,021), one-third was black (1,073), and the final third was Indian (1,194). In the early seventeenth century approximately ten thousand African slaves cared for vineyards in Pisco, Ica, and Nazca. In Lima in 1614, 42 percent of the population was Negro, whereas only 8 percent was Indian. By 1623, many Lima landowners had a hundred black slaves, but only five hundred Indians were assigned to work on Spanish farms in the entire district. Although blacks quickly replaced most Indians in the fields and cities of the Peruvian coast during the colonial period, few reached the highlands. The Andes, in the seventeenth century as today, belong to the Indian.[11]

Yet, not only in Lima but also in other settlements of the greater Lima valley, there is historical evidence for heavy immigration of laboring-age workers. The repartimiento of Comas Caravaillo, for example, situated up the Chillón valley, just over 20 kilometers from Lima, had a large population of laboring males, with a sex ratio of 129 in 1602. The repartimiento was within the truck-farming region for the supply of the Lima market, and most males were probably farm workers.[12]

Major river valley systems south of the Lima area include the Mala, Cañete, Chincha, Pisco (Humay), Ica, and Nazca. Each of these areas came under relatively early and thorough Spanish occupation. Around 1534 Francisco Pizarro granted land and the encomiendas of Chilca and Mala to Pedro de Alconchel. By the time of his death in the 1560s he had put together an estate of over 300 hectares, with a "tambo, mill, and wine chacra." When his daughter and heiress married in 1568 she had possession of about 500 head of cattle, 300 horses, and 200 goats. The local Indian population, estimated at 300 tributaries in 1549 during the Gasca division, fell to 225 in the 1570s. In 1591 the population was 166, and the *merced* was held by Josephe de Vivera. In 1602, just over a decade later, there were 142 tributaries. By 1616 the grant was held by Pablo de Montemayor, and only 118 tributaries remained. A slight recuperation in the tributary population may have begun in 1623, with an increase to 140, if the figure for that date is accurate.[13]

The Cañete valley received early Spanish attention, perhaps because of the relative abundance of land there. Indians of Huarco, the major pre-European settlement in the valley, offered major resistance to the Inca invaders from the highlands in the period from 1460 to 1480. As a result, they were ruthlessly crushed by the Inca conquerors. Cieza de León visited the valley in the 1540s and reported "mountains of bones." The Cañete valley was quickly resettled by Europeans who introduced Old World livestock. As early as 1536, according to notarial records, there were substantial numbers of pigs in the area. After the conquest Alonso Martín de Don Benito received the Indians of the valley in encomienda. Most valley residents lived in Huarco, with a small number of fishermen residing on the coast. The early population is not definitely known. One document in the Archive of the Indies reports a 1532 population of the valley of about 20,000. The Spanish chose the valley as the site for a major settlement in 1556. At that time only seventy Indian households are reported to have remained.[14] In preconquest times the valley had an extensive irrigation system. The Imperial Aqueduct was one of the largest of the coast. The system "ceased to operate by 1556, leaving the irrigated area of the valley considerably smaller than it had been. This area was further reduced when a landslide blocked the Acequia de Hualcara where it passed around the Cerro de Montalbán, a hill in the middle of the valley."[15] Neither canal was repaired until the eighteenth century. By 1556 Indians were immigrating to take up land in the valley. The north side of the river received settlers from Coayllo after the Inca conquest. On the south side Indian migrants came from Chincha and Lunahuana. Also, by 1556, Antonio Navarro was grazing large herds of cattle and horses in the valley, and the foundation of the Spanish settlement of Cañete disrupted his agricultural activities. In 1575 there were a trifling twenty-one tributaries at Huarco. By 1605 merely five were left. Yet Lunahuana, the only other repartimiento in the valley, situated upstream, retained a relatively sizable population. Pizarro had granted Lunahuana to Diego de Aguero in 1534. As late as 1617 the repartimiento remained in the same family. There is no record of the original population, but it is clear the figure of 20,000 for 1532 includes what became the two repartimientos of the valley. In the 1570s there were 740 tributaries in Lunahuana and a total population of 3,276, divided in three villages. By 1608 there were only 320 tributaries and a total population of 1,049. A 1617 census reported 265 tributaries, and one of 1625 records only 214. If the figures are accepted at face value, we see a valley drop between 1520 and 1620 in the neighborhood of 20,000:200, or 100:1. As we have seen, the Europeans moved rapidly into the Cañete valley and took over lands vacated by the Indian demographic collapse. In 1580 the corregidor of Cañete was accused of illegally using native workers to plant and cultivate his crops on their own land, without paying the Indians rent or wages. This was not an isolated case on the Peruvian coast but an example of what was taking place simultaneously in nearby valleys.[16]

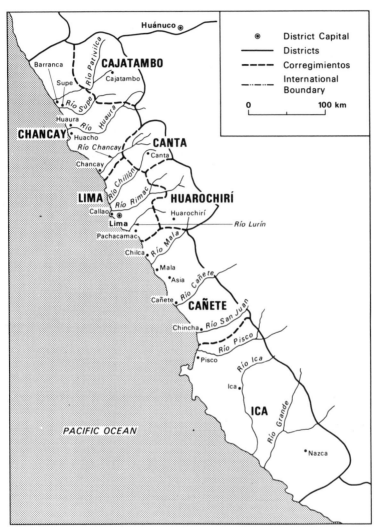

Map 7. Central coast of Peru.

The Chincha valley was one of the most important of the central Peruvian coast. The whole northwestern sector of the Inca Empire was named for it: Chinchasuyo. Pizarro may have reached as far south as Chincha by sea during the reconnoitering expedition of 1528. Cieza referred to Chincha as "the greatest and best of all." In 1532 Jerez reported the Spanish had been told that Chincha and Cuzco were the two most important Indian centers in the south of Peru. The importance of the valley is reflected in the fact that Hernando Pizarro received the Indians of Chincha as his encomienda. By 1549 it reverted to the Crown, and the Crown continued to hold it through the 1620s. The local economic base of Chincha was strong. Lizárraga divided the 30,000 households that in theory made up the valley into three equal parts: merchants and artisans, fishermen, and farmers. In pre-Columbian times local inhabitants traded painted gourds and silver objects with Indians as far away as Chucuito on the shores of Lake Titicaca. In 1549 there were some 2,000 tributaries in the royal repartimiento. By the era of Toledo there were 979 tributaries with a total population of 3,797. The number of tributaries continued to fall, to 412 in 1591, and by 1602 there were 316 tributaries and a total of 1,210 Indian inhabitants. The decline in numbers persisted through 1616, when there remained only 273 tributaries. Here, as in Cañete, the overall decline in the century following European contact approximates 100:1.[17]

In the Pisco valley, just south of Chincha, Umay suffered rapid depopulation during the period. The rate of tributary loss for the repartimiento was especially high: −5.8 percent yearly between 1575 and 1594, and −8.4 percent in the years from 1594 to 1601. Records suggest the repartimiento suffered major demographic decline during the series of severe 1589–91 epidemics. A substantial sum of money was spent from the community funds for medicines to cure the inhabitants, but local officials lamented that the results were negligible. In 1594 only 56 tributaries remained, compared with 120 in the time of Toledo's visita general. In February of 1595 the curacas of Umay were unable to pay the tribute, still based on the Toledo assessment. In March contemporary witnesses estimated only 30 to 40 tributaries remained in the valley. The drought of 1594 affected Umay just as it severely weakened irrigation-based agriculture of the repartimiento of Nazca, two valleys to the south. The corregidor in 1595 testified that it was so dry all crops were ruined. Indians left the valley, taking along with them wives and children, in a search for food and even new homes. It is possible that Spaniards used the opportunity to seize the vacated lands. Shortly after, in 1601, the corregidor of the Ica valley, Gonzalo Hernández de Hererra, was accused of planting wheat on Indian lands in the Umay valley without making just payment.[18]

The Ica valley was apparently divided between two conquerors by Pizarro in the 1530s: Juan de Barrios and Nicolás de Rivera (El Viejo).

By Toledo's era most Indian inhabitants of the valley were settled in the village of Valverde de Ica. The encomenderos Juan de Barrios and Juan Dávalos de Rivera shared Upper Ica (709 tributaries) and Lower Ica (731). The total number of Indian inhabitants of the two repartimientos of Ica in 1572 was 7,871. Males substantially outnumbered females in both repartimientos by the 1570s. The sex ratios in the first decade of the seventeenth century were 203 and 115, respectively. The heavy concentration of males is a consequence of their being used extensively for labor on nearby haciendas. In the Ica valley, as in Cañete, the corregidor Gonzalez Hernández de Herrera in 1600 was charged with planting wheat on Indian lands. The population of the area declined through the first half of the seventeenth century. A new major drought was recorded in the Ica region in the 1630s, and so many died or fled the area in 1633–4 that it was impossible to collect the annual tribute quota. In the census of Lurinica in 1626 297 tributaries were recorded, in 1634 there were 162, and in 1640 there remained fewer than 141 tributaries. Frequent water shortages were recorded through 1640. The continued shrinkage of the population of Hananica was similar: there were 214 tributaries in 1622, 113 in 1636, and 102 in 1637. The Ica valley early became tied to the production of wine for the Lima and highland markets. By the 1560s opportunistic settlers recognized that wine could yield higher profits than even wheat, but wine production in Ica was generally linked to small units of production. Both Indian commoners and curacas participated in the economic activity. The income could be substantial; Curaca Fernando Anicama held nine grape chacras when he died in 1571 (the income was willed to aid the local poor). Yet there were not enough Indians remaining in many coastal valleys by the end of the century to maintain the level of agriculture. Both Ica and Pisco (Humay) relied on 10,000 African slaves each as the major element of the labor force.[19]

Nazca, the repartimiento farthest south on the central coast, was the core of the earliest and largest sugarcane region of Peru. When Pedro Gutiérrez, probably acting on behalf of García de Salcedo, purchased the Ingenio valley from two Indian curacas in 1546 there was already cane growing there. Encomendero Salcedo constructed a sugar mill, and by 1554 he planted grapes and olives in the valley. By the early seventeenth century the area was a major producer of sugar and wine. Some records in the Archive of the Indies attribute a high aboriginal population to the valley: 20,000 to 30,000! The region, as did the other major central coastal valleys, underwent major changes during the period. In 1575 tributaries made up 21.4 percent of the population; in 1602 they composed 35.5 percent. At the later date the sex ratio was 140. In 1595 the repartimiento was in the control of Pedro Gutiérrez de Mendoza. The official in charge of protection of the Indians reported that at that time there were 300 fewer Indians than twenty years before, during the rule of Viceroy Toledo. The corregidor made strenuous efforts to collect the tribute but to no avail, for the repartimiento became practically deserted as Indians either died or fled. The number of tributaries fell from the 630 of the Toledo count to 328 in 1602 and finally to 198 in 1632. Local witnesses testified that many tributaries had fled the repartimiento, often leaving behind wives and children. The corregidor laid the blame squarely on the shoulders of the encomendero, Gutiérrez de Mendoza, charging the encomendero with severe exploitation. Mendoza had forced Indians of the repartimiento to serve on his haciendas and had not paid their wages. The Indians consequently fled, and the corregidor was unable to collect the tribute. A serious drought in the Nazca and nearby Umay valleys in 1594 also contributed to emigration. The drought continued in Nazca through 1595 with serious economic consequences. Captain Alonso Paniagua de Loaysa, the alguacil mayor of Ica, testified that indeed the corregidor had been unable to fulfill his duties, because no more than twenty Indians in the whole valley could be congregated. Instead of suspending or lowering tribute until the drought ended and conditions improved, however, colonial officials dealt with the problem by imprisoning the curaca and principales of the repartimiento in an effort to force them to produce the unpaid tribute.[20] Keith concluded the rate of depopulation of the Ica and Nazca valleys was relatively low, in spite of a rapid development of Spanish wine production. He suggests that the low rate of decline he saw might partly result from economic opportunities for Indians. The chance to advance was perhaps a great enough incentive to attract outside migrants. Keith's study of the Ica economy reveals a substantial native involvement in the wine industry; yet in the case of Nazca, if the evidence of 20,000–30,000 aboriginal inhabitants of the valley is accurate, depopulation was indeed as rapid as elsewhere.[21]

The repartimientos of the three interior corregimientos of the central coastal region – Cajatambo, Canta, and Huarochirí – are located at higher elevations on the western Andean slopes. They represented a different ecological world. Their populations were generally larger by the 1570s and afterward than the repartimientos on the coast. The size range for the five repartimientos of Cajatambo was from 2,000 to 10,000 inhabitants. There were substantially more males than females in the repartimientos of Lampas and Ocros, with a sex ratio of

111 for the former in 1605 and 233 for the latter in 1603. The other three repartimientos had large female populations: The sex ratio of Cajatambo in 1599 was 85; for Ambar in 1603 it was 80; Andax in 1602 had a sex ratio of 81. Migration was most certainly a factor in the sex ratio differences among repartimientos with more males than females and vice versa. Mining was important in the corregimiento of Cajatambo and of special significance in the repartimiento of Lampas. There, in 1577, about 80 percent of the tribute paid was in silver. Two other repartimientos contributed substantial portions of their tribute in silver: Cajatambo and Andax. It is likely that there was a strong male labor flow both toward and away from the mines. Some left to escape forced labor, whereas others were coming in to seek work. It is also evident that there was migration to the coastal haciendas and to the city of Lima. Documentary evidence is available indicating that in the 1630s large numbers of males were leaving Cajatambo to work along the coast, especially in the Chancay valley.[22]

Emigration of males is apparent in the corregimiento of Canta. There is a general, almost continuous progression from a higher number of males in the repartimientos farthest from Lima to the lower percentage in the repartimientos closest to the city. The sex ratio of the repartimiento of Hananpiscas, for example, farthest from Lima in the northeastern part of Canta, was slightly above 90 in the 1570s–1600s. The repartimiento of Canta, on the other hand, which was nearest Lima, had a sex ratio of about 80. Analysis of the origins of Indians living in Lima in 1613 reveals a significant percentage that were indeed from Canta.[23]

In the corregimiento of Huarochirí, two of three repartimientos had fewer males than females. Close contacts between the inhabitants of the repartimiento of Huarochirí and Lima have been clearly demonstrated by the research of Karen Spalding. There the sex ratio was 84 in 1602. The repartimiento of Chacalla also had fewer males than females, with a sex ratio of 90 in 1602. The repartimiento of Mama, on the other hand, had a sex ratio of 108 at the same time. The reason for the higher percentage of males in the repartimiento of Mama is probably related to the important gold and silver mines located near the villages of Mama and San Juan de Matocana. It is likely males traveled there to labor. If so, mortality was probably higher than in the other two repartimientos, for the rate of tributary population decline of Mama was greatest of the three repartimientos of Huarochirí.[24]

The native population collapse of the central coast paralleled the north coastal loss, but the rate of decline appears to have been more moderate along the central coast. One reason must be heavy immigration from other areas. The city of Lima, as is so clear in the 1614 census, acted as a magnet for Indian migrants from all parts of the realm. It is also evident coastal haciendas attracted a number of migrants, especially working males. The population pyramids of the Huaura valley for 1583 and 1623 (Figure 5) demonstrate vividly the effects of immigration. Sex ratios suggest a high number of men in both cases. Low numbers of males in nearby highland areas suggest the direction of the flow of migration. The highlands acted as a labor and demographic pool, constantly replenishing the depleted ranks of coastal inhabitants.

The impact of a severe drought in Nazca and Umay in 1594 and 1595 is indicative of the fragility of the coastal economy. Without adequate water, people were forced to move in search of sustenance. In this regard the central coast appears more vulnerable to drought than the north coast. On the central coast the Spanish were especially quick to take up lands abandoned by the Indians. Coastal lands were rapidly converted from native intensive agricultural production to livestock grazing or to European cash crops, most important from the standpoint of the colonial economic structure: sugarcane, grapes, wheat, olives, and various other fruits and vegetables for sale in the urban markets. Black slaves quickly replaced Indian workers on the larger units of production.

10

Disease, earthquakes, and droughts: south coast

In the cabildo meeting it was ordered that the irrigation canals which
have been broken and destroyed in the earthquake (February 19, 1600)
should be cleaned and repaired . . . and because Indians from nearby
villages have fled, and because those who remain are few and are occupied in their own fields which are lost and ruined . . . it is ordered
that mita Indians of the city who have fled to the province of Los
Collaguas should be sent for.

Excerpt from the Arequipa town
meeting, in Victor M. Barriga (ed.),
Los terremotos en Arequipa, pp. 55–6

As one continues down the Peruvian coast, the desert becomes more
pronounced and the river valleys fewer and farther between. Less
rainfall descends on the western slopes of the Andes as the Chilean
border is approached. Scarce water results in little land under cultivation and a small population. Even in pre-Spanish times the south
coastal population was lower than in the other coastal sectors. Another
negative factor affecting population of the area is geological instability. A series of volcanos extend from roughly 150 kilometers northwest of Arequipa to 100 kilometers southeast of the city. There are
frequent and severe seismic movements in the region, and these have
historically limited the rate of development of the afflicted area. We
shall examine these subjects in the present chapter.[1]

The south Peruvian coast underwent the most rapid rate of Indian
population decline of any area in the 1570s–1600s. The contrast
between the southern highlands and the coast is great: The Cuzco-
to-Chucuito highland region was falling at −1.1 percent annually,
whereas the south coastal area was declining at −3.8 percent each
year. Various reasons for the rapid depopulation of the south coast are
evident. Epidemics passed through the region. Natural disasters such
as droughts and earthquakes were reported with great frequency.
Moreover, Europeans turned increasing attention to that area after
1570 and settled in the irrigated valleys and the agricultural area

around Arequipa. Spanish colonists tended to dispossess the Indians of their lands, further accelerating population loss.[2]

The Acarí valley is the first major valley south of Pisco and Nazca. The area was visited by Vázquez de Espinosa around 1618, when he found roughly a hundred Indians and forty Spaniards cultivating farms in the relatively wide valley, which had an abundant supply of water. Peanuts, beans, maize, chickpeas, wheat, and fruits were the major crops. Cattle, goats, pigs, and mules were grazed on the lomas and pastured in the interior at higher elevations during part of the year. Yet the earlier population of Acarí had been much greater. The repartimiento of Acarí was originally granted by Francisco Pizarro to Captain Pedro de Mendoza. The encomienda passed through Mendoza's wife, María de Mendoza, to her second husband Pedro de Melgar. In 1580 the inhabitants were counted: There were 625 tributaries and a total population of 2,404.[3] Data from the late 1540s reveal that Mendoza had received an original grant of about eight hundred "Indians" from Pizarro.

A new and complete census of Acarí was made in 1593, following the devastation left by the epidemics that had swept the area. At that time the grant was still held by Captain Pedro de Melgar. The census was one of a series taken in neighboring areas severely affected by the epidemics. Acarí, Atiquipa, Chaparra, Molloguaca, Atico y Caravelí, and Ocoña had not been inspected since Toledo's administration, and officials reported that the Indians

> are very heavily burdened by tribute because of the death of a great many, so that the weight of payment left on the living Indians exceeds twenty and even thirty pesos, and in order to be able to pay the tax the caciques and principales of the villages pay with great vexation and difficulty, and in order to pay they have sold their fields and other possessions they have had, and have fallen in such poverty that today they have nothing left of worth to sell to pay their taxes, and for fear, many of the caciques have fled.[4]

In the ensuing census there were only 336 tributaries and a total of 1,253 inhabitants. The census results are misleading, however. A large number had emigrated to work in Ica, Nazca, Camaná, Lima, and other places. The local priest, who had served twenty years in the valley, reported that only 161 tributaries were permanently residing in Acarí. Moreover, there were many mitimaes who had entered the valley but did not pay tribute. Father Pedro de Villagra argued the principal cause for the sad economic state of the repartimiento was the requirement to contribute, especially cloth and wheat. If local mitimaes and those who had fled could be forced to pay, the situation quickly would improve, argued the priest.

The population pyramid of Acarí for 1593 reveals several significant characteristics of the demography of the area (see Figures 7 and 8; Table 38). Emigration was of major importance. The census taker recorded 43 adult males from Acarí, ranging in age from 17 to 50, who were residing in Ica; yet many of these men maintained a wife and household in the Acarí valley. Other areas of significant emigration in 1593 are nearby Nazca, with 21 adult males (ages 17–45); Camaná, the next major valley to the south, with 11 males (18–45); and, most significant, Lima, with 19, ages 18 to 45. There were 17 other emigrants, who had gone to a variety of sites relatively nearby, and 10 adult males, who apparently had fled permanently for they could not be traced by the census takers. Those absent ranged in age from 26 to 45 and had been gone from the community between five and twenty years. In all there were about 121 adult males who were not continuously residing in the valley. Their absence made it difficult for remaining Indians to maintain the required tribute payments. Of note is the fact that none was reported to have migrated to work in the major Spanish city of the south coastal area, Arequipa. Also of impor-

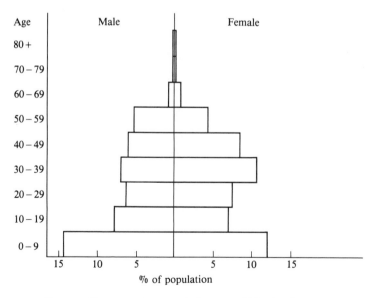

Figure 7. Ten-year cohort population pyramid for Acarí, 1593.

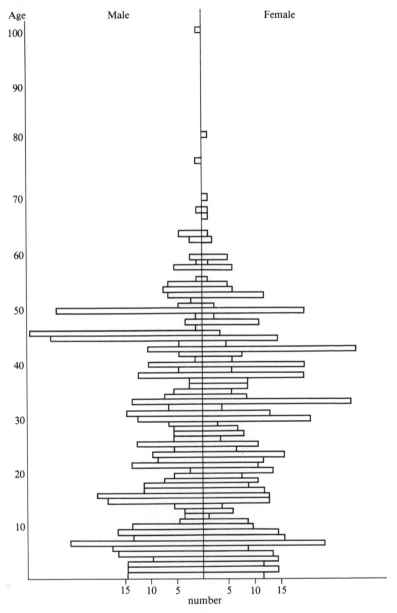

Figure 8. Population pyramid for Acarí, 1593.

Table 38. *The population of Acarí, 1593*

Cohort	Male	Percentage	Female	Percentage
80+	1	0.09	1	0.09
70–79	1	0.09	1	0.09
60–69	9	0.82	9	0.82
50–59	60	5.46	48	4.37
40–49	66	6.01	93	8.47
30–39	77	7.01	116	10.56
20–29	70	6.38	83	7.56
10–19	87	7.92	77	7.01
0–9	156	14.21	132	12.02
n.d.	—	—	11	1.00
Total	527		571	

Note: n.d. = no data.

tance is the fact that there was only one recorded child born of an Indian mother and Spanish father: "Catalina Chipana of forty years has a boy aged six, the caciques declared he is mestizo and not Indian."[5] No name for the child is listed. It is the only case in over five hundred entries where the boy's name is not included in the register. Nor is his father's name reported. In any case, the appearance of a mestizo child in Acarí in 1593 is unusual. Although miscegenation began quickly after European–Indian contact, the impact on Indian communities, even those relatively accessible along the coast, was weak. The Lima census of 1613 also demonstrated this fact.

Other characteristics of the population are notable. Given the large size of the population ages 6–9, the cohorts below these ages are too small and must reflect smallpox and measles mortality in the 1589–91 period. The cohorts ages 10–13 are exceptionally small, suggesting very high infant mortality in the years 1580 through 1583. The reasons for this are not entirely clear from the historical record. Males outnumbered females in the cohorts 0–9 and 10–19. If emigrants were included in the census, the males would also outnumber females in the cohorts through the age of 49. Males outnumbered females in the 50–59 group. There is rough parity between males and females at older ages. Also of note, the female cohorts 10–19 and 20–29 are smaller than one would expect from the size of older female cohorts. Here, heavy mortality affected the generation born between 1563 and 1583. Further, of a total repartimiento population of over one

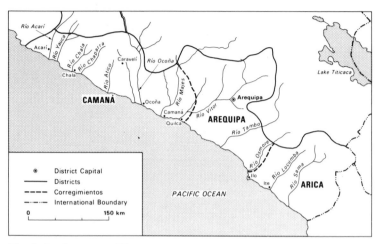

Map 8. Southern coast of Peru.

thousand, only seven survived of the generation born before European contact. Anton Tunqui, by far the oldest individual in Acarí, was reported to be 100 by the census taker. Whether or not his true age was 100 – and there is reason to doubt it – he was certainly a young man when the conquerors arrived. What stories he should have been able to tell to the children of Acarí in the 1590s! Yet Anton remained almost alone. There was one female survivor, 80 years old; a male, 76; and a female of 70.[6]

The repartimiento of Atico y Caravelí, in the corregimiento of Camaná, provides another informative example of south coastal population change. The repartimiento was composed of two population clusters: Caravelí, perhaps the most "highland" of the repartimientos of Camaná; and Atico near the coast. The Atico and Caravelí rivers bring the coastal and highland sectors together. Fernán Alvárez de Carmona was encomendero at the time of the Toledo census. Two decades later the merced had passed to his son. The economy of the grant was based on the catching and salting of large quantities of fish along the coast and their transport and sale in the sierra. There were also fig groves and vineyards in the valley. The population was declining at approximately −2.8 percent yearly in the 1570s–1600s, a less than average rate for the south coast. The percentage of tributaries was relatively stable from 1572 to 1602: 18.6 to 18.8 percent. The rate of decline in the southern section of the corregimiento of Camaná was especially pronounced. There, four small repartimientos located close to each other near the Pacific were declining in tributary population at an incredible rate of between −5.1 and −8.0 percent yearly. The repartimientos were located in an area of expanding Spanish agriculture. The region was ideal for grape vineyards.[7] Keith Davies documents quite well the early European penetration of the Camaná and Vítor–Siguas valleys. Camaná was settled even before Arequipa, but malaria led the colonists to abandon it for a more healthy area. The attraction of the two valleys was land. By the 1580s corn, wheat, olives, and especially wine were profitable local enterprises. And in the late sixteenth and early seventeenth centuries Indians were relatively willing to give up lands. Davies notes that emigration and disease mortality "left them with excess lands."[8] As early as the 1540s grapes had been planted. Vítor vineyards were only 35 kilometers from Arequipa; Siguas was 60 kilometers from the urban center, and Majes was 80. Siguas and Vítor specialized in wine and brandy production; Majes concentrated on raisins and wines. Yet the profitable industry came under heavy pressure from competition, especially from Ica in the 1580s. Vineyard expansion in Pisco and Nazca increased the competition, and by the 1590s Arequipa no longer dominated the market. Depopulation of the Majes valley continued rapidly. "In a report on the Majes valley in 1584, local informants observed that the indigenous population had dropped from over a thousand in the immediate post-conquest period to around one hundred."[9]

The city of Arequipa dominates the southern coastal area of Peru. Unlike the principal Spanish cities of the north and central regions, Trujillo and Lima, Arequipa lies some distance from the coast, at a moderate elevation. The original site was on the coast at Camaná. It was here that the Villa Hermosa was founded in the late 1530s, but a malarial climate led the settlers to opt for a more temperate area on the edge of the highlands. Arequipa, on a level area at some 2,500 meters in elevation and 100 kilometers from the Pacific, was the final site, and the cabildo celebrated the new foundation of the city on 15 August 1540. Adequate water from seasonal rains and the Chili River, plus good lands made the area attractive. Further, Arequipa was on the main transportation route from the coast to Chucuito and beyond. Little did the founders know that the nearby snow-capped peaks of Chachani and the cone of Misti that overlooked the settlement were in one of the highest earthquake zones in Peru and that their city would be destroyed several times by seismic movements.[10]

The Indian population in the countryside surrounding Arequipa was, as far as is known, not large. We know of no large urban complexes in the immediate vicinity under the Incas. The Indians who did live in the region were scattered over a relatively wide expanse of territory. Most Indians were granted to Spanish encomenderos at about the same time that the Villa Hermosa was transferred from Camaná in 1540. The congregation of Indians into European towns was initiated by Viceroy Toledo in the early 1570s. At that time Toledo brought Indians living within the city into the colonial tribute regime. About 514 men ages 18–50 were found in the city and were integrated into the system. They had not paid tribute before and worked in numerous occupations in the complex or served Spaniards. During the next years many of these Arequipa residents migrated elsewhere, and numerous Indians returned to their native communities, where they held land.[11]

The population of the Arequipa region of Peru suffered from not only the usual causes of mortality – disease, combat, famine, and so on – but also one exceptional cause: seismic activity. Arequipa is at the center of a geologically highly unstable area. The Misti volcano overshadows the nearby urban complex. Other volcanic cones are situated within a 100-kilometer radius. The Ubinas volcano historically has been especially dangerous. Frequent earthquakes and periodic volcanic eruptions have plagued the inhabitants of the area since it was first settled. Yet the soil is quite fertile and is an inducement to remain, even though the odds are unfavorable for permanent safe habitation.

The 1582 earthquake was the first major one the Spanish experienced in the valley. The records concerning the event are clear: The strong quake hit on 22 January 1582 at 11:30 a.m. It was felt over a 1,000-kilometer radius of the center, and the city was almost totally destroyed. Two churches remained standing: the Mercedarian and the Franciscan. Thirty people died (probably Europeans, because those who recorded the events were first interested in their own population); many others were injured. On the coast a large tidal wave struck. Viticulture of the coastal valleys was almost completely wiped out, and a plague of rats and flies was reported to have followed. In order to aid in the reconstruction of the center, Indians from nearby corregimientos were called on for mitayos: Condesuyos, Los Collaguas, and coastal areas as far away as Acarí. Viceroy Martín Enríquez pledged support for reconstruction but requested the inhabitants to consider another site. Nonetheless, the Arequipeños were firm in their decision to remain in the valley. Viceroy Enríquez provided a total of 1,300 mitayos for rebuilding the city for a period of one year, and the Audiencia prolonged the service six months. It was not possible to finish the job in the allotted time, so local officials requested a three-year extension of the Indian service. At that point the new viceroy, the Conde de Villar, authorized the use of 500 mitayos within a radius of 25 leagues for a period of one year. Mitayo service was continuing in 1589. A report from the corregidor of Los Collaguas that year reveals that care was taken to ensure that Indians who were living beyond 25 leagues did not serve in the rebuilding mita. It appears all construction came to a halt in 1589, when the great epidemic of measles and smallpox reached the Arequipa region. The cabildo session of 26 December of that year noted that almost all native residents had become ill and that there was insufficient Indian manpower to harvest the wheat before the arrival of the rains.[12]

On 19 February 1600 an even more devastating shock hit Arequipa. The volcano of Huaynaputina erupted, accompanied by a powerful earthquake. The cabildo asked the viceroy and the king for assistance in repairing the extensive damage to the city. Not only were buildings destroyed, but irrigation canals were broken, and heavy ash and cinders fell from the sky, covering the earth and smothering crops. The sky was darkened by a volcanic cloud, and ashes reportedly fell as far away as Cuzco. Large numbers of Indians and Europeans fled Arequipa, fearing the city would be totally destroyed. Many who remained starved because of crop losses. City officials naturally called for new mitayos, but this time their number was to be smaller, and Arequipa officials complained there were not enough Indians to do the work.[13]

There was another major earthquake on 24 November 1604, early in the afternoon. Again the quake was felt over a 1,000-kilometer radius from Arequipa. Over forty died, and the cabildo immediately requested three thousand mitayos for a three-year period for reconstruction of the city. The municipal hall and all other major buildings were destroyed during the 1604 earthquake. First on the agenda, though, was the reopening of the irrigation ditches in order to water the fields. Without moisture, "there would be another calamity, of starvation, even worse than the earthquake." All residents were to contribute to the work; Spaniards, servants, slaves, free blacks, mulattoes, mestizos, zambazgos, yanaconas, and other Indians were to assist in the required task. Once again, officials were sent to surrounding corregimientos to obtain mitayos.[14]

Other major earthquakes took place in the seventeenth century. One of the last large ones occurred on the morning of 20 October 1687. Local officials reported there was not a habitable house left in the city. Mitayos were requested; they were to be first used in the harvest of the crops before the arrival of the rainy season.[15]

Earthquakes in the Arequipa region and elsewhere could be doubly devastating to native inhabitants. There was immediate risk of mortality during the earthquake and also the threat to the ability of the community to repair destroyed irrigation systems and terraced fields. The aftershock was the Spanish attempt to force the Indians to repair damage to European structures and fields, at the very moment when all their effort should have been directed toward internal improvement. High Indian mortality during and following major earthquakes was the consequence of this double shock.

Approximately twenty-two Indian repartimientos made up the corregimiento of Caracato y Vítor that surrounded the Arequipa urban complex. Yanaconas resided within the city proper. The various repartimientos that made up the Chimba (Yanahuara) were just across the Chili River, anywhere from a five-minute to a fifteen-minute walk from the main plaza of the Spanish city. Within 20 kilometers are Tiabaya, Sachaca, Caima, Socabaya, Paucarpata, Yarabamba, Chiguata, Sabandía, Caracato, Mollebaya, Pocsi, and Guasacache. The total Indian population of these repartimientos at the time of Viceroy Toledo's inspection approached 15,000. The population density appears high for a small but rich agricultural area; yet the demography of the region is one of the least well known of Peru. Unfortunately, no new population counts were taken in the valley in the half-century following Toledo's general inspection. This lack of new censuses in the period is unusual. Counts were made in all the rest of the corregimientos of Arequipa during those years. Only the Yanaconas of Arequipa, probably city residents, came under official survey. The adult working male Yanaconas fell from 514 in 1572 to 286 in 1586 and even farther to 190 in 1593. The rate of decline between the first two censuses was −4.19 percent yearly; between 1586 and 1593 it was −5.84 percent.[16] These rates are very high and might reflect earthquake mortality in 1582 and measles and smallpox mortality between 1589 and 1591. It is also true, however, that the Yanaconas of Arequipa are a special case. Officials were attempting to limit their growth in the first place; hence, it is difficult to suggest a common demographic experience for the other 90 percent of the Indians of the Arequipa area. If, indeed, such extreme mortality faced the other Indian communities of the valley, the Arequipa elite had every reason to delay a new population count and tribute assessment. Precluding the discovery of censuses from the period, investigation of local parish registers might help throw light on the problem. Unfortunately, most of the early parish records of the region have been destroyed. Recent inventories indicate the earliest available parish register for deaths is that of Santa Marta, Arequipa, in 1608. Other Arequipa registers do not begin until the mid-seventeenth century.[17]

The Indian village of Yanahuara, located just across the bank of the Chili River north of Arequipa, may provide a good example of the population characteristics of other small communities surrounding the south coastal capital. Christianization of the Yanahuara Indians began even before the establishment of the Spanish city of Arequipa. Between 1536 and 1539 a group of missionaries, under the direction of Friar Pedro de Ulloa, initiated conversion of Indians in the Chili valley. Ulloa established a small church for the natives, which he dedicated to Saint John the Baptist. Thereafter the settlement was known either as Yanahuara or the "Villa de San Juan Bautista de la Chimba."[18] The village, officially reorganized by order of Viceroy Toledo on 16 October 1576, was administered by a curaca, two alcaldes, regidores, alguaciles, and a scribe. The first encomendero of the Yanahuaras was Diego Rodríguez Solis. By the last quarter of the sixteenth century Yanahuara was the permanent residence of many Indians who worked either in the city of Arequipa or nearby or who provided products for sale in its market. Corn, wheat, potatoes, and fruit were grown in surrounding fields. Firewood and charcoal, as well as alfalfa for livestock feed, were major commercial items. Meat from cattle that grazed in the pastures of nearby Canagua was sold to city residents. The population of Yanahuara in Toledo's time was about 8,139. The census enumerator noted that 1,986 were tributaries. Just over two centuries later, in 1792, the population was 1,466. Yanahuara retained its heavily Indian characteristics through the end of the colonial period. By the end of the eighteenth century, all other villages of the valley – Chiguata, Caracato, Caima, Tiabaya, Vitor, Paucarpata, and Tambo – had some admixture of Spanish, mestizo, mulatto, or Negro slaves; but Yanahuara remained solely Indian. Many Indian residents of Yanahuara were migrants. Parish records of the early eighteenth century reveal that many residents of the village had migrated from nearby highland repartimientos. Especially large numbers came from Los Collaguas, Condesuyos, and Ubinas, but some Indians had migrated from as far away as Cuzco, Chucuito, La Paz, and even Potosí. It is not unlikely that these migratory patterns existed in the previous century.[19]

One of the largest repartimientos of the region, Tarapacá y Arica, which was situated on the northern border of the captaincy-general of Chile and the Atacama desert, actually increased slightly in tributary population between the 1570s and the 1600s. The repartimiento's total population declined, however, but at a relatively slow rate of −0.4 percent annually. Vázquez de Espinosa reported that the Tarapacá and Arica valley is "rich in wheat, corn, wine and quantities of fish." Hispanization of the more remote sections was incomplete. The inhabitants of the area maintained in some cases pre-Spanish cult practices. Vázquez de Espinosa, during his inspection of the area, burned the village of Isquiliza "because most people there were idolaters." It is possible the relatively stable local population was the consequence of a weak contact with the Europeans up to that period. The repartimiento of Guancabamba on the northern coast also had a relatively stable population, and church observers there also reported the strength of pre-Spanish cult practices. The guano islands, just off the coast, might have also given economic stimulus to Tarapacá. Even before the arrival of the Europeans the region had become a center for the extraction of the rich fertilizer from the shores of the islands and its transport by llamas to highland areas. Dried fish and salt were also important sectors of the Tarapacá y Arica economy and were exported as far as Potosí. The development of these industries also preceded the Europeans. Furthermore, the demographic stability of the area in the period from the 1570s to the 1600s must be due in part to the economic growth of Arica. In 1572 Viceroy Toledo named Arica the port of supply for the Lima–Potosí trade. The economic impact of that decision on the growth of the other major south coastal cities is well known. The Arequipa economy stagnated between 1570 and the end of the century. Davies attributes a large part of this stagnation to Arequipa's loss of the Potosí trade to the port of Arica. If such is the case, then Arica acted as an attraction for both Indians and Europeans during its heyday. Indeed, the sex ratios of the repartimiento, 104 in 1572 and 101 in 1602, reflect the presence of a substantial number of working males, who were likely to be employed in the exploitation of the extensive fish, guano, and salt resources.[20]

The Indian population of the south coast of Peru was smaller than any other region of the country in 1570, and even smaller in 1620. A total population of about 36,500 in 1570 fell to 15,000 in 1600 and is projected to be slightly less than 10,000 in 1620. The south coastal population comprised 2.8 percent of Peru's 1570 total and only 1.5 percent in 1620. The rate of decline was highest for any region of Peru. Most inhabitants of the south coast were concentrated in the river valley systems of the Acarí, Yauca, Chala, Chapara, Atico, Caravelí, Majes, Vitor, Tambo, Osmore, Locumba, and Sama. Unlike the major urban settlements of the northern coast at the time of conquest, there were no major indigenous concentrations of population in the south. Dispersed habitations in the countryside and occasional small villages characterized south coastal population settlement. Also contrary to the north coast, whereas there was probably more cultivated farmland before the arrival of the Europeans than at present, the total southern land currently farmed is similar to that cultivated before contact. By 1620, as in the coastal regions to the north, Indian lands had been effectively usurped by European colonists. Most of the few remaining Indians along the south coast were rapidly Hispanicized.

The population pyramid of Acarí of 1593 (Figure 8) demonstrates as vividly as the pyramid of north coast Cherrepe and central coastal Huaura the impact of epidemics. In this case the 1589–91 series of epidemics had a major impact on the population, especially small children. Here, too, there are few survivors of the preconquest era. The Acarí census also shows the influence of migration on coastal communities. Large numbers of males had emigrated to other areas. Most went to Ica and Nazca on the central coast, but a substantial group had gone to Lima, and one person was reportedly residing in Cuzco. Patterns of migration pull Acarí northward, into the central coastal sector rather than Arequipa. The case of Yanahuara also illustrates the extent of migration along the south coast.

On the south coast, as elsewhere, Indian communities with relatively stable economic bases suffered least from depopulation. The stability of the Arica region during the period is a case in point. The Arica area was tied to the Potosí mining economy. Its inhabitants aided in the transport and production of supplies for the major highland silver center. Profits to be made in the traffic attracted migrants to the port city.

The south coast suffered more from earthquake-related mortality than any other region of Peru. The exact death rates for the Indian population are not available, as the Spanish kept much closer account of their own losses. Earthquakes left a lingering legacy, however: Extra labor was demanded of the natives during reconstruction. Exceptionally severe quakes shook Arequipa in 1582, 1600, 1604, and 1687. Indians from surrounding communities, also hard hit by the disasters, were forced to migrate long distances to rebuild the Europeans' buildings and estates. During such periods the ability of affected villagers to repair their own homes and agricultural systems was severely threatened.

Intermediate area: northern highlands

The jurisdiction of the provinces of the city of Chachapoyas begins from the Rio de los Balsas . . . it is a rugged land of many rivers and is very fertile . . . beyond by the road is Leimebamba, and many other small pueblos. Near Leimebamba, travelling in the direction of Chachapoyas, is the province of Cajamarquilla del Collay . . . it is a fertile and productive land where much gold is taken. They harvest much wheat, potatoes and various fruits, although at present there are few Indians because many have died, and others have escaped to the Land of War they call Los Aucaes.

> Antonio Vázquez de Espinosa,
> *Compendio y descripción de las*
> *indias occidentales,* pp. 376–7

The northern Peruvian Andes are distinct from the central and southern sections of the chain. The Andean mountains are both lower and narrower in the north than elsewhere. This fact accounts for the different ecological structure of the north and also helps explain the unique demographic development of the region. The highest point on the Ecuadorian border is only 3,726 meters. The passes between the coast and the upper Amazon basin are also lowest in the north. The cut of Porculla connecting the Olmos and Marañón valleys is a mere 2,144 meters in elevation. The transverse cuts in Figure 9 illustrate the low and broken nature of the Peruvian north. The whole of the northern sierra is also characterized by the Marañón River system. Running from south to north along the area, it divides the region into the more highland west, and the montaña to upper rain forests in the east. The river originates in the far south in the area of the Nudo de Pasco, at an elevation of about 5,750 meters. The upper Marañón picks up water from tributaries of the Cordillera Blanca. The middle Marañón passes the mining areas of Parcoi, Pataz, Buldibuyo, Huailillas, and Huancaspata, and the Nevado de Cajamarquilla, the high point on the east. Below, the western rivers of Crisnejas (Cajamarca), Utco (Celedín), Jaén, Chinchipe, and northern Huancabamba enter it. The Huancabamba is the closest to the Pacific of the

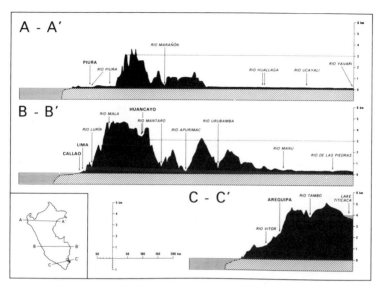

Figure 9. Transverse views of Peru.

tributaries of the Amazon and is now an area of rice cultivation. It is in the lowland northern segment of Jaén that the Marañón turns eastward to connect with the Ucayali and form the mighty Amazon. In the northeast the Utcubamba River enters the Marañón and divides Chachapoyas (elevation, 2,234 meters) and Luya in two. To the east lies Moyobamba, one of the last areas to be integrated, and then only partially, into the repartimiento system in the latter part of the sixteenth century.[1]

Because of the nature of the geography of the Peruvian north, only the repartimientos of Cajamarca, Conchucos, Huaraz, and western and southern segments of Cajamarquilla and Huamalies may be considered fully highland. Most of the high elevation repartimientos were quickly granted to Spanish colonists, and the majority of these were large in population. Further, most of the sixteenth-century highland grants can be located on modern maps. By contrast, the majority of the repartimientos in Jaén, Chachapoyas, Moyobamba, and eastern areas that can be considered lower montaña or upper Amazon basin were small in size and are today difficult to pinpoint precisely. As a consequence of the peculiar geographical structure of northern Peru, I shall first examine the historical evolution of the

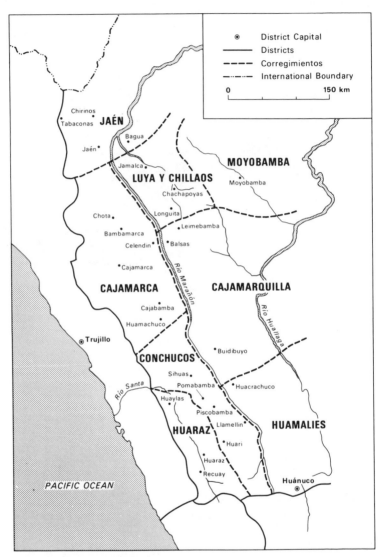

Map 9. Northern highlands of Peru.

more highland areas, then conclude with a discussion of the low elevation regions.

The Indian center of Cajamarca (2,750 meters) received the close attention of the Spanish chroniclers. Cajamarca was, after all, the site where Pizarro and the Inca Atahualpa met face to face for the first time. The city was the place where the foreigners made their initial formal claim to the Empire, where the first battle between European and Inca forces took place, and where the Inca ruler was captured and then held for ransom. Further, Cajamarca was an important pre-Columbian site because it was located on the north–south highland road between Cuzco and Quito and was near famous thermal baths. The earliest European accounts of the city are illustrative. The French report of 1530 described the Spanish arrival at "a great city which is called Caxamalca" and estimated there were over 40,000 Indian men of arms. Cristóbal de Mena, in a 1534 account, stated: "we reached a view of the pueblo which is very large." Mena reported only 400 to 500 Indian guards in the city but many women who were preparing chicha for the Inca and his men. He did report 40,000 warriors in the immediate area, however. Pedro Pizarro stated there were over 40,000; the testimony of Diego de Trujillo was the same. Estete estimated 50,000, and Francisco de Jerez reported 30,000, 40,000, or 50,000.[2] These were troops that accompanied Atahualpa, however, not necessarily the permanent residents of the urban complex of Cajamarca. Jerez described the city in detail:

Cajamarca, which is the principal place in that valley, lies at the foot of a mountain with a league of fields before it, which are crossed by two rivers. The valley is flat, with much populated land on one side and closed in by mountains on the other. It has two thousand inhabitants, and is approached by two bridges, one over each stream. The square is larger than any in Spain. It is entirely walled and has two doorways leading into the city streets. The houses have a frontage of more than two hundred yards and are very well built. The mud-brick walls around them are twenty feet high. The walls and roof are thatched with straw and the walls have wooden cappings. The houses inside are divided into eight rooms finer than those we had seen in other places. Their walls are of carefully worked blocks, and each lodging is surrounded by its own stone wall and doorways.[3]

There was a fort within the city and another on the rocky hillside above the town. "Both forts are stronger than any we had seen in the Indies," Jerez suggested. Cajamarca had a second plaza, which contained the residence of the female servants of the Inca. Further, a temple of the sun stood near the town's entrance. The Jerez estimate of 2,000 "inhabitants" seems as reliable as any, but it is likely Jerez implied adult males, household heads, or occupied houses. If so, the number of preconquest residents of Cajamarca could vary between 8,000 and 18,000 (using multipliers of 4–9). At the time of Viceroy Toledo's general census there were 15,240 Indians in Cajamarca, and in 1611 there were about 12,000 Indians living in the complex.

Cajamarca's demographic stability is unusual. Vázquez de Espinosa, who passed through the area four years later, said the settlement of Cajamarca was the largest Indian "pueblo" in Peru. There were over 100 Spaniards. Located on the main colonial highland road between Quito and Cuzco, the city was a major trade center. There was also extensive local manufacturing based on the woolen factories (obrajes) of encomenderos. The rate of population decline for the repartimiento of Cajamarca was especially low from 1575 to 1611, −0.2 percent annually. There were four repartimientos in Cajamarca with substantial populations: Cajamarca, Guarangas, Guamachuco, and Guambos. The population of all four was exceptionally stable. We have seen that the decline for Cajamarca was slight. Between the 1570s and the 1600s Guarangas declined at a rate of only −0.6 percent yearly, Guamachuco at −1.3 percent; and Guambos actually increased at a rate of 0.6 percent.[4]

To the south of Cajamarca, and slightly to the west, is situated the upper Santa river. The valley it forms is called the Callejón de Huailas. In the sixteenth century, Indians of the valley were divided into five repartimientos that composed the corregimiento of Huaraz. The Huailas valley runs parallel to the coast, in a north–south direction for about 250 kilometers. The northern part of the Huailas valley is lowest in elevation, and it is there that the Santa River breaks through the mountain chain and cascades to the Pacific less than 150 kilometers to the west. The elevation of the repartimiento of Recuay in the south is so high that only potatoes and quinoa grow. The sierra east of Yungay contained rich mines of low-grade gold ore and also some silver. Near the village of Caruas, south of Yungay, were silver mines and several woolen mills. Villages of Huaraz also manufactured woolen blankets, cloth, and other textile products. The Incas had extracted gold in the region prior to the Spanish conquest, but in the immediate postconquest decades mines elsewhere proved more alluring to the Europeans. Around the 1590s, however, the Spaniards turned close attention to the Huailas valley, and by the seventeenth century numerous mines pitted the slopes of the mountains. In November of 1593 Viceroy Cañete allowed miners to use 200 repartimiento Indians for labor in the gold source of Mataraos. One year later the viceroy named Don Diego Nuñez de Figueroa, a rich vecino of Lima with a 200,000-peso estate, the new governor of Huailas. Viceroy Cañete ordered the newly appointed governor to establish a major Spanish mining town and authorized Nuñez to use 600 Indians from surrounding repartimientos: 100 workers for the construction of the homes and public structures of the city and 500 to labor in the mines of Colqueporco. Mine labor was expected from inhabitants of both Huaraz and Conchucos, located just over the Cordillera Blanca to the east. Sex ratios of major repartimientos in both areas – Recuay, Huaraz, Marca, Huailas, Mitimas de Recuay, Piscobamba, and the two repartimientos of Conchucos – reveal small percentages of males, which suggests emigration or high masculine mortality.[5]

In spite of the fact that the Huaraz–Conchucos sector was a major early colonial mining center, large population clusters in the area did not decline at a rate substantially different from the whole of the north highland region (see Table 39). The median rate of tributary decline for the north in the 1570s–1600s was −1.9 percent each year. Of the nine figures available for Huaraz and Conchucos, only Recuay and the Mitimas de Recuay exceed the median. The rates of decline for this region are low. If we examine the cases of repartimientos for which intermediate censuses exist, however, we discern, as in the cases of Huailas, Huaraz, Recuay, and Marca, a very rapid acceleration in the rate of depopulation in the 1590s. In three cases the rate of decline from the 1590s to 1600s is double or more the rate of the 1570s–1590s period. The acceleration of the demographic loss coincided with the expansion of mining activities in the region. Nonetheless, for the whole period the highland pattern of a relatively slow decline persisted. The mine mita for Huaraz and Conchucos stood at one-seventeenth and one-twentieth of the tributary population, which was a substantially lower labor draft from the one-seventh demanded for the labor contributions for Huancavelica and Potosí in central and southern Peru.

The corregimiento of Cajamarquilla was located to the east of Cajamarca and Conchucos. The Marañón River runs along the western part of the area. The climate is moderate, and the area was covered by forest in the sixteenth century. Wheat, corn, and potatoes were grown, which indicates that the central populated area of Cajamarquilla was at a temperate climatic level. Gold and other minerals were extracted. The populations of the corregimiento were relatively large, but the tributary population was declining at a rate much higher than that of the other "highland" repartimientos of the north (see Table

Table 39. *Tributary change in the Huaraz–Conchucos mining sector*

Repartimientos	Tributaries			Rates of change		
	1575	1591	1602	(1570s–1590s)	(1590s–1600s)	(1570s–1600s)
Huaraz						
Huailas	2,690	2,368	1,859	-0.8	-2.2	-1.4
Huaraz	709	661[a]	606	-0.4	-1.0	-0.6
Recuay	3,199	2,205[b]	1,781	-2.0	-2.7	-2.2
Mitimas de Recuay	251	—	105	—	—	-3.2
Marca	910	767[c]	607[d]	-1.0	-2.1	-1.4
Conchucos						
Conchucos Pardave	873	668[a]	—	-1.5	—	—
Conchucos de Mori	760	755[c]	—	-0.0	—	—
Siguas	242	—	161	—	—	-1.5
Piscobamba	645	481	—	-1.8	—	—
Icho Guari	879	—	659[d]	—	—	-1.0
Allanca Guari	826	—	720	—	—	-0.5
Icho Pincos	368	—	—	—	—	—
Allauca Pincos	520	—	393	—	—	-1.0

Note: Dashes indicate no data available.

[a] 1593.
[b] 1594.
[c] 1592.
[d] 1603.

Table 40. *Tributary change in Cajamarquilla,*
1575–1602

	Tributaries		
Repartimiento	1575	1602	Rate of change
Leimebamba	912	413 (1600)	−3.2
Collay	584	451 (1614)	−0.7
Chilchos y Laya	353	100	−4.7
Cajamarquilla	561	306	−2.2
Buldibuyo	247	109	−3.0

40). Perhaps the reason for the rapid loss was the proximity of "free lands" just to the east. Vázquez de Espinosa corroborated this possibility when he reported, "the country contains few Indians at present, many having died off and others gone over to the hostile region which they call the Aucaes."[6]

The chief Spanish city of the southernmost part of the northern sierra was León de Huánuco. The city in fact was on the border of the north and central highlands. At the time of Viceroy Toledo's inspection three corregimientos were under its jurisdiction: Cajamarquilla, Huamalies, and Tarma. Francisco Pizarro had ordered Gómez de Alvarado in 1539 to establish a center to be used during possible future incursions in the upper Amazon. Alvarado chose Huánuco Viejo, a major Inca site at the headwaters of the Marañón, but this location was used only briefly. At an elevation too high for trees, the Inca settlement was an inauspicious jumping-off point for a search for El Dorado. Further, the Marañón flowed northward, not to the east. Therefore, Captain Pedro Varroso refounded the city farther to the south. During a 1541 Indian revolt, however, the Spanish left. After the battle of Chupas in 1542, Captain Pedro de Puelles set up yet another and final center on the banks of the upper Huallaga, which provided quicker access from Lima to the upper jungle. By 1561 there were about 300 Spanish vecinos, including 28 encomenderos. López de Velasco reported that between 23,000 and 24,000 Indian tributaries were administered from Huánuco. Wheat, corn, figs, and cattle were important products in the early 1560s, and there were several good silver mines in the region and at least one sugar mill. By 1616, when Vázquez de Espinosa visited the city, there were 100 Spaniards, 400 mestizos, and what he called "ordinary people." The

Table 41. *Tributaries in Los Huamalies, 1549–1602*

	1549	1575	1591	1602	1570s–1600s
Huamalies de Moson	—	403	372	228	−2.1
Huánuco Chobas	—	42	—	36	−0.6
Mancha	450	348	209	188	−2.3
Ancas y Yacas	—	434	381	351	−0.8
Huacarachuco	500	393	320	244	−1.8
Icho Guanuco	—	416	—	370	−0.4
Guanca	600	—	—	317	—
Allauca Guanuco	—	63	42	57	−0.4
Chachas Cascanga	—	320	—	194	−1.9
Aneyungas	—	75	—	74	−0.0
Pariaga	350	252	229	204	−0.8
Aneyungas del Rey	250	168	—	—	—
Guariguancha	250	284	207	148	−2.4
Arancay	100	110	77	48	−3.1
Ponte Anayungas	250	70	—	59	−0.6

Note: Dashes indicate no data available.

corregimiento of Los Huamalies (see Table 41), extending north from Huánuco, was rich in excellent soil. Fruit trees, such as membrillos, apples, peaches, oranges, and lemons, thrived. Conserves were exported to the coast and other highland centers. There were several cloth factories and, according to Vázquez de Espinosa, numerous unchristianized Indians to the east.[7]

One of the best of the early colonial censuses remaining is that of an Indian grant surrounding the city of Huánuco. The repartimiento of Los Chupachos was held by the encomendero Gómez Arias Dávila, and the census was taken by Íñigo Ortiz de Zúñiga in 1562. Higher-elevation sectors of Los Chupachos to the south of Huánuco may be classified as part of the central sierra. Agriculture in that area was mixed. The elevation of the eastern section of the grant was low enough for good production of maize and cotton. Further, it was close to the coca-producing area on the edge of the montaña. The total population in 1562, slightly over two thousand, provides an exceptionally clear view of the pre-Toledo demographic structure of a region.

The population pyramid (Figure 10) gives clear evidence that there was faulty age reporting. The Indians apparently did not know or

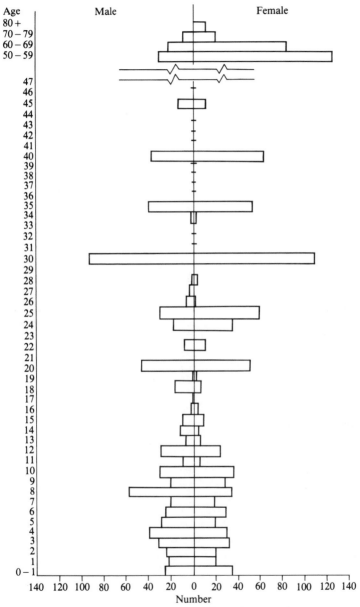

Figure 10. Population pyramid for Huánuco, 1562.

remember their exact chronological age. As in other parts of Peru where inaccurate age reporting is significant, there was a strong preference for ages ending in the digit 5. Further, the respondents reported their age in even numbers more regularly than in odd numbers. The ages of 4, 8, 12, 18, and 24 also were quite frequent. In Peru, the age of 4 is special because children are normally weaned by that age. Preference for the age of 12 may be the result of social or religious practice. Twelve years was a breaking point in the Inca census category. Traditionally, 12 marks the division between the child and the young adult in Andean societies. The Roman Catholic practice of confirmation at approximately the same age may also account for the large size of that cohort in the Chupachos census. Age heaping at 18 is stronger for males than for females and is clearly the result of the fact that males become tributaries at that age. This practice is corroborated by the scarcity of males of 16 and 17 years of age. Spanish officials often illegally classified young males as tributaries before they reached their eighteenth birthday in order to collect a greater amount of tribute. Age heaping at 24 is more pronounced for women than for men and may be related to local marriage and childbirth patterns. Age heaping in the document is indicative of the degree of error that might be expected in other statistical data in the 1562 census.

The sex ratio of Los Chupachos was 74 in 1562 and 70 in 1602. The larger number of females was similar to nearby repartimientos on the border of the north and central highland region. Even though the number of men available as husbands was small, most females of childbearing age had given birth, resulting in a child–woman ratio of 66.1 in 1562. The census demonstrates that concubinage in the Huánuco area in 1562 was widespread, in spite of attempts by Spanish authorities to prevent it. Although not enough males were present for marriage, women other than the wife lived in the same household and often had several children. The scarcity of men and the economic and social dislocations caused by their disappearance made the levirate a common practice among the Chupachos in the 1560s. Apparently, family access to land and rights to property were in this way maintained. Thus, the levirate and concubinage tended to cushion the sixteenth-century demographic crisis in the Huánuco area. The fact that concubines and near relatives occupied the same household in Los Chupachos makes it difficult to define or ascertain the size of families. Table 42 illustrates the number of people in each household of the enumerated population in 1562.

The census of Los Chupachos provides occasional evidence useful in

Table 42. *Household size in the repartimiento of Los Chupachos, 1562*

Number in household	1	2	3	4	5	6	7	8	9	10	11	12	13	14	15	16	17	18
Number of households	46	44	72	73	47	50	19	23	15	6	4	2	1	0	0	0	0	1

estimating mortality. The inspector, for example, in his returns for the pueblo of Achinga, recorded that, of forty-nine inhabitants in 1562, seven were born between 1557 and 1562, whereas ten Indians of all age categories died between the same dates. Of the ten who died, three were under the age of 3.[8] The population pyramid of Los Chupachos for 1562 (Figure 10) reveals several things about mortality in the surrounding area. First, the enumerated population of infants under the age of 3 was not large enough. The number of children in each age group (0–1, 1–2, and 2–3) should have been larger than the 3–4 group, but each cohort was substantially smaller. Under-enumeration of infants, especially under the age of 1, is common, and the inspector often failed to list some babies. It is also possible that the small number of infants was due to mortality during an epidemic that was passing through the Huánuco area concurrently with the census. This epidemic could have been related to extensive influenza in 1558–9.

The rather small group ages 12 to 19 is also probably due to European diseases. An epidemic ravaged the region in the years following 1546, and its results are well known for other areas of Peru. Mortality may have been highest for children under 4. It should be noted that the census returns for Los Chupachos list a surprising number of mute children, probably the consequence of severe cases of measles and ensuing complications.

The most interesting aspect of the population pyramid is its reflection of the preconquest condition. Anyone over 30 listed in the 1562 census manuscript would have been alive before the arrival of the European invaders. Those over 40 would have witnessed the first known European epidemic in the central Andes and the conflict between Atahualpa and Huascar over the succession to the position of Huayna Capac. This group, and their size in relation to the younger population of Los Chupachos, can reveal much of the process of the demographic transformation of Peru.

Of the whole region of the northern highlands, small repartimientos were most frequent north of Cajamarca, in the territory extending to the southern border of the Audiencia of Quito. In that area, only three of ninety repartimientos at the end of the sixteenth century had a total population exceeding one thousand. The repartimiento of Yamarasbamba illustrates the unprofitable nature of small Indian grants for the colonist. The encomendero of Yamarasbamba was Ono-rate Estévan the younger. The tribute assessment of 1584 listed ninety-six tributaries and mandated the following tribute: 96 pesos in silver; 48 pieces of cotton cloth valued at 84 pesos; 48 fanegas of corn worth 24 pesos; 48 fanegas of potatoes bringing in 12 pesos; and 96 chickens assessed at 6 pesos. The fixed expenses of the repartimiento were set at 50 pesos for the *doctrina* (for the salary and living expenses of the priest); 15 pesos for the *fabrica* (construction and upkeep of the parish church); 14 pesos for the stipend of the curacas; and 25 pesos for *justicia* (the fund for the legal defense of the Indians). In addition, tributaries were assessed a one-tomín tax (there were eight tomíns, or reales, per peso at that time) for the Indian hospital. The encomendero was left in 1584 with a profit of only 100 pesos each year, far less than the sum necessary to maintain a proper Spanish gentleman. By 1595 the population of Yamarasbamba declined to a level where the en-comendero received only 77 pesos annually.[9]

Epidemic disease also took a high toll in the northern highlands, especially in the northeastern sector. The repartimiento of Yunpit, held by Alonso Vázquez, was inspected in 1585. At that date twenty-two tributaries were enumerated. By March of 1593 only five tributaries could be found in the repartimiento. Fifteen reportedly died during the general epidemic, and two had later fled to avoid paying tribute, which was still collected at the 1585 rate. Many repartimientos in the northeast were exempted from tribute payment in the year or two following 1589 in order to aid in the restructuring of the local society and economy made necessary by the devastation caused by the epidemic.[10]

The historical demography of Jaén, the northernmost region of Peru, is poorly understood. Census records for the key dates of 1549 and the early 1570s (Toledo's) are not available; perhaps no counts of Jaén were taken at these times. Yet, according to one document, the 1532 population of Jaén included 20,000 tributaries. We do have the 1561 figure from López de Velasco, but these numbers are only approximate. Velasco reported thirty Spanish vecinos in Jaén, includ-ing twenty-four encomenderos, and from 8,000 to 10,000 tri-butaries, but the total of the ten sets of numbers in the Velasco list comes to only 7,800, indicating that the cosmographer's 1561 esti-mate for the whole area may be conservative.[11] We have already noted the low and broken terrain of the far Peruvian north. The climate of

Jaén was warm and humid, with rains from October to March. When Vázquez de Espinosa described it in the early seventeenth century, the area was completely wooded. Corn and root crops were important food items. Little wheat was grown. Tobacco, sugarcane, and various fruits plus livestock were produced. Gold was taken in substantial quantities until at least the mid-seventeenth century, especially in the Cherinos valley. Salt was evaporated from spring water in the Jolluca mountains and traded extensively. Tributary figures are available for Jaén in 1591, and a complete set of population data exists for 1606 (see Table 43). We are able to discern two main characteristics: an unusual structure of the 1606 population; and the nature of the demographic collapse of the low elevation north. First, an unusually large percentage of the 1606 population was tributary, and there was an exceptionally large number of males in the region; twenty-two of the thirty-two repartimientos in 1606 had sex ratios over 100. In some cases substantially more men than women were present, which suggests heavy immigration of males. Further, some repartimientos had abnormally low percentages of boys under 18 years of age: Jullaca Pomaca (7.7 percent); Yana en Jullaca (5 percent); Pucará (11.3 percent); and Chinchipe (4.5 percent). Such an unusually low number of young males is the result of either a severe epidemic, which destroyed the youth of the region, or the incorporation of underage males in the status of tributary. Second, the figures for the total tributaries in 1591 and 1606 reveal the demographic collapse of the north. The downward spiral of tributaries is rapid and continuous: 20,000 in the early 1530s; 8,000–10,000 three decades later; 2,000 after three more decades; and less than 1,500 in 1606. The rapid decline seems to parallel that of the Peruvian coast rather than the highlands to the south. By the early seventeenth century Jaén was almost depopulated. Only one repartimiento of the thirty-two in the corregimiento had a population that exceeded one hundred. It is not surprising that the production of gold in the region declined. Contrary to what occurred on the coast, however, the native losses in Jaén were not replaced by European settlers and black slaves. The region entered a period of almost unbroken economic stagnation.[12]

To the east of Jaén, farther in the interior, lies Chachapoyas. The Inca conquered the Chachapoyas Indians about 1475. The region was divided into Moyobamba, northern Leimebamba, and the meridian part of Cajamarquilla and Pias. The northern and eastern boundaries were defined by the Amazon jungle; the southern by the Huacarachuco; and the western limit by the Marañón. The Spanish leader Alonso de Alvarado, accompanied by four horsemen and three

Table 43. *Population change in Jaén, 1591–1606*

Repartimiento	Tributaries 1591	1606	Rate of change
Cathachina Cherinos	142	54	−6.4
Zangala Canga	60	25	−5.8
Yana	67	10	−12.7
Joroca	113	44	−6.3
Llanque	67	12	−11.5
Aconipa	106	49	−5.1
Jullaca Pomaca	40	20	−4.6
Yana en Jullaca	14	7	−4.6
Moquin	164	n.d.	—
Cunbaraca	34	n.d.	—
Jullaca Pumara	16	10	−3.3
Guamarincho Chamaya	12	3	−9.2
Chentali	43	n.d.	—
Collabarba	84	n.d.	—
Sal Cachillata	15	10	−2.7
San Pablo Caxillo	63	56	−0.8
Cherinos	206	62	−8.0
Valle de Cherinos	244	56	−9.8
Taboconas	66	81	+1.4
Guallatoca	176	269	+2.8
San Felipa Yomaco	60	58	−0.2
Pucará	41	24	−3.6
Queroato Tinoco	83	87	+0.3
Queroato Forjales	109	93	−1.1
Guallanda	17	25	+2.6
Chacainga	28(1572)	53	+1.9
Paco	91	68	−1.9
Tomependa	52	42	−1.4
Bagua	38	18	−5.0
Copallán	133	48	−6.8
Perico	50	25	−4.6
Chinchipe	15	9	−3.4
Total	2,124	1,318	

Note: Dashes indicate no data available.

foot soldiers, arrived at the Inca capital of the area, Cochapampa, in mid-1536. He was welcomed by the curaca, who swore obedience of the Chachapoyas to the ruler of Spain and gave the Spaniards gold and silver. The curaca also promised Alvarado a complete census of the inhabitants. Alonso de Alvarado then went back to Trujillo to get arms and equipment for a second expedition. He planned a large excursion into the jungle and in 1537 returned to Cochapampa. The curaca Guamán again supported Alvarado and provided 4,000 auxiliaries and allies for the exploration party. The group traveled to La Jalca, where Alvarado made a division of Indians to all Spaniards who accompanied him. The commander was to receive Cuelap, Cochapampa, Leimebamba, Pausamarca, and Chilchos, and the curaca retained La Jalca, Zuta, Puyundo, and Anaqueniche. It is possible the expedition reached interior Tomependa and Bracamoros, but the explorers were forced to leave the area when news of the conflict between Almagro the Elder and Hernando Pizarro reached them. The curaca was left in charge of local affairs as the Europeans headed toward Cuzco. Guamán was able to hold the Chachapoyas loyal to the Spanish during the ensuing rebellion of Manco Capac and was rewarded by European recognition of his chieftainship. He was renamed Don Francisco Pizarro Guaman as a mark of his highly regarded and timely support against the Incas. After the rebellion was crushed, Alonso de Alvarado returned to the northeast with 250 soldiers and planned a major expedition to El Dorado. It was on 5 September 1538 that he founded San Juan de la Frontera de Chachapoyas. Alvarado received more gold and silver and then continued eastward with 4,000 Chachapoyas aides and guides. Moyobamba was established as a result of this entrada.[13] La Gasca's division of Chachapoyas in 1549 reveals a "tributary" population of almost 18,000 for the area (see Table 44). A dozen years later the report of the cosmographer Juan López de Velasco listed a tributary population of from 16,000 to 17,000 for Chachapoyas, divided into seventeen repartimientos. There were twenty-five encomenderos and about 200 European vecinos living in San Juan de la Frontera. The corregimiento of Luya y Chillaos, located to the east of Jaén, was administered through San Juan de la Frontera. Quantities of gold were found in Luya y Chillaos, and chief agricultural products included wheat, corn, other native and Spanish cereals, potatoes, and many varieties of fruits, including figs, almonds, peaches, pippins, and apples. Vázquez de Espinosa was especially impressed by the Indians of the region and reported that they "are the shapeliest and the whitest in the whole kingdom of Peru." In the city of Chachapoyas

Table 44. *Relation of repartimientos of Chachapoyas, ca. 1549*

Name of curaca	Encomendero	Tributaries
Quinjo (serrano)	Marshall Alonso de Alvarado	1,500
Ancimga-Chilcho	Marshall Alonso de Alvarado	1,000
Dn. Gomez (serranos)	Capt. Gomez de Alvarado	700
Dn. Miguel (serranos)	Capt. Gomez de Alvarado	300
Nita (serranos)	Alonso de Chaves	500
Chupate (serranos)	Alonso de Chaves	250
Panarguara Serrano	Juan Lopez Montero	500
Guacaleba Serrano	Francisco de Fuentes	650
Chumpa (serrano)	Garcia Rodriguez de Heredia	300
2 principales Animigas	Garcia Rodriguez de Heredia	350
Quilo & Baboco	Rodrigo Bustillo	600
Colcol Serrano	Alonso Rodriguez Mercado	550
Sopla & Boboco (serranos)	Martin de Santiago	600
Chanipe & Zanza	Luis Valera	650
Jumbilla & Lonzo & Tomailte (serranos)	Pedro Ximenez	650
Azallan & Guamacocota & Miamaieque (serranos)	Alonso Calderon	600
Chuquivala (serranos)	Hernando de Mori	550
Alconamba (mitima) & Serrano natural	Melchor Ruiz	300
Nita & Quipor & Candor (serranos)	Pedro de Soramia	550
Telaco & Chebar (serranos)	Alonso Camacho	550
Zobenil	Nuestra Señora de la Merced	450
Nosquilpe & Collari (serranos)	Pedro Gomez	550
Infite & Cimia (serranos)	Martin de Salazar	500
Ponchique & Chabal (serranos)	Gonzalo Muñoz	550
Obilos (serranos)	Juan Diaz	250
Gelo (Valley of Bagua)	Juan Diaz	150
Mulos & Comedi (serranos)	Anton de Sant Pedro	550
Pulgar & Sicud (serranos)	Juan Alexandro	500
Longuin Cocota (serranos)	Honorato Estevan	550
Tibar & Macaro (serranos)	Alexo de Medina	300
Loma del Viento & Aparijo (in Pocolcha)	Alexo de Medina	600
Jomanga (serrano)	Juan de Rojas	150
Jotafe (imigas in valley of Bagua)	Juan de Rojas	150
Llanarz & Yapa (serranos)	Bernardino de Anaia[a] (now vacant)	650
Total		17,550

[a] Deceased.

Spanish and Indian women were renowned for their exquisite "point lace" of henequen fiber and also for their embroidery. The capital of Chillaos was an Indian village named Luya, which was situated five leagues from San Juan de la Frontera de Chachapoyas. The province was also famous for many livestock ranches and for the Luyan horse, reputedly one of the finest in Peru. There were a few sugar plantations and mule ranches, which supplied transport animals sold in the highlands and even as far away as Lima.[14]

At the time of Viceroy Toledo's general inspection of the viceroyalty, three corregimientos were administered through San Juan de la Frontera de Chachapoyas: Cajamarquilla, Pacllas, and Luya y Chillaos. We have already seen that Cajamarquilla presents no problems in the location of repartimientos. The administrative structure of Luya y Chillaos (predominantly, the region close to San Juan de la Frontera) and Pacllas (which includes a substantial part of Moyobamba) is confusing. From the 1570s to the 1600s there appears to be some overlap in the administration of the corregimientos. This is perhaps in keeping with the frontier and the unsettled nature of the territory. It is quite difficult to assign precise geographical locations to many of the northeasternmost repartimientos. Population counts in the western Luya y Chillaos sector were common in the 1570s to 1600s period, but farther east in Luya, and in Pacllas, censuses were concentrated in the 1575–95 era. From the fragmentary data for repartimientos in the far northeast, in the one or two decades following Toledo's census, it appears that the population decline was extremely rapid, generally more than double the north highland average. The high rates paralleled and in some cases exceeded the rates of the coast. It is therefore not surprising that in the far northeast no new censuses were attempted by Spanish officials in the early part of the seventeenth century. The region entered an era of demographic collapse and economic stagnation that lasted through the end of the colonial period.

The pueblo of Goparas, located not far from the larger settlement of Bagazán in Pacllas, furnishes an example of a typical small northeast community in the early seventeenth century. Its population was modest and was declining rapidly. The tributary population loss between 1592 and 1598 was −11.6 percent annually. A high rate of −9.6 percent continued through 1602. By the later date, there remained only eighty-five inhabitants in Goparas (Table 45). A census of 1602 provides raw material for a population pyramid (Figure 11). Here, as elsewhere, mortality was high for children. There are far too few residents under the age of 30. The 20–29 cohort appears to have

Table 45. *Age and sex discrimination of Goparas, 1602*

Age	Population Male	Population Female	% Distribution Male	% Distribution Female	Sex ratio
60+	2	2	2.35	2.35	100
50+	6	5	7.06	5.88	120
40+	4	8	4.71	9.41	50
30+	8	11	9.41	12.94	73
20+	3	4	3.53	4.71	75
10+	9	6	10.59	7.06	150
0–9	10	7	11.76	8.24	143
Total	42	43			98

been especially hard hit by demographic disaster. It is clear from the pyramid that the population of Goparas could not be maintained by internal growth. It was only a matter of time until Goparas, and other small communities like it, passed into oblivion.[15]

Another small community, San Agustín de Bagazán, within the

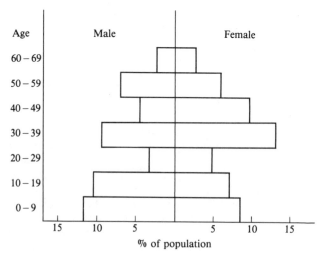

Figure 11. Population pyramid for Goparas, 1602.

jurisdiction of San Juan de la Frontera de Chachapoyas, was inspected a number of times in the latter part of the sixteenth century. Bagazán was located about 45 kilometers east of the city, near the edge of the Amazon basin. One eighteenth-century observer said that the jungle began and the mountains ended in Bagazán. It was about equidistant from Chachapoyas and Moyobamba, so there must have been considerable movement through the pueblo. At the time of Viceroy Toledo's inspection the encomendero was Francisco García Jaimes. There were 78 tributaries, and the total population was 481. By 1587 – the repartimiento was then held by Ysabel García Jaimes – the population had fallen to 424, including 63 tributaries. In a 1593 count there were only 56 tributaries, 34 reserved males, 37 boys, and 116 women. A census the ensuing year resulted in the following figures: 62 tributaries, 29 reserved, 73 boys, and 191 women. The total population made the incredible jump from 243 to 355 in one year. This increase causes us to suspect the accuracy of one of the two counts or the possibility of territorial modification of the grant. Table 46 suggests that in Bagazán in 1594 small families predominated. Over half the couples had either no offspring or just one. Child mortality must have been quite high. The epidemics of 1589–91 severely depleted the number of children.[16]

Large-scale contact with Europeans apparently came later in the more isolated frontier regions of the northern sierra than in other highland sectors. Contact and full Spanish control over Jaén and Moyobamba were especially late and proceeded at a slow pace. The first complete census records for Jaén, for example, date from the 1590s, a full two decades later than for most of the rest of Peru. The same late initial counts are true of some repartimientos in Chachapoyas. The northeastern sections of Peru offered the Spaniards less promise of easy riches than many other areas. The terrain was rugged, broken by relatively low-level mountain chains and river systems, with high humidity, heavy rainfall, and dense vegetation. The Europeans generally found the area less productive in precious metals than regions to the south. Northeastern Indian repartimientos

Table 46. *Number of children in family unit in Bagazán, 1594*

Number of children	0	1	2	3	4	5
Number of families	26	19	15	14	3	3

were scattered and of small populations. The north sierra had the second-highest number of repartimientos with a tributary population of less than 100: About 43 of 130 repartimientos fit into this category. Small repartimientos are obviously less valuable, especially in isolated regions, than are large grants.

The Indian population of the northern sierra was declining more rapidly than any other highland's area from the 1570s to 1600s. The rate of decline was −1.9 percent annually for the tributary population and −1.2 percent for the total population. The population fell from about 210,000 in 1570 to 120,000 in 1620. In 1570 the north sierra held approximately 17 percent of the Indian population of Peru, but the Indians, especially in the northeast, were scattered over a wide expanse of territory.

Internal study of the northern highlands reveals two basic trends. First, the repartimientos in low-elevation areas were rapidly losing their populations. This tendency was especially pronounced in Jaén, sections of Luya y Chillaos, and Pacllas. Here, quick depopulation parallels that of the coast, but the full extent of population loss in these areas is difficult to ascertain because of less complete statistical data. High-elevation repartimientos declined at a lower level. Even repartimientos in the mining districts of Huaraz and Conchucos fell in a relatively typical highland pattern, although the rate quickened with expansion of European mining activities.

12

Mining and population in the central sierra

> Some absent themselves from their communities to avoid going to the
> mines where they would suffer agony and martyrdom, and in order to
> avoid experiencing such hell, hardship and torment of the devils, others
> flee the mines, and still others take to the roads to avoid the mines and
> would rather chance dying suddenly rather than to suffer a slow death.
> They say that they reach such a state because contracting mercury
> sickness one dries up as a stick and has asthma, and cannot live day or
> night. It goes on in this manner a year or two and they die.
>
> Felipe Guamán Poma de Ayala, La
nueva crónica y buen gobierno, p. 333

The central Peruvian highland corregimientos are in the heart of the
Andean chain. The elevation of the area is high. The frigid,
windswept puna appears inhospitable but provides fodder for extensive flocks of llamas and alpacas, which are used for wool. Upper
sections can also produce ichu and quinoa, a native cereal. Potatoes
and other tuberous crops are grown in cool zones, and in the more
temperate valleys wheat, corn, and other crops are cultivated. The
central highlands are a major mining region of the Peruvian Andes.
The modern Cerro de Pasco mining district is in the north; minor
silver deposits were worked throughout the central highlands; famous
mercury mines are located at Huancavelica in Chocorvos; and there
was a major silver-mining center at Castrovirreyna in the southern
part of the same corregimiento. In this chapter we shall examine the
relationship between mining, which was so important in the central
sierra, and population change. As we shall see, numerous observers in
the past have stressed the deleterious consequences of mine labor.
Guamán Poma and others in the sixteenth and seventeenth centuries
have pointed out the dangers of Huancavelica and other mines. Yet,
was the relationship between exploitative labor and depopulation
stronger than the relationship between epidemic disease and the catastrophic drop in the number of natives?

The aboriginal population of the central Andean valleys was dense.
In 1570 about thirty-one of fifty repartimientos in the central high-

lands had total populations of over one thousand. Further, the population of the region appeared relatively stable in comparison with the
coastal valleys or the northern highlands.

The first European settlement in the central highlands was at Jauja.
The site was chosen because of its convenient location and its relative
proximity to the Pacific coast. Jauja became the Spanish headquarters
for the final march on Cuzco by the invading forces in 1533.[1] Jauja
was already a major city under Inca domination. Miguel de Estete,
who was there in the 1530s, described the complex as the Europeans
first viewed it:

> The town of Jauja is very large and lies in a beautiful valley. A
> great river passes near it, and its climate is most temperate. The
> land is fertile. Jauja is built in the Spanish manner with regular
> streets, and has several subject villages within sight of it. The
> population of the town and the surrounding countryside was so
> great that, by the Spaniard's reckoning, a hundred thousand
> people collected in the main square every day. The markets and
> streets were so full that every single person seemed to be there.[2]

Several historians have suggested that the figure of 100 thousand
people who congregated daily is pure conjecture. It is clear, however,
that Jauja served as a pre-Spanish center for the distribution of regional products. In the twentieth century, Huancayo, 50 kilometers
to the southeast, has superseded Jauja as an exchange depot for the
central highlands. Another important description of Jauja is found in
a letter of Hernando Pizarro of 23 November 1533 to the members of
the Royal Audiencia in Santo Domingo. Pizarro unequivocally stated
that there were 100 thousand Indians in the plaza of Jauja. Four
decades later, the total population of the seven repartimientos that
composed the corregimiento of Jauja reached fifty thousand.[3] In the
light of this information, Miguel de Estete's claim that 100 thousand
filled the Jauja marketplace does not appear extravagant, but Jauja's
resident population was clearly far less.

Pedro Cieza de León reported that the valley of Jauja contained
thirty thousand "inhabitants" when the Europeans first reached it.[4]
Other information on the native residents is more explicit: The "Relación geográfica" for the province of Jauja, which was compiled in
1582, provides figures for the population in Inca times. Curacas and
elders of the area reported that

> Hatun Xauxa then contained six thousand war Indians, and the
> repartimiento of Hurin Guanca twelve thousand war Indians,
> and Hanan Guancas nine thousand war Indians . . . and that in
> the time of the Inca they were increasing, because the Inca

awarded to brave Indians two wives, and three, and six and more and less; but commonly the Indians did not have more than one wife.[5]

Although the geographical description of Jauja was made at the bequest of royal authorities almost a half-century after conquest, its figures for the preconquest period are worthy of consideration. Research by Borah and Cook on the reliability of the numbers for the population of Mexico about 1519 in the *Relaciones* of that viceroyalty led them to conclude: "Our experiment at verification has thus shown that there is reasonable agreement between the large and varied body of testimony of the *Relaciones Geográficas* on the pre-Conquest population and our calculations which have been arrived at on the basis of a totally different body of data."[6]

By 1575 Atun Jauja's tributary population was 1,079; in 1605 it was 761; in 1617 it fell to 733; and by 1630 it stood at 326, roughly 5 percent of its initial figure. Lurin Guanca's decline was parallel: 3,374 in 1575; 2,607 in 1605; 2,258 in 1618; and 799 in 1630. In this case the last figure was 6.7 percent of the Inca-period population. Hanan Guanca fell from 2,500 in 1575 to 2,000 in 1587, 1,293 in 1602, 1,248 in 1609, 1,241 in 1618, and 556 in 1630. Here the final tributary population was 6.2 percent of the pre-Spanish. During the first three decades the annual rate of decline for Atun Jauja was −4.2 percent; Lurin Guanca's was −3.1; and Hanan Guanca's was −3.1. The annual rates of change for the 1570s to the early 1600s, however, were −1.2, −0.9, and −2.4 percent, respectively, for each repartimiento. In the period from 1617 to 1630 there was a very rapid acceleration in the rate of decline of the three repartimientos.[7]

The corregimiento of Jauja had some of the highlands' best croplands, along with close access to coastal Lima. The area was recognized as an important supplier of pork products, especially ham and bacon. There were also many local silversmiths who had established an excellent reputation for their delicate work. Sex ratios of many repartimientos in Jauja suggest male emigration. We have seen from the 1614 Lima census that the destination for some Jaujeños was the capital. Furthermore, some males migrated to work in mines, either as mitayos or as paid wage earners. Hanan Guanca, for example, was one of the repartimientos required to contribute mitayos for the mines of Huancavelica. Population loss for Hanan Guanca was pronounced for the central highlands but not nearly so high as coastal population decline. Tributaries were declining from the 1570s to the 1600s at a rate of −2.4 percent yearly. Local conditions following 1617 became especially difficult. In the 1620s curacas of Hanan Guanca were

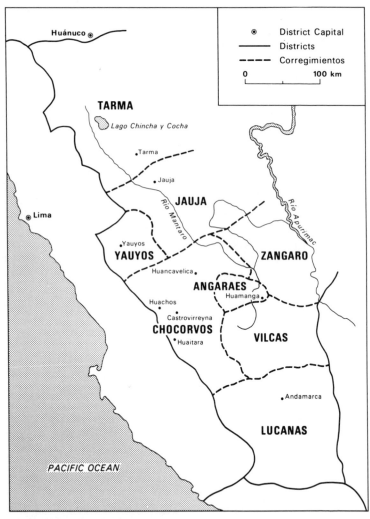

Map 10. Central highlands of Peru.

thrown into jail because they were unable to collect the tribute owed to the Spanish. The native officials lamented the fact they were unable to pay and blamed the situation on the fact that tributaries were either sick, absent, or dead. They laid the blame squarely on the disastrous consequences of Huancavelica.[8]

By 1600 the Huancavelica mercury mines had become one of the key elements of the economic structure of the entire Spanish Empire. Mercury was vital for the extraction of silver from ore. The amalgamation (also called patio) process was simple. Crushed ore was spread on the floor of a patio and mixed with mercury, copper sulfate, salt, and hot water. It was then covered and allowed to "set" for several days. Ultimately, silver from the ore combined with the mercury, which was then vaporized by relatively low levels of heat, and good quality silver was left behind. Without mercury, the refining of silver required high levels of heat, difficult to achieve in the high Andes, which were almost destitute of good combustibles. Further, lower grades of ore could be worked with good results using the amalgamation process. The method of extracting silver by using mercury had been introduced in Pachuca, New Spain, by Bartolomé de Medina in 1556. Within three years Enrique Garcés first used the method in Peru, with mercury taken at Palca, Huamanga.[9]

Native Andean residents had searched out sources of cinnabar, the ore of mercury, long before the Inca conquests. It had been used as a pigment for the decoration of their faces. The brilliant red color, resembling blood, was expected to frighten their enemies during combat. Limited deposits of mercury ore were uncovered by the Spanish before their discovery of Huancavelica. Around 1558 Garcés had located a source in Tomaca, and Gil Ramírez Dávalos discovered a vein called Tomebamba in Cuenca. By 1560 several small mines were producing in Charcas.[10]

The mines of Huancavelica had been exploited by local residents for several generations before the conquest. There are numerous versions of the European "discovery." The common element in the accounts is that the local encomendero, Amador de Cabrera, learned of the existence of the mines. Perhaps he suspected that the red cosmetic used by the women of Angaraes was cinnabar; or perhaps the curaca of Chachas (Acoria), who was Gonzalo Nahuincopa, told Cabrera of the mines in 1563. There is substantial documentation in colonial court records that the inhabitants of Conayca attempted to avoid mita service at Huancavelica because they claimed responsibility for its discovery, and the Spanish did exempt the curacas of Acoria from contribution to Huancavelica. Another version of the story, which presents the native's view of the process, describes an old Indian who wanted to share the wealth of the mine with the encomendero. The Indian revealed the secret to the Spaniard, but Cabrera failed to keep his part of the bargain and registered the mine in his name alone.[11]

Within a decade a number of miners had staked claims in the area. The largest mine was the Descubridora of Amador de Cabrera. The need for a large and stable supply of mercury was so important for the extraction of silver, however, that the Spanish government decided that it could not be left in the hands of private mining entrepreneurs. The transition from private ownership to full state control over mercury was not easy. Miners had taken great risks and invested large sums and expected to give the Crown only the traditional tax on metals – the quinto (fifth). When Viceroy Toledo arrived in Peru, he carried a royal order of 28 December 1568, for the state takeover of all mercury mines, but Toledo delayed enforcement, recognizing the disruptive consequences of any attempt by bureaucrats to operate the mines. Then, in January 1570, Toledo ordered mine discoverers to pick their primary mine plus two other sites, or, if the miner were using washing operations, he could retain up to four claims within a league (about 5.5 kilometers) of Huancavelica's center. Protests were violent against this attempt to limit free mining, and Toledo reversed the decision, but by March of 1571 he succeeded in taking for the state one-quarter of the production of the Descubridora mine. Amador de Cabrera was dissatisfied and appealed to the Council of the Indies. In November 1571 the Council declared that ownership of the Descubridora should be transferred to the Crown, in conformity with Spanish mining regulations dating back to 1387. Cabrera was allowed to continue extracting the mercury, however, and was allocated one-third of the profits after deduction of expenses. Cabrera again appealed, claiming that profits were insufficient and that he was denied the traditional benefits due a discoverer. A final Council decision was handed down in March 1572. The mercury mines were to be fully incorporated by the state, but current miners were allowed to extract the ore. The fifth was to be paid the government, and all mercury produced was to be sold to the state at a fixed price. In the future all mercury trade was to be managed by Crown officials.[12]

The new regime was instituted in February of 1573 by the official Gabriel de Loarte. The property of forty-three Huancavelica miners was expropriated. In the following month, contracts (*asientos*) were issued to individuals who would be in charge of mining operations. Four men received the first three-year contract: Amador de Cabrera, Torres de Navarra, Juan de Sotomayor, and Pedro de Contreras. They were to sell yearly 1,500 quintales of mercury to the state at a fixed price of forty-two pesos per quintal (46 kilograms). The association was granted control of an Indian mita to provide much of the labor for the extraction process. The basic mining structure continued into the next century.[13]

In the 1560s García de Castro had studied the manpower needs of the colonial mines and recognized the great necessity of employing Indian workers. Royal decrees had prohibited forced labor of native inhabitants, but Indians could be assigned for mine labor if they "volunteered" for the work and were paid. García de Castro suggested that if Indians were forced to transport supplies to mining centers they might be induced, in one way or another, to stay on. When faced with the small number of voluntary laborers, however, García allowed authorities near the mines to send Indians to be "rented out" (*alquilados*) by the miners. But free contract workers, who were paid weekly, tended to disappear late each Saturday, the day they traditionally received wages. The labor supply was too short and too unstable to allow full production at the mines. Black slaves were too expensive to satisfy the requirements of Huancavelica. Further, the mortality rate for blacks at the frigid highland center of mercury production was extremely high.[14]

Viceroy Toledo temporarily solved the demand for labor at Huancavelica by adopting the modified pre-European mita. By the viceroy's orders, and "for the good of the realm," one-seventh of the tributary population of corregimientos surrounding Huancavelica had to labor at the mines during the annual draft. The requirement was not an individual tax but a territorial requirement. Censuses were necessary to assign the appropriate number. The draft extended to 40 leagues, and the first quota was approximately three thousand. Toledo required that the workers receive one tomín of good silver daily, and there was a ration of 2.5 pounds of meat weekly and 1.5 celemines (the *celemín* equaled about one-twelfth of a fanega or 4.8 liters) of corn a month. Ultimately, a stipend was granted to cover the period of travel to and from the workplace. Individual mitayos could work no more than four months each year in Huancavelica. They were to enter the mines an hour and a half after sunrise, were given an hour off for lunch and rest, and left the mines at sunset.[15]

Laborers in the Huancavelica mine faced both immediate and long-term dangers. Cave-ins, floods, and falls as a result of slipping in the shafts posed daily threats. Intermediate health hazards were presented by a poor diet, inadequate ventilation in the underground chambers, and the sharp temperature differences between the mine interiors and the rarefied Andean atmosphere. Often sweating profusely during their ascent of a rope and timber ladder in the shaft to the main entrance, the scantily clad workers were met by the frigid twilight air of Huancavelica, 4,000 meters in elevation. Pneumonia and other bronchial and respiratory tract infections were not at all uncommon. Workers who remained for long periods in the mines perhaps suffered the worst fate of all. Dust and fine particles were released into the air of the mine by the striking of the tools used to break the ore loose. Indians inhaled the dust, which contained four dangerous substances: mercury vapors, arsenic, arsenic anhydride, and cinnabar. Long exposure, especially of the voluntary workers, resulted in death. Known as *mal de la mina,* or mine sickness, it was incurable when advanced. In less severe cases the gums were ulcerated and eaten away.[16] In many instances the entire dental system was destroyed. Arthur P. Whitaker summarizes the disastrous effects of mine labor on the Indian workers:

> The death of many mitayos in the mine and the flight of many more to escape the dread service in it led to the sharp decline in the population of all the provinces subject to the Huancavelica mita. This depopulation in turn reacted unfavorably upon the mine, for after the early part of the seventeenth century the full quota of mitayos was never supplied and by the close of the century the number actually delivered at the mine was seldom more than about half the quota.[17]

It is unnecessary to here repeat the almost constant chorus of humanitarians who have vividly depicted the horrors of Huancavelica. There is no doubt that the horrors were real. Two or three examples suffice. Don Diego de Luna, general protector of the Indians of the viceroyalty of Peru, sent a message to the king of Spain in 1629–30. He boldly affirmed his belief that the mining mitas would soon deplete the native population. He claimed that only a third of the Indians set aside for the Huancavelica mita remained when he wrote. He further charged that Huancavelica mitayos were plundered of their property and that their wives were abused by curacas, encomenderos, and oftentimes priests. Indians had no real recourse in the colonial courts. Two decades later, Don Juan Estevanez de Azebedo, in a report to the viceroy, reiterated that abuses continued and lamented the lack of laborers for the mercury mines.[18]

In Table 47 we note that the number of mitayos for Huancavelica declined almost continuously from the 1570s to the mid-seventeenth century. How much of that decline was due to actual depopulation? Here the records are not complete, for the census data for the central

Table 47. *Mitayos assigned during the Huancavelica asientos, 1573–1645*

Asiento	Mitayos	Comments
1571[a]	3,000[b]	900 during founding, 500 in winter
1573	1,400	
1581	3,280	
1586	3,000	
1590	2,274	
1598	1,600	
1604	1,600	
1608	2,300	
1618	2,200	Azangaro, Vilcas, Huachos, Soras, Lucanas, and Hanahuancas
1623	1,400	
1645	600	

[a] Based on data in Roel, *Historia, social y económica,* pp. 98–120. Asientos for other years retained the previous mitayo assessment. These figures are for the number assessed. The number who actually showed up in the mines each year was lower.
[b] Based on Lohmann, *Minas de Huancavelica,* pp. 97–8.

highlands are scarce for the post-1620 era. It would be interesting to compare the demographic experience of central highland repartimientos that did not contribute to the mercury mines with those that did, but here too the data are not clear. The maximum number of corregimientos contributing to Huancavelica reached nine: Tarma, Jauja, Angaraes, Vilcas Guaman, Chocorvos, Guanta (Zangaro), Lucanas, Andaguaylas, and Cotabambas. According to this list, only Yauyos of the central highlands escaped the mercury draft. Repartimientos in the Yauyos region did decline slightly less rapidly than other central highland units from the 1570s to the 1600s.[19]

As a whole, the rates of tributary change for most of the central highland repartimientos contributing mitayos for Huancavelica from the 1570s to the 1600s are remarkably low in comparison with the coast and the northern highlands. In spite of the requirement to contribute mitayos for Huancavelica, most repartimientos of the region were losing tributary population at a rate of about −1.3 percent yearly, and the total population was falling at −1.4 percent. By contrast, the coastal tributary decline ranged from −2.4 to −3.5 percent, and the north highland decline was −1.9 percent. With data for about 94 percent of the tributary population of the central sierra, the results should be a reasonable reflection of the actual state of affairs. The native Andean resident risked less mortality living near and, in fact, perhaps working as a mitayo at Huancavelica than did the Indian resident of Piura, Trujillo, Lima, Camaná, or elsewhere on the Peruvian coast or in the northeastern frontier of the Amazon basin. Given the nature of colonial testimony on the evils of Huancavelica, how can this be? I believe the answer lies in the fact that coastal and lowland epidemic mortality was much higher than highland mortality. A very different mortality pattern for highland and coastal lowland Mexico for the same period has been clearly demonstrated by the research of Borah and Cook. The same phenomenon was noted by MacLeod in Central America and by Freide and Colmenares in Colombia. As we have already seen, diseases spread more rapidly in warm areas, especially when there is high humidity, as in the upper Amazon basin. European diseases, for which the American resident had no natural immunity, were much more deadly than mine labor, even if it were as dangerous as that of Huancavelica. Further, the Spanish were tied to metal production. Any threat to their ability to maintain annual output, such as a decline in the labor force, received the immediate attention of colonial officials. Therefore, their reports noted in detail labor hazards at Huancavelica and consequent population decline. Also, as we have seen in the post-1620 data, the rate of tributary decline in much of the central sierra accelerated sharply.[20]

As the seventeenth century wore on, it became more and more difficult to find the mitayos subject to the Huancavelica quota. By the third quarter of the century it was impossible to locate more than 354 Indians from the corregimientos contributing to the Huancavelica mita. Viceroy Melchor de Liñán y Cisneros (1678–81) was perplexed at the sharp drop in mitayos. He believed that some had died but was convinced that there were more births in the region each year than deaths. The viceroy concluded that the natives (originarios) of the provinces had moved to nearby corregimientos that were exempt from the Huancavelica draft and that a roughly equivalent number of forasteros had replaced them. Thus, although the total population declined slowly, the mita was significantly reduced. The yanaconas were also exempt from the mita draft. Viceroy Liñán, in the face of miners' demands for mitayos and the apparent paucity of draftable tributaries, ordered a general census of all corregimientos near Huancavelica and a termination of the exemption of forasteros and yanaconas. Viceroy Liñán was unsuccessful in both, however. He was unable to complete the count or change the system.[21]

Other mines in the central sierra were exploited with the help of forced Indian labor. The silver mines of Urococha and Chocolococha were discovered in 1590. In October of the following year the viceroy established a mita quota, to be met by surrounding corregimientos, to help open the mines and establish a major Spanish city: Castrovirreyna. Pedro de Cordoba Mexía was ordered to build the city. By 1610 there were eighty-six permanent European residents; twenty-six were married, and about one-quarter were non-Spanish. According to Vázquez de Espinosa, the mines did not produce as much as their owners hoped. The Chocolococha mines were located on a snow-covered mountain about 2 leagues from the city of Castrovirreyna. The ore had to be hauled from the mines to mills (*molinos*) on the edge of a small river that flowed near the city. The silver here, as in Potosí, was extracted by the mercury amalgamation process. Labor was difficult in the high altitude and bitter cold. Castrovirreyna was one of the most frigid regions of Peru; meat could be left outside without spoiling, and unprotected wine froze at night. The climate was too harsh for wheat and barley, but ichu, tubers, and quinoa did grow. By 1610 there were several estates held by Spaniards, including four cattle ranches, four for sheep, five for goats, and one for mules. In the 1591 mita assessment, Indians were required from Parinacochas and Guaynacota (500), Los Collaguas (500), Aimaraes (500), Andaguaylas (300), and Lucanas (300), for a total of 2,100 mitayos. It is questionable if the Collaguas Indians, living about 600 kilometers to the south toward Arequipa, ever contributed. At the beginning of the seventeenth century a new and more exact mita quota was established: Aimaraes (456), Andamarcas (147), Soras (14), Parinacocha (254), Pomatambos (185), Condesuyo del Cuzco (104), Condesuyo de Arequipa (380), and Chocorvos (20), for a final total of 1,560. It appears that most of the mitayos for Castrovirreyna were drawn from provinces south of the city, probably because Huancavelica was situated not far to the north, and absorbed the available labor forces of that region. In any competition between Huancavelica and Castrovirreyna for laborers, the former was likely to win, for mercury was essential for the silver production in all parts of the viceroyalty and even in New Spain.[22]

The estimated Indian population of the central highlands in 1620 is about 125,000, approximately 20 percent of the population of Peru. Spanish officials complained loudly about the population decline in the central sierra, in spite of the fact that the central sierra Indian population clearly fell less rapidly than that in most other regions. It seems that the complaints were motivated by the growing labor shortage around the indispensable mercury mine of Huancavelica. The Spanish colonists did bemoan the fact that coastal populations were disappearing; yet with alacrity they settled on vacated Indian lands and planted European crops, often using black slaves who were less likely to die or escape to other regions. In the highland mining centers, however, the Spaniards needed the Indian because there were not enough European miners to do the work and because slaves were ineffective. Apparently blacks were no more able to provide sustained heavy labor at high altitudes without suffering prohibitively high mortality than were highland Indians able to labor on coastal plantations without almost certain sickness and death.

The rapid depletion of the ranks of central highland residents that took place following the second decade of the seventeenth century is a consequence of both deaths and migration to avoid mita service. By moving to another corregimiento, Indians, as forasteros, were exempt from mita service. As the natural population decreased, and no new censuses were taken in order to lower local assessments for the mines, it became apparent that frequent mita service would be required. Had an Indian been expected to serve only four or five times in his lifetime, as Toledo originally planned, the mita service might have been borne by the native. With the population decline and no reassessments, however, the Indian could find himself contributing every third year. At such a juncture, emigration, even if it meant giving up access to one's traditional croplands, became not only appealing but also a means of survival. By the 1680s, at the time of Viceroy Palata's administration, forasteros outnumbered originarios in many of the repartimientos that sent mitayos to Huancavelica, Castrovirreyna, Potosí, and other mining centers.

13

The Indian heartland: southern highlands

When the Spaniards arrived there (Cuzco) there was a great number of people; it would have been a pueblo of more than 40,000 vecinos, within the city alone, and what with the suburbs and districts around Cuzco, within 10 or 12 leagues, I believe that there would have been 200,000 Indians, because it was the most densely populated of all these realms.

Cristóbal de Molina, *Relación de muchas cosas acaecidas en el Perú* . . . (1553), p. 33

Almost half the Indian inhabitants of Peru, some 600 thousand, lived in the southern highlands in 1570. Many large repartimientos dotted the landscape: About 142 of the 260 holdings of the south sierra had more than a thousand residents. The largest population unit in all Peru, the Crown repartimiento of Chucuito, was composed of almost 75 thousand people at the time of Viceroy Toledo's visita general. Further, the rate of population change for the region was the lowest of all Peru from the 1570s to 1600s: The tributary population declined at only −1.1 percent annually, and the total population fell at −1.2 percent each year. Thus, the broad outlines of population change in the southern highlands are clear, but the details of the process are still poorly understood. The region is vast: It is almost a country within a country. Many communities made up each repartimiento; we are dealing with more than a thousand such population clusters. It is impossible to study them individually. Once again, we are forced to select some areas and problems to examine in greater depth. The balance must await the results of the ongoing investigation of other researchers.[1]

Essential to our understanding of the population history of the southern sierra is the population cluster of Cuzco, the Inca administrative capital and the chief center of southern Peru to the present. Even now, and with good reason, Cuzco is called the Indian capital of South America, yet there is no modern study of the demographic history of the region. Consequently, it is possible to deal with Cuzco in only the most general terms. A thorough study of the Cuzco area is of utmost importance, and until that is completed the present generalizations must be taken as tentative.

There is no definite agreement on the size and nature of Cuzco when the Europeans first reached it in 1533. The archaeologist Edward Lanning stated: "The Incas came from the rural tradition of the south. When Pachacuti and Topa Inca rebuilt Cuzco, they created it in the rural image. Its center was essentially a ceremonial center, containing temples, palaces, and government buildings but no residences for anyone but royalty, priests and their immediate retainers."[2] Borrowing on the research of John Rowe, Lanning stresses the decline of urbanism in southern Peru after the decline of the Huari in the thirteenth century. Rowe argued that no true cities were established in the south under the Incas. Beyond the ceremonial nucleus, Cuzco's population was spread in villages in the surrounding countryside; but these concentrations were separated from the main center by garden plots or farming lands. Lanning sees the villages as close enough to the center to perhaps create "a semiagglutinated city . . . If so, it was the only city ever built or occupied in the southern half of Peru between the fall of the Huari and the arrival of the Spanish."[3] John Rowe considered that Cuzco in pre-Spanish times never reached a high population, but he does agree that

> Since the service personnel in the core area probably grew to a number at least 2,000 the core itself was technically a large city by the criteria we are using [Rowe's break between "pueblo" and "city" is 2,000]. However, Pachakuti's intent appears to have been to build a ceremonial center with a cluster of small urban settlements dependent on it.[4]

Contrary to the conclusions of Rowe and Lanning, my own reading of the documentary evidence convinces me that Cuzco was a major city by whatever standards are applied. Let us review the testimony of the first Europeans to view the complex. Pedro Sancho, secretary of Francisco Pizarro, first entered Cuzco on 15 November 1533 and described the city in some detail after the Spanish "founding" in March of 1534. He was impressed by the number of large, well-built palaces, some for the staffs supporting the mummies of the imperial ancestors, others habitations for the chieftains from all parts of the realm. There were many storehouses filled with tribute goods. Pedro Sancho gives one important early clue to the population: "And in the valley in which it is situated, surrounded by hills, there are more than one hundred thousand houses."[5] Miguel de Estete saw Cuzco at the same time as Sancho, but he wrote one year later (ca. 1535). He too described temples and palaces and pictured the main plaza as neither large nor small. "This city was large, extensive and with many neighborhoods, where many lords [*señores*] have houses; it was filled with great edifices."[6] Both Estete and Sancho saw and reported on the Cuzco they had encountered prior to the great fire and destruction of the city during the Indian uprising of 1536. All who went through that experience concurred on the devastation it caused.

It is evident that the population of the city and its immediate vicinity suffered severely during the Indian revolt of 1536–7. The anonymous author of the *Relación del sitio del Cuzco* reports the European defenders and their allies faced 100,000 Indians of war and 80,000 more auxiliaries. There was high Indian mortality during the fighting. Apparently, mortality for Spanish defenders and their allies was also high. Large sections of the city were destroyed as thatched roofs were set on fire. Cuzco of 1544 was only a remnant of what it had been a decade before when the first Spaniards set foot in it. The early colonial city, southern administrative capital, never regained the wealth or opulence of the Inca center, but the urban center was not totally demolished.[7]

Pedro Cieza de León arrived in Peru in 1548, just over a decade after the Indian uprising and destruction of the city. Yet Cieza de León was very impressed by what he saw and heard from Europeans who had been in Cuzco in the early years. His description of Cuzco, written prior to 1555, is worth quoting at length:

Nowhere in this Kingdom of Peru was there a city with the air of nobility that Cuzco possessed, which (as I have said repeatedly) was the capital of the empire of the Incas and their royal seat. Compared with it, the other provinces of the Indies are mere settlements. And such towns as there are lack design, order, or polity to commend them, whereas Cuzco had distinction to a degree, so those who founded it must have been people of great worth . . .

Most of the city was settled by mitimaes . . . It was the richest city in all the Indies . . .

Although this city is cold, it is very healthy, and the best provisioned in the whole Kingdom, and the largest, where the most Spaniards hold an encomienda of Indians . . .

And as this city was full of strange and foreign people, for there were Indians from Chile, Pasto, and Cañari, Chachapoyas, Huancas, Collas, and all the other tribes to be found in the provinces we have described, each of them was established in the place and district set aside for them by the governors of the city.

They observed the customs of their own people and dressed after the fashion of their own land, *so that if there were a hundred thousand men,* they could be easily recognized by the insignia they wore about their heads.[8]

At about the same time (1553) Cristóbal de Molina wrote that Cuzco "was very large and very populous, with large edifices and districts." Molina continues, as we have seen, with the opening statement that there were 40,000 vecinos and 200,000 Indians in the area within 10 to 12 leagues. Although he wrote in the 1550s, Molina resided in the city from 1536 to 1538. He thus was able to speak with authority about the nature of the complex during its early occupation by the Europeans.[9]

Later reports of the chroniclers tend to repeat similar figures. The Mercedarian friar Martín de Morúa, for example, was in or near Cuzco in the decade following 1590. Morúa wrote:

This was a great city with one hundred thousand houses, and in each one lived two or three residents, and even ten; every five days there was a market in a wide and long plaza called Cusi-Pata, where the present convent of Nuestra Señora de las Mertedes is located . . . 100,000 people could fit in the plaza.

There were also about six thousand male and female Indians living in Cuzco who were dedicated to performing the ancient religious rites, according to Morúa.[10]

The demographic transformation of the municipality of Cuzco from Inca to colonial Spanish is as poorly understood as the true size of the aboriginal population (see Table 48). Many Europeans quickly established residence in the city and regarded it their permanent home. At the same time, many Indians who had been forced to reside in Cuzco by the Inca returned to their native lands. There was high Indian mortality in Cuzco due to disease and war. Concurrently, however, there were Indian immigrants who followed in the wake of the Spanish. The royal cosmographer Juan López de Velasco, in a description of the city as it probably was in the 1560s, reported there were around eight hundred Spanish vecinos and about 77,000 tributaries, plus many natives who escaped enumeration, living in the district. López de Velasco's *Geografía* contains a relatively graphic description of Cuzco as it must have appeared to the Spanish near the beginning of the last third of the sixteenth century. Even then it was possible to distinguish, by their residence in the city and their dress, the origin of Indian inhabitants. Indian merchants and artisans from all parts of the realm resided in Cuzco. There were two major distinctive groups, the Cañaris and Chachapoyas, who were on the Christian

Table 48. *Indian population of Cuzco, ca. 1561*

Parish	Personas
Nuestra Señora de Belém (Cayucalche)	2,400
Santiago (*plateros*)	1,000–2,000
Nuestra Señora de los Remedios	2,000
Santa Ana (Carmenga)	2,300
San Cristóbal (Colcampata)	1,800–2,000
San Blas (Totococache)	2,600
Total	(12,100–13,300)

side during the conquest and who were thereby freed from the tribute requirement. Eight from the two tribes provided a special nightly guard for the corregidor, and they were used as messengers. On the Festival of Corpus Christi 300 paraded through the city, carrying their lances and accompanying the procession. López de Velasco believed the main economic function of the city was the distribution of coca but thought the leaf's domination of the economy would end soon as a result of Viceroy Toledo's reforms. Also, all the Indians of Cuzco were *oficiales* – including more than 300 *plateros yungas* from the llanos. They were known for their excellent work in silver and gold.[11]

Viceroy Toledo, while in Cuzco during the visita general, noted that a large number of Indians resided in the city and its parishes who had not before paid tribute. By order of 11 August 1572 Toledo incorporated these Indians (called Cuzqueños and Yanaconas) into the Crown and brought them within the colonial tribute system.[12] (See Table 49.)

Baltazar Ramírez provided one last glimpse of sixteenth-century Cuzco. Writing around 1597, Ramírez reported forty-five Spanish encomenderos living in the city and more than a thousand other European vecinos. The five Indian parishes each had 400 to 500 parishioners, most of them natives of Cuzco from the pre-Spanish times. The author of the anonymous description of Peru written in the early seventeenth century gave higher numbers: 3,000 Spanish vecinos and 10,000 Indian vecinos.[13]

Vázquez de Espinosa described the population of Cuzco as it must have seemed in the second decade of the seventeenth century. By that time the chronicler estimated the Spanish population at over 3,500.

Table 49. *Toledo's count of Cuzco's tributaries*

Parish	Type of tributary	Number	Tribute (in silver pesos)
Nuestra Señora de Belém	Cuzqueños	225	765
	Yanaconas	170	510
Santiago	Cuzqueños	244	732
	Yanaconas	75	225
Hospital	Cuzqueños (Hanan and Hurin)	180	540
	Yanaconas	305	915
Santa Ana	Cuzqueños (Chachapoyas and Cañaris)	200	600
	Yanaconas	58	174
	Cañaris y Chachapoyas	265	exempt
San Cristóbal	Cuzqueños	225	675
	Yanaconas	216	648
San Blas	Cuzqueños	304	912
	Yanaconas	260	780
San Sebastián	Cuzqueños	46	138
	Yanaconas	116	348
	Undetermined number of Indians resident in San Sebastián who belong to encomenderos	—	—
San Gerónimo	Cuzqueños	40	120
	Yanaconas	204	612
Total		2,892	8,694

There were numerous mestizos, more than 14,000 Indian vecinos, and a "large number" of black slaves and mulattoes. The growth of the new sectors of Cuzco's population is continuous, although Vázquez de Espinosa's numbers are only estimates.[14] The figure of 14,000 native vecinos compares favorably with the 12,000 to 13,300 "personas" reported by López de Velasco in 1561 (Table 48). The 1571 and 1583 data on tributaries indicate the relation between the numbers of tributary and nontributary Indians in Cuzco. Using multipliers of 4 to 5 to convert "vecinos" to the total Indian population of Cuzco in the early seventeenth century, we arrive at the following figures: 56,000 to 70,000 permanent native inhabitants for the Indian capital just under a century after contact. The decline was substantial, but the city of Cuzco remained a large complex. Clearly depopulation of the Cuzco area was less rapid than that of the coast. As early as the 1560s observers noted the relatively healthy condition of the inhabitants of the region. López de Velasco, for example, wrote:

> The climate of the city and the surrounding area is moderately cold, because it is situated in the sierra, and thus is very healthy. And it is not known if there has ever been a pestilencia in it; there are some chest pains, although not dangerous: there are neither fleas nor bed-bugs, nor flies, nor mosquitos, not even rats, except a handfull. [15]

López de Velasco may exaggerate when he reports that there had never been a major epidemic, but by comparative standards Cuzco was a healthier place for the Indian to live than either the coastal or the montaña zone. Furthermore, Cuzco was a focus for migrants from the southern highlands and, as we have seen, a source of acculturated Indian residents of Lima, the viceregal capital. Unfortunately, as in the other Spanish colonial centers of Lima and Arequipa, there are very poor statistical data for the early seventeenth century. Counts of Indian residents of Spanish cities were infrequent. Most urban dwellers were able ultimately to escape the tribute collector and thus escape enumeration. European residents allowed this because of the obvious importance of the Indians who lived in the city. Whether they were skilled artisans or household servants, the urban Indians came to be viewed as a major part of early colonial society. Further research in Cuzco parish registers should help illuminate this process of social history, for here the fiscal records are inadequate and the eyewitness accounts must be verified.

Certainly the Inca knew the exact population of Cuzco when the Europeans entered Tawantinsuyu, but the census quipus no longer exist, as far as is known. Were there an inquest, as there was in Chucuito in 1566, the Cuzco quipus might have been located and their numbers recorded by Spanish scribes. Unfortunately, this was not to be the case. There is, however, enough testimony to estimate: Sancho's (1534) 100,000 houses; Estete's (1535) large and extensive city; Cieza de León's (1548) "if there were a hundred thousand men"; Molina's (1553) more than 40,000 vecinos; Morúa's (post-1590) 100,000 houses, all lead me to postulate a high aboriginal population for Cuzco, as does the archaeological evidence. Caution is necessary, however. Cuzco's population was unquestionably inflated during market days. During the frequent trade fairs the streets and plazas could have been filled with 100,000 people exchanging products and wares. These were not permanent residents of Cuzco but people who temporarily increased the number of city residents. Further, some houses and palaces had low and essentially nonproductive populations. The number of inhabitants in the residences dedicated to the worship of the Inca ancestors was limited, as was the number of priests and women who served within the religious hierarchy. There were indeed many structures in the center of the Cuzco urban complex

Map 11. Southern highlands of Peru.

dedicated to religious and administrative offices, with a low resident population. Settlement in the whole of the valley, however, and particularly in the core was dense enough that Cuzco might be considered a preindustrial city. In the city 100,000 structures were possible, but many were not inhabited by families. Molina's more than 40,000 vecinos seems an appropriate figure for 1530, and, by converting vecinos to total inhabitants, a range of between 150,000 and 200,000 is feasible.[16]

The corregimientos of Yucay and Paucartambo bordered the city of Cuzco to the north and east. Both were lower in elevation than Cuzco and produced large quantities of maize and coca. Both were located on the edge of the Peruvian montaña and were therefore ecologically distinct from the highland regions of the south. The Yucay valley was sacred to the Inca and maintained a special position during the sixteenth century. Higher slopes of Yucay were used for the pasturage of livestock, especially cattle. Crops varied, depending on ecological level. Halfway down the valley wheat, grapes, corn, and other cereals were produced, and there were several large sugar plantations, especially on the valley floor, in the early seventeenth century. Our knowledge of the historical demography of the Yucay valley is enhanced by the availability of one of the Toledo censuses for the Yanaconas of Yucay, taken in 1571 by Friar Pedro Gutiérrez Flores. The broad outlines of the history of this repartimiento are known: Francisco Pizarro first retained the Yanaconas of Yucay and used the inhabitants to cultivate coca fields in the nearby province of Los Andes. After Francisco's assassination, his son Gonzalo inherited the grant. The Crown absorbed the grant in the late 1540s when Gonzalo died, and the Yanaconas of Yucay were transferred to Sayri Tupac in 1558 in return for his support of the Spanish cause. Two years later his daughter and only child, Doña Beatriz Coya, inherited the grant. At about the same time an exceptionally powerful local curaca, Don Francisco Chilche, began to rule the area as if he were the supreme authority and challenged the administration of Doña Beatriz. After the marriage of the heiress to Captain Martín García de Loyola, the couple began to pressure the courts for full control over the Yanaconas of Yucay. During the testimony regarding the merits of the claim, a complete census was taken in 1571.[17]

The chief characteristics of the population of Yucay in 1571 can be noted in Figure 12 and 13 (Table 50). Pedro Gutiérrez Flores was clearly unable to ascertain the exact chronological age of all Yucay residents. As in the case of Huánuco, there was age heaping in even numbers, fives, and tens. In many cases the wife was assigned the age

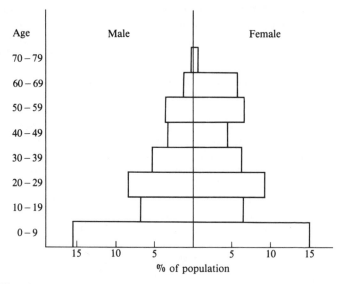

Figure 12. Ten-year cohort population pyramid for Yanaconas of Yucay, 1571.

of her spouse. The large number of 18-year-old males results from a desire to maximize the number of tributaries. It is likely that 15-, 16-, and 17-year-old boys were placed in this category. The large number of 54-year-old men suggests that prior to Toledo the tributary status was maintained until the age of 55. The small number of children younger than 3 could be the consequence of high infant mortality in the 1569-71 period. There is a marked indentation in the population pyramid for the ages of 9 to 14. The probable cause is the well-known and severe epidemics of smallpox and measles beginning in 1558. The impact of these epidemics must have been similar in other nearby repartimientos.

As with the case for the Chupachos of Huánuco in 1562, one of the most interesting aspects of the 1571 Yucay population is its reflection of the preconquest demographic structure (Figure 13). The small size of the 40-49 cohort was the result of epidemic disease and other forms of mortality in the crisis period from 1522 to 1531. Those over 50 who were still alive in Yucay in 1571 witnessed the entire period of Spanish expansion in Peru.

The 1571 census of Yucay provides excellent data for the period, but is the information representative of trends over a wide region?

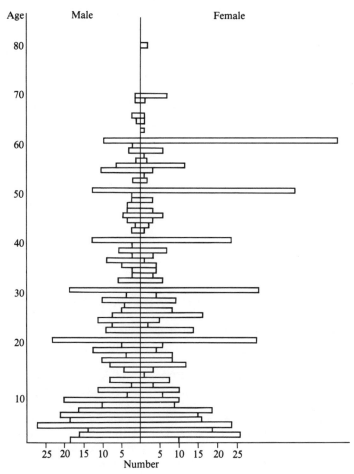

Figure 13. Population pyramid for Yanaconas of Yucay, 1571.

Certainly the total population, over 1,000, gives a sizable universe on which to base generalizations. The demographic experience of neighboring repartimientos at the time (the early 1570s) is likely to be similar to Yucay. All the various repartimientos in the cor-regimiento of Yucay were declining in population. The population of eight of the repartimientos was falling more rapidly than the south highland median. The consequences of recorded epidemics and war-

Table 50. *Age and sex distribution, Yanaconas of Yucay, 1571*

Age	Population		Percentage		Sex ratio
	Male	Female	Male	Female	
0–9	145	141	15.43	15.00	102.84
10–19	63	62	6.70	6.60	90.80
20–29	79	87	8.40	9.26	90.80
30–39	52	59	5.53	6.28	88.14
40–49	33	41	3.51	4.36	80.49
50–59	37	64	3.94	6.81	57.81
60–69	13	55	1.38	5.85	23.64
70–79	1	7	0.11	0.74	14.29
80+	—	—	—	—	—
n.d.	1	—	—	—	—
Total	424	516	45.11	54.90	82.17

fare are well known and are reflected in the Yucay example; but Yucay provides little to guide us in our analysis of the Cuzco population, or of large population clusters higher in the Andes, or of those communities called on to provide workers for Huancavelica, Potosí, or other mining centers.[18]

To the east of Yucay lies Paucartambo, well known for its production of coca leaves, which by the end of the sixteenth century were used throughout the Andes by native residents. Paucartambo was also known as Los Andes. Most of the region is rugged and is characterized by high humidity and dense vegetation. Although the region is geographically close to Cuzco, the Incas were unable to establish full control over the inhabitants of the *tierra caliente* at the base of the montaña. The Spanish also failed to fully penetrate and control the people of the upper edges of the Amazon basin. Yet, because of tremendous profits that could be made in the production of coca, the upper montaña became important and was settled.[19]

Coca had been grown in the Andean area of South America long before the rise of the Incas. Its cultivation was not limited to the eastern edges of the Andes. If the temperature was warm enough, and water ample, then varieties of the bush could be grown elsewhere. Edward Lanning found coca leaves at the site of Asia in the southern part of the central coast and dated them at 1314 ± 100 B.C. Varieties of the plant were cultivated at several locations along the coast. With the rise of the Inca, use of the leaf was restricted to members of the royal family and the local nobility. Coca was also used during local religious rites. The Inca limited consumption of the leaf to the few. After the European conquest the chewing of the leaf quickly became common for all elements of Indian society. The appeal was great: The reward was a lower feeling of fatigue; the pain of hunger and thirst slackened; the user was able to do strenuous work. Matienzo noted coca was one of the few things that could bring pleasure or contentment to an otherwise unhappy people. Observers even said coca had a good effect on the health of teeth and gums, and some elderly Spaniards picked up the habit. Blacks who chewed coca experienced the same benefit as Indians: a lessening of pain.[20]

Quickly, native Andean inhabitants became characterized by the custom of chewing the leaf. Foreign travelers report the ubiquity of the practice in the Andes well into the twentieth century. The leaves for personal consumption are generally carried in a small bag, or pouch, and are chewed along with *llipta,* a mixture of ground bone, ash, and lime. The mixture helps release small amounts of the cocaine, which affect the nervous system. "When asked why they carry the mixture in their mouths, they reply that they experience little hunger or thirst, and are more vigorous and strong."[21]

By the 1580s coca production and use had become a major part of Peru's economy. In the 1549–51 period the price of coca was so high that incredible profits could be made. The demand for coca expanded more rapidly than the supply, and high prices were the result. In early testimony Cieza de León related that some coca-producing units yielded 80,000 pesos yearly. Acosta reported the value of the Potosí coca traffic reached 500,000 pesos annually. By the late 1560s between 1,500 and 2,000 Spaniards were directly involved in the coca system. In the region of Tono, Spaniards originally planted chacras of coca that sold at 12,000–20,000 pesos each. They were later resold at 56,000–60,000 pesos![22]

Indian demand for coca became one of the driving forces of the Andean economy and its link with the wider world. Juan de Matienzo put it succinctly: "It is certain that all, or the greatest part of the silver that has gone from Peru to Spain, has been that which the Indians have given for this leaf." He went on to argue that without coca the Indian would not work in the mines or elsewhere. "Coca is the money of the Indians of this land, as cacao is in New Spain."[23] Santillán said that in spite of the problems caused by the production of coca, its trade could not be stopped because of the close link with the mining economy. Coca did present a major health hazard for Peru's Indians, but the danger was more in the actual production and distribution of the leaf than in addiction to its use.[24]

The center of coca production became the eastern montaña, a very hot and humid strip along the lower edge of the sierra that the Spanish called Los Andes. Disease was a constant danger in the area: A sickness called *mal de los Andes* (probably *uta*) ulcerated the flesh of the face, especially the nose and lips. Although it did not appear to be contagious, it was incurable. We have no statistics on the rate of occurrence, but we do know that in 1562 about two hundred were being treated in the Indian hospital in Cuzco. Viceroy Toledo, during the visita general, sent licentiate Estrada, Friar Juan de Vivero of the Augustinian order, and physician Alegría to the Andes to study and report on health conditions and illnesses in the region. Part of the health problem in the area was linked to the drinking of chicha made of yuca, which apparently was followed by various illnesses. Toledo's ordinances for the coca region prohibited further use of yuca chicha. Toledo ordinances also provided for the support of a major Indian hospital in Toayma. One of the chief avowed causes for a high rate of mortality was the change in climate, when Indians of frigid highland repartimientos descended to work in the warm and humid coca fields. Santillán reported the change was the cause for the demise of "an infinite number." Under the Inca regime workers on the coca estates were mitimaes from other areas of the tierra caliente; therefore, they did not suffer from climatic variation. Santillán also wrote that others died under the Spanish system as a result of hunger and overwork. Moreover, "there is another pestilence, greater than all the aforesaid, and this is the disorderly covetousness of the Spaniards."[25]

The method of cultivation is outlined by Matienzo: the site was chosen in the montaña, then cleared, first by slash-and-burn techniques. The small plant was then placed in the ground, and the soil was carefully hoed. After one-and-a-half to two years the bush was large enough to produce marketable leaves. Maturity is reached in about the sixth year, and the plant will yield for up to forty years, if well cared for. The hardest and most dangerous labor was the preparation of new fields and the hoeing and cleaning of already established plots. The harvesting of the leaves (called the mita) was not considered strenuous and was done three times a year, or four times each fourteen months. At each picking laborers also worked and cleaned the soil. Toledo, in an effort to protect the health of the workers, ordered that the cleaning be done before 9:00 a.m., the picking until 3:00 p.m., then the hard labor again until sunset. An hour was set aside for eating. After harvesting, the leaves were placed in covered baskets (*cestos*) holding approximately 8 kilograms of leaves, and transported quickly to the highlands in order to avoid excess humidity. The head and shoulder harnesses and the weight of the cesto brought the total to 10 kilograms. The leaves then had to be dried in the sun, and, ideally, were to retain their green color. The best-quality leaves could be stored for up to a year.[26]

Various systems of coca production operated simultaneously in the montaña. Coca land in Inca times had been controlled by the Inca and curacas. The Crown had changed that system. By 1567 several types could be discerned: Some coca lands and repartimientos had been granted to individual encomenderos; others were held by the remnants of the Inca nobility (Doña Beatriz Coya, for example) or local chieftains (Don Francisco Chilche); other lands were purchased by Spaniards who used Indian workers from their own highland repartimientos or rented labor from curacas; also, some Indians migrated from the highlands or elsewhere and worked as permanent coca producers. Matienzo reported that the last group existed in the region "in great numbers." Many left wives in the sierra and remarried or took concubines in their new homes. Others brought along wives and children. If they survived the diseases they soon contracted, they generally were much healthier than later immigrants. The new resident allegedly had few children, however, and they were usually "of a poor color."[27]

By the 1570s, during harvest time, the region was filled with migrants. In addition to abundant Indian merchants, there were Spaniards, various types of Indian laborers, curacas, and "mestizos, mulattos, and free Black vagabonds." Such a diverse population caused problems. Viceroy Toledo, hoping to protect Indians from abuses, ordered the mestizos, mulattoes, and blacks out of the coca-producing region in 1572. Matienzo argued that treatment of Indians was best in places like Tono, where there was a large Indian population and close supervision of legislation.[28]

Was mortality exceptional in the coca area? Santillán reported that many villages were depopulated because of deaths in the coca production of Los Andes. Matienzo argued otherwise. He noted that some observers claimed, as in the case of Chuquiapo, that the coca labor was so unhealthy that, when ten Indians entered it, not even six returned; but he continued that such observations must not be allowed to become part of the historical record. Matienzo concluded that, even if the Spanish ordered the Indians not to work in the coca fields, they would go anyway.

Parish records for the coca area in the sixteenth century have not been located, but we do have the Toledo figure for the 1570s. Figures for approximately 1602 have been found for four of sixteen coca-producing repartimientos in the Cuzco region. These four communities (Gualla, Paucartambo, Amaybamba, and Matinga) were declining substantially more rapidly than the median rate of change for the south sierra for the 1572–1602 period. For Gualla, the number of tributaries of Doña Beatriz Coya fell from 190 to 70 during the period. In Paucartambo, the tributary population of Antonio Pereyra declined only from 242 to 228, but the total population fell from 1,531 to 952. Unfortunately, the data are not adequate to verify the generalization of either Santillán or Matienzo. It does appear that the numbers given for the coca region are not so accurate as those for most highland repartimientos. Indeed, at the time of Toledo's visita general, some groups in the area had not yet been inspected and taxed by the Spanish. The written record indicates a highly fluid population. With such a large number of migrants, some temporary and some permanent in the coca region, it is difficult to estimate mortality rates. Certainly, mortality rates could be high, yet the total population could appear relatively stable, if there were a large number of immigrants. Small highland villages involved in coca production could have suffered high losses due to the emigration of residents participating in the coca trade. It is clear that extra-hazardous health conditions awaited new workers in the coca zone. One unknown factor is the number of workers who might have fled to lower elevations to escape the excesses of the colonial regime. It would be especially easy to follow the flow of the rivers and quickly go beyond the effective jurisdiction of Spaniards. Future research on the historical demography of the coca area may help to shed light on the solutions to these enigmas.[29]

The corregimiento of Carabaya was also located on the edge of the montaña. Carabaya was a region rich in gold nuggets. The nuggets were taken by a modified washing process. Vast reservoirs were constructed, then broken so that the water cut away the earth piled in front of them, leaving the gold behind. Large amounts of gold were also washed from the Inambari River. Two Spanish towns were located in Carabaya, the most important San Juan del Oro, and there were several mining camps. The Indians of the corregimiento were not subject to the mitas of the major mines to the south or west. They were definitely used for the strenuous local mine labor, however. There were only six repartimientos in Carabaya, and only Carabaya itself had more than a thousand residents (1,374). From 1559 to 1573 the tributary population of Carabaya declined at a rapid rate of −4.54 percent annually. As with Paucartambo, which was subject to labor in the coca fields, and the corregimientos providing the bulk of mitayos for Potosí, population records are bad. No census was taken after Toledo's visita general through the early seventeenth century. Population change in the corregimiento is still a mystery. Contact between Carabaya and the outside world was via two highland communities; Asillo and Huancané, connected by roads to the gold-producing areas. The two trade centers acted as public markets for Carabaya.[30]

Andaguaylas, on the border of the central highlands, contributed mitayos for both Huancavelica and Castrovirreyna. Vázquez de Espinosa noted that the corregimiento was large, with many villages, and that it had an excellent climate and fertile soil. He reported that Andaguaylas had once been densely populated, but the civil wars between the Spaniards had reduced its population. Testimony taken at the residencia of the corregidor in 1634 related that Indians had been fleeing for the previous twenty years in order to avoid service, especially mine labor. Some Indians were reported to have gone on to the puna region and provinces up to 60 leagues away, and others were leaving with their families for the eastern montaña. The mestizo chronicler, Guamán Poma de Ayala, vividly depicted the extreme response to the constant pressure of forced labor:

> Victims of such grievances and suffering many of them have committed suicide, following the example of the Chanchas in Andaguaylas where some male and female Indians grouped on a small hill and willed to die at one time, not wishing to be surrounded by such evil and suffering.[31]

The largest repartimiento in the corregimiento was Andaguaylas la Grande, with a total population of almost 30,000 in 1573. Its rate of decline between 1573 and 1603 was −2.5 percent yearly for the tributary population and −2 percent for the total population. Both figures are much higher than the average for the central and southern highlands. The second-largest repartimiento was Cayara, with 3,000 residents. For the same period its tributary population was slipping at −2.1 percent annually, also substantially above the average.[32]

The corregimiento of Los Aimaraes, just to the south, bordered the central highland region, as did Andaguaylas. Los Aimaraes was situated at a moderately high elevation; the terrain was broken and crossed by mountain ranges. In the early seventeenth century the region was thickly settled with villages built on the slopes, about one day's journey from each other. The chief agricultural products were potatoes, wheat, corn, fruits, cereals, and livestock. A number of important mines of gold, silver, lead, and other metals dotted the countryside. The Indians of Aimaraes were subject to the Castrovirreyna mita. By the end of the 1620s the population had fallen to the point that it was impossible to collect the assessed tribute or to find mitayos for the mine labor. A major cause for concern was the fact that the Indians were forced to contribute at old rates, because new tribute assessments had not been made. In 1627 the repartimiento of Collana Aimara was still taxed at the Toledo rate of 4 March 1580. Taipe Aimara was paying on the basis of the 8 July 1605 assessment. In worse condition were the tributaries of Cayao Aimara, who were forced to contribute the 16 October 1575 quota! In 1625 the tribute rate per individual reached about seven pesos, roughly twice that owed by a tributary in Toledo's era. In 1626 the curacas of Cayao were jailed, and colonial officials held a public sale of the property of the curacas to help pay uncollected tribute. During a new inspection of the repartimiento of Challaunca in 1627 the visitadores reported that the area was being rapidly depopulated. Indians were traveling to the silver mines of Chocolococha in Castrovirreyna and were not returning. In 1627 the corregidor of Los Aimaraes complained that he was unable to collect the tribute from the 456 Indians of the corregimiento who were required to work in the mine because they had moved. The same problem existed in the repartimientos of Mutca y Pariaca, Quichuas y Tintay, Guamanpalpas, and Atancanas.[33]

Indians from the corregimiento of Cotabambas were also subject to the mita draft of Huancavelica. Cotabambas was separated from the central sierra by the corregimientos of Andaguaylas, Aimaraes, and Abancay, so the distance to the mercury mines was great, approximately 300 kilometers. The elevation of Cotabambas was relatively high, and the most important agricultural commodities were llamas, potatoes and other root crops, and corn. In 1630 colonial officials compiled a list of all mitayos to serve as reference for the payment of the travel stipend. The tributary population was also recorded (see Table 51). Eight of the nine repartimientos of Cotabambas were large, with populations of more than a thousand. The sex ratios of all indicate a substantial lack of males. The two largest repartimientos, Cotabambas and Omasayos, both had a total population of more than 10,000 in 1573, yet their sex ratios were 73. There were even fewer males in the decade of the 1590s, with the sex ratio of Cotabambas 69 and Omasayos 52. Such sex ratios, if the data are accurate, reflect a substantial disproportion between the sexes. Males either died, migrated, or avoided record keepers. The sexual imbalance must have influenced family establishment and the number of children born and

Table 51. *Huancavelica mitayos from Cotabambas, 1630*

Repartimiento	Tributaries	Mitayos	Period	Annual tributary decline	Period	Annual tributary decline
Cotaneras	321	45	(1575–1605)	−1.3	(1605–1630)	−1.2
Guayllamisa	26	3	(1572–1599)	−1.3	(1599–1630)	−1.7
Cotabambas	800	114	(1573–1599)	−1.0	(1607–1630)	−1.8
Aquira	623	89	(1578–1609)	−0.7	(1609–1630)	−1.1
Piti Yanaguaras	596	76	(1571–1591)	0.1	(1605–1630)	−0.6
Maray Yanaguaras	320	45	(1571–1640)	−2.3		
Guancallo y Chacaro	180	25	(1572–1599)	−0.8	(1599–1630)	−1.1
Anocallas (?)	86	12				

must have contributed to further population decline. Full census category returns are available for the repartimiento of Omasayos in 1573 and 1594. The figures provide the best insight we have of what occurred in the area during the 1589–91 epidemic period. The number of tributaries fell from 1,781 in 1573 to 1,165 in 1594. The most catastrophic decline took place in the young male category. Here the change was from 2,088 to 432 just twenty-one years later! At the same time, the number of old and disabled males increased from 431 to 557. One generation of children was, for practical purposes, wiped out. The rates of change for the tributary population of the corregimiento of Cotabambas were relatively near the −1.1 percent average for the region in the period from about 1572 to 1600 but in most cases accelerated slightly from the later date to 1630.[34]

The corregimiento of Parinacochas, south of Aimaraes, also sent mitayos to work in the silver mines of Castrovirreyna. Part of the region had a mild climate, allowing for considerable production of corn. Native and Spanish cereals, including wheat, and potatoes and fruit were grown, and there were ranches for various types of livestock. Much of the area was rich in gold and silver deposits. The repartimiento of Parinacocha, with a total population of 11,072 in 1572, was required to pay 11,231 pesos in tribute. Of that figure, 7,657 pesos were contributed in gold and silver, which were probably produced locally. Tribute requirements suggest the climate of Parinacocha was mild: 600 fanegas of corn, 100 fanegas of wheat, and 159 fanegas of chuño. The sex ratios demonstrate a preponderance of males: 103 in 1572 and 121 in 1602. The tributary population of Parinacocha actually increased between 1572 and 1591, at +0.34 percent; yet fell a catastrophic −22.49 percent in the epidemic year 1591–2, then continued to decline at the rate of −1.66 percent annually during the next decade.[35]

The corregimiento of Condesuyos situated to the southeast of Parinacochas also contributed mitayos for the silver mines of Castrovirreyna. Because of the location of Condesuyos, mitayos had to work in the city of Arequipa as well. There were several mines in Condesuyos, and llama and alpaca production was high. All twelve repartimientos in Condesuyos contained over a thousand inhabitants in the 1570s. Data are available to calculate rates of change from the early 1570s to 1602 for nine of the twelve repartimientos of Condesuyos. In seven cases the rate of tributary population exceeds the median figure for the southern sierra. In two cases, Achamarcas and Achanquillo Yanque, the rate is higher than 3 percent yearly. The tributary population of Achamarcas fell from 385 to 138 between

1571 and 1602; that of Achanquillo Yanque declined from 317 to 102 for the same period. The tributary figures for the repartimiento of Viraco are especially complete. In Viraco the rate of change from 1572 to 1591 was −1.46 percent; then, −1.74 percent between 1591 and 1599; −2.58 from 1599 to 1624; and finally −3.69 between 1624 and 1645. The figures for the corregimiento of Condesuyos suggest excessively high population loss during the period. There were more females than males. It is possible that male population loss was occurring during the Castrovirreyna mita, that other men migrated to and remained in Arequipa, and that some may have migrated to the south coastal region. Most repartimientos of Condesuyos were located on or near the various tributaries of the Majes River, which flows into the Pacific at Camaná. Connections between Condesuyos and the coast were close throughout the period.[36]

To the southeast of Condesuyos and north of the city of Arequipa lay the corregimiento of Los Collaguas. The five repartimientos that made up the region were large, ranging in size in the time of Toledo from 2,400 to 17,000. In 1591 mitayos had been briefly ordered to serve in Castrovirreyna, but the continuous demand for laborers for the building in Arequipa and for work in surrounding fields brought about revocation of the order, and in fact the Collaguas Indians were spared from all major mining mitas until the discovery of local mines at Cailloma in the early seventeenth century. The alliance between the Spanish residents of the southern capital and the Indians of Los Collaguas proved to be a mixed blessing, for labor conditions in and around Arequipa were often hard. Yet the population of the Río Colca valley apparently declined less rapidly than in other areas. The largest of the repartimientos, Yanque Collaguas, with a total population of 17,000 in 1572, declined slowly, at −0.8 percent. The smallest repartimientos, Cavana de la Torre, declined most rapidly at −1.5 percent.[37]

A number of censuses for the Collaguas region have been discovered and are currently being analyzed by several scholars. The 1591 census of the Hurinsaya moiety of Yanque Collaguas provides a clear case of the population characteristics of a southern highland community during the period. The Indians were expected to contribute silver, cloth, and livestock. The count, taken by the corregidor licenciate Gaspar de Colmenares, was initiated on 31 August 1591. The official was assisted by scribe Pedro de Quiroz and interpreter Diego Coro Inga. The remaining record is incomplete, but the total population enumerated exceeds 2,000, enough to provide an ample universe for statistical generalization for the region. The results are recorded in Table 52 and

Table 52. *The 1591 population of Los Collaguas, 10-year-cohorts*

Age	Population		Percentages		
	Men	Women	Men	Women	Sex ratio
0–9	302	276	13.49	12.33	109.42
10–19	130	126	5.80	5.63	103.17
20–29	293	219	13.09	9.79	103.79
30–39	94	90	4.20	4.02	104.44
40–49	204	181	9.12	8.09	112.70
50–59	76	106	3.40	4.74	71.70
60–69	32	50	1.43	2.23	64.00
70–79	27	21	1.21	0.94	128.57
80+	7	1	0.31	0.04	700.00
No age data	1	2	0.04	0.09	50.00
Total	1,116	1,072	52.10	47.90	108.77

Figures 14 and 15. As has already been noted in the case of Lima, Acarí, Huánuco, and Yucay, the age data are faulty. Age-heaping patterns in the 1591 Collaguas census parallel the others. There is no

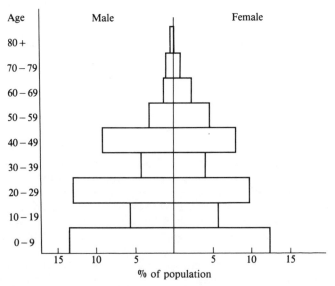

Figure 14. Ten-year cohort population pyramid for the Collaguas, 1591.

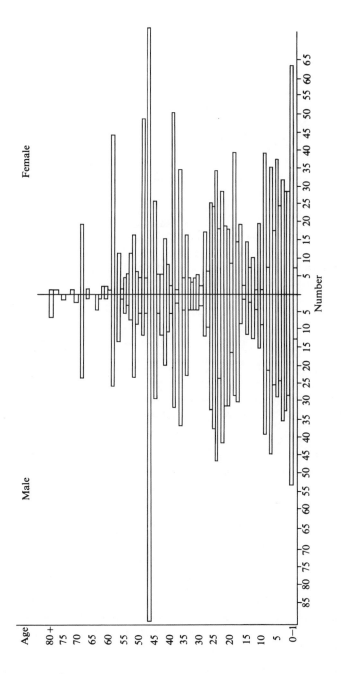

Figure 15. Population pyramid for the Collaguas, 1591.

major change with respect to the time or place, although it appears that certain enumerators had their own peculiar preferences. The ninety men age 48 present another attempt of the royal fiscal agents to maximize the amount of tribute collected. Many of the ninety might be expected to be over the legal tribute-paying age. The large number of women in the cohort age 48 is evidently a consequence of the fact that the enumerator often assigned the wife the same age as her spouse. At the 50-year cohort there were forty-eight women as opposed to eleven men. Part of the difference must be accounted for by the inclusion of men older than 50 in the tributary ranks.

The 0–9 cohort is the largest in the population pyramid, yet the group of small babies is significantly smaller than it should be, compared with the group ages 1 to 2. Underenumeration of the newly born and high infant mortality are the likely explanations. The 10–19 cohort is significantly smaller than it should have been. Mortality during the 1585–91 epidemic period is unlikely to be the only cause for the small size of the group. The 30–39 cohort is also smaller than one would expect from the size of the 20–29 and 40–49 groups. The small size of the 10–19 cohort is related to the equally small 30–39 cohort. The 30–39 generation experienced heavy mortality in the 1558–9 epidemics of measles, smallpox, and influenza that affected them as small children. Close examination of the full population pyramid reveals that the two small generations are spaced approximately fourteen years apart. The total number of children born in a small population will obviously be small. The consequences of an epidemic go far beyond the generation immediately infected. Likewise, the large 20–29 cohort is a reflection of the large group ages 40–49 counted in 1591. Those who were 40 to 49 in 1591 passed through the period of greatest fertility (18 to 34) without suffering significantly from disease. The relatively large cohort 0–9 represents the fertility of the 20–29 group. From the age of 40 upward through the eighties there is a general progression. It should be noted, based on the record of survivors of later cohorts, that the number of those 70 and over was larger than expected. These fifty-six inhabitants of the area would have been born before 1521. There is rough parity between males and females at the age of 70 plus. Had demographic conditions been "normal" the population in 1591 should have been sharply larger than recorded.

The 1591 Collaguas census reveals other important aspects of the population. The number of children per couple is recorded in Table 53. If the data are correct, there is a surprisingly small number of large families in the Collaguas region in the period. The average number of

Table 53. *Number of children per couple, Collaguas, 1591*

Number of children	0	1	2	3	4	5	6
Number of couples	152	130	104	64	19	3	2

children per couple was 1.33. The size of the completed family was larger. Some older siblings set up their own households, and high infant mortality also affected the total number of children currently living in a family. Nonetheless, given the small number of offspring in each family, the total population would be likely to continue to decline for some time into the future.[38]

The Collaguas pyramid once again demonstrates the demographic consequences of European disease. An epidemic affected not only those immediately infected but also the whole population structure through its life cycle. The total population of the Collaguas region was large, and the Collaguas never became extinct, in contrast to many coastal peoples. Nonetheless, in the first century after European contact, the Collaguas population continued its moderate decline.

The corregimiento of Ubinas was located in the highlands southeast of the city of Arequipa. In the sixteenth century it was part of the district of Arequipa. There were ten repartimientos in Ubinas, and most were small: Only Carumas Grande, Pocosi, and Ubinas exceeded 1,000 inhabitants during the administration of Viceroy Toledo. The elevation of the region was high, the terrain was broken, and it was an area of intense earthquake activity. Tribute for the Ubinas repartimiento was required in silver and wool and cotton cloth, not in other agricultural products. For Carumas the tribute was in silver, cotton cloth, wheat (40 fanegas), corn (20 fanegas), and chickens. The Indians of Pocosi, including a few inhabitants living along the seacoast near Arequipa, contributed silver, corn, and service in the fields of the encomendero. The Ubinas region was shaken by a major earthquake and volcanic eruption in 1600. A contemporary wrote, "It left the whole country, crops and stock, burned and devastated, and some villages in the provinces were destroyed; the land remained scorched and burned, and nothing would grow for a long time, its fertility having been impaired."[39] We already studied the impact of the earthquake on the south coast, where it nearly destroyed the city of Arequipa and where the fields were reportedly covered in places with a meter of volcanic ash and cinders. The sky was darkened as far away as Cuzco by the clouds of ash swept northward by the southerly winds.

Of the three largest repartimientos, we have good data only for Ubinas. The tributary rate of decline there jumped from −0.83 percent annually in 1573–91 to −1.70 percent between 1591 and 1602. For that same period (1591–1602) the rate of decline of tributaries for Cochuna was −6.3 percent, a very rapid decline that was probably related to the earthquake. Seven rates of the ten repartimientos can be calculated for the period from 1573 to 1602, and all tributary rates but one are above the median rate of decline for the southern highlands.[40]

Six corregimientos located within the boundary of modern Peru contributed to the famed mita of Potosí in the seventeenth century: Quispicanche, Azangaro or Collasuyo, Urcosuyo or Atuncolla, Canas y Canches, Paucarcolla, and Chucuito. The repartimiento closest to the silver-mining center was Chucuito on the shores of Lake Titicaca. Yet Chucuito is located more than 500 kilometers from Potosí. Quispicanche bordered the city of Cuzco and was 200 kilometers farther to the north. Although Potosí is situated in what is now Bolivia, in the altiplano some 500 kilometers from the Peruvian border, a survey of the development of that complex is necessary because of its obvious impact on the demography of Peru.[41]

The great silver mine of Potosí was discovered around 1545. Spaniards had begun exploitation of silver at the Inca-period mine of Colqueporco in 1543, only 30 kilometers from Potosí. In April of 1545 mine operators at Porco discovered the source of silver being taken by an Indian and filed claims to the land. By July of 1545 Spanish pressure for Indian labor at Potosí resulted in a revolt of the village of nearby Cantumarca and those inhabiting neighboring valleys. Indians charged that Spaniards were illegally forcing them to build houses, and in the ensuing skirmishes three Europeans and fifty natives were killed. By September 1545 there were 170 Spaniards and 3,000 Indians settled at the base of the *cerro* of Potosí. Two years later there were approximately 2,500 houses and 14,000 inhabitants. Potosí was not laid out on the typical colonial urban gridiron pattern. Streets were narrow and crooked, as are those of many mining towns. Until the introduction of the mercury amalgamation process, refining was by the traditional native practice: wind furnaces (*huayras*) were placed at or near the tops of hills to use the high winds. The fuel could be charcoal or ichu, and wind velocity could be controlled to reach the desired temperatures in miniature "blast furnaces." The melted silver was then cooled and transported down the hills for two final refining processes. Indian labor was at first by free wage earners. Production, especially after the conclusion of the civil wars, grew slowly until

1566, when the best veins were exhausted. Two factors helped bring about the economic recovery of Potosí after the early 1570s. One was the introduction of the mercury amalgamation process for the extraction of silver from the ore. The other was Viceroy Toledo's order assigning Indian mitayos for mine labor.[42]

When described by López de Velasco in the early 1560s, Potosí included 400 houses of Spaniards, almost all of whom were merchants or miners. Indians were living in their "ranches" or ayllus and numbered between 30,000 and 50,000. Spanish homes were often two stories high with tile roofs, whereas the traditional Indian habitations were low and covered with straw. The elevation is too high for trees or food crops, and all goods had to be imported. López de Velasco stated Potosí had been from the first a major market for Indians and Spaniards. Goods were exchanged for the mined silver. Several small streams passed through the city, and there were mills and washings (*lavaderos*) for the metal. The mills were necessary to crush the ore in preparation for the amalgamation process. By the end of the sixteenth century there were 150 mills, thirty powered by animals, the remainder using water power. Large amounts of water were also used in the patio process, as we have seen in the discussion of Huancavelica. By 1611 the population of Potosí reached 160,000. The composition of the population included 76,000 Indians, 6,000 blacks and mixed bloods, 35,000 Creoles, and 3,000 *peninsulares*.[43]

A key factor in understanding the impact of the Potosí mita on the Indians is that mita labor was only one form of work at the mines. A 1603 report stated that of 58,800 Indians working at Potosí, 5,100 were mitayos, or less than one in ten. In addition to the mitayos there were 10,500 *mingas* (contractual workers) and 43,200 free wage earners. Yet mitayos were required to do the work others refused: predominantly the transport of the ore up the shafts to the mouth of the mine.[44]

Causes of death of the Potosí mitayos were similar to those for mine workers in other areas of the Americas. Mortality from one major cause of deaths in Huancavelica, mercury poisoning, was not so dangerous in Potosí, save in the actual amalgamation process. Frequent cave-ins took their toll. In 1595 the Mendieta mine collapsed, killing 300 Indians and two Spanish miners. Few escaped in such catastrophes. In 1616 eight Indian miners were buried in a Potosí mine but managed to clamber out sixteen days later; the escape was heralded as a major "miracle." Deep shafts, with inadequate ventilation, were slowly filled with carbon monoxide from the burning candles, and the respiration of the workers used up available oxygen.

As in Huancavelica, the ore had to be carried from the warm mine caverns to the frigid exterior, and pneumonia and respiratory infections were common. One of the greatest hardships of Potosí was the difficulty of carrying the ore up to the surface. Near the entrance was a great central shaft, which extended to a depth of about 250 meters. It was necessary to ascend or descend using a pair of ladders, with leather steps at 55-centimeter intervals. This was the most strenuous work in the mine and was left to the mitayos. The daily quota for each worker was twenty-five sacks of ore, weighing about 45 kilograms each. The journeys up and down were dangerous, and falling rock could kill or injure the worker; or one of the steps could break. Rodrigo de Loaisa wrote in 1586: "If twenty healthy Indians enter on Monday, half may emerge crippled on Saturday."[45]

Natural disasters occurred frequently. An eleven-day snowstorm in August 1557 left many people frozen in the streets. In 1567 a severe storm hit Potosí; hail was reported to be as large as pigeon eggs, and in a flood that followed thirty Indians were swept away. In 1588 intense rains again flooded Potosí; seventy-two houses were washed away, and thirty-six people drowned. In February of 1597, twenty-eight were killed during a hail and lightning storm. A drought struck in 1606; many died of thirst, and the water-powered mills could not crush the ore. In 1591–2 a general famine and crop failure made conditions especially difficult in the mining center because all goods had to be imported. Indians apparently did not suffer one type of mortality that hit the European population. Due to the high elevation, during the first years of settlement Spanish children died within a few hours of birth. The first boy to survive was born in 1584. European women generally migrated to lower valleys when their confinements approached.

Two of the worst disasters occurred in 1624 and 1626. In the 1574–7 period dams had been constructed and filled with water from runoffs during the rainy season. The water was to be stored to provide drinking water for the inhabitants and year-round power for the mills. At 5:00 p.m. on 17 March 1624 the San Salvador dam broke and destroyed much of the Indian sector of the city; approximately two hundred drowned. Then, at 1:30 p.m. on 15 March 1626 the Lake Caricari dam gave way and pushed down hardest on the Spanish side of the city. A total of 4,000 inhabitants died in the second catastrophe, 58 Spanish and 52 Indian blocks were wiped out, and 120 mills were destroyed.[46]

Epidemics must also have been a major cause of Indian mortality, but only one in the period prior to 1620 is mentioned in the *Anales* of

Potosí: that of 1560. In October of that year an unknown type of "peste" infected the population. Some people who contracted the disease died within twenty-four hours, their legs doubled to their stomachs. Others had a high fever and expired in two days. Still others were covered with boils with yellowish secretions. The epidemic lasted into the early months of 1561, but with the arrival of the rains it gradually subsided. There is, however, a striking lack of correlation between epidemics and silver production at Potosí (see Figure 16). There appears to be no appreciable change in metal output even during the 1589–91 epidemic period. Several possible explanations may be noted. First, the non-Indian resident population, which was high, may have filled the manpower gap, thus maintaining the level of production. Second, rapid Indian immigration could have continued and made up the difference between disease deaths and the labor requirement. Third, Potosí was situated at a very high elevation, and epidemic mortality levels are lowest at high elevations. It may be that the 1589–91 epidemics missed Potosí altogether. Had they decimated the city, mention of the fact would be expected in the city annals, but there is no record in the standard contemporary account of the mining center. There is, of course, a long-term decline in Potosí's output and the Indian population, but a direct correlation between the two deserves further study before definitive conclusions are warranted.[47]

One type of mortality was peculiar to Potosí. Almost from the beginning of settlement the miners were battling each other. Potosí quickly became one of the most hazardous cities of the Indies in which to live. During the civil wars of the conquerors the village of Cantumarca was burned by Francisco de Canteno for allegedly harboring troops of the traitor Marcos Gutiérrez. Strife broke out between various Spaniards in 1548, and approximately forty died. In 1564 there were conflicts between factions: Castillians versus Andalusians and Portuguese versus Extremadurans; twenty-three were killed. Intermittent strife continued. In 1582 there were fights between Basques and Extremadurans in which eighteen died. In one conflict the Basques set fire to the Extremaduran barrio and eight houses were destroyed. In 1587 the daughter of the corregidor of Potosí died in a fire set during factional strife. In 1588 there were battles among Andalusians, Extremadurans, and Spaniards born in Peru, as well as fights involving Basques, Navarrese, and Gallegos; in all, eighty-five were killed that year. In 1593 battles broke out among Basques, Extremadurans, and the young 16–18-year-old Criollos of Potosí; sixteen died. In 1600 there were new fights between the Basques and

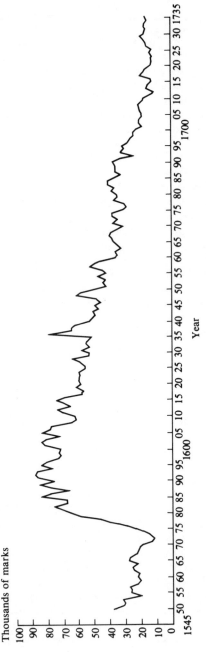

Thousands of marks

Year

Figure 16. Registered silver production in the Potosí district, 1550–1735. (From Bakewell, "Registered Silver Production," pp. 86–7.)

the Andalusians; several were killed, thirty wounded. The next year saw skirmishes between Basques and Criollos in which many died. In 1604 there were fights involving Basques, Andalusians, and Criollos. The viceroy ordered the corregidor to disarm participants after a battle between Andalusians and Vizcayans in 1605 over a young lady. More bloodshed occurred in 1608 in the Indian village of Cantumarca and resulted in the death of fifty-two Basques, twelve Criollos, and seven Portuguese. The first report of Indian casualties after Toledo dates from 1609, when five Indians were killed during a battle in which three Basques and two Criollos succumbed. It is likely Indians were killed in preceding fights. Renewed outbreaks occurred in 1614: In a battle between Basques and Criollos, seventy of the former and twenty of the latter perished. The Civil War, as one observer called it, resulted in thirty dead the following year. More battles took place in 1616. Between 1617 and 1618, 120 died, with warfare continuing into 1619. In 1620 a new "game" was added to the hazardous streets of Potosí. At strategic corners of the main plaza gangs of ten to twelve youths guarded the streets. Those who wanted to pass had to prove their skill with the sword. Consequently, there were more dead and wounded. Violence did not diminish, despite continued efforts of the colonial officials and the clergy. In 1621 sixty were killed, 210 wounded. In 1622 the strife assumed the full proportions of a civil war. As had been the tendency in preceding years, conflict rotated around the Basques, on one hand, versus the Criollos and others on the other. The Basques, with their mining expertise and economic acumen, had managed by the end of the sixteenth century to dominate much of the economic life of Potosí. This position, coupled with traditional local Spanish loyalties, had been the source of much of the Potosí conflict. On 10 June 1622 the War of the Vicuña began. Criollos dressed in vicuña cloth attacked the Basques throughout the region. For the year, the European dead reached 381, most of them Basques. A total of 1,000 Indians, mestizos, mulattoes, and blacks also perished in the conflict. The 1623 toll included 1,600 Europeans in Potosí, 300 Indians, blacks, and mulattoes, with an additional 35 dead in Chuquisaca and 400 in the area surrounding Potosí. Battles continued in 1624 and left a total of 400 Spanish dead, plus 2,000 Indians, blacks, and mulattoes.[48]

It is difficult to ascertain Indian mortality during the street fighting in Potosí. It seems likely that mitayos from the corregimientos of Peru tried to avoid the conflict as much as possible. They were required to labor in the mines, and when they emerged from the shafts each evening they probably went directly to their quarters and kept out of the Spanish sector of the city. It is much more likely that permanent Indian residents of Potosí, those who worked for one mine owner or another, could be brought into the fray on the side of their employer. It is also true that a local encomendero could attempt to use his charges as aides during the skirmishes. From the little data available, admittedly inadequate for statistical generalization, roughly half the deaths, when categories other than Europeans are included, were Indians, mulattoes, and blacks. Some mitayos from Peru could have been among these. In the early seventeenth century, however, only 10 percent of the Indian population of Potosí were mitayos. Hence, conflict mortality of Peruvian Indians laboring in Potosí to fulfill the mita requirements was probably not great, clearly far less than deaths from such causes as cave-ins, floods, and epidemics.

The Crown repartimiento of Chucuito, located on the southwestern shore of Lake Titicaca, was the largest Indian repartimiento in the viceroyalty, with a total population of 74,988 in 1573. The sex ratio of Chucuito in 1573 was 93, the composition of the population was in a "normal" range, with tributaries making up 23.71 percent, muchachos 22.20 percent, the old and disabled males 2.19 percent, and women 51.89 percent. According to records, the tributary population of Chucuito actually increased from 1567 to 1573, at a rate of +2.39 percent, then slowly decreased to 1613 at −0.71 percent yearly. Still, the population decline did affect the Potosí mita and vice versa. In 1617, Don Pedro Cutipa, curaca of the pueblo of Acoria and acting "captain" of the Indians of Chucuito, complained that he was able to supply only 1,194 mitayos of the 1,854 that had been established as the quota in 1613.[49]

Alfonso Messia, who wrote around 1600, chronicles the impact of the Potosí mita on the inhabitants of Chucuito. The curaca of each community issued a notice of the coming mita two months before the deadline for departure. The approximately 2,200 mitayos who left each year from Chucuito normally took with them wives and children.

> I have twice seen them and can report that there must be 7,000 souls. Each Indian takes at least eight ot ten llamas and a few alpacas to eat. On these they transport their food, maize and chuño, sleeping rugs and straw pallets to protect them from the cold, which is severe, for they always sleep on the ground. All this cattle normally exceeds 30,000 head.[50]

The 480-kilometer trip from the shore of Lake Titicaca to Potosí took about two months to complete. The mitayos earned forty-six pesos during seventeen weeks of work at the mining center, but it cost them a hundred pesos for their journey and tribute. In all, they were at

Potosí about six months and spent four months in transit. "Only some two thousand people return: of the other five thousand some die and others stay at Potosí or the nearby valleys because they have no cattle for the return journey."[51]

Paucarcolla in the sixteenth century was administered from La Paz. Situated across Lake Titicaca from Chucuito, its boundaries extended toward the Amazon basin. Most residents of its repartimientos gained a living through wool production or through the mining of local silver ore. Unfortunately, with one exception no new censuses were taken in the immediate post-Toledo era, so the local impact of forced labor at Potosí is difficult to measure. Urcosuyo, also called Atuncolla or Cabana and Cabanilla, was another center for textile production. Here, too, information is weak. Recounts were taken for eight of fifteen repartimientos, and five actually increased in population. Were officials selectively conducting new enumerations in grants they expected to remain stable or increase? Collasuyo (Azangaro and Asillo) was situated between Urcosuyo and Paucarcolla on Lake Titicaca's north shore. Most grants were large, and few counts were taken after Toledo's visita general. Here, also, there appears to be a tendency to avoid taking a new count because of the possible negative impact on tribute and the mitayo labor force.[52]

The corregimiento of Canas y Canches was located on the Cuzco–Potosí road north of Urcosuyo. There were eighteen repartimientos in the district, and twelve had over a thousand inhabitants. Vázquez de Espinosa described the Indians of Canas y Canches in the early seventeenth century:

> These are very reasonable Indians, unassuming and great workers; for their mita they go to Potosí, which is 200 leagues away. They have large llama ranches, and wear native costume, like the others, made of llama wool; they have good fields for their wheat, corn, potatoes, and other cereals and root crops . . . The province of Los Canas contains vast level meadows which they call savannas or pampas, and they have great numbers of llama and sheep ranches on them, on account of their wide pasturage. The pampas are very cold and yield no crop but potatoes.

New counts of repartimientos of the period were made in ten of the eighteen cases. In eight, the recorded tributary population actually increased, one decreased at a rate less than the south highland median, and one decreased at a more rapid rate.[53]

Quispicanche, between the borders of Cuzco and Canas y Canches, is also reported to have contibuted mitayos for Potosí, about 700 kilometers to the south. The corregimiento was relatively high in elevation and was broken by the Yucay River, which flows northward to the Urubamba. Unlike the other corregimientos, Quispicanche was made up of a relatively large number of small repartimientos. Approximately twenty of thirty had under a thousand inhabitants during the 1570s, and only two grants had over two thousand residents. The proximity to the city of Cuzco apparently accounts for the small size of grants. The corregimientos of Chilques, Abancay, Paucartambo, and Yucay, which also surrounded Cuzco, were characterized by numerous petty grants. Around Lima the repartimientos also had a small number of inhabitants. The competition for grants of Indians near major colonial centers was intense. Spaniards desired to maintain formal access to Indian workers, as we have seen. The encomendero's residence was in the colonial city, and he used inhabitants of nearby communities for a variety of personal services, often in spite of specific legal prohibitions against such practices. In order to reward as many claimants as possible, the Crown often granted a small repartimiento near a major Spanish city, in additon to a larger repartimiento situated in the distant rural countryside. For nine of the repartimientos of Quispicanche two sets of tributary censuses are available, and the population between the 1570s and the 1600s declined in all cases but one. In only three cases did the rate exceed the median for the region.[54]

Several trends in the population change of the southern highlands emerge from the cases we have studied. First, in the post-Inca period the urban complex of Cuzco attracted Indian migrants, just as did other major colonial administrative centers. The fact that the capital was a focus of migration neutralized the local effects of the general demographic contraction. Cuzco was, and remains, the Indian capital of the Americas. Although its native population was shrunken during the colonial era, it was not abandoned, as were many lesser centers.

The coca-producing areas situated to the north and east of Cuzco on the edge of the Peruvian montaña also acted as a magnet, attracting all elements of colonial society who wished to share in the immense potential profits of the leaf. Natives actively participated in the process. Mortality of highland migrants to the warm, humid valleys was high, although the true extent cannot be ascertained, given the poor quality of early regional data. Permanent migrants who survived the first year experienced mortality similar to the long-time residents of the tierra caliente. At any rate, the possible gain from the coca trade outweighed the risks in the minds of many Indians who continued to move toward the area.

Several corregimientos in the western sector of the southern highlands contributed mitayos to the Huancavelica and Castrovirreyna mines located in the central highlands. Andaguaylas, Aimaraes, Cotabambas, Parinacochas, and Condesuyos all sent workers, oftentimes over relatively long distances, to labor in the mines to the north. The population loss of Andaguaylas, which sent mitayos to both mining centers, was especially pronounced and accelerated rapidly after 1608. Complete new post-Toledo censuses of Aimaraes were generally not made; consequently, the extent of depopulation of that area cannot be measured. There are, however, ample sources showing the impact of decline on local communities. The decline of Cotabambas appears to parallel the loss of most south Andean areas, as does that of Parinacochas. Condesuyos, however, which was in the unfortunate position of sending workers to Castrovirreyna and the city of Arequipa to the south, fell more rapidly than most.

The large population clusters in Los Collaguas avoided contributions of mitayos for the major mining centers, at least until the local discovery of silver at Cailloma in the early seventeenth century. Workers were sent to the city of Arequipa, but the population of most repartimientos in the region remained relatively stable. As the 1591 population pyramid (Figure 15) indicates, however, the area did not totally escape the severe consequences of epidemic disease.

Several Peruvian corregimientos sent mitayos to the silver mines of Potosí, located up to 700 kilometers to the south in what is now highland Bolivia. Potosí grew rapidly after its discovery in 1545. The Indian population jumped from about 3,000 in 1545 to 30,000–50,000 in 1561 to around 76,000 in 1611. Most of the inhabitants were permanent residents. The 1603 report delineates the relationship between the temporary mitayos and the full-time inhabitants: 5,100 mitayos of 58,800 Indians working at Potosí. The majority of Potosí's resident Indians had probably immigrated from the corregimientos of La Paz and Charcas, but it is clear that many of the mitayos who had come from Peru stayed on in the city.

For the southern highlands as a whole, there is a clear indication that European disease was less lethal at high elevations. Some diseases, especially those carried by insects such as malaria and yellow fever, could not be a significant problem in the higher sectors of the Andes, although they could be endemic in humid lowland areas. Also, it might be postulated that the contact between the Indian and the European was less in the highlands than in other regions. Dense Indian settlements would be less prone to disruption by Spaniards because the ratio of Spaniards to Indians would be smaller than elsewhere. Further, traditional patterns of marriage and childbearing would be more enduring where the aboriginal population remained relatively dense.

The low rate of decline calculated for the southern highlands could have been higher in reality, were more complete data available for the coca-producing region of Yucay and Paucartambo, the gold-mining area of Carabaya, and the six southern corregimientos that contributed mitayos for the silver mines of Potosí. It is probable that in these critical areas colonial officials and local economic interest groups blocked post-Toledo repartimiento population counts in order to keep tribute and mita quotas as high as possible. In most of the other corregimientos of the southern sierra, reassessments were made with some frequency.

By 1620, as a statistical consequence of the rapid decline of other regions of Peru, the population of the southern highlands comprised approximately 50 percent of all the Indian inhabitants of Peru. There were almost 600,000 Indians living in the southern highlands in 1570; in 1620 there were 350,000, of a total estimated 670,000 Indians in all of Peru.

14

An overview

The magnitude of the decline varies with the figures given for 1530; but in any case, it does not fundamentally alter the shape of the curve: whether the population diminished by half or three-quarters, the effects of this fall on social structures were every bit as devastating.

Nathan Wachtel, *Vision of the Vanquished*, p. 87

The demographic transformation of Peru was almost complete by the end of the first century after the Spanish arrived at coastal Tumbez. "Collapse" most aptly describes the process along the Pacific desert strip. With few exceptions, a once dense native population was wiped out and partially replaced by Europeans, Africans, and migrants from other regions. Remaining Indians were quickly integrated into the lower strata of colonial society. Collapse also occurred in the low-lying areas of the northern highlands. In the north and northeast, fewer outsiders immigrated to establish permanent settlements. That area therefore remained economically and socially outside the mainstream of the historical development of Peru during the colonial perod. The highlands proper, from Cajamarca, Conchucos, and Huailas southward to Lake Titicaca, also entered into the downward spiral, but in a less pronounced fashion. The highland population was more evenly spread over vast distances in contrast with the coastal populations, which were concentrated in narrow valleys. Population decline of the central and southern sierra was considerable; but not catastrophic as elsewhere. Large populations allowed the highland Indian to maintain social and economic institutions long after they were lost on the coast and in the far north. Much of the contemporary Peruvian highlands, in fact, retains a largely indigenous culture, in spite of contact with the Spanish and the wider western world for the past four-and-a-half centuries.

We have seen that the population contraction was selective even in coastal areas. Some valleys declined much more rapidly than others. The Lambayeque irrigated valley system fared considerably better than most nearby coastal agricultural areas. A reliable water supply and a sound economic base seem to have helped sustain the Lambayeque population. Transportation and communication centers, such as Olmos on the north coast and Arica on the south coast, even reversed the downward trend and increased, if only slightly, their populations. The major Spanish colonial administrative centers in the coastal area attracted Indian migrants from both the surrounding countryside and the highlands. In Lima the Indian population was scattered throughout the city and in the nearby Indian village of El Cercado. The same pattern existed in Arequipa, with many Indian immigrants living in Yanahuara. Trujillo, in the north, attracted its share of migrants. The major Spanish cities provided opportunities for advancement that were limited in traditional communities. Many of the immigrants were artisans and craftsmen, as is so vividly demonstrated in the 1614 Lima census. Others were house servants or agriculturalists who provided vegetables and other foodstuffs for urban residents. The early seventeenth-century Indian census of Lima should indicate the nature of other urban Indians in the period: large numbers of young adult working men, many unmarried residents, very small families, and a population that is increasing only as a result of continued heavy immigration. Censuses of the small agricultural communities of Huacho and Végueta, not far from Lima, also show the effects of heavy immigration of adult males. The larger populations of Cherrepe and Acarí, on the north and south coasts, illustrate the consequences of both migration and European epidemics that swept the region.

The availability of water was a key to the population stability of coastal valleys. The ecological balance was fragile, and large variations had great impact on coastal communities. The droughts in the Nazca and Umay valleys in the early 1590s caused much devastation, and survivors fled to other places where food was available. In an economic system where full reciprocity existed, as in the Inca state, temporary local crises were met by distribution of foodstuffs to needy areas from regions in which surpluses had been stored. In the Spanish colonial regime, however, this type of reciprocity was destroyed, and affected inhabitants were left either to starve or to migrate to communities not influenced by the drought. By emigrating, however, the Indians often lost the right to their land and found it difficult to return to native homes at the conclusion of the dry period. On the other hand, infrequent floods could have an equally devastating effect on the ecological structure of valley systems. The flood that afflicted residents of the north coastal Jequetepeque valley in 1578 is a case in point. Destroyed homes and irrigation systems required vast amounts of human labor to reconstruct. Economic and social dislocation lasted far longer than the actual inundation. Earthquakes were another type of natural disaster with an impact on Peru's population. The south coast was particularly vulnerable to seismic catastrophe. Volcanic eruptions and earthquakes occurred in the Arequipa area in 1582, 1600, and 1604. Perhaps the dual shock of drought and earthquake, on top of the epidemic deaths, explains why the sharpest demographic fall in Peru took place in the south coastal sector.[1]

In the highlands demographic diminution was also selective. The frontiers in the north and northeast, consisting of Jaén, Chachapoyas, and Moyobamba, rapidly lost their populations. The low elevation of the area and its high humidity were conducive to the spread of dangerous diseases. In addition to smallpox, measles, and influenza, which equally affected the natives at higher elevations, the diseases carried by insects spread rapidly. Yellow fever, malaria, and illnesses native to the upper Amazon basin took their toll.[2] The Europeans suffered equally and never established a complete hold over the area. Likewise, Spanish domination of the central and southern highlands extended only into the foothills, or montaña, of the upper Amazon. Neither had the Incas been able to control the land beyond the montaña. The flat floodplains and dense jungles of the area were only partially penetrated by European missionaries in the mid-seventeenth century. The initial reconnaissance by Spanish explorers in search of El Dorado in the sixteenth century gave way to intermittent expeditions with few practical results. Gold in the Chachapoyas area provided the inducement for consistent Spanish efforts in that region. In the south, the rich gold-producing sectors of Carabaya presented a similar opportunity, and both Europeans and Indian laborers were active. Nearer Cuzco, in Yucay and Paucartambo, the cultivation of coca and the tremendous profits to be made in its preparation and sale acted as a magnet for Indian migrants. Many settled there permanently and devoted their lives to the production of the leaf. Yucay and Paucartambo became centers of immigration in spite of the very high mortality in the warm and humid areas where coca flourished.

Colonial highland administrative cities also attracted Indian residents. Cuzco, the seat of the Inca Empire, had been a focus of migration prior to the conquest, but the freedom to move to Cuzco during the Inca regime was severely limited. After the conquest, as the Spanish converted the native capital into a colonial administrative center, large numbers of Indians entered it. At the same time, many who had been required to live in the city by the Inca returned to their homelands. In the early period of European domination Cuzco must have experienced constant movement in and out of the city. Huánuco, Cajamarca, and Huamanga (now Ayacucho) also attracted reasonable numbers of Indians from the rural countryside.

The greatest flow of highland migrants was directed toward the major mining centers. The weakest drift was probably in the north and was geared toward the silver mines in Huailas and Conchucos. The mercury mines of Huancavelica in the central highlands required a large labor force. The work requirements were met by permanent contract laborers, who either had lived nearby or had migrated to take work, or by mitayos after the labor reforms of Viceroy Toledo in the early 1570s. In the case of both permanent workers and mitayos, mortality in the mines was high. Floods, cave-ins, falls, pneumonia contracted in part because of the great temperature differences between the relatively warm mine interior and the very cold Andean atmosphere, and various forms of mercury poisoning contributed to a high death rate. It appears that mitayos suffered more than hired miners, perhaps because they were required to do the most dangerous work. Other mines, such as the Castrovirreyna silver center, also attracted permanent workers and used mitayos from other corregimientos. The surprising feature of highland mortality is that, in spite of hard mine labor, the population loss of the area was sharply less than that of the coast. The differential is highest in the south, where the coastal tributary population was falling at about -3.5 percent yearly from the 1570s to 1600s, whereas the highland was declining at -1.1 percent.

Indian migration was extensive during the period, and it varied from local travel of a few kilometers for nearby agricultural labor to a large-scale move to work in mines almost 1,000 kilometers distant. Some migration was seasonal, but often it was permanent. Some migration was forced, as with mita service; other was voluntary, such as the movement to urban areas or to native fields located in various ecological niches. Migration involved Peruvians and other Indians from as far away as Mexico and Chile. Viceroy Toledo's reducciones, the forced resettlement of Indians from scattered hamlets in Spanish-style towns, were also a form of forced local migration. Spaniards who usurped Indian lands created migrants, although little documentary evidence of such displaced persons is available in the sixteenth century, except along the coast.

Migration was selective: Males of an economically productive age changed residence most often and for the greatest distances. An Indian skilled in a needed craft, for example, might be more successful in an urban environment than in his native village. Women often moved to cities to work as domestics in Spanish homes, and many also became concubines of their masters. Indian migration tended to be oriented toward the coast from highland repartimientos. The migratory current was also directed toward urban and mining centers in the sierra; and Indians often moved eastward to the montaña region bordering the effective administrative jurisdiction of the Spaniards.[3]

The consequences of migration were great. Because men were the primary migrants, the resulting imbalance between the sexes adversely influenced the number of children born. Migration weakened traditional kinship patterns, especially the ayllu, because of the total disappearance of some units. Migration tended to break down customary barriers between isolated groups. Migration aided the rapid growth of cities and provided labor when and where it was needed most. Migration was also responsible for the death of thousands of Indians. Whether population movement was forced, as by the mita system, or voluntary, an Indian who left his home high in the Andes to work in coastal cities and plantations or to labor in coca-producing regions of the montaña faced increased susceptibility to disease and a higher risk of death due to the sudden change in environment. One observer, perhaps greatly exaggerating, suggested that yearly some two or three thousand Indians died in Lima from disease and starvation. Another reported in 1574 that over half the mitayos who descended to the coastal cities from the highlands died.[4]

| One of the most significant migratory flows in colonial American history resulted from the mita for Potosí. The purpose of the required movement of one-seventh of the tributary population of affected corregimientos was the extraction of silver from the mountain of Potosí. Spain's need for silver, to support its vast bureaucracy and military and to finance its dynastic designs in Europe and elsewhere, led to a compromise of the commitment to the welfare of its native American subjects.| Chucuito, on the edge of Lake Titicaca, was about 480 kilometers from Potosí, yet it was closest of the Peruvian corregimientos that ultimately became subject to the draft. Quispicanche, on the border of Cuzco and more than 800 kilometers from the silver mine, was required to send workers. Potosí quickly grew to be one of the largest seventeenth-century cities in the Americas, and over half its population was composed of Indians. Although most native permanent residents of Potosí were probably from La Paz and Charcas, a sizable number must have come from corregimientos within Peru proper. It is not yet possible to ascertain the exact figure, but future parish research may help to shed light on the issue. In spite of the harsh conditions in the Potosí mine and the difficulties incurred

during the annual trips to the center, Peruvian repartimientos contributing workers appear to have been declining at a rate comparable
to other central and southern highland areas. Perhaps if more post-
1570 censuses for the Potosí corregimientos were available, the rate
would be higher. It appears, however, that officials resisted new
population counts in southern Peru in corregimientos subject to the
Potosí draft. The effort was intentional: The purpose was to maintain
a high tribute and mita quota as long as possible.[5]

The child–woman ratios for several regions and periods further
demonstrate the differing demographic experience of the coast and
highlands. The ratio in Cherrepe on the north coast was 41 in 1572; in
south coastal Acarí the figure was 41.4 in 1593; and for the capital of
Lima it stood a relatively close 37.4 in 1614. The highland range was
likewise narrow: For Huánuco in 1562 the child–woman ratio was
66.1; Yucay's in 1571 was 74.2; and for Los Collaguas the ratio was
71.2 in 1591. In the high-elevation repartimientos a larger proportion of children survived than on the Peruvian coast in the early
colonial period. Children, just as adults in the highlands, suffered less
from diseases than did lowland residents. This explains, at least in
part, why the sierra could act as a pool for migrants to the coastal
sector. Central coastal Huacho, with a child–woman ratio of 83.6 in
1583, is a variant. As we have seen, the high ratio there follows a
decade free of major epidemics. It will be informative to compare
these results with the child–woman ratios for later periods when new
information becomes available.

The various population pyramids we have examined illustrated
vividly the consequences of the passage of epidemics through the
Andean area. In almost all cases children suffered from disease
mortality. Entire cohorts of infants and young children were wiped
out. With the exception of Lima in 1614, which presents an unusual
case because of heavy immigration of working males, it is possible to
trace the impact of epidemics using population pyramids. The effects
of an epidemic lasted long beyond the year in which the disease
infected local residents. The shrunken generation, as it passed
through its years of fertility, left fewer children of its own, and that
following generation also produced a small number of children. The
downward spiral, once it began, would continue until a new balance
was reached. In the cases of some coastal areas an equilibrium was
never achieved, and small population units became extinct.

It is evident that Indian mortality in early colonial Peru was very
high. The Indian death rate was certainly higher, primarily because of

the lack of immunity, than for other groups in the population, although black slave mortality may have been as high under severe labor conditions. Infant mortality was very high, just as it still is among Peruvian Indians. Sixteenth-century vital statistics are usually not complete enough to calculate Indian birth or death rates, but there is no doubt that Indian mortality was especially high during epidemics. In severe epidemics, as in the 1589–91 period, substantial segments of the population could be wiped out. It is apparent that children, mainly the very young, suffered a much higher rate of death than their parents. Mortality was also sex selective. Women almost always outnumbered men in the higher Andes in the sixteenth century. The pattern of above-average death rates for men living at high altitudes persists in the Andes in the twentieth century.

The birth rate was high in the sixteenth and early seventeenth centuries. The very rapid growth of the young male group, evident in the census returns for years following major epidemics, suggests a high birth rate. The imbalanced sex ratio and Spanish attempts to enforce the Catholic ideal of monogamy are factors that would depress the birth rate. Both, however, were circumvented by the Indian practice of concubinage. Even after persistent attempts, Spanish priests were able to suppress neither the indigenous custom nor idolatry in the first century after contact between the two peoples.[6]

By 1620 Indian Peru was highland Peru, especially from Cajamarca to Lake Titicaca. In this vast region the culture and language of native inhabitants were not destroyed but only transformed during the early colonial era. The Indian population of the highland region fell from 1.045 million to 585,000 in the half-century following 1570. In the same period the coastal population collapsed from 250,000 to 87,000. Although under severe pressure, the highland Indian was able to survive the shock of the Old World invasion. The Spaniard brought death through military combat, overwork, and forced migration. The new regime resulted in an increased dependence on alcohol and coca and contributed to suicides among the natives. Most of all, the European brought pestilence, such as had never before been experienced by the Andean peoples. The legend reported by the Indian chronicler Juan Santa Cruz Pachacuti in the early seventeenth century presents the native view of the introduction of epidemic diseases and the agony of demographic collapse. In the story, Huayna Capac was returning to Quito from northern conquests:

And when he approached the sea with his army, he saw clearly at midnight nearly a billion people, and no one knew who they

were. To this it is reported that he said they were the souls of the
living, that God had pointed out that they signify, in the coming pestilence, many would have to die; the souls said that they
came against the Inca, from which the ruler understood that it
[pestilence] was his enemy.

Huayna Capac continued with his army to Quito.

And then, at mealtime, a messenger in a black cloak arrived, and
reverently kissed the Inca, and gave the Inca a *putti,* or a closed
box with a key, and the Inca ordered the envoy to open the box.
But the emissary asked pardon, saying that the Creator ordered
that only the Inca could open it. The Inca, seeing the truth,
opened the box, and from it flew butterflies or moths scattering
until they disappeared. It was the pestilence of measles, and
within two days general Mihacnacamayta along with many other
captains died, all their faces covered with *caracha* [scabs]. Having seen what occurred, the Inca ordered the construction of a
stone house to hide in, and afterward concealed himself in it,
covering it with the same stone, and therein died.[7]

The legend is reminiscent of the story of Pandora's box of classical
antiquity. Perhaps Santa Cruz Pachacuti borrowed and embellished a
myth he had heard from a Spanish priest. Nonetheless, whether indigenous or partly transformed by the European experience, the tale
vividly portrays a universe on the edge of chaos. The European
epidemics were destined to shake the foundation of the Andean
World, and the best explanation for this sudden catastrophe that the
Indians could fathom was intervention by a supernatural power.

Yet the Indian in the highlands persisted. Why was he able to
survive while the coastal resident succumbed to the onslaught?
Spaniards were more prone to settle in coastal areas, near the sea, and
only entered the highlands in large numbers to search for and extract
mineral wealth. The Europeans tended to congregate in urban areas,
rather than live permanently in the countryside. By law, encomenderos were forbidden to live with their charges. Highland repartimientos were large enough in population for the encomenderos
usually to reside comfortably in the chief administrative cities, living
from their income. Consequently, Indo–Spanish contact was limited.
Furthermore, by sheer numbers the Indians overwhelmed the
Spaniards in the highlands. Large populations can more readily maintain traditional customs. We have seen the example of the inability of
bureaucrats and clergymen to stamp out concubinage. The evolution
of the colonial Spanish hacienda, and its concomitant impact on the
Indian community, took place later in the central and southern high-

lands than it did on the coast. And, most important for the demographic survival of the Andean people in the sierra, the high elevation and cool climate lessened the impact of disease, and the lower population density as the century progressed slowed the spread of epidemics.

Abbreviations used in notes

AGI   Archivo General de Indias (Seville)
AHC   Archivo Histórico (Cuzco)
ANP   Archivo Nacional del Perú (Lima)
BNL   Biblioteca Nacional (Lima)
BNM   Biblioteca Nacional (Madrid)
CDIHE   L. Torres de Mendoza (ed.), *Colección de documentos inéditos para la historia de España*
HAHR   *Hispanic American Historical Review*
HSAI   Julian H. Steward (ed.), *Handbook of South American Indians*

Notes

The problem in perspective

1. For a recent review of the state of the debate, see William M. Denevan (ed.), *The Native Population of the Americas in 1492* (Madison: Univeristy of Wisconsin Press, 1976), pp. 1–12, 35–42, 77–84, 151–6, 235–42, 289–92. Angel Rosenblat, *La población de América en 1492: viejos y nuevos cálculos* (Mexico City: Colegio de México, 1967), is critical of high estimates. High numbers are defended by Henry F. Dobyns, "Estimating Aboriginal American Population: An Appraisal of Techniques with a New Hemispheric Estimate," *Current Anthropology* 7 (1966):395–449. The best overview of population history is Nicolás Sánchez-Albornoz, *The Population of Latin America: A History* (Berkeley: University of California Press, 1974).

2. David Henige, "On the Contact Population of Hispaniola: History as Higher Mathematics," *HAHR* 58 (1978):217–37, clearly presents the argument against using mathematical models to estimate the pre-Columbian population. R. A. Zambardino, "Critique of David Henige's 'On the Contact Population of Hispaniola: History as Higher Mathematics,' " *HAHR* 58 (1978): 700–8, points out the value of the use of statistical methods in historical research. On a broader level, the debate on quantification in history has led to a partial division of the profession into those who do and those who do not. Literature on the conflict is extensive.

3. Bartolomé de las Casas was read widely in Europe in the sixteenth century. His description of the Spanish treatment of the Indians fueled anti-Spanish sentiments in England and elsewhere. The "Brief Relation" depicts a dense and developed native population cruelly exploited by the rapacious European. He reports very large numbers for the aboriginal population and chronicles rapid depopulation. The *Brevísima relación de la destrucción de las Indias* was written around 1542 but was published in 1552. The *Apologética historia* was in manuscript by 1552–60. The celebrated de Bry edition appeared as *Narratio regionum indicarum per Hispanos quosdam devastatorum verissima* in 1598.

4. Henige, "Contact Population of Hispaniola," p. 237; Angel Rosenblat, "The Population of Hispaniola at the Time of Columbus," in Denevan, *Native Population*, pp. 43–66; Charles Verlinden, "La population de l'Amérique précolumbienne: une question de méthode," in *Méthodologie de l'histoire et des sciences humaines: Mélanges en honneur de Fernand Braudel* (Paris, 1973), pp. 453–62, and the same author's "Le 'repartimiento' de Rodrigo de Alburquerque à Española en 1514: aux origines d'une importante institution économico-sociale de l'empire colonial espagnol," in *Mélanges offerts à G. Jacquemyns* (Brussels: Université Libre de Bruxelles, 1968), pp. 633–46; Manuel A. Amiama, "La población de Santo Domingo," *Clio* 115 (1959):116–34; Woodrow Borah and Sherburne F. Cook, "The Aboriginal Population of His-

paniola," in Borah and Cook, *Essays in Population History: Mexico and the Caribbean*, 3 vols. (Berkeley: University of California Press, 1971–7), 1:376–410; Alejandro Lipschutz, "La despoblación de los indios después de la conquista," *América indígena* 26 (1966):229–47; Efrén Córdova, "La encomienda y la desaparición de los indios en las Antillas mayores," *Caribbean Studies* 8 (1968):23–49; Frank Moya Pons, *Española en el siglo XVI, 1493–1520* (Santiago, 1971); and Zambardino, "Critique," p. 704.

5. Sherburne F. Cook and Lesley Byrd Simpson, *The Population of Central Mexico in the Sixteenth Century*, Ibero-Americana, no. 31 (Berkeley: University of California Press, 1948); Woodrow Borah and Sherburne F. Cook, *The Population of Central Mexico in 1548*, Ibero-Americana, no. 43 (Berkeley: University of California Press, 1960), *The Indian Population of Central Mexico, 1531–1610*, Ibero-Americana, no. 44 (Berkeley: University of California Press, 1960), and *The Aboriginal Population of Central Mexico on the Eve of the Spanish Conquest*, Ibero-Americana, no. 45 (Berkeley: University of California Press, 1963).

6. Angel Rosenblat, *La población indígena y el mestizaje en América*, 2 vols. (Buenos Aires: Editorial Nova, 1954), 1:102; William T. Sanders, "The Population of the Central Mexican Symbiotic Region, the Basin of Mexico, and the Teotihuacán Valley in the Sixteenth Century," in Denevan, *Native Population*, pp. 85–150.

7. Denevan estimates 18.3 million for Central Mexico, based on the average of Borah and Cook's 25.2 million amd Sanders's projected 11.4 million. See Denevan, *Native Population*, p. 291. In a critical review of Borah and Cook's method, Rudolph A. Zambardino, "Mexico's Population in the Sixteenth Century: Demographic Anomaly or Mathematical Illusion?" *Journal of Interdisciplinary History* 11 (1980):1–27, the author posits a range of 5 million to 10 million.

8. Murdo J. MacLeod, *Spanish Central America: A Socioeconomic History, 1520–1720* (Berkeley: Univeristy of California Press, 1973), esp. pp. 52, 71, 93, 332; William L. Sherman, *Forced Native Labor in Sixteenth-Century Central America* (Lincoln: University of Nebraska Press, 1979), pp. 4–6, 347–55; David R. Radell, "The Indian Slave Trade and Population of Nicaragua during the Sixteenth Century," in Denevan, *Native Population*, pp. 67–76; Howard E. Daugherty, "Man-Induced Ecologic Change in El Salvador" (Ph.D. diss., University of California at Los Angeles, 1969); and Rodolfo Barón Castro, *La población de El Salvador* (Madrid: Instituto Gonzalo Fernández de Oviedo, 1942), and the same author's "El desarrollo de la población hispanoamericana (1492–1950)," *Cahiers d'histoire mondiale* 5 (1959):325–43.

9. Rolando Mellafe, "Problemas demográficos e historia colonial hispanoamericana," in *Temas de historia económica hispanoamericana* (Paris: Colección Nova Americana, 1965), 1: 45–55; Marcello Carmagnani, "Colonial Latin American Demography: Growth of Chilean Population, 1700–1830," *Journal of Social History* 1 (1967):179–91; Horacio Larrain Barros, "La población indígena de Tarapacá (norte de Chile) entre 1538 y 1581," *Norte grande* (Santiago) 1 (1975):269–300; David Graham Sweet, "The Population of the Upper Amazon Valley, Seventeenth and Eighteenth Centuries" (M.A. thesis, Univeristy of Wisconsin, 1969); and John Hemming, *Red Gold: The Conquest of the Brazilian Indians* (Cambridge, Mass.: Harvard University Press, 1978).

10. See Nicolás Sánchez-Albornoz, *El indio en el Alto Perú a fines del siglo XVII* (Lima, 1973), and *Indios y tributos en el Alto Perú* (Lima: Instituto de Estudios Peruanos, 1978); Herbert S. Klein, "The Impact of the Crisis in Nineteenth Century Mining on Regional Economies: The Example of the Bolivian Yungas, 1786–1838," in David J. Robinson (ed.), *Social Fabric and Spatial Structure in Colonial Latin America* (Ann Arbor: University Microfilms, 1979), pp. 315–38; and Klein's "Hacienda and Free Community in Eighteenth-Century Alto Peru: A Demographic Study of the Aymara Population of the Districts of Chulumani and Pacajes in 1786," *Journal of Latin American Studies* 7 (1975):193–220.

11. John L. Phelan, *The Kingdom of Quito in the Seventeenth Century* (Madison: University of Wisconsin Press, 1967), pp. 44–6; Hugo Burgos-Guevara, "La población del Ecuador en la encrucijada de los siglos XVI y XVII," in *Atti del XL Congresso Internazionale degli Americanisti* (Rome, 1972), 2:483–7; and Michael T. Hamerly, "La demografía histórica de Ecuador, Perú, y Bolivia: una bibliografía preliminar," *Revista del Archivo Histórico de Guayas* 3-6 (1974):24–63; the same author's *Historia social y económica de la antigua provincia de Guayaquil, 1763–1842* (Guayaquil, 1973), "La demografía histórica del distrito de Cuenca, 1778–1838," *Boletín de la Academia Nacional de Historia* 53-116 (1970):203–29, and "Registros parroquiales e inventarios de iglesias del litoral," *Revista del Archivo Histórico de Guayas* 12 (1977):25–69. See also Julio Estrada Ycaza, "Migraciones internas en el Ecuador," *Revista del Archivo Histórico de Guayas* 11 (1977):5–26.

12. Robert C. Eidt, "Aboriginal Chibcha Settlement in Colombia," *Annals of the Association of American Geographers* 49 (1959):374–92; James J. Parsons, *Antioqueño Colonization in Western Colombia,* 2nd ed. (Berkeley: University of California Press, 1968); Jaime Jaramillo Uribe, "La población indígena de Colombia en el momento de la conquista y sus transformaciones posteriores," *Anuario Colombiano de historia social y de la cultura* 1 (1964):239–93; Julian Bautista Ruíz Rivera, *Fuentes para la demografía histórica de Nueva Granada* (Seville: Escuela de Estudios Hispano-Americanos, 1972); Juan A. and Judith E. Villamarín, "Chibcha Settlement under Spanish Rule, 1537–1810," in Robinson, *Social Fabric,* pp. 25–84; Germán Colmenares, *Encomienda y población en la provincia de Pamplona (1549–1650)* (Bogotá: Universidad de los Andes, 1969), and the same author's *La provincia de Tunja en el Nuevo Reino de Granada: ensayo de historia social (1539–1800)* (Bogotá: Universidad de los Andes, 1970); Silvia Padilla Altamirano, María Luisa López Arellano, and Adolfo Luís González Rodrígues, *La encomienda en Popayán (tres estudios)* (Seville: Escuela de Estudios Hispano-Americanos, 1977); and Juan Friede, *Los Quimbayas bajo la dominación española: estudio documental (1539–1810)* (Bogotá: Banco de la República, 1963), and "Algunas consideraciones sobre la evolución demográfica en la provincia de Tunja," *Anuario Colombiano de historia social y de la cultura* 2, no. 3 (1965):5–19.

13. Denevan, *Native Population,* p. 155.

14. Ibid.; Woodrow Borah, "The Historical Demography of Aboriginal and Colonial America: An Attempt at Perspective," in Denevan, *Native Population,* pp. 13–34; Borah, "America as Model: The Demographic Impact of European Expansion upon the Non-European World," *Actas y memorias, XXXV Congreso Internacional de Americanistas* 3 (1964):379–87, and "The Historical Demography of Latin America:

Sources, Techniques, Controversies, Yields," in Paul Deprez (ed.), *Population and Economics: Proceedings of Section V of the Fourth Congress of the International Economic History Association* (Winnipeg: University of Manitoba Press, 1970), pp. 173–205; Rosenblat, *Población en 1492;* Dobyns, "Estimating Aboriginal Population"; and Sánchez-Albornoz, *Population of Latin America.*

15. Borah, "Attempt at Perspective," p. 31.

16. Edward P. Lanning, *Peru before the Incas* (Englewood Cliffs, N.J.: Prentice-Hall, 1967), presents the clearest outline of the cultural evolution of Peru prior to the fourteenth century; see esp. pp. 96, 115–16, 121, 127–35, 141–53.

17. See Nicolás Sánchez-Albornoz, "Les registres paroissiaux en Amérique Latine: quelques considérations sur leur exploitation pour la démographie historique," *Revue suisse d'histoire* 17 (1967):60–71; Claude Morin, "Los libros parroquiales como fuente para la historia demográfia y social novohispana," *Historia mexicana* 21 (1972):389–418; Rosemary D. F. Bromley, "Parish Registers as a Source in Latin American Demographic and Historical Research," *Bulletin of the Society for Latin American Studies* 19 (1974):14–21; Claude Mazet, "Population et société à Lima aux XVIᵉ et XVIIᵉ siècles," *Cahiers des Amériques Latines* 13-14 (1976):51–102; Noble David Cook, "La población de la parroquia de Yanahuara, 1738–47: un modelo para el estudio de las parroquias coloniales peruanas," in Franklin Pease (ed.), *Collaguas I* (Lima: Universidad Católica, 1977), pp. 13–34; and the same author's "Eighteenth Century Population Change in Andean Peru: The Parish of Yanque," paper presented at the XLIII International Congress of Americanists (Vancouver, B.C., 1979).

Part I. Peru's preconquest population

1. Pedro Cieza de León, *El señorio de los Incas* (Lima: Instituto de Estudios Peruanos, 1967), p. 62; and John Howland Rowe, "Inca Culture at the Time of the Spanish Conquest," *HSAI*, 2:262–4, 272–3, 325–7.

2. *CDIHE,* 50:206–20; see also José Toribio Medina (ed.), *La imprenta en Lima (1584-1824)* (Santiago de Chile, 1904), 1:202.

3. For Inca counting and age classification, see Ake Wedin, *El sistema decimal en el imperio incaico* (Madrid; Insula, 1965); and John V. Murra, *Formaciones económicas y políticas del mundo andino* (Lima: Instituto de Estudios Peruanos, 1975), pp. 243–54; also Waldemar Espinosa Soriano (ed.), *Visita hecha a la provincia de Chucuito por Garcí Diez de San Miguel en el año 1567* (Lima: Talleres Gráficos Quiros, 1964).

4. See Alonso Caso, "El mapa de Teozacoalco," *Cuadernos americanos* 8-5 (1949):3–40, and the same author's "Valor histórico de los códices mixtecos," *Cuadernos americanos* 19-2 (1960):139–47; Philip Dark, *Mixtec Ethnography: A Method of Analysis of the Codical Art* (London: Oxford University Press, 1958); J. Eric S. Thompson, *Maya Hieroglyphic Writing: An Introduction,* 2nd ed. (Norman: University of Oklahoma Press, 1960); and Borah, "Demography of Latin America," pp. 174–5.

5. T. H. Hollingsworth, *Historical Demography* (Ithaca: Cornell University Press, 1969), p. 299.

6. Similar approaches have been used by others in attempting to estimate populations where the data are late, as anthropologists have been forced to do for years. Cook and Borah, Sanders, and others have done so for Mesoamerica. This is, however, the

first comprehensive approach to the problem in the Andean setting. Hollingsworth attempted to use plague mortality to study population size of cities; see his *Historical Demography,* pp. 355–74.

1. The ecological approach

1. Sherburne F. Cook, "Human Sacrifice and Warfare as Factors in the Demography of Pre-Colonial Mexico," *Human. Biology* 18 (1946):81–103; Philip Ziegler, *The Black Death* (New York: John Day, 1969); and A. R. Bidbury, "The Black Death," *Economic History Review* 26 (1973):577–92. See also Ezra B. W. Zubrow, "Carrying Capacity and Dynamic Equilibrium in the Prehistoric Southwest," *American Antiquity* 36 (1971):127–38; and Paul Tolstoy, "Settlement and Population Trends in the Basin of Mexico (Ixtapaluca and Zacatenco Phases)," *Journal of Field Archaeology* 2 (1975):331–49.

2. See W. R. Aykroyd et al., "Protein Requirements: Report of the FAO Committee, Rome, Italy, October 24–31, 1955," *Nutritional Studies,* no. 16 (Rome: Food and Agriculture Organization of the United Nations, 1957); J. M. Weiner, "Nutritional Ecology," in G. A. Harrison (ed.), *Human Biology: An Introduction to Human Evolution, Variation, and Growth* (New York: Oxford University Press, 1964); and Michael A. Glassow, "Considerations in Estimating Prehistoric California Coastal Populations," *American Antiquity* 32 (1967):354–9.

3. Study of climatic variations in Peru since 1520 is incomplete. Preliminary research for the prehistoric era has been done; see Taiji Yazawa, "Climatological Survey in the Central Andes," in *Andes: Report of the University of Tokyo Scientific Expedition to the Andes in 1958* (Tokyo: University of Tokyo, 1960), pp. 414–17. There is no equivalent for Gustaf Utterström, "Climate Fluctuations and Population Problems in Early Modern History," *Scandinavian Economic Review* 3 (1955):3–47; or for E. LeRoy Ladurie, *Histoire du climat depuis l'an mil* (Paris: Flammarion, 1967). Nor has there been a study of agricultural prices in Peru. Had we a series, as Enrique Florescano has generated for Mexico in *Precios del maíz y crises agrícolas en México, 1708–1810* (Mexico City: Colegio de México, 1969); Charles Gibson, *The Aztecs under Spanish Rule: A History of the Indians of the Valley of Mexico, 1519–1810,* (Stanford, Calif.: Stanford University Press, 1964), pp. 314, 452–9; and Woodrow Borah and Sherburne F. Cook, *Price Trends of Some Basic Commodities in Central Mexico, 1531–1570,* Ibero-Americana, no. 40 (Berkeley: University of California Press, 1958), then closer parallels between agriculture and demography might be drawn. Guillermo Lohmann Villena's "Apuntaciones sobre el curso de los precios de los artículos de primera necesidad en Lima durante el siglo XVI," *Revista histórica* 29 (1966):79–104, is premature.

4. Sanders, "Mexican Symbiotic Region," p. 138.

5. Gibson, *Aztecs,* p. 307.

6. Alfred W. Crosby, *The Columbian Exchange: Biological and Cultural Consequences of 1492,* (Westport, Conn.: Greenwood Press, 1972), pp. 171–5.

7. Sherburne F. Cook, *The Historical Demography and Ecology of the Teotlalpan,* Ibero-Americana, no. 33, (Berkeley: University of California Press, 1949), pp. 39–41.

8. Sanders, "Mexican Symbiotic Region," p. 139.

9. Ibid., pp. 139–42.

10. Lanning, *Peru before the Incas,* pp. 16–17; Rowe, "Inca Culture," pp. 210–21; and Wendell C. Bennett, "The Andean Highlands," *HSAI,* 2:5. For Mexico, see Gibson, *Aztecs,* pp. 316, 554–5.

11. For economic organization, see Murra, *Formaciones económicas,* and the same author's "Economic Organization of the Inca State," (Ph.D. diss., University of Chicago, 1956); Nathan Wachtel, *Sociedad e ideología: ensayos de historia y antropología andinas* (Lima: Instituto de Estudios Peruanos, 1973); and María Rostworowski de Diez Canseco, *Etnía y sociedad: costa peruana prehispánica* (Lima: Instituto de Estudios Peruanos, 1977).

12. Gordon R. Willey, *Prehistoric Settlement Patterns in the Virú Valley, Peru,* Bureau of American Ethnology Bulletins, no. 155 (Washington, D.C.: Smithsonian Institution, 1953); and Paul Kosok, *Life, Land, and Water in Ancient Peru* (New York: Long Island University Press, 1965).

13. Robert G. Keith, *Conquest and Agrarian Change: The Emergence of the Hacienda System on the Peruvian Coast* (Cambridge, Mass.: Harvard University Press, 1976), p. 23.

14. David L. Browman, "Pastoral Nomadism in the Andes," *Current Anthropology* 15 (1974):190.

15. Lanning, *Peru before the Incas,* pp. 14–18.

16. See Carlos Monge M., *Acclimatization in the Andes: Confirmation of Climate Aggression in the Development of Andean Man* (Baltimore: Johns Hopkins University Press, 1948), and the same author's joint work with Carlos Monge C., *High Altitude Diseases: Mechanism and Management* (Springfield, Ill.: Charles C. Thomas, 1976).

17. Browman, "Pastoral Nomadism", p. 188; and Jorge Flores Ochoa, *Los pastores de Paratía,* Instituto Indigenista Interamericano, Serie Antropología Social, no. 10 (Mexico City, 1968).

18. Browman, "Pastoral Nomadism", p. 195.

19. William M. Denevan, "Aboriginal Drained-Field Cultivation in the Americas," *Science* 169 (1970):653.

20. *Production Yearbook, 1962* (Rome: Food and Agriculture Organization of the United Nations, 1963), pp. 4–5; and Keith, *Conquest and Agrarian Change,* p. 23.

21. Julian H. Steward and Louis C. Faron, *Native Peoples of South America* (New York: McGraw-Hill, 1959), p. 121.

22. Julian H. Steward, "The Native Population of South America," *HSAI,* 5:656, actually suggests 6 million for the Inca area.

23. Sanders, "Mexican Symbiotic Region," p. 139.

24. Murra, *Formaciones económicas,* pp. 36–41, 59–115.

25. C. T. Smith, "Depopulation of the Central Andes in the 16th Century," *Current Anthropology* 11 (1970):453–64.

26. Richard P. Schaedel, "Formation of the Inca State," in *III Congreso peruano: el hombre y la cultura andina* (Lima: Ramiro Matos, 1978), p. 124.

27. Cecilia Andrea Rabell and Carlos Sempat Assadourian, "Self-regulating Mechanisms of the Population in a Pre-Columbian Society: The Case of the Inca Empire," in *International Population Conference, Mexico 1977* (Liège, Belgium: Derouaux, 1977), 3: 31–2.

28. Rowe, "Inca Culture," pp. 274–82; J. Alden Mason, *The Ancient Civilizations of Peru,* 2nd ed. (New York: Penguin, 1968), pp. 193–200; and Gordon J. Hadden, "Un ensayo de demografía histórica y etnológica en Huánuco," in John V. Murra (ed.), *Visita de la provincia de León de Huánuco* (Lima: Villanueva, 1967), 1:272, 278.

29. Rabell and Assadourian, "Self-regulating Mechanisms," pp. 30, 38: Rowe, "Inca Culture," p. 282; and Mason, *Ancient Civilizations,* p. 151.

30. Rabell and Assadourian, "Self-regulating Mechanisms," pp. 36, 38; Rowe, "Inca Culture," pp. 282, 99; and Mason, *Ancient Civilizations,* p. 185.

31. Rabell and Assadourian, "Self-regulating Mechanisms," p. 37; Rowe, "Inca Culture," pp. 283–6; and Mason, *Ancient Civilizations,* p. 154. The average age at marriage given by the chroniclers varies. The colonial visitas and parish registers often provide more exact information, but it is likely that earlier patterns were substantially modified during the demographic crisis of the first century of European rule.

2. Population and archaeology

1. Noble David Cook, "La población indígena en el Perú colonial," *Anuario del Instituto de Investigaciones Históricas* 8 (1965):73–110, "The Indian Population of Peru, 1570–1620" (Ph.D. diss., University of Texas, 1973), and "Estimaciones sobre la población del Perú en el momento de la conquista," *Histórica* 1 (1977):37–60.

2. There are numerous works relevant to this question. See J. Lawrence Angel, "The Bases of Paleodemography," *American Journal of Physical Anthropology* 30 (1969):427–35; W. W. Howells, "Estimating Population Numbers through Archaeological and Skeletal Remains," in S. F. Cook and R. F. Heizer (eds.), *The Application of Quantitative Methods in Archaeology* (Chicago: Quadrangle, 1960), pp. 158–85; C. O. Lovejoy, "Methods for the Detection of Census Error in Paleodemography," *American Anthropologist* 73 (1971):101–9; Zubrow, "Carrying Capacity and Dynamic Equilibrium," pp. 127–38, and the same author's *Prehistoric Carrying Capacity: A Model* (Menlo Park, Calif.: Cummings, 1975). Excellent reviews are to be found in Sherburne F. Cook, *Prehistoric Demography* (Reading, Mass.: Addison-Wesley, 1972); and Claude Masset, "La démographie des populations inhumées: essai de paléodémographie," *L'homme* 13 (1973):95–131.

3. Angel, "Paleodemography," p. 428.

4. Henri V. Vallois, "Vital Statistics in Prehistoric Populations as Determined from Archaeological Data," in Cook and Heizer, *Quantitative Methods,* pp. 187, 194–5.

5. Angel, "Paleodemography," p. 428.

6. Raoul Naroll, "Floor Area and Settlement Population," *American Antiquity* 27 (1962):587–9.

7. See Steven Le Blanc, "An Addition to Naroll's Suggested Floor Area and Settlement Population Relationship," *American Antiquity* 36 (1971):210–11.

8. Study by N. C. Nelson, cited by Glassow, "Considerations," p. 354.

9. See Howells, "Population Numbers," p. 163.

10. S. F. Cook and A. E. Treganza, *The Quantitative Investigation of Indian Mounds, with Special Reference to the Relation of the Physical Components to the Probable Material*

Culture. University of California Publications in American Archaeology and Ethnology, vol. 40, no. 5 (Berkeley, 1950).

11. Howells, "Population Numbers," pp. 163–5; Glassow, "Considerations," pp. 354–5; and Robert Ascher, "A Prehistoric Population Estimate Using Midden Analysis and Two Population Models," *Southwestern Journal of Anthropology* 15 (1959):173.

12. Howells, "Population Numbers," p. 164.

13. Glassow, "Considerations," p. 357.

14. Mark Nathan Cohen, "Some Problems in the Quantitative Analysis of Vegetable Refuse, Illustrated by a Late Horizon Site on the Peruvian Coast," *Nawpa Pacha* 10–12 (1972–4):49.

15. Sherburne F. Cook, "Can Pottery Residues Be Used as an Index to Population?" *Contributions of the University of California Archaeological Research Facility, Miscellaneous Papers on Archaeology*, no. 14 (Berkeley, 1975), p. 27.

16. Ibid., pp. 27–29, 37.

17. Oliver G. Ricketson and Edith Bayles, *Uaxactún, Guatemala, Group E, 1926–1931,* Carnegie Institutions of Washington, Publication no. 477 (Washington, D.C., 1937), p. 16; from Dobyns, "Estimating Aboriginal Population," p. 400.

18. Sylvanus G. Morley, *The Ancient Maya* (Stanford, Calif.: Stanford University Press, 1947), p. 317; cited in Dobyns, "Estimating Aboriginal Population," p. 401.

19. George S. Brainerd revised and published Morley's *Ancient Maya* in 1958; see p. 262 and Dobyns, "Estimating Aborginal Population," p. 401.

20. George L. Cowgill, cited in Howells, "Population Numbers," p. 161.

21. J. Eric S. Thompson, "Estimates of Maya Population: Deranging Factors," *American Antiquity* 36 (1971):214–16.

22. See Anthony P. Andrews, "The U-Shaped Structures at Chan Chan, Peru," *Journal of Field Anthropology* 1 (1974):242–64; Michael E. Moseley, "Chan Chan: Andean Alternative of the Pre-industrial City," *Science* 187 (1975):219–25; and Richard W. Keatinge, "Urban Settlement Systems and Rural Sustaining Communities: An Example from Chan Chan's Hinterland," *Journal of Field Archaeology* 2 (1975):215–27.

23. Richard W. Keatinge and Kent C. Day, "Socio-economic Organization of the Moche Valley, Peru, during the Chimu Occupation of Chan Chan," *Journal of Anthropological Research* 29 (1973):275–82.

24. See Michael West, "Community Settlement Patterns at Chan Chan, Peru," *American Antiquity* 35 (1970):84.

25. Ibid.

26. Ibid.

27. Moseley, "Chan Chan," p. 223. See John H. Rowe, "The Kingdom of Chimor," *Acta americana* 6 (1948):26–59.

28. Robert R. Kautz and Richard W. Keatinge, "Determining Site Function: A North Peruvian Coastal Example," *American Antiquity* 42 (1977):86–97.

29. Ibid., p. 95.

30. Jeffrey R. Parsons and Norbert P. Psuty, "Sunken Fields and Prehispanic Subsistence on the Peruvian Coast, *American Antiquity* 40 (1975):259–82.

31. Denevan, "Aboriginal Drained-Field Cultivation," p. 653.

32. Lanning, *Peru before the Incas*, p. 150.

33. Ibid., p. 151; see also Alfred Kidder, "Settlement Patterns, Peru," in Gordon R. Willey (ed.), *Prehistoric Settlement Patterns in the New World,* Viking Fund Publications in Anthropology, no. 23 (New York, 1956), pp. 148–55.

34. John Howland Rowe, "Urban Settlements in Ancient Peru," *Nawpa Pacha* 1 (1963):1–27.

35. Ibid. See Dorothy Menzel, "The Inca Occupation of the South Coast of Peru," *Southwestern Journal of Anthropology* 15 (1959):125–42; and the same author's "Archaism and Revival on the South Coast of Peru," in Daniel R. Gross (ed.), *Peoples and Cultures of Native South America* (Garden City, N.Y.: Doubleday, 1973), pp. 19–27.

36. John Howland Rowe, *An Introduction to the Archaeology of Cuzco,* Papers of the Peabody Museum of American Archaeology and Ethnology, Harvard University, vol. 27, no. 2 (Cambridge, Mass., 1944), pp. 5–6.

37. John Howland Rowe, "What Kind of a Settlement Was Inca Cuzco? *Nawpa Pacha* 5 (1967):60–1.

38. William Peterson, "A Demographer's View of Prehistoric Demography," *Current Anthropology* 16 (1975):227.

3. Depopulation ratios

1. Rowe, "Inca Culture," 2:184–5; Dobyns, "Estimating Aboriginal Population," pp. 412–16; Smith, "Depopulation of the Central Andes," pp. 453–64; and Nathan Wachtel, *La vision des vaincus: les indiens du Pérou devant la conquête espagnole, 1530–1570* (Paris: Gallimard, 1971), and the English translation, *Vision of the Vanquished: The Spanish Conquest of Peru through Indian Eyes, 1530–1570* (Hassocks, Sussex: Harvester Press, 1977).

2. Rowe, "Inca Culture," 2:184.

3. Espinosa Soriano, *Visita de Chucuito,* f. 31v., 35v., and 39r.

4. Rowe, "Inca Culture," 2:184.

5. For the Toledo data, see Noble David Cook (ed.), *Tasa de la visita general de Francisco de Toledo* (Lima: San Marcos, 1975); Roberto Levillier, *Gobernantes del Perú, cartas y papeles, siglo XVI* (Madrid: Juan Pueyo, 1925), 9:114–230; and Víctor M. Maúrtua, *Juicio de límites entre el Perú y Bolivia, prueba peruana* (Barcelona, 1906), 1:153–280.

6. Rowe, "Inca Culture," 2:184–5.

7. Dobyns, "Estimating Aboriginal Population," p. 414.

8. Ibid., p. 413.

9. Sánchez-Albornoz, *Indios y tributos,* pp. 19–34.

10. Gabriel Fernández de Villalobos, *Vaticinios de la pérdida de las Indias y Mano de Relox* (Caracas: Instituto Panamericano de Geografía e Historia, 1949); and Dobyns, "Estimating Aboriginal Population," p. 413.

11. See the biographical notes of Joaquín Gabaldon Márquez to the study of Fernández de Villalobos, *Vaticinios de la pérdida,* pp. 9–12.

12. Smith, "Depopulation of the Central Andes," pp. 453–64; and Espinosa Soriano, *Visita de Chucuito.*

13. Smith, "Depopulation of the Central Andes," p. 459.

14. See Espinosa Soriano, *Visita de Chucuito,* f. 35v., 39r., and 46r.

15. John V. Murra's critique of Dobyns in *Current Anthropology* 7 (1966):462.

16. Smith, "Depopulation of the Central Andes," p. 457.

17. Smith might have considered use of stable population analysis, made possible by the tables devised by Ansley J. Coale and Paul Demeny, *Regional Model Life Tables and Stable Populations* (Princeton, N.J.: Princeton University Press, 1966).

18. Smith, "Depopulation of the Central Andes," pp. 456–9.

19. Wachtel, *Vision of the Vanquished,* p. 88; see Cook, *Tasa de la visita general,* pp. xxviii–xliii.

20. Wachtel, *Vision of the Vanquished,* pp. 217–20.

21. Ibid. p. 89.

22. Ibid.

23. Ibid., p. 90.

24. Borah and Cook, *Aboriginal Population of Central Mexico,* pp. 4, 88.

25. Dobyns, "Estimating Aboriginal Population," pp. 405–8; Rosenblat, *Población indígena,* 1:102, and *Población en 1492,* pp. 23–81; Denevan, *Native Population,* pp. 77–83; and Sánchez-Albornoz, *Population of Latin America,* pp. 35–6.

26. We shall treat this subject in greater depth in Chapter 5.

4. Estimates from social organization

1. E. A. Wrigley, *Population and History* (New York: McGraw-Hill, 1969), pp. 42–59.

2. Robert L. Carneiro, "On the Relationship between Size of Population and Complexity of Social Organization," *Southwestern Journal of Anthropology* 23 (1967):240.

3. D. E. Dumond, "Population Growth and Cultural Change," *Southwestern Journal of Anthropology* 21 (1965):315; and Michael J. Harner, "Population Pressure and the Social Evolution of Agriculturalists," *Southwestern Journal of Anthropology* 26 (1970):67–86.

4. Julian H. Steward, *Theory of Culture Change: The Methodology of Multilinear Evolution* (Urbana: University of Illinois Press, 1973), pp. 78–87, 191–205.

5. Philip Ainsworth Means, *Ancient Civilizations of the Andes* (New York: Charles Scribner's Sons, 1931), p. 296.

6. Mason, *Ancient Civilizations,* pp. 176–9.

7. Dobyns, "Estimating Aboriginal Population," p. 409.

8. Schaedel, "Formation of the Inca State," pp. 123–4.

9. Wendell C. Bennett and Junius B. Bird, *Andean Culture History* (New York: Museum of Natural History, 1960), p. 153; and Rowe, "Inca Culture," pp. 184–93.

10. Dobyns, "Estimating Aboriginal Population," p. 409.

5. Disease mortality models

1. Henry F. Dobyns, "An Outline of Andean Epidemic History to 1720," *Bulletin of the History of Medicine* 37 (1963):493–515; Juan B. Lastres, *Historia de la medicina*

peruana, 3 vols. (Lima: San Marcos, 1951); and José Toribio Polo, "Apuntes sobre las epidemias del Perú," *Revista histórica* 5 (1913):50–109.

2. Frederick F. Cartwright, *Disease and History* (London: Rupert Hart-Davis, 1972), p. 116.

3. T. Aidan Cockburn, "Infectious Diseases in Ancient Populations," *Current Anthropology* 12 (1971):50.

4. Ibid.

5. Jacques M. May, *The Ecology of Human Diseases* (New York: MD Publications, 1958), p. 267.

6. Frank MacFarlane Burnet, *The Integrity of the Body: A Discussion of Modern Immunological Ideas* (Cambridge, Mass.: Harvard University Press, 1962), p. 4.

7. Cockburn, "Infectious Diseases," p. 51.

8. Crosby, *Columbian Exchange,* p. 44.

9. Francis Borgia Steck, *Motolinía's "History of the Indians of New Spain"* (Richmond, Va.: William Byrd, 1951), pp. 87–8.

10. Cockburn, "Infectious Diseases," p. 51; mortality varied among cities from 1 in 5.5 to 1 in 6.7 births. See also John Duffy, *Epidemics in Colonial America* (Baton Rouge: Louisiana State University Press, 1953), p. 20.

11. Z. Deutschmann, "The Ecology of Smallpox," in Jaques M. May (ed.), *Studies in Disease Ecology* (New York: Hafner, 1961), p. 1.

12. Cartwright, *Disease and History,* pp. 117–21; and Hans Zinnser, *Rats, Lice, and History* (New York: Blue Ribbon Books, 1934), pp. 255–6.

13. May, *Ecology of Human Diseases,* p. 266.

14. Zinnser, *Rats, Lice, and History,* p. 67.

15. Ibid., p. 251.

16. John M. Cooper, "The Yahgan," *HSAI,* 1:83.

17. John M. Cooper, "The Ona," *HSAI,* 1:108–9.

18. May, *Ecology of Human Diseases,* p. 267.

19. Ibid., pp. 267–78.

20. See the data in Cook, "Indian Population of Peru," pp. 348–68.

21. Robert S. Katz, "Influenza, 1918–1919: A Study in Mortality," *Bulletin of the History of Medicine* 48 (1974):416–18.

22. D. I. Pool, "The Effects of the 1918 Pandemic of Influenza on the Maori Population of New Zealand," *Bulletin of the History of Medicine* 47 (1973):281, 273–7.

23. Katz, "Influenza," p. 420.

24. Dobyns, "Andean Epidemic History," pp. 499–500.

25. Zinnser, *Rats, Lice, and History,* pp. 183, 256–7.

26. Alfred A. Buck, Tom T. Sasaki, and Robert I. Anderson, *Health and Disease in Four Peruvian Villages: Contrasts in Epidemiology* (Baltimore: Johns Hopkins University Press, 1968), pp. 81–2.

27. Ibid., p. 57.

28. Ibid., pp. 34, 57–8; Crosby, *Columbian Exchange,* p. 208; and Cartwright, *Disease and History,* pp. 141–5. Crosby states that malaria was also in America in 1492. Saul Jarcho, "Some Observations on Disease in Prehistoric North America," *Bulletin of the History of Medicine* 38 (1964):1–19, reports that malaria was probably not native to the Americas.

29. Geoffrey Marks and William K. Beatty, *Epidemics* (New York: Charles Scribner's Sons, 1976), p. 138.

30. Alwin M. Pappenheimer, "The Diphtheria Bacilli," in René J. Dubos and James G. Hirsch (eds.), *Bacterial and Mycotic Infections of Man*, 4th ed. (Philadelphia: J. B. Lippincott, 1965), p. 469.

31. Alice Lorraine Smith, *Microbiology and Pathology*, 10th ed. (Saint Louis: C. V. Mosby, 1972), pp. 190-5.

32. Cockburn, "Infectious Diseases," p. 51.

33. Ibid.

34. Ibid., p. 50; see A. B. Sabin, "Nature of Inherited Resistance to Viruses Affecting the Nervous System," *Proceedings of the National Academy of Sciences* 38 (1952):540-6; and, with regard to measles among the American Indians, James V. Neel, "Genetic Aspects of the Ecology of Disease in the American Indian," in Francisco M. Salzano (ed.), *The Ongoing Evolution of Latin American Populations* (Springfield, Ill.: Charles C. Thomas, 1971), pp. 561-92.

35. Kenneth A. Bennett's critique of Cockburn, "Infectious Diseases," p. 54; see David Pimentel, "Population Regulation and Genetic Feedback," *Science* 159 (1968):1432-7.

36. T. D. Stewart, "A Physical Anthropologist's view of the Peopling of the New World," *Southwestern Journal of Anthropology* 16 (1960):265.

37. Paul T. Baker, "Ecological and Physiological Adaptation in Indigenous South Americans," in Paul T. Baker and J. S. Weiner (eds.), *The Biology of Human Adaptability* (Oxford: Oxford University Press, Clarendon Press, 1966):pp. 276-77; and the same author's "Adaptation Problems in Andean Human Populations," in Salzano, *Ongoing Evolution*, pp. 475-507; R. B. Mazess, "Variation in Neo-natal Mortality and Altitude in Peru," *American Journal of Physical Anthropology* 23 (1965):209-14 and Monge, *Acclimatization in the Andes*.

38. Norman T. J. Bailey, *The Mathematical Theory of Infectious Diseases and Its Applications* (New York: Hafner, 1975), p. viii.

6. Census projections

1. George W. Barclay, *Techniques of Population Analysis* (New York: John Wiley, 1958); and Mortimer Spiegelman, *Introduction to Demography*, rev. ed. (Cambridge, Mass.: Harvard University Press, 1968).

2. Cook, "Indian Population of Peru," pp. 11-52.

3. Carlos A. Romero, "Libro de la visita general del Virrey Francisco de Toledo," *Revista histórica* 7 (1924):115-216; Roberto Levillier, *Don Francisco de Toledo, supremo organizador del Perú* (Madrid: Espasa-Calpe, 1935), 1:78, 98-100; and Cook, *Tasa de la visita general*, pp. ix-xiii.

4. Cook, *Tasa de la visita general*, pp. 217-18.

5. See Dobyns, "Andean Epidemic History," pp. 493-515. George Kubler's conclusion that "not until 1720 did any great losses through pestilence occur in Peru" is unfounded. See Kubler, "The Quechua in the Colonial World," *HSAI*, 2:334; and Luís de Morales Figueroa, "Relación de los indios tributarios que hay al presente en estos reinos y provincias del Pirú; fecho por mandado del Señor Marqués de Cañete,"

CDIHE, 6:41–61. The best copy, still unpublished, is found in "Manuscritos del Marqués del Risco," Biblioteca Central de la Universidad de Sevilla, vol. 4.

6. Kubler, "The Quechua," 2:337.

7. See Rosenblat, *Población indígena,* 1:254; Alberto Tauro's introduction to Enrique Torres Saldamando, *Apuntes históricos sobre las encomiendas en el Perú* (Lima: San Marcos, 1967), p. 9; Kubler, "The Quechua," 2:337–9; Günter Vollmer, *Bevölkerungspolitik und Bevölkerungsstruktur im Vizekönigreich Peru zu Ende der Kolonialzeit, 1741–1821,* Beiträge zur Soziologie und Sozialkunde Lateinamerikas, Cosal 2 (Bad Homburg vor der Höhe, 1967); and Daniel E. Shea, "A Defense of Small Population Estimates for the Central Andes in 1520," in Denevan, *Native Population,* pp. 157–80.

8. Noble David Cook and Franklin Pease, "New Research Opportunities in Los Collaguas, Peru," *Latin American Research Review* 10 (1975):201–2; and Pease, *Collaguas I.*

9. See the biographical notes of Charles Upson Clark in Antonio Vázquez de Espinosa, *Compendio y descripción de las Indias occidentales,* Smithsonian Miscellaneous Collections, vol. 108 (Washington, D.C., 1948), pp. iii–xii.

10. Torres Saldamando, *Apuntes,* p. 9.

11. Rosenblat, *Población indígena,* 1:254.

12. Vollmer, *Bevölkerungspolitik,* pp. 281–2.

13. Kubler, "The Quechua," 2:338.

14. Wachtel, *Vision of the Vanquished,* pp. 217–20, 272.

15. ANP, Residencias, leg. 2, cuad. 5; leg. 7, cuad. 16; leg. 22, cuad. 57; Maúrtua, *Juicio de límites,* pp. 240, 254; Manuscritos del Marqués del Risco, vol. 4; Vázquez de Espinosa, *Compendio,* p. 645; and BNL, B893.

16. Toribio Alfonso de Mogrovejo, "Diario de la segunda visita pastoral que hizo de su arquidiocesis," *Revista del Archivo Nacional del Perú* 1 (1920):51–81, 227–79, 401–19; 2 (1921):37–78; and Manuscritos del Marqués del Risco, vol. 4.

17. Kubler, "The Quechua," 2:377–8.

18. Karen Spalding, "Indian Rural Society in Colonial Peru: The Example of Huarochirí" (Ph.D. diss., University of California, 1967), pp. 111–12.

19. AGI, Contaduría 1786; and ANP, Residencias, leg. 4.

20. BNM, 3032; Murra, "Economic Organization," pp. 219, 270–1, 289–90; and BNL, B44. The number of Cañaris must have been relatively stable. In 1594 there were fifteen Cañari males ages 18 to 50 living in the village of Chiara in the corregimiento of Vilcas. At the time of Viceroy Palata's census (1687) there were twenty-five. The population of the same Cañari cohort in the pueblo of Pallcayaco in 1594 was sixteen and in 1687 it was twenty-four. Juan López de Velasco, *Geografía y descripción universal de las Indias* (Madrid, 1894), p. 480.

21. See Cook, *Tasa de la visita general.*

22. Archivo Parroquial de Yanque.

23. Spalding suggests that, although the migrant had no access to the land or social benefits of the ayllu, he left his native repartimiento to escape the forced labor in Potosí and Huancavelica, "Indian Rural Society," p. 110. See also John H. Rowe, "The Incas under Spanish Colonial Institutions," *HAHR* 37 (1957):180.

24. Sánchez-Albornoz, *Indios y tributos,* pp. 46–7.

25. BNM, 3004.

26. BNL, C1156; Sánchez-Albornoz, *Indios y tributos*, p. 49.

27. Sánchez-Albornoz, *Indios y tributos*, p. 32.

28. Ibid., pp. 49, 51–2.

29. Viceroys and lesser Crown officials generally concurred in their complaints about the disappearance of mitayos.

30. Sánchez-Albornoz, *Indios y tributos*, pp. 46–7; see Marcos Jiménez de la Espada (ed.), *Relaciones geográficas de Indias, Perú*, 3 vols., rev. ed. (Madrid: Atlas, 1965), 2:319–20; and Manuel Atanasio Fuentes (ed.), *Memorias de los virreyes que han gobernado el Perú, durante el tiempo del colonaje español*, 6 vols. (Lima, 1859), 1:118–19.

31. Kubler, "The Quechua," 2: 376.

32. Sánchez-Albornoz, *Indios y tributos*, pp. 69–151.

33. Diez de San Miguel, in Murra, *Visita de Huánuco*.

34. See George Kubler, *The Indian Caste of Peru, 1795–1940*, Smithsonian Institution, Institute of Social Anthropology, Publication no. 14 (Washington, D.C., 1952); and *Informe demográfico del Perú, 1970* (Lima: Centro de Estudios de Población y Desarollo, 1972), pp. 332–5.

35. Maúrtua, *Juicio de límites*, 1:257; and Vázquez de Espinosa, *Compendio*, p. 649.

36. Computer assisted studies of topics in modern demography are common. For applications in eighteenth-century Latin America, see David J. Robinson, "Distribution and Structure of the Population in the Spanish Empire, 1750–1810: The Joint Syracuse–Oxford Project," *Latin American Population History Newsletter* 1 (1978–9): 17–22; David G. Browning, "Distribution and Structure of the Population in Spanish America, 1750–1810: Identification and Retrieval of Data," Paper presented at the XLI International Congress of Americanists (Mexico City, 1974); and T. Brady and J. Lombardi, "The Application of Computers to the Analysis of Census Data: The Bishopric of Caracas, 1780–1820," in Deprez, *Population and Economics*, pp. 271–8.

37. There are several useful geographical descriptions of Peru. See the nineteenth-century work of Mariano Felipe Paz Soldán, *Diccionario geográfico estadístico del Perú* (Lima: Imprenta del Estado, 1877), and his *Atlas geográfico del Perú* (Paris: Fermin Didot Hermanos, 1865); Germán Stiglich's *Diccionario geográfico peruano*, 3 vols. (Lima: Torres Aguirre, 1922), is still helpful. One of the best modern geographical surveys of Peru is Emilio Romero, *Geografía económica del Perú*, 5th ed. (Lima, 1966).

38. An assessment of all models will be made at the conclusion to Part I.

39. Shea, "Defense of Small Population Estimates," pp. 157–80.

40. Cook, "Indian Population of Peru," and *Tasa de la visita general*.

41. Means, *Ancient Civilizations*, p. 296; and Dobyns, "Estimating Aboriginal Population," p. 414. Loayza's means for derivation of 45 million is worth outlining: "1,500,000 inhabitants, according to Viceroy Toledo, were living forty years after the Conquest, as a result of a depopulation of 30 percent of a given people. In order to find the exact population of the realm you multiply the first quantity by 30, and you obtain the searched for result; that is, the total population of the Inca Empire before the Conquest, which is forty-five million. 45,000,000, not a person more or less, because numbers are numbers!" See Francisco A. Loayza (ed.), *Las crónicas de los Molinas* (Lima: Miranda, 1943), p. 82.

42. See *Manual IV: Methods of Estimating Basic Demographic Measures from Incomplete*

Data, Department of Economic and Social Affairs, Population Studies, no. 42 (New York: United Nations, 1967); and Coale and Demeny, *Regional Model Life Tables and Stable Populations.* Thomas H. Hollingsworth, "Examples of Stable Populations in the Historical Record," in *International Population Conference, Mexico 1977,* 3 vols. (Liège, Belgium: Derouaux, 1977), 3:65–76, points out some difficulties in studying stable populations. A recent study, with an excellent bibliography, is Michael R. Haines, "The Use of Model Life Tables to Estimate Mortality for the United States in the Late Nineteenth Century," *Demography* 16 (1979):289–312.

43. José Luis Rénique and Efraín Trelles, "Aproximación demográfica, Yanque-Collaguas 1591," in Pease, *Collaguas I,* p. 175.

7. Conclusion

1. William M. Denevan, "The Aboriginal Population of Amazonia," in Denevan, *Native Population,* pp. 205–34; and Perú, Dirección Nacional de Estadística y Censos, *Sexto censo nacional de población levantado el 2 de julio de 1961: resultados de primera prioridad* (Lima, 1964).

2. *Historical Statistics of the United States: Colonial Times to 1970,* 2 vols. (Washington, D.C.: U.S. Government Printing Office, 1975), .1:1. In 1960 the undercount was 2.7 percent, down from 1950's 3.3 percent.

8. First contact: north coast

1. There are several useful studies of Peru's geography. The following discussion is based primarily on Romero, *Geografía económica,* the same author's *Historia económica del Perú,* 2 vols. (Lima, 1968), and his more recent *Perú: una nueva geografía,* 2 vols. (Lima: Studium, 1973); Thomas R. Ford, *Man and Land in Peru* (Gainesville, Fla.: University of Florida Press, 1955); Keith, *Conquest and Agrarian Change;* and Kosok, *Life, Land, and Water.* For the location of communities, many of which no longer exist, Paz Soldán's *Atlas geográfico* was helpful, along with the same author's *Diccionario geográfico.* Especially useful was Stiglich's *Diccionario geográfico.* The *Map of Hispanic America,* 1:1,000,000, of the American Geographical Society was of little help, but the various maps of the Instituto Geográfico Militar in Lima, especially the 1:200,000 scale, were invaluable.

2. The best general study of Peru's north coastal geography is that of Kosok, *Life, Land, and Water.*

3. See Chapter 6.

4. John Hemming, *The Conquest of the Incas* (London: Sphere Books, 1972), p. 26.

5. Agustín de Zárate, *Historia del descubrimiento y conquista del Perú* (Lima: Miranda, 1944), pp. 23–4.

6. See Raúl Porras Barrenechea (ed.), *Cedulario del Perú, siglos XVI, XVII, y XVIII* (Lima: Torres Aguirre, 1948), pp. 18–58, for the agreements concerning the discovery of Peru.

7. Zárate, *Historia,* pp. 54–5.

8. Miguel de Estete, *Relación de la conquista del Perú* (Lima: Sanmartí, 1924), p. 20.

9. Raúl Porras Barrenechea (ed.), *Las relaciones primitivas de la conquista del Perú,*

2nd ed. (Lima: Minerva, 1967), p. 71. In this report the number of Indian prisoners is set at 800.

10. Rafael Loredo, *Los repartos* (Lima: Miranda, 1958), pp. 265, 274.

11. Maúrtua, *Juicio de límites,* 1:260; and Manuscritos del Marqués del Risco, vol. 4.

12. Estete, *Relación,* p. 21.

13. Porras Barrenechea, *Relaciones primitivas,* p. 71.

14. Loredo, *Repartos,* pp. 265–75.

15. López de Velasco, *Geografía y descripción,* pp. 441–3.

16. Maúrtua, *Juicio de límites,* 1:258–60; Manuscritos del Marqués del Risco, vol. 4; and Vázquez de Espinosa, *Compendio,* p. 652.

17. Maúrtua, *Juicio de límites,* 1:256–7; and Kosok, *Life, Land, and Water,* pp. 146, 163, 180.

18. Vázquez de Espinosa, *Compendio,* pp. 369–70.

19. Keith, *Conquest and Agrarian Change,* p. 105; Maúrtua, *Juicio de límites,* 1:256–7; Juan Bromley, *La fundación de la ciudad de los Reyes* (Lima: Excelsior, 1935), pp. 108–10; Manuscritos del Marqués del Risco, vol. 4; Loredo, *Repartos,* p. 271; and Vázquez de Espinosa, *Compendio,* p. 649. See Sebastián de la Gama, "Visita hecha en el valle de Jayanca (Trujillo) (1540)," *Historia y cultura* 8 (1974): 215–28.

20. Loredo, *Repartos,* pp. 268–71; Maúrtua, *Juicio de límites,* 1:257; Manuscritos del Marqués del Risco, vol. 4; and Vázquez de Espinosa, *Compendio,* p.649.

21. Domingo de Angul (ed.), "La fundación y población de la villa de Zaña," *Revista del Archivo Nacional del Perú* 1 (1920):280–301; and Maúrtua, *Juicio de límites,* 1:256.

22. Manuel Burga, *De la encomienda a la hacienda capitalista: el valle del Jequetepeque del siglo XVI a XX* (Lima: Instituto de Estudios Peruanos, 1976), pp. 50–1, 64, 73–9, 91–4. See also Susan E. Ramírez-Horton, "Chérrepe en 1572: un análisis de la visita general del Virrey Francisco de Toledo," *Historia y cultura* 11 (1978):79–122.

23. Kosok, *Life, Land, and Water,* p. 88.

24. Miguel Cabello de Balboa, *Miscelánea antártica: una historia del Perú antiguo* (Lima: San Marcos, 1951), pp. 319–20; quoted in Kosok, *Life, Land, and Water,* p. 81.

25. Kosok, *Life, Land, and Water,* pp. 82–3.

26. Vázquez de Espinosa, *Compendio,* pp. 365–6.

27. Zárate, *Historia,* p. 33; see *Monografía de la Diócesis de Trujillo,* 3 vols. (Trujillo: Centro de Estudios de Historia Eclesiástica del Perú, 1930–1); Marco A. Cabero, "El corregimiento de Saña y el problema histórico de la fundación de Trujillo," *Revista histórica* 1 (1906):151–91, 337–73, 486–514; and "Fragmentos de una historia de Trujillo," *Revista histórica* 8 (1925):86–118.

28. Rómulo Cúneo-Vidal, *Vida del conquistador del Perú, don Francisco Pizarro* (Barcelona: Maucci, 1925), pp. 339–46; Loredo, *Repartos,* pp. 250–2; Bromley, *La fundación,* p. 107; and ANP, Residencias, leg. 22, cuad. 57.

29. Katherine Coleman, "Provincial Urban Problems: Trujillo, Peru, 1600–1784," in Robinson, *Social Fabric,* pp. 369–408; and Cabero, "El corregimiento de Saña," pp. 496–502.

30. Cabero, "El corregimiento de Saña," p. 359.

31. Coleman, "Urban Problems: Trujillo," p. 398.
32. Quote from ibid., p. 400.
33. Ibid., pp. 376–9.
34. See *Revista histórica* 8 (1925):91–3; and compare with the figures in Cabero, "El corregimiento de Saña," p. 345.
35. Kosok, *Life, Land, and Water*, p. 29.
36. Vázquez de Espinosa, *Compendio*, pp. 364–6; BNL, A574; ANP, Residencias, leg. 2, cuad. 5; leg. 22, cuad. 57; Manuscritos del Marqués del Risco, vol. 4; and Maúrtua, *Juicio de límites*, 1:254.
37. See Chapter 2.

9. Center of Spanish control: middle coast

1. The best recent work on the early colonial development of the central coast is Keith's *Conquest and Agrarian Change*.
2. Bromley, *La fundación*, pp. 105–9.
3. ANP, Residencias, leg. 23, cuad. 58; BNL, B1923, B1936; Manuscritos del Marqués del Risco, vol. 4; and Maúrtua, *Juicio de límites*, 1:242.
4. For a discussion of developments in the population of the area for the period to the administration of Viceroy Palata, see Noble David Cook, "The Indian Population of Végueta, 1623–1683: A Case Study of Population Change in the Central Coastal Region of Peru in the Seventeenth Century," *Atti del XL Congresso Internazionale degli Americanisti* (Rome, 1972), 4:309–16.
5. Wachtel, *Vision of the Vanquished*, pp. 114–55; and Keith, *Conquest and Agrarian Change*, p. 35.
6. See Juan Bromley and José Barbagelati, *Evolución urbana de la ciudad de Lima* (Lima, 1945); Ralph A. Gakenheimer, "Determinants of Physical Structure of the Peruvian Town of the Sixteenth Century" (Ph.D. diss., University of Pennsylvania, 1964); Rosenblat, *Población indígena*, pp. 225–7, 255–6; and Rolando Mellafe, "The Importance of Migration in the Viceroyalty of Peru," in Deprez, *Population and Economics*, pp. 303–13.
7. Rubén Vargas Ugarte, *Historia del Perú: virreinato siglo XVII* (Buenos Aires: López, 1954), pp. 92–3.
8. BNM, 3032. For the published text, see Noble David Cook (ed.), *Padrón de los indios de Lima en 1613* (Lima: San Marcos, 1968). See the same author's "Les indiens immigrés à Lima au début de XVIIᵉ siècle," *Cahiers des Amériques Latines* 13/14 (1976):33–50.
9. Spalding, in "Indian Rural Society," studies the relationship of Lima and that region.
10. Frederick Park Bowser, "Negro Slavery in Colonial Peru, 1529–1650," (Ph.D. diss., University of California, 1967), p. 128; and James Lockhart, *Spanish Peru, 1532–1560: A Colonial Society* (Madison, Wisc.: University of Wisconsin Press, 1968), p. 217. Lockhart reports: "Indian group life was disrupted by the quick turnover of the migratory population and the diseases and starvation which, one contemporary thought, in the 1540's caused the deaths of two or three thousand Indians in Lima every year."

11. Bowser, "Negro Slavery," 32, 124, 165–7; and Rubén Vargas Ugarte, *Biblioteca peruana: manuscritos peruanos en la Biblioteca Nacional de Lima* (Lima, 1940), 3:86–7. See Monge, *Acclimatization in the Andes*. In the early seventeenth century there were over 100 migrants from Asia residing in Lima. See Cook, *Padrón*, pp. 525–47.

12. Manuscritos del Marqués del Risco, vol. 4; Maúrtua, *Juicio de límites*, 1:242; and Vázquez de Espinosa, *Compendio*, p. 644.

13. Keith, *Conquest and Agrarian Change*, pp. 57, 73, 77; Bromley, *La fundación*, p. 105; Loredo, *Repartos*, p. 225; Maúrtua, *Juicio de límites*, 1:241; Manuscritos del Marqués del Risco, vol. 4; BNL, B893; and ANP, Residencias, leg. 27, cuad. 75.

14. AGI, Charcas 136; Keith, *Conquest and Agrarian Change*, pp. 17, 57, 90.

15. Keith, *Conquest and Agrarian Change*, pp. 17, 88.

16. Bromley, *Fundación*, p. 105; Keith, *Conquest and Agrarian Change*, pp. 57, 73; Maúrtua, *Juicio de límites*, 1:240; Vázquez de Espinosa, *Compendio*, p. 645; Manuscritos del Marqués del Risco, vol. 4; BNL, B893; and ANP, Residencias, leg. 27, cuad. 75.

17. Keith, *Conquest and Agrarian Change*, pp. 23, 24; Loredo, *Repartos*, p. 224; AGI, Charcas 136; Maúrtua, *Juicio de límites*, 1:239; Vázquez de Espinosa, *Compendio*, p. 645; BNL, B893; and ANP, Residencias, leg. 27, cuad. 75. See also Juan Carlos Crespo, "La relación de Chincha," *Historia y cultura* 8 (1974):91–104.

18. ANP, Residencias, leg. 12, cuad. 30; leg. 13, cuad. 36; leg. 16, cuad. 45; Manuscritos del Marqués del Risco, vol. 4; Vázquez de Espinosa, *Compendio*, p. 644; and Maúrtua, *Juicio de límites*, 1:240–53.

19. ANP, Residencias, leg. 12, cuad. 30; leg. 30, cuad. 84; Manuscritos del Marqués del Risco, vol. 4; Vázquez de Espinosa, *Compendio*, p. 644; Maúrtua, *Juicio de límites*, 1:239; Keith, *Conquest and Agrarian Change*, pp. 97–102; and Bromley, *La fundación*, pp. 106–9.

20. AGI, Charcas 136; ANP, Residencias, leg. 13, cuad. 36; leg. 29, cuad. 83; Keith, *Conquest and Agrarian Change*, pp. 75–6, 99–101; Bromley, *La fundación*, p. 107; and Alberto Rossel Castro, *Historia regional de Ica* (Lima: San Marcos, 1964), p. 100.

21. Keith, *Conquest and Agrarian Change*, p. 47.

22. AGI, Lima 200; BNL, B493; ANP, Residencias, leg. 16, cuad. 43; leg. 18, cuad. 49; leg. 23, cuad. 60; ANP, Derecho indígena y encomiendas, leg. 8, cuad. 112; Manuscritos del Marqués del Risco, vol. 4; Bromley, *La fundación*, p. 180; Vázquez de Espinosa, *Compendio*, p. 648; Loredo, *Repartos*, pp. 220–31; and Maúrtua, *Juicio de límites*, 1:243–8.

23. ANP, Residencias, leg. 11, cuad. 28; leg. 12, cuad. 33; ANP, Testamentos de indios; Manuscritos del Marqués del Risco, vol. 4; Vázquez de Espinosa, *Compendio*, p. 645; Loredo, *Repartos*, pp. 219–21; Bromley, *La fundación*, p. 109; and Maúrtua, *Juicio de límites*, 1:238.

24. BNL, A332; Manuscritos del Marqués del Risco, vol. 4; Jiménez de la Espada, *Relaciones geográficas*, 1:162–4; Vázquez de Espinosa, *Compendio*, p. 648; Maúrtua, *Juicio de límites*, 1:236; Bromley, *La fundación*, p. 106; Loredo, *Repartos*, pp. 223–4; and Spalding, "Indian Rural Society."

10. Disease, earthquakes, and droughts: south coast

1. See the appropriate sections of Romero's *Nueva geografía*.

2. A good introduction to the economic transformation of the southern coastal sector may be found in Keith Arfon Davies, "The Rural Domain of the City of Arequipa, 1540–1665" (Ph.D. diss., University of Connecticut, 1974).

3. Vázquez de Espinosa, *Compendio*, pp. 460–1; and Cook, *Tasa de la visita general*, p. 250.

4. "Visita de Acarí (1593)," *Historia y cultura* 7 (1973):131.

5. Ibid., p. 187.

6. Ibid., pp. 129–209.

7. AGI, Contaduría 1786; Maúrtua, *Juicio de límites*, 1:222; Manuscritos del Marqués del Risco, vol. 4; and Vázquez de Espinosa, *Compendio*, p. 656.

8. Davies, "Rural Domain," pp. 53–4.

9. Ibid., pp. 170, 98–121.

10. Ibid., pp. 1–3; Vázquez de Espinosa, *Compendio*, pp. 465–7; and Germán Leguía y Martínez, *Historia de Arequipa*, 2 vols. (Lima: El Lucero, 1913). The best collection of documents relating to early colonial Arequipa is that of Víctor M. Barriga (ed.), *Documentos para la historia de Arequipa*, 3 vols. (Arequipa, 1939–55), and his *Memorias para la historia de Arequipa*, 4 vols. (Arequipa, 1952).

11. Alejandro Málaga Medina, "Consideraciones económicas sobre la visita de la provincia de Arequipa," in Cook, *Tasa de la visita general*, pp. 299–311; the same author's "Los Collaguas en la historia de Arequipa en el siglo XVI," in Pease, *Collaguas I*, pp. 93–130; and Menzel, "Inca Occupation."

12. Víctor M. Barriga (ed.), *Los terremotos en Arequipa, 1582–1868* (Arequipa: La Colmena, 1951), pp. 3–9, 20–1, 32–43, 47.

13. Ibid. pp. 55–163.

14. Ibid., pp. 187–98.

15. Ibid., pp. 237–59.

16. AGI, Contaduría 1786; ANP, Residencias, leg. 4, cuad. 8; ANP, Derecho indígena y encomiendas, leg. 2, cuad. 10; Manuscritos del Marqués del Risco, vol. 4; and Vázquez de Espinosa, *Compendio*, p. 657.

17. See Fernando Ponce and Eusebio Quiroz Paz-Soldán, "Observaciones críticas a la información demográfico-histórica de Arequipa, 1549–1820," *Latin American Research Review* 13 (1978):170–81; and the same authors' *Informe de datos bibliográficos-documentales de orden demográfico de la ciudad de Arequipa, Perú* (Mexico City: Celade, 1975).

18. Leguía y Martínez, *Arequipa*, 1:49–58, 166; and Barriga, *Memorias de Arequipa*, 4:65.

19. See Cook, "La población de Yanahuara," pp. 13–34.

20. Vázquez de Espinosa, *Compendio*, pp. 480–4, 587, 656–7; Davies, "Rural Domain," p. 6; Manuscritos del Marqués del Risco, vol. 4; Maúrtua, *Juicio de límites*, 1:216; and AGI, Contaduría 1786.

11. Intermediate area: northern highlands

1. Romero, *Nueva geografía*, 1:153–6, 256–64; 2:185.

2. Porras Barrenechea, *Relaciones primitivas,* pp. 71–2, 83–4.

3. The English translation of Jerez is from J. M. Cohen's edition of Agustín de Zárate, *The Discovery and Conquest of Peru* (Baltimore: Penguin, 1968), pp. 91–2.

4. Waldemar Espinosa Soriano, "El primer informe etnológico sobre Cajamarca, año de 1540," *Revista peruana de cultura* 11/12 (1967):5–41; AGI, Escribanía de Cámara 500A, 500B; ANP, Derecho indígena y encomiendas, leg. 3, cuad. 37; leg. 4, cuad. 51; ANP, Superior gobierno, leg. 2, cuad 12; Manuscritos del Marqués del Risco, vol. 4; Maúrtua, *Juicio de límites,* 1:258; and Vázquez de Espinosa, *Compendio,* pp. 373–6, 651–2.

5. ANP, Residencias, leg. 19, cuad. 50; leg. 26, cuad. 72; ANP, Real Hacienda, leg. 4; BNL, A163, B825; Manuscritos del Marqués del Risco, vol. 4: Levillier, *Gobernantes,* 13:111, 251; Loredo, *Repartos,* pp. 232–3; Maúrtua, *Juicio de límites,* 1:246–7; Vázquez de Espinosa, *Compendio,* pp. 646–7; and Noble David Cook, "La visita de los Conchucos por Cristóbal Ponce de León, 1543," *Historia y cultura* 10 (1976–7):23–46.

6. Vázquez de Espinosa, *Compendio,* pp. 376–7, 650; ANP, Residencias, leg. 15, cuad. 39; Maúrtua, *Juicio de límites,* 1:262; and Manuscritos del Marqués del Risco, vol. 4.

7. López de Velasco, *Geografía y descripción,* p. 473; Vázquez de Espinosa, *Compendio,* pp. 452–7; Rolando Mellafe, "Consideraciones históricas sobre la visita de Iñigo Ortiz de Zúñiga," in Murra, *Visita de Huánuco,* p. 329; Loredo, *Repartos,* p. 235; Manuscritos del Marqués del Risco, vol. 4; and Maúrtua, *Juicio de límites,* 1:248–9.

8. Murra, *Visita de Huánuco,* p. 187.

9. ANP, Residencias, leg. 17.

10. Ibid.

11. *CDIHE,* 9:357; López de Velasco, *Geografía y descripción,* pp. 440–1.

12. Luís Antonio Eguiguren, *Invincible Jaén* (Lima: Torres Aguirre, 1943), pp. 64–70; Loredo, *Repartos,* p. 274; AGI, Lima 199, 200; Manuscritos del Marqués del Risco, vol. 4; and Vázquez de Espinosa, *Compendio,* pp. 367, 380–1.

13. Rogger Ravines, "Los caciques de Pausamarca: algo más sobre las etnías de Chachapoyas," *Historia y cultura* 6 (1973):217–18; and Waldemar Espinosa Soriano, "Los señorios étnicos de Chachapoyas y la alianza hispano–chacha," *Revista histórica* 30 (1967):272–5.

14. Loredo, *Repartos,* pp. 259–64; López de Velasco, *Geografía y descripión,* pp. 471–3; and Vázquez de Espinosa, *Compendio,* pp. 376–80, 651.

15. BNL, B10, B20; Manuscritos del Marqués del Risco, vol. 4; and ANP, Residencias, leg. 17.

16. ANP, Derecho indígena y encomiendas, leg. 3, cuad. 34; ANP, Residencias, leg. 17; Maúrtua, *Juicio de límites,* 1:264; and Espinosa Soriano, "Señorios étnicos," p. 231.

12. Mining and population in the central sierra

1. Hemming, *Conquest,* pp. 93–6. The ceremonial foundation of Jauja took place on 25 April 1534. José Antonio del Busto Duthurburu, *Francisco Pizarro, el marqués gobernador* (Madrid: Rialp, 1966), pp. 191–3.

2. English quotation from Cohen's edition of Zárate, *Discovery and Conquest,* p. 123.

3. Hernando Pizarro, in his report about Pachacamac, also mentions his visit to Jauja in 1533. He stated: "We mounted a hill overlooking Jauja, and saw in the plaza a large black mass that we thought was something that had burned. We asked what it was, and they told us they were Indians . . . The next morning the people came to the plaza, they were *indios de servicio,* and I tell the truth that there were over one hundred thousand souls." Pizarro wrote in November of 1533; see Horacio H. Urteaga (ed.), *Informaciones sobre el antiguo Perú* (Lima: Sanmartí, 1920), p. 179.

4. Pedro de Cieza de León, *The Incas* (Norman: University of Oklahoma Press, 1959).

5. Jiménez de la Espada, *Relaciones geográficas,* 1:167.

6. Sherburne F. Cook and Woodrow Borah, "On the Credibility of Contemporary Testimony on the Population of Mexico in the Sixteenth Century," in *Homenaje a Roberto J. Weitlaner* (Mexico: Instituto Nacional Antropológica de México, 1966), p. 237.

7. ANP, Derecho indígena y encomiendas, leg. 3, cuad. 36; ANP, Residencias, leg. 27, cuad. 73; Manuscritos del Marqués del Risco, vol. 4; Maúrtua, *Juicio de límites,* 1:234–5; and Vázquez de Espinosa, *Compendio,* p. 648.

8. Vázquez de Espinosa, *Compendio,* pp. 442–4; AGI, Lima 199; ANP, Derecho indígena y encomiendas, leg. 3, cuad. 36; and ANP, Residencias, leg. 27, cuad. 73.

9. J. R. Fisher, *Silver Mines and Silver Miners in Colonial Peru, 1776–1824* (Liverpool: Centre for Latin-American Studies, 1977), p. 3.

10. Guillermo Lohmann Villena, *Las minas de Huancavelica en los siglos XVI y XVII* (Seville: Escuela de Estudios Hispano-Americanos, 1949), pp. 11–22.

11. Ibid.; see also Arthur P. Whitaker, *The Huancavelica Mercury Mine* (Cambridge, Mass: Harvard University Press, 1941).

12. Lohmann Villena, *Minas de Huancavelica,* pp. 34–45, 51, 64–5.

13. See Virgilio Roel Pineda, *Historia social y económica de la colonia* (Lima: Gráfica Labor, 1970), pp. 102–3.

14. Lohmann Villena, *Minas de Huancavelica,* pp. 91–2.

15. Ibid., pp. 97–8.

16. Ibid., pp. 173–4.

17. Whitaker, *Huancavelica Mercury Mines,* pp. 20, 108.

18. See Philip Ainsworth Means, *Fall of the Inca Empire and the Spanish Rule in Peru, 1530–1720* (New York: Charles Scribner's Sons, 1932), pp. 181–6.

19. Fuentes, *Memorias de los virreyes,* 1:308–10.

20. See Chapter 5.

21. Fuentes, *Memorias de los virreyes,* 1:308–10.

22. AGI, Lima 272; AGI, Contaduría 1786, 1827; ANP, Residencias, leg. 12, cuad. 32; leg. 28, cuad. 77; leg. 33, cuad. 96; Boleslao Lewin (ed.), *Descripción del virreinato del Perú* (Rosario: Universidad Nacional del Litoral, 1958), pp. 83–6; and Vázquez de Espinosa, *Compendio,* pp. 490–1, 535, 664. There were several non-Spanish residents of Castrovirreyna: eleven from Genoa, seven Corsicans, three Portuguese, one Savoyard, and one Levantine.

13. The Indian heartland: southern highlands

1. A good outline of the historical evolution of the Cuzco region can be found in Magnus Mörner, *Perfil de la sociedad rural del Cuzco a fines de la colonia* (Lima: Universidad del Pacífico, 1978).

2. Lanning, *Peru before the Incas,* p. 162.

3. Ibid., p. 163.

4. Rowe, "Urban Settlements," p. 18.

5. Raúl Porras Barrenechea (ed.), *Antología del Cuzco* (Lima: Librería Internacional, 1961), pp. 3–5.

6. Ibid., pp. 7–8.

7. Horacio H. Urteaga (ed.), *Relación del sitio del Cusco* (Lima, 1934), p. 14.

8. Cieza de León, *The Incas,* pp. 144, 47–8.

9. Loayza, *Crónicas de los Molinas,* p. 33.

10. Martín de Morúa, *Historia de los Incas, reyes del Perú* (Lima: Sanmartí, 1925), p. 13.

11. López de Velasco, *Geografía y descripción,* pp. 479–81.

12. Cook, *Tasa de la visita general,* pp. 210–12.

13. Porras Barrenechea, *Antología,* pp. 114–16; and Urteaga, *Relación del sitio,* p. 93.

14. Vázquez de Espinosa, *Compendio,* pp. 553–6.

•15. López de Velasco, *Geografía y descripción,* p. 481.

16. See also the section on Cuzco archaeology in Chapter 2.

17. AHC, Genealogía de Sayri Tupac, libro 2, índ. 4, ff. 318v–352r. See also Wachtel, *Sociedad e ideología,* pp. 101–13; and Horacio Villanueva Urteaga, "Documentos sobre Yucay en el siglo XVI," *Revista del Archivo Histórico del Cuzco* 13 (1970):1–149.

18. See Hemming, *Conquest,* pp. 269, 284–6, 513, 590, for an outline of the history of the grant; and Wachtel, *Vision of the Vanquished,* pp. 86–93, 109–14.

19. One of the best general accounts of the production of coca in early colonial Peru is that of Joseph A. Gagliano, "The Coca Debate in Colonial Peru," *The Americas* 20 (1963):43–63.

20. Juan de Matienzo, *Gobierno del Perú* (*1567*) (Paris: Institut Français d'Etudes Andines, 1967), pp. 163–4; and Lanning, *Peru before the Incas,* pp. 72–7.

21. Matienzo, *Gobierno del Perú,* p. 162.

22. Ibid., pp. 164–74; and Hemming, *Conquest,* p. 368.

23. Matienzo, *Gobierno del Perú,* pp. 162–4.

24. Fernando de Santillán, *Relación de su gobierno* (Lima: Sanmartí, 1927), pp. 108–9.

25. Ibid., p. 108; and Francisco de Toledo, *Fundación española del Cusco y ordenanzas para su gobierno* (Lima: Sanmartí, 1926), pp. 115, 133.

26. Matienzo, *Gobierno del Perú,* pp. 167–8.

27. Ibid., pp. 169–74; and Cook, *Tasa de la visita general,* pp. 169, 201–2.

28. Matienzo, *Gobierno del Perú,* pp. 171–9; and Toledo, *Fundación del Cusco,* p. 123.

29. Santillán, *Relación,* p. 108; and Matienzo, *Gobierno del Perú,* p. 171.

30. Vázquez de Espinosa, *Compendio*, pp. 561, 659; Manuscritos del Marqués del Risco, vol. 4; AHC, Archivo de la Sociedad de Beneficencia, 1ª Sala, Est. 5, Ana 7–18, 1575, Per. #3, Libro de Encomiendas; and Cook, *Tasa de la visita general*, pp. 106–7.

31. Felipe Guamán Poma de Ayala, *La nueva crónica y buen gobierno* (Lima: Editorial Cultura, 1956), 3:181.

32. AGI, Contaduría 1826, 1827; Manuscritos del Marqués del Risco, vol. 4; ANP, Derecho indígena y encomiendas, leg. 4, cuad. 50; ANP, Real Hacienda, leg. 2, cuad. 6; ANP, Residencias, leg. 28, cuad. 81; BNL, B500; Vázquez de Espinosa, *Compendio*, p. 664; and Cook, *Tasa de la visita general*, pp. 115–16.

33. AGI, Contaduría 1826, 1827; Manuscritos del Marqués del Risco, vol. 4; ANP, Residencias, leg. 12, cuad. 32; leg. 28, cuad. 77; leg. 33, cuad. 96; Vázquez de Espinosa, *Compendio*, p. 663; and Cook, *Tasa de la visita general*, pp. 116–19, 124–8.

34. AGI, Contaduría 1826, 1827; Manuscritos del Marqués del Risco, vol. 4; ANP, Derecho indígena y encomiendas, leg. 3, cuad. 21; ANP, Residencias, leg. 29, cuad. 82; BNL, B1481; Vázquez de Espinosa, *Compendio*, p. 662; and Cook, *Tasa de la visita general*, pp. 118–19, 135–6, 163–5.

35. AGI, Lima 150; Manuscritos del Marqués del Risco, vol. 4; ANP, Residencias, leg. 5, cuad. 11; leg. 14, cuad. 38; ANP, Testamentos de indios; BNL, A236, A238; Vázquez de Espinosa, *Compendio*, pp. 512–13; and Cook, *Tasa de la visita general*, pp. 120–3.

36. AGI, Contaduría 1786; AGI, Indiferente general 1660; AGI, Lima 199, 200; Manuscritos del Marqués del Risco, vol. 4; ANP, Residencias, leg. 33, cuad. 93; Maúrtua, *Juicio de límites*, 1:217–18; and Vázquez de Espinosa, *Compendio*, pp. 655–6.

37. Manuscritos del Marqués del Risco, vol. 4; Maúrtua, *Juicio de límites*, 1:219; Vázquez de Espinosa, *Compendio*, pp. 467–8, 655; Cook, *Tasa de la visita general*, pp. 220–7; and Jiménez de la Espada, *Relaciones geográficas*, 1:326–33.

38. See Rénique and Trelles, "Aproximación demográfica," pp. 169–90; and Franklin Pease, *Del Tawantinsuyu a la historia del Perú* (Lima: Instituto de Estudios Peruanos, 1978), pp. 141–79.

39. Vázquez de Espinosa, *Compendio*, pp. 468–74; and Cook, *Tasa de la visita general*, pp. 218, 236–42.

40. AGI, Lima 199; Manuscritos del Marqués del Risco, vol. 4; ANP, Derecho indígena y encomiendas, leg. 2, cuad. 10; Maúrtua, *Juicio de límites*, 1:218–20; and Vázquez de Espinosa, *Compendio*, p. 655.

41. See Josep M. Barnadas, *Charcas: orígenes históricos de una sociedad colonial* (La Paz: Universo, 1973), pp. 266–7.

42. Bartolomé Martínez y Vela, *Anales de la villa imperial de Potosí* (La Paz: Artística, 1939), pp. 9–12; and Fisher, *Silver Mines*, pp. 2–4.

43. López de Velasco, *Geografía y descripción*, pp. 502–4; Joseph Baquijano, "Historia del descubrimiento del Cerro de Potosí," *Mercurio peruano* 7 (1793):28–48; and Roel, *Historia social y económica*, p. 100.

44. Robert C. Padden (ed.), *Tales of Potosí* (Providence, R.I.: Brown University Press, 1975), p. xx.

45. Martínez y Vela, *Anales,* pp. 50, 74–6; Hemming, *Conquest,* p. 372.
46. Martínez y Vela, *Anales,* pp. 22, 31–56, 108–26.
47. Ibid., pp. 23–5.
48. Ibid., pp. 11–112.
49. Manuscritos del Marqués del Risco, vol. 4; Maúrtua, *Juicio de límites,* 1:190–1; Vázquez de Espinosa, *Compendio,* p. 670; Cook, *Tasa de la visita general,* pp. 78–83; and Espinosa Soriano, *Visita de Chucuito.*
50. Hemming, *Conquest,* p. 408.
51. Ibid.; Kubler, "The Quechua," pp. 372–3; and Pease, *Del Tawantinsuyu,* pp. 115–40.
52. See Cook, "Indian Population of Peru," pp. 191–5.
53. AGI, Contaduría 1826, 1827; Manuscritos del Marqués del Risco, vol. 4; Vázquez de Espinosa, *Compendio,* pp. 558–9, 659; and Cook, *Tasa de la visita general,* pp. 134–50.
54. AGI, Contaduría 1826, 1827; AGI, Indiferente General 1660; AGI, Lima 199; Manuscritos del Marqués del Risco, vol. 4; and ANP, Residencias, leg. 35, cuad. 98.

14. An overview

1. Were it not for the proximity of nearby dense highland populations, which tended to migrate in the direction of Arequipa, the collapse of this sector would probably have been complete.
2. Denevan has stated: "The reasons for the more rapid population decline in the lowlands are not entirely clear. The introduction of Old World tropical diseases such as malaria, which were less destructive in the highlands, is generally thought to have been a major reason for the difference. On the other hand, the main highland killers, smallpox and measles, may have been even more virulent in the lowlands. Some viruses tend to survive better in warmer climates. Also, different dietary patterns may have been the key factor. In the lowlands, where starchy tubers were the staples, malnutrition would have been more likely to have occurred when hunting and fishing, the main protein sources, were disrupted by Spanish labor demands than in the highlands where maize and beans (Mesoamerica) or potatoes with *quinoa* (Andes) provided balanced diets." *Native Population,* p. 41.
3. Mellafe's study of colonial Peruvian migration is still the best available: "Importance of Migration," pp. 303–13.
4. See Cook, "Indian Population of Peru," pp. 201–36.
5. On the other hand, as Sánchez-Albornoz points out, the increase in the number of forasteros becomes more significant as a factor as the seventeenth century progresses. See *Indios y Tributos.*
6. See Franklin Pease, *El dios creador andino* (Lima: Mosca Azul, 1973); and Pierre Duviols, *La lutte contre les religions autochtones dans le Pérou colonial: l'extirpation de l'idolatrie entre 1532 et 1660* (Paris: Institut Français d'Etudes Andines, 1971).
7. Juan Santa Cruz Pachacuti, *Historia de los Incas* (Lima: Sanmartí, 1927), pp. 215–16.

Bibliography

Published sources of population information on sixteenth- and seventeenth-century Peru are often filled with errors, and correct census dates are generally not given. Modern demographic studies, which have relied heavily on published rather than archival research, must be used with caution. Demographic data are most often found in association with economic information relating to the collection of tribute, which was required of adult Indian males between the ages of 18 and 50. Such sources are usually scattered; the amassing of a sizable amount of population figures is consequently a slow process.

The Archivo General de Indias in Seville clearly is the best single depository for administrative documents of Spanish America. The fiscal information in the Contaduría section was especially valuable, and the Audiencia of Lima material provided useful supplementary information on the working of Peruvian repartimiento-encomienda. The less widely used Biblioteca Central of the University of Seville contains the important manuscript collection of Juan Luis López, the Marqués del Risco and secretary while in Peru to Viceroy Duque de la Palata (1681–9). Volume 4 of this collection contains the Luis de Morales Figueroa list of Peruvian encomiendas in 1591. Two important manuscript collections at the Royal Academy of History in Madrid with sixteenth-century population numbers are the Muñoz and the Mata Linares collections. The Manuscript Collection of the Biblioteca Nacional in Madrid contains the 1613 census of the Indians living in Lima, taken by Viceroy Marqués de Montesclaros.

Peruvian population material is much more extensive than that to be found in Spain. Most *legajos* in the Residencia section of the National Archive in Lima provide information on numbers, as well as excellent material on ethnohistory. Tribute records in the Real Hacienda and in the Derecho Indígena y Encomiendas sections are valuable sources of population figures. The manuscript room of the Biblioteca Nacional in Lima houses several complete or partial censuses of Indian grants. The Archivo Arzobispal in the same city has good population records for Lima, but the coverage for Indians in the sixteenth century is relatively weak. Provincial archives in Arequipa and Cuzco contain some helpful information, and the parish archive of the community of Yanque includes some sixteenth- and seventeenth-century census material for the five repartimientos of the Collaguas.

Amiama, Manuel A. "La población de Santo Domingo." *Clio* 115 (1959):116–34.
Andrew, Anthony P. "The U-Shaped Structures at Chan Chan, Peru." *Journal of Field Anthropology* 1 (1974):242–64.
Angel, J. Lawrence, "The Bases of Paleodemography." *American Journal of Physical Anthropology* 30 (1969):427–35.

Angulo, Domingo de, ed. "La fundación y población de la villa de Zaña." *Revista del Archivo Nacional del Perú* 1 (1920):280–301.

Ascher, Robert. "A Prehistoric Population Estimate Using Midden Analysis and Two Population Models." *Southwestern Journal of Anthropology* 15 (1959):168–78.

Aykroyd, W. R., et al. "Protein Requirements: Report of the FAO Committee, Rome, Italy, October 24–31, 1955." *Nutritional Studies,* no. 16. Rome: Food and Agriculture Organization of the United Nations, 1957.

Bailey, Norman T. J. *The Mathematical Theory of Infectious Diseases and Its Applications.* New York: Hafner, 1975. ·

Baker, Paul T. "Adaptation Problems in Andean Human Populations." in *The Ongoing Evolution of Latin American Populations,* edited by Francisco M. Salzano, pp. 475–507. Springfield, Ill.: Charles C. Thomas, 1971.

Baker, Paul T. "Ecological and Physiological Adaptation in Indigenous South Americans." In *The Biology of Human Adaptability,* edited by Paul T. Baker and J. S. Weiner, pp. 275–303. Oxford: Oxford University Press, Clarendon Press, 1966.

Baker, Paul T. , and Weiner, J. S., eds. *The Biology of Human Adaptability.* Oxford: Oxford University Press, Clarendon Press, 1966.

Bakewell, Peter J. "Registered Silver Production in the Potosí District, 1550–1735." *Jahrbuch für Geschichte von Staat, Wirtschaft und Gesellschaft Lateinamerikas* 12 (1975):67–103.

Baquijano, Joseph. "Historia del descubrimiento del Cerro de Potosí." *Mercurio peruano* 7 (1793):28–48.

Barclay, George W. *Techniques of Population Analysis.* New York: John Wiley, 1958.

Barnadas, Josep M. *Charcas: orígenes históricos de una sociedad colonial.* La Paz: Universo, 1973.

Barón Castro, Rodolfo. "El desarrollo de la población hispanoamericana (1492–1950)." *Cahiers d'histoire mondiale* 5 (1959):325–43.

Barón Castro, Rodolfo. *La población de El Salvador.* Madrid: Instituto Gonzalo Fernández de Oviedo, 1942.

Barriga, Víctor M., ed. *Documentos para la historia de Arequipa.* 3 vols. Arequipa, 1939–55.

Barriga, Víctor M., ed. *Memorias para la historia de Arequipa.* 4 vols. Arequipa, 1952.

Barriga, Víctor M., ed. *Los terremotos en Arequipa, 1582–1868.* Arequipa: La Colmena, 1951.

Bennett, Wendell C. "The Andean Highlands." In *Handbook of South American Indians,* edited by Julian H. Steward, 2:1–60. 7 vols. Bureau of American Ethnology Bulletins, no. 143. Washington, D.C., 1946–59.

Bennett, Wendell C., and Bird, Junius B. *Andean Culture History.* New York: Museum of Natural History, 1960.

Bidbury, A. R. "The Black Death." *Economic History Review* 26 (1973):577–92.

Borah, Woodrow. "America as Model: The Demographic Impact of European Expansion upon the Non-European World." *Actas y memorias, XXXV Congreso Internacional de Americanistas* 3:379–87. Mexico City, 1964.

Borah, Woodrow. "The Historical Demography of Aboriginal and Colonial America:

An Attempt at Perspective." In *The Native Population of the Americas in 1492*, edited by William M. Denevan, pp. 13–34. Madison: University of Wisconsin Press, 1976.

Borah, Woodrow. "The Historical Demography of Latin America: Sources, Techniques, Controversies, Yields." In *Population and Economics: Proceedings of Section V of the Fourth Congress of the International Economic History Association*, edited by Paul Deprez, pp. 173–205. Winnipeg: University of Manitoba Press, 1970.

Borah, Woodrow, and Cook, Sherburne F. *The Aboriginal Population of Central Mexico on the Eve of the Spanish Conquest*. Ibero-Americana, no. 45. Berkeley: University of California Press, 1963.

Borah, Woodrow, and Cook, Sherburne F. *Essays in Population History: Mexico and the Caribbean*. 3 vols. Berkeley: University of California Press, 1971–7.

Borah, Woodrow, and Cook, Sherburne F. *The Indian Population of Central Mexico, 1531–1610*. Ibero-Americana, no. 44. Berkeley: University of California Press, 1960.

Borah, Woodrow, and Cook, Sherburne F. *The Population of Central Mexico in 1548*. Ibero-Americana, no. 43. Berkeley: University of California Press, 1960.

Borah, Woodrow, and Cook, Sherburne F. *Price Trends of Some Basic Commodities in Central Mexico, 1531–1570*. Ibero-Americana, no. 40. Berkeley: University of California Press, 1958.

Bowser, Frederick Park. "Negro Slavery in Colonial Peru, 1529–1650." Ph.D. dissertation, University of California, 1967.

Brady, T., and Lombardi, J. "The Application of Computers to the Analysis of Census Data: The Bishopric of Caracas, 1780–1820." In *Population and Economics: Proceedings of Section V of the Fourth Congress of the International Economic History Association*, edited by Paul Deprez, pp. 271–8. Winnipeg: University of Manitoba Press, 1970.

Bromley, Juan. *La fundación de la ciudad de los Reyes*. Lima: Excelsior, 1935.

Bromley, Juan, and Barbagelati, José. *Evolución urbana de la ciudad de Lima*. Lima, 1945.

Bromley, Rosemary D. F. "Parish Registers as a Source in Latin American Demographic and Historical Research." *Bulletin of the Society for Latin American Studies* 19 (1974):14–21.

Browman, David L. "Pastoral Nomadism in the Andes." *Current Anthropology* 15 (1974):188–96.

Browning, David G. "Distribution and Structure of the Population in Spanish America, 1750–1810: Identification and Retrieval of Data." Paper presented at the XLI International Congress of Americanists. Mexico City, 1974.

Buck, Alfred A.; Sasaki, Tom T.; and Anderson, Robert I. *Health and Disease in Four Peruvian Villages: Contrasts in Epidemiology*. Baltimore: Johns Hopkins University Press, 1968.

Burga, Manuel. *De la encomienda a la hacienda capitalista: el valle del Jequetepeque del siglo XVI a XX*. Lima: Instituto de Estudios Peruanos, 1976.

Burgos-Guevara, Hugo. "La población del Ecuador en la encrucijada de los siglos XVI y XVII." In *Atti del XL Congresso Internazionale degli Americanisti*, 2:483–7. Rome, 1972.

Burnet, Frank MacFarlane. *The Integrity of the Body: A Discussion of Modern Immunological Ideas.* Cambridge, Mass.: Harvard University Press, 1962.

Busto Duthurburu, José Antonio del. *Francisco Pizarro, el marqués gobernador.* Madrid: Rialp, 1966.

Cabello de Balboa, Miguel. *Miscelánea antártica: una historia del Perú antiguo.* Lima: San Marcos, 1951.

Cabero, Marco A. "El corregimiento de Saña y el problema histórico de la fundación de Trujillo." *Revista histórica* 1 (1906):151–91, 337–73, 486–514.

Cabero, Marco A. "Fragmentos de una historia de Trujillo." *Revista histórica* 8 (1925):86–118.

Carmagnani, Marcello. "Colonial Latin American Demography: Growth of Chilean Population, 1700–1830." *Journal of Social History* 1 (1967):179–91.

Carneiro, Robert L. "On the Relationship between Size of Population and Complexity of Social Organization." *Southwestern Journal of Anthropology* 23 (1967):234–43.

Cartwright, Frederick F. *Disease and History.* London: Rupert Hart-Davis, 1972.

Casas, Bartolomé de las. *Apologética historia de las Indias.* Madrid, 1909.

Casas, Bartolomé de las. *Brevísima relación de la destrucción de las Indias.* Buenos Aires, 1973.

Caso, Alonso. "El mapa de Teozacoalco." *Cuadernos americanos* 8-5 (1949):3–40.

Caso, Alonso. "Valor histórico de los códices mixtecos." *Cuadernos americanos* 19-2 (1960):139–47.

Castro, Alberto Rossel. *Historia regional de Ica.* Lima: San Marcos, 1964.

Cieza de León, Pedro. *The Incas.* Norman: University of Oklahoma Press, 1959.

Cieza de León, Pedro. *El señorío de los Incas.* Lima: Instituto de Estudios Peruanos, 1967.

Coale, Ansley J., and Demeny, Paul. *Regional Model Life Tables and Stable Populations.* Princeton, N.J.: Princeton University Press, 1966.

Cockburn, T. Aidan. "Infectious Diseases in Ancient Populations." *Current Anthropology* 12 (1971):45–62.

Cohen, Mark Nathan. "Some Problems in the Quantitative Analysis of Vegetable Refuse, Illustrated by a Late Horizon Site on the Peruvian Coast." *Ñawpa Pacha* 10-12 (1972–4):49–60.

Coleman, Katherine. "Provincial Urban Problems: Trujillo, Peru, 1600–1784." In *Social Fabric and Spatial Structure in Colonial Latin America,* edited by David J. Robinson, pp. 369–408. Ann Arbor, Mich.: University Microfilms, 1979.

Colmenares, Germán. *Encomienda y población en la provincia de Pamplona (1549–1650).* Bogotá: Universidad de los Andes, 1969.

Colmenares, Germán. *La provincia de Tunja en el Nuevo Reino de Granada: ensayo de historia social (1539–1800).* Bogotá: Universidad de los Andes, 1970.

Cook, Noble David. "Eighteenth Century Population Change in Andean Peru: The Parish of Yanque." Paper presented at the XLIII International Congress of Americanists. Vancouver, B.C., 1979.

Cook, Noble David. "Estimaciones sobre la población del Perú en el momento de la conquista." *Histórica* 1 (1977):37–60.

Cook, Noble David. "The Indian Population of Peru, 1570–1620." Ph.D. dissertation, University of Texas, 1973.

Cook, Noble David. "The Indian Population of Végueta, 1623–1683: A Case Study of Population Change in the Central Coastal Region of Peru in the Seventeenth Century." In *Atti del XL Congresso Internazionale degli Americanisti*, 4:309–16. Rome, 1972.

Cook, Noble David. "Les indiens immigrés à Lima au début du XVIIᵉ siècle." *Cahiers des Amériques Latines* 13/14 (1976):33–50.

Cook, Noble David. "La población indígena en el Perú colonial." *Anuario del Instituto de Investigaciones Históricas* 8 (1965):73–110.

Cook, Noble David. "La población de la parroquia de Yanahuara, 1738–47: un modelo para el estudio de las parroquias coloniales peruanas." In *Collaguas I*, edited by Franklin Pease, pp. 13–34. Lima: Universidad Católica, 1977.

Cook, Noble David. "La visita de los Conchucos por Cristóbol Ponce de León, 1543." *Historia y cultura* 10 (1976–7):23–46.

Cook, Noble David, ed. *Padrón de los indios de Lima en 1613*. Lima: San Marcos, 1968.

Cook, Noble David, ed. *Tasa de la visita general de Francisco de Toledo*. Lima: San Marcos, 1975.

Cook, Noble David, and Pease, Franklin. "New Research Opportunities in Los Collaguas, Peru." *Latin American Research Review* 10 (1975):201–2.

Cook, Sherburne F. "Can Pottery Residues Be Used as an Index to Population?" *Contributions of the University of California Archaeological Research Facility*. Miscellaneous Papers on Archaeology, no. 14. Berkeley, 1975.

Cook, Sherburne F. *The Historical Demography and Ecology of the Teotlalpan*. Ibero-Americana, no. 33. Berkeley: University of California Press, 1949.

Cook, Sherburne F. "Human Sacrifice and Warfare as Factors in the Demography of Pre-Colonial Mexico." *Human Biology* 18 (1946):81–103.

Cook, Sherburne F. *Prehistoric Demography*. Reading, Mass.: Addison-Wesley, 1972.

Cook, Sherburne F., and Borah, Woodrow. "On the Credibility of Contemporary Testimony on the Population of Mexico in the Sixteenth Century." In *Homenaje a Roberto J. Weitlaner*, pp. 229–39. Mexico: Instituto Nacional Antropológica de México, 1966.

Cook, S. F., and Heizer, R. F., eds. *The Application of Quantitative Methods in Archaeology*. Chicago: Quadrangle, 1960.

Cook, Sherburne F., and Simpson, Lesley Byrd. *The Population of Central Mexico in the Sixteenth Century*. Ibero-Americana, no. 31. Berkeley: University of California Press, 1948.

Cook, S. F., and Treganza, A. E. *The Quantitative Investigation of Indian Mounds, with Special Reference to the Relation of the Physical Components to the Probable Material Culture*. University of California Publications in American Archaeology and Ethnology, vol. 40, no. 5. Berkeley, 1950.

Cooper, John M. "The Ona." In *Handbook of South American Indians*, edited by Julian H. Steward, 1:107–26. 7 vols. Bureau of American Ethnology Bulletins, no. 143. Washington, D.C., 1946–59.

Cooper, John M. "The Yahgan." In *Handbook of South American Indians*, edited by Julian H. Steward, 1:81–106. 7 vols. Bureau of American Ethnology Bulletins, no. 143. Washington, D.C., 1946–59.

Córdova, Efrén. "La encomienda y la desaparición de los indios en las Antillas mayores." *Caribbean Studies* 8 (1968):23–49.

Crespo, Juan Carlos. "La relación de Chincha." *Historia y cultura* 8 (1974):91–104.

Crosby, Alfred W. *The Columbian Exchange: Biological and Cultural Consequences of 1492.* Westport, Conn.: Greenwood Press, 1972.

Cúneo-Vidal, Rómulo. *Vida del conquistador del Perú, don Francisco Pizarro.* Barcelona: Maucci, 1925.

Dark, Philip. *Mixtec Ethnography: A Method of Analysis of the Codical Art.* London: Oxford University Press, 1958.

Daugherty, Howard E. "Man-Induced Ecologic Change in El Salvador." Ph.D. dissertation, University of California at Los Angeles, 1969.

Davies, Keith Arfon. "The Rural Domain of the City of Arequipa, 1540–1665." Ph.D. dissertation, University of Connecticut, 1974.

Denevan, William M. "Aboriginal Drained-Field Cultivation in the Americas." *Science* 169 (1970):647–54.

Denevan, William M. "The Aboriginal Population of Amazonia." In *The Native Population of the Americas in 1492,* edited by W. M. Denevan, pp. 205–34. Madison: University of Wisconsin Press, 1976.

Denevan, William M., ed. *The Native Population of the Americas in 1492.* Madison: University of Wisconsin Press, 1976.

Deprez, Paul, ed. *Population and Economics: Proceedings of Section V of the Fourth Congress of the International Economic History Association.* Winnipeg: University of Manitoba Press, 1970.

Deutschmann, Z. "The Ecology of Smallpox." In *Studies in Disease Ecology,* edited by Jacques M. May, pp. 1–14. New York: Hafner, 1961.

Dobyns, Henry F. "Estimating Aboriginal American Population: An Appraisal of Techniques with a New Hemispheric Estimate." *Current Anthropology* 7 (1966):395–449.

Dobyns, Henry F. "An Outline of Andean Epidemic History to 1720." *Bulletin of the History of Medicine* 37 (1963):493–515.

Dubos, René J., and Hirsch, James G., eds. *Bacterial and Mycotic Infections of Man.* 4th ed. Philadelphia: J. B. Lippincott, 1965.

Duffy, John. *Epidemics in Colonial America.* Baton Rouge: Louisiana State University Press, 1953.

Dumond, D. E. "Population Growth and Cultural Change." *Southwestern Journal of Anthropology* 21 (1965):302–24.

Duviols, Pierre. *La lutte contre les religions autochtones dans le Pérou colonial: l'extirpation de l'idolatrie entre 1532 et 1660.* Paris: Institut Français d'Etudes Andines, 1971.

Eguiguren, Luís Antonio. *Invincible Jaén.* Lima: Torres Aguirre, 1943.

Eidt, Robert C. "Aboriginal Chibcha settlement in Colombia." *Annals of the Association of American Geographers* 49 (1959):374–92.

Espinosa Soriano, Waldemar. "El primer informe etnológico sobre Cajamarca, año de 1540." *Revista peruana de cultura* 11/12 (1967):5–41.

Espinosa Soriano, Waldemar. "Los señoríos étnicos de Chachapoyas y la alianza hispano-chacha." *Revista histórica* 30 (1967):224–332.

Espinosa Soriano, Waldemar, ed. *Visita hecha a la provincia de Chucuito por Garcí Diez de San Miguel en el año 1567.* Lima: Talleres Gráficos Quiros, 1964.

Estete, Miguel de. *Relación de la conquista del Perú.* Lima: Sanmartí, 1924.

Estrada Ycaza, Julio. "Migraciones internas en el Ecuador." *Revista del Archivo Histórico de Guayas* 11 (1977):5–26.

Fernández de Villalobos, Gabriel. *Vaticinios de la pérdida de las Indias y Mano de Relox.* Caracas: Instituto Panamericano de Geografía e Historia, 1949.

Fisher, J. R. *Silver Mines and Silver Miners in Colonial Peru, 1776–1824.* Liverpool: Centre for Latin-American Studies, 1977.

Flores Ochoa, Jorge. *Los pastores de Paratía.* Instituto Indigenista Interamericano, Serie Antropología Social, no. 10. Mexico City, 1968.

Florescano, Enrique. *Precios del maíz y crises agrícolas en México, 1708–1810.* Mexico City: Colegio de México, 1969.

Ford, Thomas R. *Man and Land in Peru.* Gainesville, Fla.: University of Florida Press, 1955.

Friede, Juan. "Algunas consideraciones sobre la evolución demográfica en la provincia de Tunja." *Anuario Colombiano de historia social y de la cultura* 2, no. 3 (1965):5–19.

Friede, Juan. *Los Quimbayas bajo la dominación española: estudio documental (1539–1810).* Bogotá: Banco de la República, 1963.

Fuentes, Manuel Atanasio, ed. *Memorias de los virreyes que han governado el Perú, durante el tiempo del colonaje español.* 6 vols. Lima, 1859.

Gagliano, Joseph A. "The Coca Debate in Colonial Peru." *The Americas* 20 (1963):43–63.

Gakenheimer, Ralph A. "Determinants of Physical Structure of the Peruvian Town of the Sixteenth Century." Ph.D. dissertation, University of Pennsylvania, 1964.

Gama, Sebastián de la. "Visita hecha en el valle de Jayanca (Trujillo) (1540)." *Historia y cultura* 8 (1974):215–28.

Gibson, Charles. *The Aztecs under Spanish Rule: A History of the Indians of the Valley of Mexico, 1519–1810.* Stanford, Calif.: Stanford University Press, 1964.

Glassow, Michael A. "Considerations in Estimating Prehistoric California Coastal Populations." *American Antiquity* 32 (1967):354–9.

Gross, Daniel R., ed. *Peoples and Cultures of Native South America.* Garden City, N.Y.: Doubleday, 1973.

Hadden, Gordon J. "Un ensayo de demografía histórica y etnológica en Huánuco." In *Visita de la provincia de León de Huánuco (1562),* edited by John V. Murra, 1:369–80. 2 vols. Lima: Villanueva, 1967, 1972.

Haines, Michael R. "The Use of Model Life Tables to Estimate Mortality for the United States in the Late Nineteenth Century." *Demography* 16 (1979):289–312.

Hamerly, Michael T. "La demografía histórica del distrito de Cuenca, 1778–1838." *Boletín de la Academic Nacional de Historia* 53–116 (1970):203–29.

Hamerly, Michael T. "La demografía histórica de Ecuador, Perú, y Bolivia: una bibliografía preliminar." *Revista del Archivo Histórico de Guayas* 3–6 (1974):24–63.

Hamerly, Michael T. *Historia social y económica de la antigua provincia de Guayaquil, 1763–1842.* Guayaquil, 1973.

Hamerly, Michael T. "Registros parroquiales e inventarios de iglesias del litoral." *Revista del Archivo Histórico de Guayas* 12 (1977):25–69.

Harner, Michael J. "Population Pressure and the Social Evolution of Agriculturalists." *Southwestern Journal of Anthropology* 26 (1970):67–86.

Harrison, G. A., ed. *Human Biology: An Introduction to Human Evolution, Variation, and Growth.* New York: Oxford University Press, 1964.

Hemming, John. *The Conquest of the Incas.* London: Sphere Books, 1972.

Hemming, John. *Red Gold: The Conquest of the Brazilian Indians.* Cambridge, Mass.: Harvard University Press, 1978.

Henige, David. "On the Contact Population of Hispaniola: History as Higher Mathematics." *Hispanic American Historical Review* 58 (1978):217–37.

Historical Statistics of the United States: Colonial Times to 1970. 2 vols. Washington, D.C.: U.S. Government Printing Office, 1975.

Hollingsworth, Thomas H. "Examples of Stable Populations in the Historical Record." In *International Population Conference, Mexico 1977,* 3:65–76. 3 vols. Liège, Belgium: Derouaux, 1977.

Hollingsworth, Thomas H. *Historical Demography.* Ithaca, N.Y.: Cornell University Press, 1969.

Howells, W. W. "Estimating Population Numbers through Archaeological and Skeletal Remains." In *The Application of Quantitative Methods in Archaeology,* edited by S. F. Cook and R. F. Heizer, pp. 158–85. Chicago: Quadrangle, 1960.

Informe demográfico del Perú, 1970. Lima: Centro de Estudios de Población y Desarollo, 1972.

Jaramillo Uribe, Jaime. "La población indígena de Colombia en el momento de la conquista y sus transformaciones posteriores." *Anuario Colombiano de historia social y de la cultura* 1 (1964):239–93.

Jarcho, Saul. "Some Observations on Disease in Prehistoric North America." *Bulletin of the History of Medicine* 38 (1964):1–19.

Jiménez de la Espada, Marcos, ed. *Relaciones geográficas de Indias, Perú.* 3 vols. Rev. ed. Madrid:Atlas, 1965.

Katz, Robert S. "Influenza, 1918–1919: A Study in Mortality." *Bulletin of the History of Medicine* 48 (1974):416–22.

Kautz, Robert R., and Keatinge, Richard W. "Determining Site Function: A North Peruvian Coastal Example." *American Antiquity* 42 (1977):86–97.

Keatinge, Richard W. "Urban Settlement Systems and Rural Sustaining Communities: An Example from Chan Chan's Hinterland." *Journal of Field Archaeology* 2 (1975):215–27.

Keatinge, Richard W., and Day, Kent C. "Socio-Economic Organization of the Moche Valley, Peru, during the Chimu Occupation of Chan Chan." *Journal of Anthropological Research* 29 (1973):275–82.

Keith, Robert G. *Conquest and Agrarian Change: The Emergence of the Hacienda System on the Peruvian Coast.* Cambridge, Mass.: Harvard University Press, 1976.

Kidder, Alfred. "Settlement Patterns, Peru." In *Prehistoric Settlement Patterns in the New World,* edited by Gordon R. Willey, pp. 148–55. Viking Fund Publications in Anthropology, no. 23. New York, 1956.

Klein, Herbert S. "Hacienda and Free Community in Eighteenth-Century Alto Peru: A Demographic Study of the Aymara Population of the Districts of Chulumani and Pacajes in 1786." *Journal of Latin American Studies* 7 (1975):193–220.

Klein, Herbert S. "The Impact of the Crisis in Nineteenth Century Mining on Regional Economies: The Example of the Bolivian Yungas, 1786–1838." In *Social Fabric and Spatial Structure in Colonial Latin America,* edited by David J. Robinson, pp. 315–38. Ann Arbor, Mich.: University Microfilms, 1979.

Kosok, Paul. *Life, Land, and Water in Ancient Peru.* New York: Long Island University Press, 1965.

Kubler, George. *The Indian Caste of Peru, 1795–1940.* Smithsonian Institution, Institute of Social Anthropology, Publication no. 14. Washington, D.C., 1952.

Kubler, George. "The Quechua in the Colonial World." In *Handbook of South American Indians,* edited by Julian H. Steward, 2:331–410. 7 vols. Bureau of American Ethnology Bulletins, no. 143. Washington, D.C., 1946–59.

Lanning, Edward P. *Peru before the Incas.* Englewood Cliffs, N.J.: Prentice-Hall, 1967.

Larrain Barros, Horacio. "La población indígena de Tarapacá (norte de Chile) entre 1538 y 1581." *Norte grande* (Santiago) 1 (1975):269–300.

Lastres, Juan B. *Historia de la medicina peruana.* 3 vols. Lima: San Marcos, 1951.

Le Blanc, Steven. "An Addition to Naroll's Suggested Floor Area and Settlement Population Relationship." *American Antiquity* 36 (1971):210–11.

Leguía y Martínez, Germán. *Historia de Arequipa.* 2 vols. Lima: El Lucero, 1913.

Le Roy Ladurie, Emmanuel. *Histoire du climat depuis l'an mil.* Paris: Flammarion, 1967.

Levillier, Roberto. *Don Francisco de Toledo, supremo organizador del Perú.* Madrid: Espasa-Calpe, 1935.

Levillier, Roberto, ed. *Gobernantes del Perú, cartas y papeles, siglo XVI.* 14 vols. Madrid: Juan Pueyo, 1925.

Lewin, Boleslao, ed. *Descripción del virreinato del Perú.* Rosario: Universidad Nacional del Litoral, 1958.

Lipschutz, Alejandro. "La despoblación de los indios después de la conquista." *América indígena* 26 (1966):229–47.

Loayza, Francisco A., ed., *Las crónicas de los Molinas.* Lima: Miranda, 1943.

Lockhart, James. *Spanish Peru, 1532–1560: A Colonial Society.* Madison, Wisc.: University of Wisconsin Press, 1968.

Lohmann Villena, Guillermo. "Apuntaciones sobre el curso de los precios de los artículos de primera necesidad en Lima durante el siglo XVI." *Revista histórica* 29 (1966):79–104.

Lohmann Villena, Guillermo. *Las minas de Huancavelica en los siglos XVI y XVII.* Seville: Escuela de Estudios Hispano-Americanos, 1949.

López de Velasco, Juan. *Geografía y descripción universal de las Indias.* Madrid, 1894.

290   *Bibliography*

Loredo, Rafael. *Los repartos.* Lima: Miranda, 1958.

Lovejoy, C. O. "Methods for the Detection of Census Error in Paleodemography." *American Anthropologist* 73 (1971):101–9.

MacLeod, Murdo J. *Spanish Central America: A Socioeconomic History, 1520–1720.* Berkeley: University of California Press, 1973.

Málaga Medina, Alejandro. "Los Collaguas en la historia de Arequipa en el siglo XVI." In *Collaguas I,* edited by Franklin Pease, pp. 93–130. Lima: Universidad Católica, 1977.

Málaga Medina, Alejandro. "Consideraciones económicas sobre la visita de la provincia de Arequipa." In *Tasa de la visita general de Francisco de Toledo,* edited by Noble David Cook, pp. 299–311. Lima, San Marcos, 1975.

Manual IV: Methods of Estimating Basic Demographic Measures from Incomplete Data. Department of Economic and Social Affairs, Population Studies, no. 42. New York: United Nations, 1967.

Marks, Geoffrey, and Beatty, William K. *Epidemics.* New York: Charles Scribner's Sons, 1976.

Martínez y Vela, Bartolomé. *Anales de la villa imperial de Potosí.* La Paz: Artística, 1939.

Mason, J. Alden. *The Ancient Civilizations of Peru.* 2nd ed. New York: Penguin, 1968.

Masset, Claude. "La démographie des populations inhumées: essai de paléodémographie." *L'homme* 13 (1973):95–131.

Matienzo, Juan de. *Gobierno del Perú (1567).* Paris: Institut Français d'Etudes Andines, 1967.

Maúrtua, Víctor M. *Juicio del límites entre el Perú y Bolivia, prueba peruana.* 12 vols. Barcelona, 1906.

May, Jacques M. *The Ecology of Human Diseases.* New York: MD Publications, 1958.

May, Jacques M., ed. *Studies in Disease Ecology.* New York: Hafner, 1961.

Mazess, R. B. "Variation in Neo-natal Mortality and Altitude in Peru." *American Journal of Physical Anthropology* 23 (1965):209–14.

Mazet, Claude. "Population et société à Lima aux XVIe et XVIIe siècles." *Cahiers des Amériques Latines* 13-14 (1976):51–102.

Means, Philip Ainsworth. *Ancient Civilizations of the Andes.* New York: Charles Scribner's Sons, 1931.

Means, Philip Ainsworth. *Fall of the Inca Empire and the Spanish Rule in Peru, 1530–1720.* New York: Charles Scribner's Sons, 1932.

Medina, José Toribio, ed. *La imprenta en Lima (1584–1824).* 4 vols. Santiago de Chile, 1904–7.

Mellafe, Rolando. "Consideraciones históricas sobre la visita de Iñigo Ortiz de Zúñiga." In *Visita de la provincia de León de Huánuco (1562),* edited by John V. Murra, 1:323–44. 2 vols. Lima: Villanueva, 1967, 1972.

Mellafe, Rolando. "The Importance of Migration in the Viceroyalty of Peru." In *Population and Economics: Proceedings of Section V of the Fourth Congress of the International Economic History Association,* edited by Paul Deprez, pp. 303–13. Winnipeg: University of Manitoba Press, 1970.

Mellafe, Rolando. "Problemas demográficos e historia colonial hispanoamericana." In *Temas de historia económica hispanoamericana*, 1:45–55. Paris: Colección Nova Americana, 1965.

Menzel, Dorothy. "Archaism and Revival on the South Coast of Peru." In *Peoples and Cultures of Native South America*, edited by Daniel R. Gross, pp. 19–27. Garden City, N.Y.: Doubleday, 1973.

Menzel, Dorothy. "The Inca Occupation of the South Coast of Peru." *Southwestern Journal of Anthropology* 15 (1959):125–42.

Mörner, Magnus. *Perfil de la sociedad rural del Cuzco a fines de la colonia*. Lima: Universidad del Pacífico, 1978.

Mogrovejo, Toribio Alfonso de. "Diario de la segunda visita pastoral que hizo de su arquidiocesis." *Revista del Archivo Nacional del Perú* 1 (1920):51–81, 227–79, 401–19; 2 (1921):37–78.

Monge M., Carlos. *Acclimatization in the Andes: Historical Confirmation of Climate Aggression in the Development of Andean man*. Baltimore: Johns Hopkins University Press, 1948.

Monge M., Carlos, and Monge C., Carlos. *High Altitude Diseases: Mechanism and Management*. Springfield, Ill.: Charles C. Thomas, 1976.

Monografía de la Diócesis de Trujillo. 3 vols. Trujillo: Centro de Estudios de Historia Eclesiástica del Perú, 1930–1.

Morales Figueroa, Luís de. "Relación de los indios tributarios que hay al presente en estos reinos y provincias del Pirú; fecho por mandado del Señor Marqués de Cañete." In *Colección de documentos inéditos relativos al descubrimiento, conquista y colonización de las posesiones españolas en América y Oceania*, edited by L. Torres de Mendoza, 6:41–61. 42 vols. Madrid, 1864–84.

Morin, Claude. "Los libros parroquiales como fuente para la historia demográfica y social novohispana." *Historia mexicana* 21 (1972):389–418.

Morley, Sylvanus G. *The Ancient Maya*. Stanford, Calif.: Stanford University Press, 1947.

Morley, Sylvanus G. *The Ancient Maya*. 3rd rev. ed. by George W. Brainerd. Stanford, Calif.: Stanford University Press, 1958.

Morúa, Martín de. *Historia de los Incas, reyes del Perú*. Lima: Sanmartí, 1925.

Moseley, Michael E. "Chan Chan: Andean Alternative of the Pre-industrial City." *Science* 187 (1975):219–25.

Moya Pons, Frank. *Española en el siglo XVI, 1493–1520*. Santiago, 1971.

Murra, John V. "Economic Organization of the Inca State." Ph.D. dissertation, University of Chicago, 1956.

Murra, John V. *Formaciones económicas y políticas del mundo andino*. Lima: Instituto de Estudios Peruanos, 1975.

Murra, John V., ed. *Visita de la provincia de León de Huánuco (1562)*. 2 vols. Lima: Villanueva, 1967, 1972.

Naroll, Raoul. "Floor Area and Settlement Population." *American Antiquity* 27 (1962):587–9.

Navarrete, Martín Fernández de, ed. *Colección de documentos inéditos para la historia de España*. 112 vols. Madrid, 1842–95.

Neel, James V. "Genetic Aspects of the Ecology of Disease in the American Indian." In *The Ongoing Evolution of Latin American Populations,* edited by Francisco M. Salzano, pp. 561–92. Springfield, Ill.: Charles C. Thomas, 1971.

Padden, Robert C., ed. *Tales of Potosí.* Providence, R.I.: Brown University Press, 1975.

Padilla Altamirano, Silvia; López Arellano, María Luisa; and González Rodrigues, Aldolfo Luís. *La encomienda en Popayán (tres estudios).* Seville: Escuela de Estudios Hispano-Americanos, 1977.

Pappenheimer, Alwin M. "The Diphtheria Bacilli." In *Bacterial and Mycotic Infections of Man,* edited by René J. Dubos and James G. Hirsch, pp. 468–89. 4th ed. Philadelphia: J. B. Lippincott, 1965.

Parsons, James J. *Antioqueño Colonization in Western Colombia.* 2nd ed. Berkeley: University of California Press, 1968.

Parsons, Jeffrey R., and Psuty, Norbert P. "Sunken Fields and Prehispanic Subsistence on the Peruvian Coast." *American Antiquity* 40 (1975):259–82.

Paz Soldán, Mariano Felipe. *Atlas geográfico del Perú.* Paris: Fermin Didot Hermanos, 1865.

Paz Soldán, Mariano Felipe. *Diccionario geográfico estadístico del Perú.* Lima: Imprenta del Estado, 1877.

Pease, Franklin. *El dios creador andino.* Lima: Mosca Azul, 1973.

Pease, Franklin. *Del Tawantinsuyu a la historia del Perú.* Lima: Instituto de Estudios Peruanos, 1978.

Pease, Franklin, ed. *Collaguas I.* Lima: Universidad Católica, 1977.

Perú, Dirección Nacional de Estadística y Censos. *Sexto censo nacional de población levantado el 2 de julio de 1961: resultados de primer prioridad.* Lima, 1964.

Peterson, William. "A Demographer's View of Prehistoric Demography." *Current Anthropology* 16 (1975):227–45.

Phelan, John L. *The Kingdom of Quito in the Seventeenth Century.* Madison: University of Wisconsin Press, 1967.

Pimentel, David. "Population Regulation and Genetic Feedback." *Science* 159 (1968):1432–7.

Polo, José Toribio. "Apuntes sobre las epidemias del Perú." *Revista histórica* 5 (1913):50–109.

Poma de Ayala, Felipe Guamán. *La nueva crónica y buen gobierno.* 3 vols. Lima: Editorial Cultura, 1956.

Ponce, Fernando, and Quiroz Paz-Soldán, Eusebio. *Informe de datos bibliográficos-documentales de orden demográfico de la ciudad de Arequipa, Perú.* Mexico City: Celade, 1975.

Ponce, Fernando, and Quiroz Paz-Soldán, Eusebio. "Observaciones críticas a la información demográfico-histórica de Arequipa, 1549–1820." *Latin American Research Review* 13 (1978):170–81.

Pool, D. I. "The effects of the 1918 Pandemic of Influenza on the Maori Population of New Zealand." *Bulletin of the History of Medicine* 47 (1973):273–81.

Porras Barrenechea, Raúl, ed. *Antología del Cuzco.* Lima: Librería Internacional, 1961.

Porras Barrenechea, Raúl, ed. *Cedulario del Perú, siglos XVI, XVII, y XVIII.* Lima: Torres Aguirre, 1948.

Porras Barrenechea, Raúl, ed. *Las relaciones primitivas de la conquista del Perú.* 2nd ed. Lima: Minerva, 1967.

Production Yearbook, 1962. Rome: Food and Agriculture Organization of the United Nations, 1963.

Rabell, Cecilia Andrea, and Assadourian, Carlos Sempat. "Self-regulating Mechanisms of the Population in a Pre-Columbian Society: The Case of the Inca Empire." In *International Population Conference, Mexico 1977,* 3:25–42. 3 vols. Liège, Belgium: Derouaux, 1977.

Radell, David R. "The Indian Slave Trade and Population of Nicaragua during the Sixteenth Century." In *The Native Population of the Americas in 1492,* edited by William M. Denevan, pp. 67–76. Madison: University of Wisconsin Press, 1976.

Ramírez-Horton, Susan E. "Chérrepe en 1572: un análisis de la visita general del Virrey Francisco de Toledo." *Historia y cultura* 11 (1978):79–122.

Ravines, Rogger. "Los caciques de Pausamarca: algo más sobre las etnías de Chachapoyas." *Historia y cultura* 6 (1973):217–48.

Rénique, José Luis, and Trelles, Efraín. "Approximación demográfica, Yanque-Collaguas 1591." In *Collaguas I,* edited by Franklin Pease, pp. 169–89. Lima: Universidad Católica, 1977.

Ricketson, Oliver G., and Bayles, Edith. *Uaxactún, Guatemala, Group E, 1926–1931.* Carnegie Institutions of Washington, Publication no. 477. Washington, D.C., 1937.

Robinson, David J. "Distribution and Structure of the Population in the Spanish Empire, 1750–1810: The Joint Syracuse–Oxford Project." *Latin American Population History Newsletter* 1 (1978–9):17–22.

Robinson, David J., ed. *Social Fabric and Spatial Structure in Colonial Latin America.* Ann Arbor, Mich.: University Microfilms, 1979.

Roel Pineda, Virgilio. *Historia social y económica de la colonia.* Lima: Gráfica Labor, 1970.

Romero, Carlos A. "Libro de la visita general del Virrey Francisco de Toledo." *Revista histórica* 7 (1924):115–216.

Romero, Emilio. *Geografía económica del Perú.* 5th ed. Lima, 1966.

Romero, Emilio. *Historia económica del Perú.* 2 vols, Lima, 1968.

Romero, Emilio. *Perú: una nueva geografía.* 2 vols. Lima: Studium, 1973.

Rosenblat, Angel. *La población de América en 1492: viejos y nuevos cálculos.* Mexico City: Colegio de México, 1967.

Rosenblat, Angel. *La población indígena y el mestizaje en América.* 2 vols. Buenos Aires: Editorial Nova, 1954.

Rosenblat, Angel. "The Population of Hispaniola at the Time of Columbus." In *The Native Population of the Americas in 1492,* edited by William M. Denevan, pp. 43–66. Madison: University of Wisconsin Press, 1976.

Rostworowski de Diez Canseco, María. *Etnía y sociedad: costa peruana prehispánica.* Lima: Instituto de Estudios Peruanos, 1977.

Rowe, John Howland. "Inca Culture at the Time of the Spanish Conquest." In *Handbook of South American Indians,* edited by Julian H. Steward, 2:183–330. 7 vols. Bureau of American Ethnology Bulletins, no. 143. Washington, D.C., 1946–59.

Rowe, John Howland. "The Incas under Spanish Colonial Institutions." *Hispanic American Historical Review* 37 (1957):155–99.

Rowe, John Howland. *An Introduction to the Archaeology of Cuzco.* Papers of the Peabody Museum of American Archaeology and Ethnology, Harvard University, vol. 27, no. 2. Cambridge, Mass., 1944.

Rowe, John Howland. "The Kingdom of Chimor." *Acta americana* 6 (1948):26–59.

Rowe, John Howland. "Urban Settlements in Ancient Peru." *Nawpa Pacha* 1 (1963):1–27.

Rowe, John Howland. "What Kind of a Settlement Was Inca Cuzco?" *Nawpa Pacha* 5 (1967):59–77.

Rowe, John H., and Menzel, Dorothy, eds. *Peruvian Archaeology: Selected Readings.* Palo Alto, Calif.: Peek Publications, 1967.

Ruíz Rivera, Julian Bautista. *Fuentes para la demografía histórica de Nueva Granada.* Seville: Escuela de Estudios Hispano-Americanos, 1972.

Sabin, A. B. "Nature of Inherited Resistance to Viruses Affecting the Nervous System." *Proceedings of the National Academy of Sciences* 38 (1952):540–6.

Salzano, Francisco M., ed. *The Ongoing Evolution of Latin American Populations.* Springfield, Ill.: Charles C Thomas, 1971.

Sánchez-Albornoz, Nicolás. *El indio en el Alto Perú a fines del siglo XVII.* Lima, 1973.

Sánchez-Albornoz, Nicolás. *Indios y tributos en el Alto Perú.* Lima: Instituto de Estudios Peruanos, 1978.

Sánchez-Albornoz, Nicolás. *The Population of Latin America: A History.* Berkeley: University of California Press, 1974.

Sánchez-Albornoz, Nicolás. "Les registres paroissiaux en Amérique Latine: quelques considérations sur leur exploitation pour la démographie historique." *Revue suisse d'histoire* 17 (1967):60–71.

Sanders, William T. "The Population of the Central Mexican Symbiotic Region, the Basin of Mexico, and the Teotihuacán Valley in the Sixteenth Century." In *The Native Population of the Americas in 1492,* edited by William M. Denevan, pp. 85–150. Madison: University of Wisconsin Press, 1976.

Santa Cruz Pachacuti, Juan. *Historia de los Incas.* Lima: Sanmartí, 1927.

Santillán, Fernando de. *Relación de su gobierno.* Lima: Sanmartí, 1927.

Schaedel, Richard P. "Formation of the Inca State." In *III Congreso peruano: el hombre y la cultura andina,* 1:112–56. Lima: Ramiro Matos, 1978.

Shea, Daniel E. "A Defense of Small Population Estimates for the Central Andes in 1520." In *The Native Population of the Americas in 1492,* edited by William M. Denevan, pp. 157–80. Madison: University of Wisconsin Press, 1976.

Sherman, William L. *Forced Native Labor in Sixteenth-Century Central America.* Lincoln: University of Nebraska Press, 1979.

Smith, Alice Lorraine. *Microbiology and Pathology.* 10th ed. Saint Louis: C. V. Mosby, 1972.

Smith, C. T. "Depopulation of the Central Andes in the 16th Century." *Current Anthropology* 11 (1970):453–64.

Spalding, Karen. "Indian Rural Society in Colonial Peru: The Example of Huarochirí." Ph.D. dissertation, University of California, 1967.

Spiegelman, Mortimer. *Introduction to Demography.* Rev. ed. Cambridge, Mass.: Harvard University Press, 1968.

Steck, Francis Borgia. *Motolinía's "History of the Indians of New Spain.* Richmond, Va.: William Byrd, 1951.

Steward, Julian H. "The Native Population of South America." In *Handbook of South American Indians,* edited by J. H. Steward, 5:655–68. 7 vols. Bureau of American Ethnology Bulletins, no. 143. Washington, D.C. 1946–59.

Steward, Julian H. *Theory of Culture Change: The Methodology of Multilinear Evolution.* Urbana: University of Illinois Press, 1973.

Steward, Julain H., ed. *Handbook of South American Indians.* 7 vols. Bureau of American Ethnology Bulletins, no. 143. Washington, D.C., 1946–59.

Steward, Julian H., and Faron, Louis C. *Native Peoples of South America.* New York: McGraw-Hill, 1959.

Steward, T. D. "A Physical Anthropologist's View of the Peopling of the New World." *Southwestern Journal of Anthropology* 16 (1960):259–73.

Stiglich, Germán. *Diccionario geográfico peruano.* 3 vols. Lima: Torres Aguirre, 1922.

Sweet, David Graham. "The Population of the Upper Amazon Valley, Seventeenth and Eighteenth Centuries." M.A. thesis, University of Wisconsin, 1969.

Thompson, J. Eric S. "Estimates of Maya Population: Deranging Factors," *American Antiquity* 36 (1971):214–16.

Thompson, J. Eric S. *Maya Hieroglyphic Writing: An Introduction.* 2nd ed. Norman: University of Oklahoma Press, 1960.

Toledo, Francisco de. *Fundación española del Cusco y ordenanzas para su gobierno.* Lima: Sanmartí, 1926.

Tolstoy, Paul. "Settlement and Population Trends in the Basin of Mexico (Ixtapaluca and Zacatenco Phases)." *Journal of Field Archaeology* 2 (1975):331–49.

Torres de Mendoza, L., ed. *Colección de documentos inéditos relativos al descubrimiento, conquista, y colonización de las posesiones españolas en América y Oceania.* 42 vols. Madrid, 1864–84.

Torres Saldamando, Enrique. *Apuntes históricos sobre las encomiendas en el Perú.* Lima: San Marcos, 1967.

Urteaga, Horacio H., ed. *Informaciones sobre el antiguo Perú.* Lima: Sanmartí, 1920.

Urteaga, Horacio H., ed. *Relación del sitio del Cusco.* Lima, 1934.

Utterström, Gustaf. "Climate Fluctuations and Population Problems in Early Modern History." *Scandinavian Economic Review* 3 (1955):3–47.

Vallois, Henri V. "Vital Statistics in Prehistoric Populations as Determined from Archaeological Data." In *The Application of Quantitative Methods in Archaeology,* edited by S. F. Cook and R. F. Heizer, pp. 186–222. Chicago: Quadrangle, 1960.

Vargas Ugarte, Rubén. *Biblioteca peruana: manuscritos peruanos en la Biblioteca Nacional de Lima.* Lima, 1940.

Vargas Ugarte, Rubén. *Historia del Perú: virreinato siglo XVII*. Buenos Aires: López, 1954.

Vázquez de Espinosa, Antonio. *Compendio y descripción de las Indias occidentales*. Smithsonian Miscellaneous Collections, vol. 108. Washington, D.C., 1948.

Verlinden, Charles. "La population de l'Amérique précolumbienne: une question de méthode." In *Méthodologie de l'histoire et des sciences humaines: mélanges en honneur de Fernand Braudel*, pp. 453–62. Paris, 1973.

Verlinden, Charles. "Le 'repartimiento' de Rodrigo de Alburquerque à Española en 1514: aux origines d'une importante institution économico-sociale de l'empire colonial espagnol." In *Mélanges offerts à G. Jacquemyns*, pp. 633–46. Brussels: Université Libre de Bruxelles, 1968.

Villamarín, Juan A., and Villamarín, Judith E. "Chibcha Settlement under Spanish Rule, 1537–1810." In *Social Fabric and Spatial Structure in Colonial Latin America*, edited by David J. Robinson, pp. 25–84. Ann Arbor, Mich.: University Microfilms, 1979.

Villanueva Urteaga, Horacio. "Documentos sobre Yucay en el siglo XVI." *Revista del Archivo Histórico del Cuzco* 13 (1970):1–149.

"Visita de Acarí (1593)." *Historia y cultura* 7 (1973):129–209.

Vollmer, Günther. *Bevölkerungspolitik und Bevölkerungsstruktur im Vizekönigreich Peru zu Ende der Kolonialzeit, 1741–1821*. Beiträge zur Soziologie und sozialkunde Lateinamerikas, Cosal 2. Bad Homburg vor der Höhe, 1967.

Wachtel, Nathan. *Sociedad e ideología: ensayos de historia y antropología andinas*. Lima: Instituto de Estudios Peruanos, 1973.

Wachtel, Nathan. *Vision of the Vanquished: The Spanish Conquest of Peru through Indian Eyes, 1530–1570*. Hassocks, Sussex: Harvester Press, 1977.

Wedin, Ake. *El sistema decimal en el imperio incaico*. Madrid: Insula, 1965.

Weiner, J. M. "Nutritional Ecology." In *Human Biology: An Introduction to Human Evolution, Variation, and Growth*, edited by G. A. Harrison, pp. 413–40. New York: Oxford University Press, 1964.

West, Michael. "Community Settlement Patterns at Chan Chan, Peru." *American Antiquity* 35 (1970):74–86.

Whitaker, Arthur P. *The Huancavelica Mercury Mine*. Cambridge, Mass.: Harvard University Press, 1941.

Willey, Gordon R., *Prehistoric Settlement Patterns in the Virú Valley, Peru*. Bureau of American Ethnology Bulletins, no. 155. Washington, D.C.: Smithsonian Institution, 1953.

Willey, Gordon R., ed. *Prehistoric Settlement Patterns in the New World*. Viking Fund Publications in Anthropology, no. 23. New York, 1956.

Wrigley, E. A. *Population and History*. New York: McGraw-Hill, 1969.

Yazawa, Taiji. "Climatological Survey in the Central Andes." In *Andes: Report of the University of Tokyo Scientific Expedition to the Andes in 1958*, pp. 414–17. Tokyo: University of Tokyo, 1960.

Zambardino, Rudolph A. "Critique of David Henige's 'On the Contact Population of Hispaniola: History as Higher Mathematics.'" *Hispanic American Historical Review* 58 (1978):700–8.

Zambardino, Rudolph A. "Mexico's Population in the Sixteenth Century: Demographic Anomaly or Mathematical Illusion?" *Journal of Interdisciplinary History* 11 (1980):1–27.

Zárate, Agustín de. *The Discovery and Conquest of Peru*. Baltimore: Penguin, 1968.

Zárate, Agustín de. *Historia del descubrimiento y conquista del Perú*. Lima: Miranda, 1944.

Ziegler, Philip. *The Black Death*. New York: John Day, 1969.

Zinnser, Hans. *Rats, Lice, and History*. New York: Blue Ribbon Books, 1934.

Zubrow, Ezra B. W. "Carrying Capacity and Dynamic Equilibrium in the Prehistoric Southwest." *American Antiquity* 36 (1971):127–38.

Zubrow, Ezra B. W. *Prehistoric Carrying Capacity: A Model*. Menlo Park, Calif.: Cummings, 1975.

Index

Acarí, 166-70, 172; migration from, 167; population of, 167-70, 177
Acequia de Hualcara, 158
Achamarcas, 230-1
Achanquillo Yanque, 230-1
Achinga, 189
Acoria (Chachas), 203
Acosta, José de, 223
administration: colonial, 76, 78, 81, 84, 128, 150, 204; Inca, *see* Inca administration; of Yanahuara, 175
agriculture, 15, 17, 18, 20, 22, 93, 125, 131, 141, 145, 149, 157, 160, 164, 186; and altitude, 22, 182, 199; coca, *see* coca; land under cultivation, 23, 28, 165; livestock, 125, 130, 157, 158, 164, 166, 175, 178, 191, 195, 199, 209, 219, 227, 228, 230, 243; products, 22, 125, 130, 134, 138-9, 144, 146, 157, 161, 164, 166, 170, 171, 175, 178, 182, 183, 185-6, 191, 193, 199, 209, 219, 227, 228, 230, 243; ridged-field cultivation, 23, 28, 37-8; soil fertility, 172, 178, 186, 201, 235; sunken-field, 23, 28, 37
Aguero, Diego de, 158
Aimaraes, 227-8, 245
Alconchel, Pedro de, 157
Alegría (physician), 224
Almagro, Diego de, 121, 122, 123, 137, 149
alpaca, *see* cameloids
alquilados, 205
altitude, 54, 73, 210; and agriculture, 22, 182, 199; and disease, 59, 62, 68, 73, 143, 239, 245; and fertility, 73, 238; physiological adaptations to, 22, 73-4, 133, 156
Alvarado, Alonso de, 138, 191-3
Alvárez de Carmona, Fernán, 170
amalgamation process, 203, 209, 236, 237

Amazon basin, 68, 111, 178-9, 197
Amazon river, 179
Ambar, 163
Ancón Necropolis, 33
Andaguaylas, 227, 245
Andaguaylas la Grande, 66-7, 227
Andax, 163
Andes, ecology of, 119, 120, 178
Andes, Los, *see* Paucartambo
Angel, J. Lawrence, 31
Anicama, Fernando, 161
archaeology, 30, 132, 143; burial sites, 31; cultural records, 30-1; Cuzco, 39-40; skeletal remains, 30, 31, 40; as tool to estimate Peruvian population, 30, 40, 108-9
architecture, 39; used to estimate population, 35-6
Arequipa, 82, 85, 87, 154, 165, 167, 171-4; climate, 171; earthquakes in, 165, 171, 172-4; economy of, 176; epidemics, 173; mitayos in, 172-3, 231; population of, 172, 174; Yanaconas, 174; *see also* Yanahuara
Arias Dávila, Gómez, 186
Arica, port of, 176, 177
artisans, 153, 156, 160; pre-Columbian, 160; silversmiths, 201, 215
Ascher, Robert, 32-3
Asia valley (Peru), 37
Asillo, 227
Assadourian, Carlos Sempat, 25, 27
Atahualpa, 82, 112, 181, 189
Atavillos, 80
Atico y Caravelí, 166, 170
Atun Jauja, 200, 201
Aucaes (Land of War), 178, 185
Audiencia of Lima, 77, 173
Australia, 72
Avendaño, Pedro de, 77
ayllu, 27, 56, 77, 79, 237
Aymaras, 45, 74

298

Foster, George M., 34
fruits, 166, 175, 186, 193
Fuentes, Francisco de, 138

Garcés, Enrique, 203
García de Castro, Lope, 205
García Jaimes, Francisco, 197
García Jaimes, Ysabel, 197
garua, 119
Gasca, Pedro de la, 76-7, 97, 113
Glassow, Michael A., 33
gold: mining, 178, 182-3, 191, 193; as
    tribute payment, 230; washing pro-
    cess, 226
Gómez de Alvarado, 185
González de Ayala, Pedro, 133
Goparas, 195-6
grapes, 125, 138, 144; *see also* wine
Guadalupe, 134
Gualla, 226
Guamachuco, 139, 182
Guamanga (Ayacucho), *see* Huamanga
Guambos, 182
Guancabama, 176
Guanchaco, 130, 138, 141-2
guano, *see* fertilizer
Guarangas, 182
Guayaquil, 120-1, 153, 156
guinea pigs, *see* cavies
Gutiérrez, Pedro, 161
Gutiérrez Flores, Friar Pedro, 219
Gutiérrez de Mendoza, Pedro, 162

hacienda, 145, 146, 164; labor force,
    157, 161, 164
Hananhuanca, (Hanan Guanca), 51,
    200, 201-3
Hananica, 161
Hananpiscas, 163
Harner, Michael J., 55-6
hatunruna, 20, 48, 58; *see also* Inca age
    categories
Henige, David, 2, 14
Hernández de Hererra, Gonzalo, 160,
    161
Hispaniola, 2
Hoces, Juan de, 134
Hollingsworth, T. H., 41
honokoraka, 41, 42
horses, 157, 158, 195
hospital, 125, 130, 190, 224
household dwelling area: used to esti-
    mate population, 32

Huacho, population of, 149-50
Huachos Chocorvos, 69
Huamalies, 179, 186
Huamanga, 87, 95, 154, 203
Huancabamba river, 178-9
Huancané, 227
Huancas, 41-3, 49, 213
Huancavelica, 84, 85, 113, 199,
    203-8, 209, 237; and the Crown,
    204-5; discovery of mines, 203-4;
    mita, 183, 201, 205-6, 207, 208;
    and Viceroy Toledo, 204, 205
Huandoval, 69
Huánuco, 26, 51, 57, 95, 100-4, 154,
    185-6; population of Los Chupachos,
    186-9; *see also visita* of Huánuco
Huánuco Viejo, 185
Huaraz, 179, 182-3, 198
Huarco, 157-8
Huari, 212
Huarmey, 120, 149
Huarochirí, 82, 162, 163
Huaura, 145, 149
Huayna Capac (Inca ruler), 62, 82,
    189, 253-4
Huaynaputina, eruption of, 173
Hudson Bay (Canada), 66
Humboldt current, 119-20
Hurtado de Mendoza, García, *see* Ca-
    ñete, marqués de

Ica, 157, 160-1, 162, 166, 167; wine
    production, 161, 162, 171
Iceland: smallpox epidemic, 64
immunity, *see* disease, immunity to
Inca: administration, 4, 10-11, 25, 42,
    56-7, 58, 81, 108; age categories,
    11, 20, 42, 45-8, 52, 57; architec-
    ture, 39, 122, 123, 181-2; celibacy,
    27, 28; census, 10-11, 45, 217;
    cities, 39, 121, 123, 181-2, 200-1,
    217-19; civil war, 82, 112, 121,
    189; conquest of Chachapoyas, 191;
    conquest of Chan Chan, 137, 143;
    expansion, 143, 145, 157, 222;
    farming, 24, 108, 145; highways, 4;
    irrigation system, 128, 158; mar-
    riage customs, 27, 201; practices as-
    sociated with childbirth, 26; reli-
    gion, 39, 122, 137, 145, 218, 223;
    status during colonial times, 83, 89;
    treatment of children, 26; treatment
    of conquered enemies, 26, 57, 82,
    137, 157; tribute, 25, 42; use of cin-

Cambridge Latin American Studies

309